TOOLKIT FOR INTERMEDIATE ACCOUNTING
SEVENTH CANADIAN EDITION

 W9-CGX-119

Diagram of Lessee's Criteria for Lease Classification

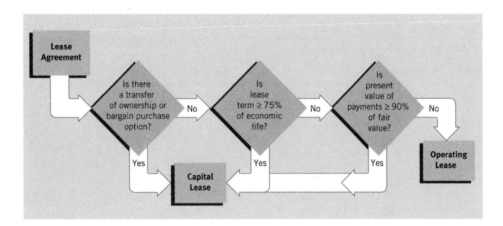

Flowchart of Lessor's Criteria for Lease Classification

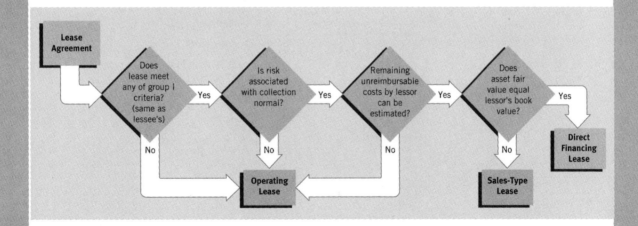

©2005 John Wiley & Sons Canada, Ltd

TOOLKIT FOR INTERMEDIATE ACCOUNTING
SEVENTH CANADIAN EDITION

DEFINITIONS

These definitions are central to qualitative analysis of financial reporting issues. To that extent, this chart should be referred to and used when doing case analysis or analysing issues. Ideally, these concepts/criteria and definitions should be committed to memory as they form the core of intermediate accounting.

	Reference	Definition	Recognition—General Rule	Measurement General rule*
ASSETS	HB 1000.29-.31	• **future benefit** • entity **controls** access to benefit or has **risks and rewards** of ownership • **transaction or event has occurred**	• meets definition AND • **probable/likely** AND • **measurable**	• at historical cost with write down if impairment in value (see Subsequent Revaluation of Assets) • see also industry practice • at transaction cost or best estimate
LIABILITIES	HB 1000.32-.34	• **obligation**/duty to pay • little or **no discretion to avoid** • **transaction or event obligating entity has occurred**	• meet definition AND • **probable/likely** AND • **measurable**	
EQUITY	HB 1000.35-.36	• **ownership** interest in net assets	• **transaction has occurred AND** • **measurable**	• at transaction cost
REVENUES	HB 1000.37 HB 3400.03	• **increases in economic resources** (from **ordinary operations**)	• **performance/risks and rewards** of ownership passed • reasonable assurance as to **measurement** • reasonable assurance as to **collectibility**	• at transaction cost
EXPENSES	HB 1000.38	• **decreases in economic resources** (from **ordinary operations**)	• if asset **no longer has future benefit**, OR • expense (not linked to specific revenues) **occurred in period** OR, • in order to **match** with revenues	• at transaction cost or best estimate
GAINS	HB 1000.39	• **increases in net assets** from **peripheral/incidental** transactions	• when **realized**	• at transaction cost
LOSSES	HB 1000.40	• **decreases in net assets** from **peripheral/incidental** transactions	• when **likely/** measurable	• at best estimate
CONTIN-GENCIES	HB 3290	• **existing condition involving uncertainty as to possible gain or loss that will be resolved by future event**	• loss-when likely and measurable • gain-may not recognize even if likely	• at best estimate

*see also HB I508 for measurement uncertainty—must disclose nature of uncertainty and amount.

©2005 John Wiley & Sons Canada, Ltd

SEVENTH CANADIAN EDITION

STUDY GUIDE TO ACCOMPANY

Intermediate Accounting

VOLUME 2:   CHAPTERS 14 - 24

Donald E. Kieso, PhD, CPA
KPMG Peat Marwick Emeritus Professor of Accounting
Northern Illinois University
DeKalb, Illinois

Jerry J. Weygandt, PhD, CPA
Arthur Andersen Alumni Professor of Accounting
University of Wisconsin
Madison, Wisconsin

Terry D. Warfield, PhD
PricewaterhouseCoopers Research Scholar
University of Wisconsin
Madison, Wisconsin

Nicola M. Young, MBA, FCA
Saint Mary's University
Halifax, Nova Scotia

Irene M. Wiecek, CA
University of Toronto
Toronto, Ontario

Study Guide prepared by Peter J. Thomas

John Wiley & Sons Canada, Ltd.

Copyright © 2005 by John Wiley & Sons Canada, Ltd

Copyright 2001 by John Wiley & Sons Inc. All rights reserved. No part of this work covered by the copyrights herein may be reproduced or used in any form or by any means-graphic, electronic, or mechanical-without the prior written permission of the publisher.

Any request for photocopying, recording, taping or inclusion in information storage and retrieval systems of any part of this book shall be directed to The Canadian Copyright Licensing Agency (Access Copyright). For an Access Copyright licence, visit www. accesscopyright.ca or call toll-free, 1-800-893-5777.

Care has been taken to trace ownership of copyright material contained in this text. The publishers will gladly receive any information that will enable them to rectify any erroneous reference or credit line in subsequent editions.

National Library of Canada Cataloguing in Publication Data

Thomas, Peter J.
    Study guide to accompany Intermediate accounting, 7th Canadian edition

ISBN 0-470-83493-5 (v. 1).-ISBN 0-470-83494-3 (v. 2)

    1. Accounting-Problems, exercises, etc. I. Title.

HF5635.I573 2004 Suppl. 1   657'.044   C2004-900303-8

Production Credits
Editorial Manager: Karen Staudinger
Publishing Services Director: Karen Bryan
Sr. Marketing Manager: Janine Daoust
New Media Editor: Elsa Passera
Developmental Editors: Leanne Rancourt and Amanjeet Chauhan
Interior Text Design: Natalia Burobina
Cover Design: Interrobang Graphic Design
Printing & Binding: Tri-Graphic Printing Limited

Printed and bound in Canada
10 9 8 7 6 5 4 3 2 1

John Wiley & Sons Canada, Ltd.
6045 Freemont Blvd.
Mississauga, Ontario L5R 4J3

Visit our website at: www.wiley.com/canada

C O N T E N T S

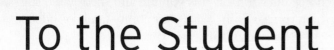

PREFACE

To the Student

The purpose of this *Study Guide* is to help you to improve your success rate in solving accounting homework assignments and in answering accounting exam questions. For each chapter we include the following:

OVERVIEW To briefly introduce the chapter topics and their importance.

STUDY STEPS To discuss the business transactions or issues pertinent to the chapter topics, including an analysis of the key recognition, measurement and disclosure issues.

TIPS To alert you to common pitfalls and misconceptions and remind you of important terminology, concepts, and relationships that are relevant to answering specific questions of solving certain problems.

To help you to understand the intricacies of a problematic situation and tell you what to do in similar circumstances.

EXERCISES To provide you with a selection of problems representative of homework assignments that an intermediate accounting student may encounter.

MULTIPLE CHOICE To provide you with a selection of multiple-choice questions which are representative of common exam questions covering topics in the chapter.

PURPOSES To identify the essence of each question or exercise and link them to the text material.

SOLUTIONS To show you the appropriate solution for each exercise and multiple-choice question presented.

EXPLANATIONS To give you the details of how selected solutions were derived and explain why things are done as shown.

APPROACHES To coach you on the particular model, computational format, or other strategy to be used to solve particular problems.
To teach you how to analyse and solve multiple-choice questions.

This book will be a welcome teaching/learning aid because it provides you with the opportunity to solve accounting problems in addition to the ones assigned by your instructor without having to rely on your teacher for solutions. Many of the exercises and questions contained herein are very similar to items in your intermediate accounting textbook; the difference is, the ones in this book are accompanied with detailed clearly laid out solutions.

The use of the multiple choice questions in this volume and the related suggestions on how to approach them can easily increase your ability (and confidence in your ability) to deal with exam questions of this variety.

HOW TO STUDY ACCOUNTING

The successful study of accounting requires a different approach than most other subjects. In addition to reading a chapter, applying the material through the completion of exercises or problems is necessary to develop a true and lasting understanding of the concepts introduced in the text chapter. The study of accounting principles is a combination of theory and practice; theory describes what to do and why, and practice is the application of guidelines to actual situations. We use illustrations to demonstrate how theory works and we use theory to explain why something is done in practice. Therefore, it is impossible to separate the two in the study of accounting.

Learning accounting is a cumulative process. It is difficult to master chapter 4 until you are thoroughly familiar with Chapters 1-3, and so on. Therefore, it is imperative that you keep up with class assignments. And, because accounting is a technical subject, you must pay particular attention to terminology.

Accounting is the language of business. It is an exciting subject that provides a challenge for most business majors. Your ultimate success in life may well depend on your ability to grasp financial data. The effort you expend now will provide rewards for years to come.

We encourage you to follow the four steps for study outlines below to give yourself the best possible chance for a successful learning experience and to make the most efficient use of your time. These steps provide a system of study for each new chapter in your text.

Step 1

- Scan the learning objectives at the beginning of each chapter.
- Scan the chapter (or chapter section) rather quickly.
- Glance over the questions at the end of the chapter.

The first step will give you an overview of the material to be mastered.

Step 2

- Read the assigned pages slowly.
- Study carefully and mark for later attention any portions not clearly understood.
- Pay particular attention to examples and illustrations.
- Try to formulate tentative answers to end-of-chapter questions.

During this phase, you will be filling in the "outline" you formed in Step 1. Most of the details will fall into place during this part of your study. The remaining steps are necessary, however, for a keen understanding of the subject.

Step 3

- Carefully read the **Overview**, **Study Steps**, and **Tips** sections of this *Study Guide*.
- Do the **Exercises** and **Cases** in this *Study Guide* that pertain to the same topics as your homework assignments.
- Review the relevant **Illustrations** in this book.
- Do the **Multiple-Choice Questions** in the *Study Guide* that pertain to the same concepts as your homework assignments.
- Refer back to the sections of the chapter in the text that you marked as unclear, if any. It is likely that any confusion or questions on your part will have been cleared up through your in the *Study Guide*. If a section remains unclear, carefully reread it and rework relevant pages of the *Study Guide*.
- Repeat this process for each assigned topic area.

Step 4

- Write out formal answers to homework assignments in the text.

This step is crucial because you find out whether you can independently apply the material you have been studying to fresh situations. You may find it necessary to go back to the text and/or the *Study Guide* to restudy certain sections. This is common and merely shows that the study assignments are working for you.

Additional comments to help you get the most out of this *Study Guide* are as follows:

The **Study Steps** and **Tips**, along with the **Illustrations**, will aid your understanding and retention of the material. **Exercises** provide examples of application of the text material. These should be very valuable in giving you guidance in completing homework assignments that are often similar in nature and content.

The **Approach** stated for an exercise or question is likely the most valuable feature of this *Study Guide* because it tells you how to think through the situation at hand. This thought process can then be used for similar situations. It is impossible to illustrate every situation you may encounter. You can, however, handle new situations by simply applying what you know and making modifications where appropriate. Many students make the mistake of attempting to memorize their way through an accounting book. That, too, is an impossible feat. **Do not rely on memorization**. If this material is going to be useful to you, you must think about what you are reading and always be thinking of why things are as they are. If you know the reasoning for a particular accounting treatment, it will be much easier to remember that treatment and reconstruct it even weeks after your initial study of it.

Explanations are provided for exercise and questions. These are very detailed so that you will thoroughly understand what is being done and why. These details will serve you well when you complete your homework assignments.

Always make an honest effort to solve the exercises and answer the questions contained in this *Study Guide* **before** you look at the solutions. Answering the questions on your own will maximize the benefits you can expect to reap from this book.

The **Multiple-Choice Questions** are self-tests to give you immediate feedback on how well you understand the material. Study the **Approaches** suggested for answering these questions in the *Study Guide*. Practice them when answering the multiple-choice questions in the text. Apply them when taking examinations. By doing so, you will learn to calmly, methodically, and successfully process examination questions. This will definitely improve your exam scores. When you work an **Exercise** or **Case** in the *Study Guide* or in the text, always read the instructions **before** you read all of the given data. This allows you to determine what you are to accomplish. Therefore, as you now tread through the data, you can begin to process it because you can determine its significance and relevance. If you read the data before the instructions, you are likely to waste your time because you will have to reread the facts once you find out what you are to do with them. Also, more importantly, you are likely to begin to anticipate what the problem is about, which will often cause you to do things other than what is requested in the questions.

Good luck and best wishes for a positive learning experience!

Current Liabilities and Contingencies

Overview

Initially, the resources (assets) of a business have to come from entities outside of the particular organization. Two main sources of resources are creditor sources (liabilities) and owners' sources (owners' equity). In this chapter, we begin our in-depth discussion of liabilities.

Due to the nature of some business activities, it is common to find some goods and services being received while payment for these items is made days or weeks later. Therefore, at a specific point in time, such as a balance sheet date, we may find that a business has obligations for merchandise received from suppliers (accounts payable), for money it has borrowed (notes payable), for interest incurred (interest payable), for property taxes (property taxes payable), for sales tax charged to customers which has not yet been remitted to the government (sales taxes payable), for salaries and wages (salaries and wages payable), and for other amounts due to government agencies in connection with employee compensation. Such payables are reported as current (short-term) liabilities, because they will fall due within the next 12 months and will require the use of current assets (cash, in these cases) to liquidate them.

Other liabilities are more difficult to estimate due to the uncertainty involved in either the likelihood of being incurred and/or the measurement of the liability. These estimated and "contingent" liabilities require extensive analysis of the relevant facts to determine proper treatment.

Accounting for current financial and contingent liabilities is discussed in this chapter.

Study Steps

Understanding the Nature of Liabilities

Liabilities

Liabilities represent claims upon the company. By definition (*CICA Handbook*, Section 1000), they have the following characteristics:

- They embody a duty or responsibility to others.
- The responsibility cannot be avoided (i.e., if the employee has earned vacation pay by law or under the employment arrangement, the company must pay it).
- The underlying event that caused the duty to arise has already occurred (i.e., the act of the employee working causes the vacation pay obligation to arise).

Liabilities need not be legally enforceable to be considered a liability. They may arise out of moral or ethical obligations.

Often, the key to the analysis is determining the "event" that gives rise to a liability.

A current liability is an obligation that must be discharged within a year or the operating cycle of business (*CICA Handbook*, Section 1510)

Contingencies

Existing conditions involving uncertainty (as to possible gain or loss) that will be resolved in the future by the occurrence or nonoccurrence of a confirming event.

It is very important to focus on the uncertainty surrounding a possible liability. The more uncertain, the less likely it is that a liability and, therefore, a loss will in fact be realized.

It is also important to focus on the fact that the condition causing possible loss already exists and that the future event is really just a confirming event and not the event itself.

Asset Retirement Obligations

CICA Handbook Section 3110 requires a company to recognize legal liabilities for the costs of retiring an asset, despite the fact that these obligations may be years away. Examples of where this is most common include nuclear facilities, oil and gas properties, mining, and landfills. With these type of assets, the company usually has a legal obligation to restore the asset and surrounding area to its original condition. A best estimate of the fair value of the cost to retire the asset is made when known and measurable, and is added to the carrying value of the related asset. This cost is then depreciated over the useful life of the asset. This provides better matching of costs to expected benefits, as well as better predictability of future obligations.

Understanding How the Transaction Fits into the Financial Reporting Model

Financial Statement Analysis

The presentation of liabilities between current and long-term is a very important issue, as it impacts key ratios such as the current ratio and quick or acid-test ratio. There may be a bias to show liabilities as long-term, or, in the case of contingent liabilities, avoid recording them altogether.

Key ratios are:

$$\text{Current ratio} = \frac{\text{Current Assets}}{\text{Current Liabilities}}$$

$$\text{Quick ratio} = \frac{\text{Cash + marketable securities + receivables (net)}}{\text{Current Liabilities}}$$

$$\text{Current cash debt coverage ratio} = \frac{\text{Net cash provided by operating activities}}{\text{Average current liabilities}}$$

In terms of benchmarking, often if a company's current ratio exceeds 2:1, this is normally considered acceptable. Care should be taken however to look at the business of the company and how quickly current assets are realized in interpreting this ratio. Developing industry "standards" is also useful in evaluating ratios.

The quick or acid-test ratio benchmark is generally below 2:1 since, by definition, the formula focuses on more liquid assets only.

The net cash provided by operating activities looks at whether cash generated is capable of meeting required payments (i.e., current liabilities). The higher this ratio, the better.

Tips on Chapter Topics

Current liabilities are often called **short-term liabilities** or **short-term debt**. **Noncurrent liabilities** are often called **long-term liabilities** or **long-term debt**.

TIP!

Current liabilities are obligations whose liquidation is reasonably expected to require the use of resources properly classifiable as current assets, or the creation of other current liabilities. **Noncurrent liabilities** are obligations which do not meet the criteria to be classified as current.

TIP!

An estimated loss from a loss contingency should be accrued by a charge to expense and a credit to a liability if both of the following conditions are met: (1) it is **likely** that a liability has been incurred at the date of the balance sheet, and (2) the amount of the loss can be **reasonably estimated (measured)**. If the loss is likely but not measurable, or if its existence is not determinable, it should be disclosed in the

TIP!

notes (but not accrued). If it is only **unlikely** that a liability has been incurred, no accrual or note disclosure is required.

TIP!   Self-insurance is not insurance; rather, it is no insurance and therefore a significant risk assumption. Any company that assumes its own risks puts itself in the position of incurring expenses or losses as they occur. However, it is **not** generally acceptable to report a liability before the occurrence of damage, since a company cannot record an obligation to itself. Disclosure of this situation is considered desirable only. (*CICA Handbook* 3290.16).

Exercise 14-1

PURPOSE: This exercise tests your ability to distinguish between current and noncurrent (long-term) liabilities.

Instructions

Indicate how each of the following items would be reported on a balance sheet being prepared at December 31, 2005.

1. Obligation to supplier for merchandise purchased on credit. (Terms 2/10, n/30) *CL*
2. Note payable to bank maturing 90 days after balance sheet date. *CL*
3. Bonds payable due January 1, 2008. *non Current*
4. Property taxes payable. *Curr*
5. Interest payable on long-term bonds payable. *Curr*
6. Income taxes payable. *Curr*
7. Portion of lessee's lease obligations due in years 2007 through 2011. *non-Curr*
8. Revenue received in advance, to be earned over the next six months. *Curr*
9. Salaries payable. *Curr*
10. Rent payable. *Curr*
11. Short-term notes payable. *Curr*
12. Instalment loan payment due three months after balance sheet date. *Curr*
13. Instalment loan payments due after one year. *non-Curr*
14. Portion of lessee's lease obligations due within a year after the December 31, 2005 balance sheet date. *Curr*
15. Bank overdraft. *Curr*
16. Accrued officer bonus.
17. Coupon offers outstanding.
18. Cash dividends declared but not paid.
19. Unearned rent revenue.
20. Stock dividends distributable.
21. Bonds payable due June 1, 2006.
22. Bonds payable due July 1, 2006 for which a sinking fund will be used to pay off the debt. The sinking fund is classified as a long-term investment.

23. Discount to the bonds payable in item 3 above.
24. Current maturities of long-term debt.
25. Accrued interest on notes payable.
26. Customer deposits.
27. Sales taxes payable.
28. Employee payroll withholdings.
29. Contingent liability (likely but not measurable).
30. Contingent liability (likely and measurable).
31. Obligation for warranties.
32. Unearned warranty revenue.
33. Gift certificates outstanding.
34. Loan from shareholder.

Solution to Exercise 14-1

Apply the definition of a current liability. Analyse each situation and determine if the liability will fall due within a year (or operating cycle) of the balance sheet date and whether it will require the use of current assets or the incurrence of another current liability to be liquidated. If so, it is current; if not, it is long-term. Recall that current assets include cash and assets expected to be converted to cash or sold or consumed within the next year or operating cycle, whichever is longer.

TIP!

1. Current liability (called Accounts Payable).
2. Current liability.
3. Noncurrent liability.
4. Current liability.
5. Current liability; interest on bonds is usually due semi-annually or annually.
6. Current liability.
7. Noncurrent liability.
8. Current liability.
9. Current liability.
10. Current liability.
11. Current liability.
12. Current liability.
13. Noncurrent liability.
14. Current liability.
15. Current liability (assuming no other bank accounts with positive balances in the same bank).
16. Current liability.
17. Current liability; may also classify a portion as a noncurrent liability.
18. Current liability.
19. Current liability or noncurrent liability, depending on when the revenue is expected to be earned.
20. Does not meet the definition of a liability. Usually reported in shareholder's equity.
21. Current liability.
22. Noncurrent liability; even though it is coming due within a year, it will not require the use of current assets to be liquidated.

23. Contra noncurrent liability (deducted from the related bonds payable).
24. Current liability.
25. Current liability, generally; in rare cases may be noncurrent.
26. Current liability or noncurrent liability, depending on the time left before they are to be returned or earned.
27. Current liability.
28. Current liability.
29. Note disclosure only.
30. Current liability or noncurrent liability, depending on the date settlement is expected.
31. Current liability and/or noncurrent liability, depending on term of warranty (this account title is used with the expense warranty method).
32. Current liability and/or noncurrent liability, depending on term of warranty (this account title is used with the sales warranty method).
33. Current liability, most likely; could have a portion as a noncurrent liability.
34. Current liability or noncurrent liability, depending on the due date of the loan; loans with related parties are required to be separately disclosed; if this loan is due on demand, the payable must be classified as a current liability.

Exercise 14-2

PURPOSE: This exercise will provide an example of the proper accounting for an obligation to an agency of the provincial or federal government—unremitted sales taxes.

During the month of September, Chelsea's Boutique had cash sales of $702,000 and credit sales of $411,000, both of which include the 6% sales tax that must be remitted to the provincial government by October 15. Sales taxes on September sales were lumped with the sales price and recorded as a credit to the Sales Revenue account.

Instructions

(a) Prepare the adjusting entry that should be recorded to fairly present the financial statements at September 30.

(b) Prepare the entry to record the remittance of the sales taxes on October 5 if a 2% discount is allowed for payments received by the provincial government by October 10.

Solution to Exercise 14-2

(a) 9/30   Sales Revenue   63,000
                    Sales Taxes Payable   63,000
                           Calculation:
                           Sales plus sales tax
                               ($702,000 + $411,000) $1,113,000
                           Sales exclusive of tax
                               ($1,113,000 ÷ 1.06)   <u>1,050,000</u>
                           Sales tax   <u>$ 63,000</u>

(b) 10/5   Sales Taxes Payable   63,000
                    Cash (98% x $63,000)   61,740
                    Gain on Sales Tax Collections (2% x $63,000)   1,260

EXPLANATION: Sales taxes on transfers of tangible personal property and on certain services must be collected from customers and remitted to the proper government authority. A liability is set up to provide for taxes collected from customers but as yet unremitted to the tax authority. The Sales Taxes Payable account should reflect the liability for sales taxes due to the government.

When the sales tax collections credited to the liability account are not equal to the liability as calculated by the governmental formula, an adjustment of the liability account may be made by recognizing a gain or a loss on sales tax collections.

Exercise 14-3

PURPOSE: This exercise will provide you with two examples of the proper treatment of short-term debt expected to be refinanced.

Situation 1

On December 31, 2004, Mayor Frederick Specialty Foods Company had $1 million of short-term debt in the form of notes payable due February 4, 2005. On January 22, 2005, the company issued 20,000 shares of its common shares for $40 per share, receiving $800,000 proceeds after brokerage fees and other costs of issuance. On February 4, 2005, the proceeds from the share sale, supplemented by an additional $200,000 cash, are used to liquidate the $1 million debt. The December 31, 2004 balance sheet is issued on February 20, 2005.

Situation 2

Included in Hubbard Corporation's liability account balances on December 31, 2004 were the following:

14% note payable issued October 1, 2001, maturing
    September 30, 2005 $500,000

16% note payable issued April 1, 2001, payable in six annual
instalments of $200,000 beginning April 1, 2002   600,000

Hubbard's December 31, 2004 financial statements were issued on March 31, 2005. On January 13, 2005, the entire $600,000 balance of the 16% note was refinanced by issuance of a long-term obligation payable in a lump sum. In addition, on March 8, 2005, Hubbard consummated a noncancellable agreement with the lender to refinance the 14%, $500,000 note on a long-term basis, with readily determinable terms that have not yet been implemented. Both parties are financially capable of honouring the agreement, and there have been no violations of the agreement's provisions.

Instructions

Situation 1: Show how the $1 million of short-term debt should be presented on the December 31, 2004 balance sheet, including note disclosure.

Situation 2: Explain how the liabilities should be classified on the December 31, 2004 balance sheet. How much should be classified as a current liability?

Solution to Exercise 14-3

Situation 1

Mayor Frederick Specialty Foods Co.
PARTIAL BALANCE SHEET
December 31, 2004

Current liabilities:
    Notes payable (Note 1) $ 200,000
Long-term debt:
    Notes payable refinanced in February 2002 (Note 1)   800,000

Note 1—Short-term debt refinanced
As of December 31, 2004, the Company had notes payable totalling $1 million due on February 4, 2005. These notes were refinanced on their due date to the extent of $800,000 received from the issuance of common shares on January 22, 2005. The balance of $200,000 was liquidated using current assets.

OR

Current liabilities:
    Notes payable (Note 1) $ 200,000
Short-term debt expected to be refinanced (Note 1)   800,000
Long-term debt   XXX,XXX
    (Same Note as above)

Situation 2
The entire $600,000 balance of the 16% note is properly excluded from short-term obligations since before the balance sheet was issued Hubbard refinanced the

note by issuance of a long-term obligation. The $500,000, 14% note is properly excluded from short-term obligations due to the fact that, before the balance sheet was issued, Hubbard entered into a financing agreement that clearly permits Hubbard to refinance the short-term obligation on a long-term basis with terms that are readily determinable.

APPROACH AND EXPLANATION: Review the criteria which will require an enterprise to exclude a short-term obligation from current liabilities and apply the criteria to the situation at hand.

In accordance with Canadian GAAP (see S.1510.06), an enterprise is allowed to exclude a short-term obligation from current liabilities if the following conditions are met:
1. It must **intend to refinance** the obligation on a long-term basis, and
2. It must **demonstrate an ability** to consummate the refinancing.

Intention to refinance on a long-term basis means the enterprise intends to refinance the short-term obligation so that the use of working capital will not be required during the ensuing fiscal year or operating cycle, if longer. The **ability** to consummate the refinancing must be demonstrated by:
(a) **Actually refinancing** the short-term obligation by issuance of a long-term obligation or equity securities after the date of the balance sheet but before it is issued; or
(b) Entering into a **financing agreement** that clearly permits the enterprise to refinance the debt on a long-term basis with terms that are readily determinable.

If an actual refinancing occurs, the portion of the short-term obligation to be excluded from current liabilities may not exceed the proceeds from the new obligation or equity securities issued that are to be used to retire the short-term obligation. When a financing agreement is relied upon to demonstrate ability to refinance a short-term obligation on a long-term basis, the amount of short-term debt that can be excluded from current liabilities cannot exceed the amount available for refinancing under the agreement.

> By excluding short-term debt expected to be refinanced from the current liability classification, the company's working capital position and its current ratio are improved.

TIP!

Exercise 14-4

PURPOSE: This exercise will review accounting for compensated absences.

Marsha Diebler Company began operations on January 2, 2004. It employs nine individuals who work 8-hour days and are paid hourly. Each employee earns 10 paid vacation days and six paid sick days annually. Vacation days may be taken after

January 15 of the year following the year in which they are earned. Sick days may be taken as soon as they are earned; unused sick days accumulate but do not vest. Additional information is as follows:

Actual Hourly Wage Rate		Vacation Days Used by Each Employee		Sick Days Used By Each Employee	
2004	2005	2004	2005	2004	2005
$7.00	$8.00	0	9	4	5

Marsha Diebler has chosen not to accrue paid sick leave until used, and has chosen to accrue paid vacation time at expected future rates of pay without discounting. The company used the following projected rates to accrue vacation time:

Year in Which Vacation Time Was Earned	Projected Future Pay Rates Used to Accrue Vacation Pay
2004	$7.90
2005	8.60

Instructions

(a) Prepare journal entries to record transactions related to compensated absences during 2004 and 2005.
(b) Calculate the amounts of any liability for compensated absences that should be reported on the balance sheet at December 31, 2004 and 2005.

Solution to Exercise 14-4

(a) **2004**

To accrue the expense and liability for vacations:	Wages Expense	5,688 (1)	
	Vacation Wages Payable		5,688
To record sick time paid:	Wages Expense	2,016 (2)	
	Cash		2,016
To record vacation time paid:	No entry.		

2005

To accrue the expense and liability for vacations:	Wages Expense	6,192 (3)	
	Vacation Wages Payable		6,192
To record sick time paid:	Wages Expense	2,880 (4)	
	Cash		2,880
To record vacation time paid:	Wages Expense	65	
	Vacation Wages Payable	5,119 (5)	
	Cash		5,184 (6)

Illustration 14-1   11

(1)   9 employees x $7.90/hr. x 8 hrs./day x 10 days = $5,688.
(2)   9 employees x $7.00/hr. x 8 hrs./day x 4 days = $2,016.
(3)   9 employees x $8.60/hr. x 8 hrs./day x 10 days = $6,192.
(4)   9 employees x $8.00/hr. x 8 hrs./day x 5 days = $2,880.
(5)   9 employees x $7.90/hr. x 8 hrs./day x 9 days = $5,119.
(6)   9 employees x $8.00/hr. x 8 hrs./day x 9 days = $5,184.

(b) Accrued liability at year-end:

	2004 Vacation Wages Payable	2005 Vacation Wages Payable
Jan. 1 balance	$ 0	$ 5,688.00
+ accrued	5,688.00	6,192.00
– paid	(0)	(5,119.20)
Dec. 31 balance	$ 5,688.00 (1)	$ 6,760.80 (2)

(1)   9 employees x $7.90/hr. x 8 hrs./day x 10 days   = $ 5,688.00

(2)   9 employees x $7.90/hr. x 8 hrs./day x 1 day   = $ 568.80
        9 employees x $8.60/hr. x 8 hrs./day x 10 days   =   6,192.00
                                                                $ 6,760.80

The expense and related liability for compensated absences should be recognized in the year in which the employees earn the rights to those absences. Vacation and holiday pay must be accrued if it vests or accumulates. Sick pay must be accrued only if it vests.

TIP!

Illustration 14-1
Accounting Treatment of Loss Contingencies

Loss Related to	Usually Accrued	Not Accrued	May Be Accrued*
1. Collectibility of receivables	X		
2. Obligations related to product warranties and product defects	X		
3. Premiums offered to customers	X		
4. Risk of loss or damage of enterprise property by fire, explosion, or other hazards		X	
5. General or unspecified business risks		X	
6. Risk of loss from catastrophes assumed by property and casualty insurance companies, including reinsurance companies		X	

Loss Related to	Usually Accrued	Not Accrued	May Be Accrued*
7. Threat of expropriation of assets			X
8. Pending or threatened litigation			X
9. Actual or possible claims and assessments**			X
10. Guarantees of indebtedness of others			X
11. Obligations of commercial banks under "standby letters of credit"			X
12. Agreements to repurchase receivables (or the related property) that have been sold			X

* Should be accrued when both criteria are met (likely and measurable).

**Estimated amounts of losses incurred prior to the balance sheet date but settled subsequently should be accrued as of the balance sheet date.

Exercise 14-5

PURPOSE: This exercise will enable you to practise analysing situations to determine whether a liability should be reported, and if so, at what amount.

Cleese Inc., a publishing company, is preparing its December 31, 2005 financial statements and must determine the proper accounting treatment for each of the following situations:

1. Cleese sells subscriptions to several magazines for a two- or three-year period. Cash receipts from subscribers are credited to Unearned Magazine Subscriptions Revenue. This account had a balance of $5,300,000 at December 31, 2005, before adjustment. An analysis of outstanding subscriptions at December 31, 2005 shows that they expire as follows:

During 2006:	$ 800,000
During 2007:	900,000
During 2008:	1,200,000

2. A suit for breach of contract seeking damages of $1,000,000 was filed by an author against Cleese on June 1, 2005. The company's legal counsel believes that an unfavourable outcome is likely. A reasonable estimate of the court's award to the plaintiff is in the range between $200,000 and $800,000. The company's legal counsel believes the best estimate of potential damages is $350,000.

3. On January 2, 2005, Cleese discontinued collision, fire, and theft coverage on its delivery vehicles and became self-insured for these risks. Actual losses of $40,000 during 2005 were charged to Delivery Expense. The 2004 premium for the discontinued coverage amounted to $75,000, and the controller wants

to set up a reserve for self-insurance by a debit to Delivery Expense of $35,000 and a credit to Liability for Self-insurance of $35,000.

4. During December 2005, a competitor company filed suit against Cleese for copyright infringement, claiming $600,000 in damages. In the opinion of management and company counsel, it is possible that damages will be awarded to the plaintiff. The best estimate of potential damages is $175,000.

Instructions

For each of the situations above, prepare the journal entry that should be recorded as of December 31, 2005, or explain why an entry should not be recorded. Show supporting calculations in good form.

Solution to Exercise 14-5

1. Unearned Magazine Subscription Revenue   2,400,000*
        Magazine Subscriptions Revenue   2,400,000
            (To adjust the unearned revenue account)

    *Liability account:
    Book balance at December 31, 2005 $ 5,300,000
    Adjusted balance ($800,000 +
        $900,000 + $1,200,000)   2,900,000
    Adjustment required $ 2,400,000

2. Estimated Loss from Pending Lawsuit   350,000
        Estimated Liability from Pending Lawsuit   350,000
            (To record estimated minimum damages on
            breach-of-contract litigation)

This situation involves a contingent liability. Because it is **likely** that a liability has been incurred and the loss is reasonably measurable, the loss should be accrued. When the expected loss amount is in a range, the best estimate within the range is used for the accrual. When no amount within the range is a better estimate than any other amount, the dollar value at the low end is accrued and the dollar amount at the high end of the range is disclosed in the notes.

3. No entry should be made to accrue for an expense because the absence of insurance coverage does not mean that an asset has been impaired or a liability has been incurred as of the balance sheet date. Cleese may, however, appropriate retained earnings for self-insurance as long as actual costs or losses are not charged against the appropriation of retained earnings and no part of the appropriation is transferred to income. Appropriation of retained earnings and/or disclosure in the notes to the financial statements are not required, but are recommended.

4. No entry should be made for this loss contingency, because it is not likely that an asset has been impaired or a liability has been incurred as of the balance sheet date. The loss contingency (along with the best estimate of amount) should be disclosed in the notes to financial statements because the likelihood of loss cannot be determined.

Exercise 14-6 ✓

PURPOSE: This exercise will provide an example of accounting for premium claims outstanding.

Beiler Corporation includes one coupon in each box of cereal that it packs and 10 coupons are redeemable for a premium (a toy). In 2005, Beiler purchased 9,000 premiums at 90 cents each and sold 100,000 boxes of cereal at $2.00 per box; 40,000 coupons were presented for redemption in 2005. It is estimated that 60% of the coupons will eventually be presented for redemption. This is the first year for this premium offering.

Instructions

Prepare all the entries that would be made relative to sales of cereal and to the premium plan in 2005.

Solution to Exercise 14-6

Inventory of Premiums (9,000 x $.90)	8,100	
Cash		8,100
Cash (100,000 x $2.00)	200,000	
Sales		200,000
Premium Expense	3,600	
Inventory of Premiums [(40,000 ÷ 10) x $.90]		3,600
Premium Expense	1,800*	
Estimated Liability for Premiums		1,800

*[(100,000 x 60%) − 40,000] ÷ 10 x $.90 = $1,800

EXPLANATION: The first entry records the purchase of 9,000 toys which will be used as premiums. The second entry records the sales of cereal (100,000 boxes). The third entry records the redemption of 40,000 coupons, with customers receiving one premium for every 10 coupons. The cost of the 4,000 toys distributed to these customers is recorded by a debit to expense. The fourth entry is an adjusting entry at the end of the accounting period to accrue the cost of additional premiums included in boxes of cereal sold this period that are likely to be redeemed in future periods. This is an application of the matching principle. The expense of a premium should be recognized in the same period as the related revenue which, in this case, is from the sale of cereal boxes containing the coupons that customers will redeem for a premium.

Exercise 14-7

PURPOSE: This exercise will provide an example of the journal entries involved in accounting for a warranty that is included with the sale of a product (warranty is not sold separately). Two methods are examined—the cash basis and the expense warranty method (an accrual method).

Colleen Mahla Corporation sells laptop computers under a two-year warranty contract that requires the corporation to replace defective parts and to provide the necessary repair labour. During 2004 the corporation sells for cash 400 computers at a unit price of $2,000. On the basis of past experience, the two-year warranty costs are estimated to be $90 for parts and $100 for labour per unit. (For simplicity, assume that all sales occurred on December 31, 2004, rather than evenly throughout the year.)

Instructions

(a) Record any necessary journal entries in 2004, applying the cash basis method.
(b) Record any necessary journal entries in 2004, applying the expense warranty accrual method.
(c) What liability relative to these transactions would appear on the December 31, 2004 balance sheet and how would it be classified if the cash basis method is applied?
(d) What liability relative to these transactions would appear on the December 31, 2004 balance sheet and how would it be classified if the expense warranty accrual method is applied?

In 2005 the actual warranty costs to Colleen Mahla Corporation were $14,800 for parts and $18,200 for labour.
(e) Record any necessary journal entries in 2005, applying the cash basis method.
(f) Record any necessary journal entries in 2005, applying the expense warranty accrual method.
(g) Under what conditions is it acceptable to use the cash basis method? Explain.

Solution to Exercise 14-7

(a)	Cash (400 x $2,000)	800,000	
	Sales of Computers		800,000

(b)	Cash (400 x $2,000)	800,000	
	Sales of Computers		800,000
	Warranty Expense [400 x ($90 + $100)]	76,000	
	Estimated Liability Under Warranties		76,000

(c) No liability would be disclosed under the cash basis method relative to future costs due to warranties on past sales.

(d) Current Liabilities:
    Estimated Liability Under Warranties $38,000 ᴺ

    Long-term Liabilities:
    Estimated Liability Under Warranties $38,000 ᴺ

(e)	Warranty Expense	33,000	
	Parts Inventory		14,800
	Wages Payable		18,200

(f)	Estimated Liability Under Warranties	33,000	
	Parts Inventory		14,800
	Wages Payable		18,200

(g) The cash basis is used for income tax purposes. Theoretically, the accrual basis (expense warranty method in this case) should be used for financial reporting purposes. However, the cash basis is often justifiably used for accounting purposes when warranty costs are immaterial or when the warranty period is relatively short.

Exercise 14-8

PURPOSE: This exercise will exemplify the journal entries involved in accounting for a warranty that is sold separately from the related product. The sales warranty accrual method is used for such situations.

Trent Company sells scanners for $800 each and offers to each customer a three-year warranty contract for $90 that requires the company to perform periodic services and to replace defective parts. During 2004, the company sold 500 scanners and 400 warranty contracts for cash. It estimates the three-year warranty costs as $30 for parts and $50 for labour and accounts for warranties on the sales warranty accrual method. Assume all sales occurred on December 31, 2004, and revenue from the sale of the warranties is to be recognized on a straight-line basis over the life of the contract.

Instructions

(a) Record any necessary journal entries in 2004.
(b) What liability relative to these transactions would appear on the December 31, 2004 balance sheet and how would it be classified?

In 2005, Trent Company incurred actual costs relative to 2004 scanner warranty sales of $3,800 for parts and $6,000 for labour.

(c) Record any necessary journal entries in 2005 relative to 2004 scanner warranties.
(d) What amounts relative to the 2004 scanner warranties would appear on the December 31, 2005 balance sheet and how would they be classified?

Solution to Exercise 14-8

(a) Cash ($400,000 + $36,000)   436,000
          Sales of Scanners (500 x $800)   400,000
          Unearned Warranty Revenue (400 x $90)   36,000

(b) Current Liabilities:
          Unearned Warranty Revenue $12,000
              (Note: Warranty costs are assumed to be
              incurred equally over the three-year period)

     Long-term Liabilities:
          Unearned Warranty Revenue $24,000

(c) Warranty Expense   9,800
          Parts Inventory   3,800
          Wages Payable   6,000

     Unearned Warranty Revenue   12,000
          Revenue from Warranties   12,000

(d) Current Liabilities:
          Unearned Warranty Revenue $12,000

     Long-term Liabilities:
          Unearned Warranty Revenue $12,000

Exercise 14-9

PURPOSE: This exercise will show you how to calculate a bonus under two different agreements.

Merry Rawls, president of the Merry Music Company, has a bonus arrangement with the company under which she receives 15% of the net income (after deducting taxes and bonus) each year. For the current year, the net income before deducting either the provision for income taxes or the bonus is $719,400. The bonus is deductible for tax purposes, and the effective income tax rate is 40%.

Instructions

(a) Calculate the amount of Merry's bonus.
(b) Calculate the appropriate provision for federal income taxes for the year.
(c) Recalculate the amount of Merry's bonus if the bonus is to be 15% of income after bonus but before tax. (Round to the nearest dollar.)

Solution to Exercise 14-9

(B = bonus; T = taxes)

(a)

$$B = .15 (\$719{,}400 - B - T)$$
$$T = .40 (\$719{,}400 - B)$$
$$B = .15 [\$719{,}400 - B - .4 (\$719{,}400 - B)]$$
$$B = .15 (\$719{,}400 - B - \$287{,}760 + .4B)$$
$$B = .15 (\$431{,}640 - .6B)$$
$$B = \$64{,}746 - .09B$$
$$1.09B = \$64{,}746$$
$$\text{Bonus} = \underline{\$59{,}400}$$

(b)

$$T = .40 (\$719{,}400 - B)$$
$$T = .40 (\$719{,}400 - \$59{,}400)$$
$$T = .40 (\$660{,}000)$$
$$\text{Taxes} = \underline{\$264{,}000}$$

(c)

$$B = .15 (\$719{,}400 - B)$$
$$B = \$107{,}910 - .15B$$
$$1.15B = \$107{,}910$$
$$\text{Bonus} = \underline{\$93{,}835}$$

TIP! Examine the equation to calculate the bonus. Make sure it is consistent with the wording of the agreement. For instance, if the bonus is based on income **after** bonus and **after** taxes, then income must be reduced by both bonus and taxes in your formula (Income − B − T) [see part (a)]. But if the bonus is to be based on income after bonus and before taxes, then taxes are not part of your equation [see part (c)].

Always "prove" the bonus figure calculated.		**TIP!**
Proof—parts (a) and (b)		
Income before bonus and before taxes	$ 719,400	
Bonus	(59,400)	
Income before taxes	660,000	
Income taxes (40% x $660,000) [agrees with (b)]	(264,000)	
Income after bonus and after taxes	396,000	
Bonus rate	15%	
Bonus [agrees with (a)]	$ 59,400	
Proof—part (c)		
Income before bonus and before taxes	$ 719,400	
Bonus	(93,835)	
Income before taxes	625,565	
Bonus rate	15%	
Bonus [agrees with (c)]	$ 93,835	

Analysis of Multiple-Choice Type Questions

Question

1. A current liability is an obligation that:
   a. was paid during the current period.
   b. will be reported as an expense within the year or operating cycle that follows the balance sheet date, whichever is longer.
   c. will be converted to a long-term liability within the next year.
   d. is expected to require the use of current assets or the creation of another current liability to liquidate it.

EXPLANATION: Before you read the answer selections, write down the definition for "current liability." Compare each answer selection with your definition. A **current liability** is an obligation which will come due within one year and whose liquidation is reasonably expected to require the use of existing resources properly classifiable as current assets or the creation of other current liabilities. (Solution = d.)

Question

2. Reynolds Company borrowed money from Andersen Company for nine months by issuing a zero-interest-bearing note payable with a face value of $106,000. The proceeds amounted to $100,000. In recording the issuance of this note, what account should Reynolds debit for $6,000?
   a. Interest Payable
   b. Interest Expense

c. Prepaid Interest
d. Discount on Note Payable

EXPLANATION: The excess of the face value of a zero-interest-bearing note payable and the proceeds collected upon its issuance is the cost of borrowing. This cost of borrowing (interest expense) should be recognized over the months the loan is outstanding. Therefore, the total interest ($6,000) is initially debited to a Discount on Note Payable Account. The balance of that account is then amortized (allocated) to interest expense over the life of the note. (Solution = d.)

TIP! A **zero-interest-bearing note** is often called a **non-interest-bearing-note**.

Question

3. Martha's Boutique sells gift certificates. These gift certificates have no expiration date. Data for the current year are as follows:

Gift certificates outstanding, January 1	$225,000
Gift certificates sold	750,000
Gift certificates redeemed	660,000
Gross profit expressed as percentage of sales	40%

At December 31, Martha should report unearned revenue of:
a. $90,000.
b. $126,000.
c. $261,000.
d. $315,000.

EXPLANATION: Draw a T-account for the liability and enter the data given.

Gift Certificates Outstanding

Redeemed	660,000	Beginning Balance		225,000
		Sold		750,000
		Ending Balance		315,000

(Solution = d.)

TIP! The gross profit percentage is not used in the solution for the balance of unearned revenue. Revenue and unearned revenue are gross amounts, not net amounts.

Question

4. A local retailer is required to collect a 6% sales tax for the province's department of revenue and remit in the month that follows the sale. The retailer does not use a separate Sales Taxes Payable account; rather the sales price of products sold and the related sales tax is all credited to Sales Revenue. During the month of March, 2004, credits totalling $25,440 were made to the

Sales Revenue account. The amount to be remitted to the government in April for sales taxes collected during the month of March:

a. is $1,526.40.
b. is $1,440.00.
c. is $2,696.64.
d. cannot be determined from the data given.

EXPLANATION: Set up an algebraic expression to describe the relationships between the data given and solve.

$$\text{Sales} + .06 \ \text{Sales} = \$25,440$$

$$1.06 \ \text{Sales} = \$25,440$$

$$\text{Sales} = \frac{25,440}{1,06}$$

$$\text{Sales} = \$24,000$$

$$\$25,440 \ \text{Total} - \$24,000 \ \text{Sales} = \underline{\underline{\$1,440}} \ \text{Sales Tax} \quad (\text{Solution} = \text{b.})$$

Question

5. Included in Arnold Howell Company's liability accounts at December 31, 2005 was the following:

12% Note payable issued in 2003 for cash and
due in May 2006 $2,000,000

On February 1, 2006 Arnold issued $5 million of five-year bonds with the intention of using part of the bond proceeds to liquidate the $2 million note payable maturing in May. On March 2, 2006, Arnold used $2 million of the bond proceeds to liquidate the note payable. Arnold's December 31, 2005 balance sheet is being issued on March 15, 2006. How much of the $2 million note payable should be classified as a current liability on the balance sheet?

a. $0
b. $800,000
c. $1,000,000
d. $2,000,000

EXPLANATION: Mentally review the definition of a current liability and the guidelines for reporting short-term debt expected to be refinanced. At the date the balance sheet is issued, we have evidence of the intent and ability to refinance the debt on a long-term basis. That evidence is the post balance sheet issuance of long-term debt securities. The proceeds from the bond issuance exceed the reported amount of the note. Therefore, the entire $2 million note payable should be classified as a long-term liability. (Solution = a.)

Question

6. An employee's net (or take-home) pay is determined by gross earnings minus amounts for income tax withholdings and the employee's:
    a. portion of employment insurance.
    b. and employer's portion of employment insurance.
    c. portion of employment insurance, and Canada Pension Plan deductions.
    d. portion Canada Pension Plan deductions.

EXPLANATION: Before you read the answer selections, write down the model for the net (take-home) pay calculation. Then find the answer selection that agrees with your model.

Employee's gross earnings for the current period
 – Income tax withholdings
 – Canada Pension Plan
 – Employment insurance
 = Net (or take-home) pay   (Solution = c.)

TIP! | The employer must also contribute Canada Pension Plan and Employment Insurance premiums on behalf of each employee.

Question

7. An example of a contingent liability is:
    a. sales taxes payable.
    b. accrued salaries.
    c. property taxes payable.
    d. a pending lawsuit.

EXPLANATION: Mentally define contingent liability and think of examples before you read the alternative answer selections. A contingent liability is a situation involving uncertainty as to possible loss or expense that will ultimately be resolved when one or more future events occur or fail to occur. Examples are pending or threatened lawsuits and product warranties. Accrued salaries result in an actual liability. Sales taxes payable and property taxes payable are both actual liabilities if they exist at a balance sheet date. (Solution = d.)

Question

8. A contingent loss with an outcome that cannot be determined should be:

	Accrued	Disclosed
a.	Yes	Yes
b.	Yes	No
c.	No	Yes
d.	No	No

EXPLANATION: A contingent loss that is likely and measurable is to be accrued. A contingent loss that cannot be determined should be disclosed, but it should not be accrued. A contingent loss that is unlikely need not be accrued or disclosed. (Solution = c.)

Question

9. Mayberry Co. has a loss contingency to accrue. The loss amount can only be reasonably estimated within a range of outcomes. No single amount within the range is a better estimate than any other amount. The amount of loss accrual should be:
    a. zero.
    b. the minimum of the range.
    c. the mean of the range.
    d. the maximum of the range.

EXPLANATION: It is *CICA Handbook* Section 3290.12 that calls for the accrual of a loss contingency when it is likely and estimable. Then paragraph .13 of Section 3290 states that, when the reasonable estimate of loss is a range and some amount within the range appears at the time to be a better estimate than any other amount within the range, that amount shall be accrued. When no amount within the range is a better estimate then any other amount, however, the minimum amount in the range should be accrued. (Solution = b.)

Question

10. Scott Corporation began operations at the beginning of 2004. It provides a two-year warranty with the sale of its product. Scott estimates that warranty costs will equal 4% of the selling price the first year after sale and 6% of the selling price the second year after the sale. The following data are available:

	2004	2005
Sales	$400,000	$500,000
Actual warranty expenditures	10,000	38,000

The balance of the warranty liability at December 31, 2005 should be:
    a. $12,000.
    b. $42,000.
    c. $44,000.
    d. $50,000.

EXPLANATION: Draw a T-account and enter the amounts that would be reflected in the account and determine its balance.

Estimated Liability Under Warranties			
(2) Expenditures in 2004	10,000	(1) Expense for 2004	40,000
(4) Expenditures in 2005	38,000	(3) Expense for 2005	50,000
		12/31/05 Balance	42,000

(Solution = b.)

(1) $400,000 x (4% + 6%) = $40,000 expense for 2004.
The total warranty cost related to the products sold during 2004 should be recognized in the period of sale (matching principle).
(2) Given data. Actual expenditures during 2004.
(3) $500,000 x (4% + 6%) = $50,000 expense for 2005.
(4) Given data. Actual expenditures during 2005.

TIP! Because some items are sold near the end of the year and the warranty is for two years, a portion of the warranty liability should be classified as a current liability (the amount pertaining to the actual expenditures estimated to occur in 2006) and the remainder as a long-term liability.

Question

11. Crazy Pete Theme Park is self-insured. Premiums for insurance used to cost $100,000 per year before Crazy Pete discontinued coverage. During 2005, Crazy Pete suffered losses of $39,000 that used to be (but are no longer) covered by insurance. Crazy Pete thinks this was a "light" year and greater losses in future years will offset the lower amount sustained in 2005. In order to avoid volatility in earnings due to being self-insured, Crazy Pete wants to set up a Liability for Self-insurance. A reasonable estimate of losses to be incurred in 2006 is $120,000. The liability to be reported by Crazy Pete at December 31, 2005 due to this situation is:
    a. $0.
    b. $61,000.
    c. $100,000.
    d. $120,000.

EXPLANATION: Even if the amount is estimable, the future losses from self-insurance do not result in liabilities at the December 31, 2005 balance sheet date because the losses in the future will result from future events, not from a past event. It is not generally acceptable to accrue future losses from self-insurance. (Solution = a.)

TIP! Crazy Pete should report $39,000 of losses on its 2005 income statement.

Question

12. Powercell, a manufacturer of batteries, offers a cash rebate to buyers of its size D batteries. The rebate offer is good until June 30, 2004. At December 31, 2003, the balance sheet should include an estimated liability for unredeemed rebates in order to comply with the:
    a. Revenue recognition principle.
    b. Expense recognition principle.
    c. Matching principle.
    d. Time-period assumption.

EXPLANATION: Premium, coupon, and rebate offers are made to stimulate sales, and their costs should be charged to expense in the period of the sale that benefits from the premium plan. At the end of the accounting period, many of these premium, coupon, and rebate offers may be outstanding and, when presented in subsequent periods, must be redeemed. The number of outstanding premium, coupon, and rebate offers that will be presented for redemption must be estimated in order to reflect the existing current liability and to match expenses with revenues. An adjusting entry is made with a debit to Rebate Expense and a credit to Estimated Liability for Rebates. (Solution = c).

Question

13. The ratio of current assets to current liabilities is called the:
    a. current ratio.
    b. acid-test ratio.
    c. current asset turnover ratio.
    d. current liability turnover ratio.

EXPLANATION: Two major ratios used to measure liquidity of an entity are the (1) current ratio and the (2) acid-test ratio. The current ratio is calculated by dividing current assets by current liabilities. The acid-test ratio is calculated by dividing quick assets (cash + marketable securities + net receivables) by current liabilities. Marketable securities in this context refer to short-term (temporary) investments. The current ratio is sometimes called the working capital ratio; the acid-test ratio is often called the quick ratio. (Solution = a).

Question

14. Gary Brooks, a manager of a local business, is to receive an annual bonus equal to 10% of the company's income in excess of $100,000 before income taxes but after deduction of the bonus. If income before income taxes and bonus is $820,000 and the tax rate is 40%, the amount of the bonus would be:
    a. $22,800.
    b. $36,981.
    c. $65,455.
    d. $72,000.

EXPLANATION: Carefully write an equation that expresses the agreement. Notice what should be deducted from income before the bonus percentage is applied—$100,000 and the bonus (but not taxes). Solve for bonus. Prove your answer.

B	=	10% ($820,000 − $100,000 − B)
B	=	$82,000 − $10,000 − .1B
1.1 B	=	$72,000
B	=	$72,000 ÷ 1.1
B	=	$65,455 (Solution = c.)

Proof:	Income before taxes and bonus	$ 820,000
	Exclusion	(100,000)
	Bonus expense	(65,455)
	Income after bonus and before taxes	654,545
	Bonus rate	10%
	Bonus	$ 65,455

Question

✗ 15. The definition of a liability includes all but which of the following?
  a. An obligation or duty to another party.
  b. Little or no discretion to avoid.
  c. Legally enforceable.
  d. The transaction or event giving rise to the obligation that has occurred.

EXPLANATION: *CICA Handbook* Section 1000 provides the definition of a liability. The transaction need not be legally enforceable to be an obligation. (Solution = c.)

Question

16. It is important to present current liabilities separately from other liabilities for the following reason:
  a. When netted against current assets, it shows the working capital position of the company.
  b. It helps assess liquidity of the company since it shows the ability of the company to realize its operating assets for payment of its operating liabilities.
  c. It helps users predict cash flow needs.
  d. All of the above.

EXPLANATION: It is very important for cash flow prediction, liquidity assessment, and assessment of whether the company has enough working capital (defined as current assets minus current liabilities). (Solution = d.)

Question

17. Debt that is currently due but that is expected to be refinanced through long-term debt may be classified as long-term if which of the following set of conditions holds:
  a. There is a non-cancellable agreement (that extends beyond one year) with a financially solvent lender. The company is not in violation of any of the terms of the contract.
  b. The company fully intends to refinance and has contacted several interested parties all of whom are financially solvent.
  c. There is a signed agreement to refinance the loan through a demand loan

facility with a financially solvent lender. The company is not in violation of any of the covenants under the agreement.

d. The company fully intends to refinance and has a verbal agreement with a financially solvent party. The company is not in violation of any terms of the agreement. Under the terms of the contract, the company may cancel the agreement at any time.

EXPLANATION: The key in deciding the best answer is the concept of non-cancellable. Answer (b) is based on intent and does not provide sufficient assurance; (c) is a demand loan which is technically another current liability; (d) allows the company to back out of the agreement. (Solution = a.)

Question

18. A company lacks fire insurance. Which of the following statements is true:
    a. This represents a loss contingency and should be provided for in the financial statements if estimable and note disclosed if not.
    b. This constitutes an uncertainty as to amounts and timing of losses; however, it should not be recorded since no impairment of an asset or incurrence of a liability can exist prior to the event (the fire).
    c. This represents a contingent loss where the outcome is not determinable and therefore should be disclosed.
    d. This represents a condition involving uncertainty where it is unlikely that a future event will confirm that an asset has been impaired or liability incurred; however, note disclosure is required.

EXPLANATION: *CICA Handbook* Section 3290 states that acts such as fires are random in occurrence and unpredictable. Therefore, note disclosure is not required (although it may be desirable) since the event giving rise to a potential loss has not yet happened nor may ever happen. Lack of insurance on key assets does represent a significant exposure that users may wish to be aware of (full disclosure principle). (Solution = b.)

Question

19. When analysing the liquidity of a company which of the following statements is most true?
    a. The current ratio is the best ratio and as long as the ratio is greater than 2:1 the company is fine.
    b. The current ratio is a good measure of liquidity but it does not take into account the relative liquidity and illiquidity of current assets.
    c. Ratios do not give useful information and users should focus on the cash flow statement instead.
    d. Ratios such as the current and quick or acid-test ratios provide definitive quantitative information and therefore other information such as the nature of the business need not be looked at.

EXPLANATION: The benchmark of 2:1 is often used however, it is an imprecise benchmark when taken in isolation. Factors such as (i) the nature of the business, as well as (ii) whether the company is in a startup state or mature state must be taken into consideration as well as other factors. While the cash flow statement provides significant information, a better analysis would incorporate assessment of ratios as well as the factor noted above. The quick or acid-test ratios incorporate the fact that some current assets are more liquid than others. They are therefore more sensitive ratios. (Solution = b.)

CHAPTER 15

Long-Term Financial Liabilities

Overview

Sources of assets include current liabilities, long-term liabilities, and owners' equity. Liabilities are considered a "temporary" source of assets; whereas, owners' equity is a more "permanent" source of assets. When a company borrows money, it does so with the expectation of using the borrowed funds to acquire assets that can be used to generate more income. The objective is to generate an amount of additional income which exceeds the cost of borrowing the funds (interest).

Long-term debt consists of probable future sacrifices of economic benefits arising from present obligations that are not payable within a year or the operating cycle of the business, whichever is longer. Bonds payable, long-term notes payable, mortgages payable, pension liabilities, and lease obligations are examples of long-term liabilities. This chapter will focus on the first three of these.

Although the subject of accounting for bonds is included in the principles of an introductory accounting course, many intermediate students don't remember the details of the procedures and look upon this topic as one of the most difficult they have encountered. Perhaps they have problems with the material because they try to memorize their way through the topic. As a result, it is imperative that you think about the time value of money concepts introduced elsewhere in the text and grasp how they are applied in the calculations involved in accounting for long-term debt. When you see the logic and rationale of the accounting procedures, you will find it easier to recall these guidelines years from now.

Study Steps

Understanding the Underlying Business Transactions

Bonds

Bonds are instruments used to raise financing. They are considered liabilities of the company as they generally require repayment along with interest on the principal. Bonds usually have a face value (i.e., the value at which the bonds will be redeemed at maturity) and a stated interest rate. If the market interest rate (i.e., the current interest rate for similar bonds with similar risk) is the same as the stated rate on the bond, the bond trades at face value (e.g., a bond with a face value of $100 and a stated interest rate of 10% will be bought and sold for $100 assuming that current market interest rates are 10%).

If market interest rates are lower than the stated rates, the bond becomes more valuable to investors and therefore would trade at a premium (would be bought and sold for greater than $100 in the example). Likewise, if the market interest rate is higher, the bond would trade at a discount.

The market value of a bond varies with demand and current market interest rates and, therefore, it is rare that a bond's market value would be the same as its face value or carrying value.

Bond premium is the excess value attributed to the bond, often primarily due to the fact that the stated interest rate on the bond exceeds the market interest rate.

Bond discount is the decrease in value (from face value), often primarily due to the fact that the bond's stated interest rate is less than the market rate.

Extinguishment of Debt

Extinguishment of debt involves paying off debt before it becomes due. This assumes that the debt agreement allows for early repayment.

Often, early repayment is not an allowable option under the terms of the agreement or there are stiff penalties for early repayment. One way around this is by entering into a transaction/business arrangement called debt defeasance. Defeasance occurs when the company takes the funds that it would have otherwise used to extinguish the debt, if it could, and puts them in investments that are then held to be used solely to pay off the debt. In other words, the investment and the return on the investment may only be used to make the scheduled repayments on the old debt as they come due.

Legal defeasance occurs when the company gets the creditors (from original debt) to agree to this arrangement and to release the company from further liability. The creditors would want to ensure that the investment funds will be used only for repayment and, therefore, they would normally require that the funds be placed in trust.

In-substance defeasance occurs when the creditors do not agree to release the company from any further liability relating to the debt or they do not know about the defeasance arrangement.

The difference between legal and in-substance defeasance is primarily that with legal defeasance, the creditors give up their legal claim on the company, and look solely to the trust for repayment. Because of this, GAAP does not allow "in-substance" defeasance of debt to be removed from the balance sheet. They are therefore not popular in practice any longer.

Off-Balance-Sheet Financing

Off-balance-sheet financing entails a company obtaining some sort of financing without recording debt on the balance sheet. Indeed, often the sole purpose of these arrangements is to avoid recording debt. For example, if a company needs cash, there are many creative ways to obtain financing without actually borrowing the funds. They could sell their inventory for cash up front and agree to buy it back over time. They could transfer their receivables while retaining the risks and rewards of ownership or they could finance the purchase of equipment through a lease, etc. There are many more examples.

Always scrutinize complex business arrangements that are entered into for the purposes of raising funds. Management intent is key to understanding the economic substance of the transaction.

Impairment and Restructuring of Loans

This topic is covered both from the creditor's perspective and the debtor's perspective. A loan receivable is impaired when there is no reasonable assurance that the original amounts will no longer be collected. Thus a provision is accrued for the non-collectible portion.

Sometimes these instruments are renegotiated such that the terms are changed. In some cases, however, the creditor forecloses on the loan and takes back the underlying security.

From the debtor's perspective, there may be difficulty in determining whether the debt has been repaid and replaced by new debt or whether the old debt still exists but under new terms. This is a significant difference since it determines whether a gain or loss will be recognized at the date of the transaction and also future interest expense.

Becoming Proficient in Related Calculations and Accounting Skills

Three main areas involve fairly complex calculations:

- Bond accounting
- Loan impairment
- Troubled debt restructuring

Use the illustrations and exercises below to ensure competence has been achieved on the nature of the calculations as well as the reasoning behind them.

Ratio analysis

Interpreting ratios correctly can only come from a detailed understanding of the GAAP that resulted in their presentation (or lack of presentation!) on the financial statements.

There are two key ratios that users calculate to determine whether the company has undue liquidity/solvency risk associated with debt:

Debt to total assets: total debt/total assets

Times interest earned: Income before taxes and interest/interest expense

The former measures what percentage of assets are financed by this more risky source of financing. Note that many companies do not necessarily use "total debt" in the calculation. It may be that long-term debt is more important. The higher this ratio, the higher the risk of default. Care should be taken when comparing company to company. Note also that not all debt is reflected in the total debt number on the balance sheet. Off-balance-sheet financing would not be included; however, good analysts would adjust the calculation to incorporate off-balance-sheet debt as well.

Times interest earned focuses on the company's ability to cover its interest obligation. The higher this ratio, the better.

Tips on Chapter Topics

TIP! The denomination of a bond is called the **face value**. Synonymous terms are **par value, principal amount, maturity value,** and **face amount**.

TIP! Bond prices are quoted in terms of percentage of par. Thus, a bond with a par value of $4,000 and a price quote of 102 is currently selling for a price of $4,080 (102% of $4,000). A bond with a quote of 100 is selling for its par value.

TIP! The bond contract is called an **indenture**. This term is often confused with the term "debenture." A **debenture** bond is an unsecured bond.

TIP! The interest rate written in the bond indenture and ordinarily appearing on the bond certificate is known as the **stated rate**. Synonymous terms are **coupon rate, nominal rate**, and **contract rate**.

TIP! The rate of interest actually earned by bondholders is called the **effective, yield**, or **market rate**.

TIP! A bond's **issuance price** is determined by the present value of all of the future cash flows promised by the bond indenture. The future cash flows include the face value and interest payments. The bond's present value is determined by using the market rate of interest at the date of issuance. An excess of the issuance price over par is called a **premium**; an excess of par value over the issuance price is called a **discount**.

TIP! In computing the present value of a bond's (1) maturity value and (2) interest payments, the **same** interest rate is used. That rate is the effective interest rate on a per interest period basis. As an example, if a ten-year bond has a stated rate of 10%, pays interest semiannually, and is issued to yield 12%, a 6% rate is used to perform **all** of the present value calculations.

Illustration 15-1   33

Bond prices vary inversely with changes in the market rate of interest. This means that as the market rate of interest goes down, bond prices go up; and as the market rate of interest goes up, bond prices go down. It also means that at the date of issuance, if the market rate of interest is below the stated rate, the price will be above par; likewise, if the market rate is above the stated rate, the issuance price will be below par. Hence, **a premium or a discount is an adjustment to interest via an adjustment to price**. The adjustment to interest is recorded by the process of amortizing the premium or discount over the periods the bond is outstanding.

TIP!

Interest payments on notes payable are generally made on a monthly or quarterly basis. Interest payments on bonds payable are usually made semiannually. Despite these common practices, interest rates generally are expressed on an annual basis. Therefore, care must be taken that the annual rate be converted to a "rate per period" before other calculations are performed.

TIP!

The **Discount on Bonds Payable account** is a contra liability account so its balance should be deducted from Bonds Payable on the balance sheet. The **Premium on Bonds Payable account** is an adjunct type valuation account so its balance should be added to the balance of Bonds Payable on the balance sheet. Unamortized Bond Issuance Costs are to be classified as a deferred charge in the "Other Assets" classification on the balance sheet; they should be amortized over the bond's life using the straight-line method.

TIP!

The **effective interest method** of amortization is sometimes called the **interest method** or the **present value method** or the **effective method**. When the effective interest method is used, the bond's carrying value will equal its present value (assuming the amortization is up to date).

TIP!

When the accounting period ends on a date other than an interest date, the amortization schedule for a bond or a note payable is unaffected by this fact. That is, the schedule is prepared and calculations are made according to the bond periods, ignoring the details of the accounting period. The interest expense amounts shown in the amortization schedule are then apportioned to the appropriate accounting period(s). As an example, if the interest expense for the six months ending April 30, 2003 is $120,000, then $40,000 (2/6) of that amount would go on the income statement for the 2002 calendar year and $80,000 (4/6) of it should be reflected on the income statement for the 2003 calendar year.

TIP!

Illustration 15-1
Calculation and Proof of Bond Issuance Price

Gemple Company issues a 5-year bond on January 1, 2005 (maturity date is January 1, 2010), with a stated interest rate of 6%. The market rate of interest at the date of issuance is 5%, the par value is $1,000, and interest is due annually on January 1.

The bond is a promise to pay $1,000 on January 1, 2010 and $60 (6% x $1,000) every January 1 beginning January 1, 2006 and ending January 1, 2010. The price of the bond is determined by the present value of all future cash flows related to the bond. The present value of the bond is found by discounting all of the promised payments at the market rate of interest (5%). This process is illustrated by the following timeline and present value calculations:

$$
\begin{array}{ll}
\text{PV} & \$259.77 \\
\text{PV} & \underline{783.53} \\
\text{Total PV} & \underline{\$1,043.30}
\end{array}
\qquad \$1,000
$$

$n=5; i=5\%$

Present value of an ordinary annuity of $60 per period for five years at 5% interest ($60 x 4.32948)	$ 259.77
Present value of $1,000 due in five periods at 5% interest ($1,000 x .78353)	783.53
Total present value	$ 1,043.30

TIP! The factor of .78353 was derived from the Present Value of 1 table and the factor of 4.32948 was derived from the Present Value of an Ordinary Annuity of 1 table.

Thus, the bond price would be $1,043.30. Theoretically, this is the sum that would be required to be invested now at 5% compounded annually (market rate) to allow for the periodic (annual in this case) withdrawal of $60 (stated amount of interest) at the end of each of five years and the withdrawal of $1,000 at the end of five years. The following is proof that $1,043.30 is the amount required in this case.

Jan. 1, 2005	$1,043.30		$1,043.30	
	+ 52.17	interest at 5%	x .05	**market rate**
	1,095.47		52.1650	**effective interest**
1st interest payment on 1/1/06	− 60.00			
	1,035.47		1,035.47	
	+ 51.77		x .05	
	1,087.24		51.7735	
2nd interest payment on 1/1/07	− 60.00			
	1,027.24		1,027.24	
	+ 51.36		x .05	
	1,078.60		51.3620	
3rd interest payment on 1/1/08	− 60.00			
	1,018.60		1,018.60	
	+ 50.93		x .05	
	1,069.53		50.9300	
4th interest payment on 1/1/09	− 60.00			
	1,009.53		1,009.53	
	+ 50.48		x .05	
	1,060.01		50.4765	
5th interest payment on 1/1/10	− 60.00			
	1,000.01			
Principal payment	−1,000.00			
	$ .01	Rounding error		

Illustration 15-2   35

An amortization schedule can be constructed using the calculations above. It would appear as follows:

Date	Stated Interest	Effective Interest	Premium Amortization	Carrying Value
1/1/05				$ 1,043.30
1/1/06	$ 60.00	$ 52.17	$ 7.83	1,035.47
1/1/07	60.00	51.77	8.23	1,027.24
1/1/08	60.00	51.36	8.64	1,018.60
1/1/09	60.00	50.93	9.07	1,009.53
1/1/10	60.00	50.47 *	9.53	1,000.00
	$300.00	$256.70	$ 43.30	

*The rounding error of $.01 is plugged to interest expense in the last interest period.

Illustration 15-2
Formats for Common Calculations Involving Bonds Payable

1. Cash Interest Per Period.

    Par value
    x   Stated rate of interest per period
    =   Cash interest per period

    Cash interest is always a constant amount each period.

2. Interest Expense Using Straight-Line Amortization Method.

    Cash interest for the period
    +   Discount amortization for the period
    OR − Premium amortization for the period
    =   Interest expense for the period

    Interest expense is a constant amount each period using this method.

3. Amortization Amount Using Straight-Line Method.

    Issuance premium or discount ÷ Periods in bonds life = Amortization per period

4. Interest Expense Using Effective Interest Method.

    Carrying value at the beginning of the period
    x   Effective rate of interest per interest period
    =   Interest expense for the interest period

    The carrying value changes each interest period so the interest expense changes each period.

5. Amortization Amount Using Effective Interest Method.

    Interest expense for the interest period
    −   Cash interest for the interest period
    =   Amortization of discount for the interest period

    OR

    Cash interest for the interest period
    −   Interest expense for the interest period
    =   Amortization of premium for the interest period

    Interest expense is greater than cash interest for bonds issued at a discount.

    Cash interest is greater than interest expense for bonds issued at a premium.

6.   Carrying Value and Net Carrying Value.
         Par value
      –   Unamortized discount

OR +   Unamortized premium
      =   Carrying value
      –   Unamortized debt issue costs
      =   Net carrying amount

> The process of amortization decreases the unamortized amount of discount or premium; hence the carrying value moves toward the par value.

7.   Gain or Loss on Redemption.
         Net carrying amount
      –   Redemption price
      =   Gain if positive, that is, if net carrying value is the greater
OR =   Loss if negative, that is, if redemption price is the greater

TIP!   An **interest payment** promised by a bond is calculated by multiplying the bond's par value by its stated interest rate. This amount is often referred to as the **cash interest** or **stated interest**.

TIP!   Using the **straight-line method of amortization**, interest expense is determined by either adding the amount of discount amortization to the cash interest or deducting the amount of premium amortization from the cash interest. The periodic amount of amortization is determined by dividing the issuance premium or discount by the number of periods in the bond's life.

TIP!   The **life** of a bond is measured by the time between the date of issuance and the date of maturity. The bond's life is shorter than the term of the bond if the bond is issued on a date later than it is dated.

TIP!   The **effective interest expense** (interest expense using the effective interest method of amortization) is determined by multiplying the bond's carrying value at the beginning of the period by the effective interest rate. The difference between the interest payment (cash interest) and the effective interest expense for a period is the amount of premium or discount amortization for the period. The amount of amortization for a period causes a reduction in the balance of the unamortized premium or unamortized discount which in turn causes the carrying value to change.

TIP!   A bond's **carrying value (book value, carrying amount)** is equal to the (1) par value plus any unamortized premium, or (2) par value minus any unamortized discount. When the effective interest method of amortization is used and the amortization is up to date, the bond's carrying value will equal its present value (determined by using the bond's effective interest rate to discount all remaining interest payments and par value). A bond's **net carrying value** is equal to its carrying value minus any related unamortized bond issuance costs.

TIP!   The pattern of interest expense using the effective interest method may be compared to the pattern of interest expense using the straight-line method for both a bond issued at a discount and a bond issued at a premium by reference to the graph in **Illustration 15-3**. The relationship between interest expense and cash interest should also be noted. The difference between the cash interest and interest expense for a period is the amount of amortization for the period. The pattern of the periodic amount of amortization is also depicted by the graph.

Exercise 15-1

PURPOSE: This exercise will illustrate (1) the calculations and journal entries throughout a bond's life for a bond issued at a discount and (2) the accounting required when bonds are called prior to their maturity date.

Howell Company issued bonds with the following details:

Face value	$100,000
Stated interest rate	7%
Market interest rate	10%
Maturity date	January 1, 2008
Date of issuance	January 1, 2005
Bond issue costs	$8,000
Call price	102
Interest payments due	Annually on January 1
Method of amortization	Effective interest

Instructions

(a) Calculate the amount of issuance premium or discount.
(b) Prepare the journal entry for the issuance of bonds.
(c) Prepare the amortization schedule for these bonds.
(d) Prepare all of the journal entries (subsequent to the issuance date) for 2005 and 2006 that relate to these bonds. Assume the accounting period coincides with the calendar year. Assume reversing entries are not used.
(e) Prepare the journal entry to record the retirement of bonds assuming they are called on January 1, 2007.

Solution to Exercise 15-1

(a) $100,000 par x 7% stated rate = $7,000 annual cash interest
Factor for present value of a single sum, $i = 10\%$, $n = 3$ .75132
Factor for present value of an ordinary annuity, $i = 10\%$, $n = 3$ 2.48685

$100,000 x .75132 =	$ 75,132.00
$7,000 x 2.48685 =	17,407.95
Issuance price	$ 92,539.95
Face value	$ 100,000.00
Issuance price	92,539.95
Discount on bonds payable	$ 7,460.05

(b)

Cash ($92,539.95 – $8,000.00)	84,539.95	
Discount on Bonds Payable	7,460.05	
Unamortized Bond Issue Costs	8,000.00	
Bonds Payable		100,000.00

EXPLANATION: Always start with the easiest part of a journal entry. The issuance of a bond is **always** recorded by a credit to the Bonds Payable account for the par value of the bonds ($100,000 in this case). Because the issuance price is less than par, a contra type valuation account must be established; it is titled Discount on Bonds Payable and is debited for the issuance discount of $7,460.05. The $8,000 issuance costs are to be amortized over the periods benefited by the loan in order to comply with the matching principle; hence they are initially charged to an asset account. Cash was received for the issuance price less the issuance costs (fees to attorneys, accountants, printers, and underwriters) so debit Cash for the net proceeds of $84,539.95.

TIP! The Unamortized Bond Issue Costs account can be titled Bond Issue Costs. The Discount on Bonds Payable account is sometimes called Unamortized Bond Discount. Regardless of whether the word unamortized appears in the account titles or not, the balances of these accounts at a balance sheet date (after adjustments) represent the unamortized amounts.

(c)

Date	7% Stated Interest	10% Interest Expense	Discount Amortization	Carrying Value
1/1/05				$ 92,539.95
1/1/06	$ 7,000.00	$ 9,254.00	$ 2,254.00	94,793.95
1/1/07	7,000.00	9,479.40	2,479.40	97,273.35
1/1/08	7,000.00	9,726.65 [a]	2,726.65	100,000.00
	$ 21,000.00	$ 28,460.05	$ 7,460.05	

[a]Includes rounding error of $.69.

EXPLANATION: Stated interest is determined by multiplying the par value ($100,000) by the contract rate of interest (7%). Interest expense is calculated by multiplying the carrying value at the beginning of the interest period by the effective interest rate (10%). The amount of discount amortization for the period is the excess of the interest expense over the stated interest (cash interest) amount. The carrying value at an interest payment date is the carrying value at the beginning of the interest period plus the discount amortization for the period.

TIP! The amount of interest expense of $9,479.40 appearing on the "1/1/07" payment line is the amount of interest expense for the interest period ending on that date. Thus, in this case, $9,479.40 is the interest expense for the 12 months preceding the date 1/1/07, which would be the calendar year of 2006.

TIP! Any rounding error should be plugged to (included in) the interest expense amount for the last interest period. Otherwise, there would forever be a small balance left in the Discount on Bonds Payable account long after the bonds were extinguished.

TIP! Notice that the total interest expense ($28,460.05) over the three-year period equals the total cash interest ($21,000.00) plus the total issuance discount ($7,460.05). Thus, you can see that the issuance discount represents an additional amount of interest to be recognized over the life of the bonds.

(d) **December 31, 2005**

Bond Interest Expense	9,254.00	
Interest Payable		7,000.00
Discount on Bonds Payable		2,254.00
Bond Issue Expense	2,666.67	
Unamortized Bond Issue Costs		2,666.67
($8,000.00 ÷ 3 = $2,666.67)		

January 1, 2006

Interest Payable	7,000.00	
Cash		7,000.00

December 31, 2006

Bond Interest Expense	9,479.40	
Interest Payable		7,000.00
Discount on Bonds Payable		2,479.40
Bond Issue Expense	2,666.67	
Unamortized Bond Issue Costs		2,666.67

(e) **January 1, 2007**

Interest Payable	7,000.00	
Bonds Payable	100,000.00	
Loss on Redemption of Bonds (4)	7,393.31	
Discount on Bonds Payable (1)		2,726.65
Unamortized Bond Issue Costs (2)		2,666.66
Cash ($102,000 (3) + $7,000)		109,000.00

(1) ($7,460.05 – $2,254.00 – $2,479.40 = $2,726.65 unamortized discount)
(2) ($8,000.00 – $2,666.67 – $2,666.67 = $2,666.66 unamortized issue costs)
(3) ($100,000.00 x 102% = $102,000.00 price to retire)
(4) ($100,000.00 – $2,726.65 = $97,273.35 carrying value)
    ($97,273.35 – $2,666.66 = $94,606.69 net carrying value)
    ($102,000.00 – $94,606.69 = $7,393.31 loss)

There was a **call premium** (amount in excess of par required) of $2,000.00 in this situation which is included in the loss calculation.

TIP!

Illustration 15-3
Graph to Depict Interest Patterns for Bonds

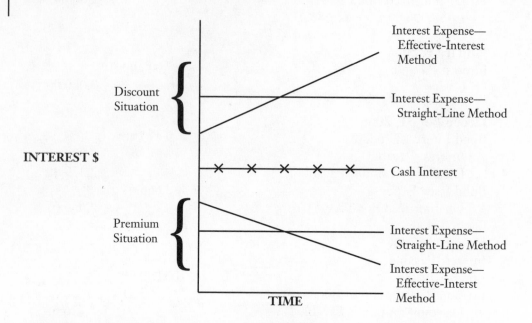

TIP! Regardless of whether the straight-line method of amortization or the effective interest method of amortization is used, the following will occur:
1. The amount of cash interest (stated interest) is a constant amount each period.
2. The bond's carrying amount increases over the bond's life if it is issued at a discount, due to the amortization of the discount.
3. The bond's carrying amount decreases over the bond's life if it is issued at a premium, due to the amortization of the premium.

TIP! If the straight-line method of amortization is used, the following relationships will exist:
1. The amount of amortization is a constant amount each period.
2. The amount of interest expense is a constant amount each period.

TIP! If the effective interest method of amortization is used, the following relationships will exist:
1. The effective interest rate is constant each period.
2. The interest expense is an increasing amount each period if the bond is issued at a discount (because a constant rate is applied to an increasing carrying amount each period).
3. The interest expense is a decreasing amount each period if the bond is issued at a premium (because a constant rate is applied to a decreasing carrying amount each period).
4. The amount of amortization **increases** each period because the difference between the effective interest expense and the cash interest widens each period.

Exercise 15-2

PURPOSE: This exercise will serve as an example for both the issuance of bonds between interest payment dates and the use of the straight-line method of amortization.

On May 1, 2005, Pan Tools Corporation issued bonds payable with a face value of $1.4 million at 104 plus accrued interest. They are registered bonds dated January 1, 2005, bear interest at 9% payable semiannually on January 1 and July 1, and mature January 1, 2015. The company uses the straight-line method of amortization.

Instructions

(a) Calculate the amount of bond interest expense to be reported on Pan's income statement for the year ended December 31, 2005. (Round calculations to the nearest dollar.)

(b) Calculate the amount of bond interest payable to be reported on Pan's balance sheet at December 31, 2005.

(c) Calculate the amount of bond interest expense to be reported on Pan's income statement for the year ended December 31, 2006.

Solution to Exercise 15-2

(a) Interest paid on July 1, 2005 ($1,400,000 x 9% x 6/12) $ 63,000
     Premium amortized on July 1, 2005 ($56,000 x 2/116)   (966)
     Accrued interest collected on May 1, 2005
       ($1,400,000 x 9% x 4/12)   (42,000)
     Interest accrued on December 31, 2005 ($1,400,000 x 9% x 6/12)   63,000
     Premium amortized on December 31, 2005 ($56,000 x 6/116)   (2,897)
      Total bond interest expense for the year ending
      December 31, 2005 $ 80,137

APPROACH AND EXPLANATION: Prepare the journal entries to record the issuance of the bonds, the payment of interest and amortization of premium on July 1, 2005, and the year-end adjusting entry. Post the entries to the Interest Expense account and determine its balance at December 31, 2005.

May 1, 2005

Cash	1,498,000 [c]	
Bonds Payable		1,400,000
Premium on Bonds Payable		56,000 [a]
Bond Interest Expense		42,000 [b]
(To record sale of bonds at a premium plus		
accrued interest)		

^{a} (104% x $1,400,000) – $1,400,000 = $56,000 issuance premium.
^{b} 9% x $1,400,000 x 4 months/12 months = $42,000 accrued interest (for January through April 2005).
^{c} $1,400,000 face value x 104% = $1,456,000 issuance price.
$1,456,000 issuance price + $42,000 accrued interest = $1,498,000 cash proceeds.

July 1, 2005

Bond Interest Expense ($63,000 – $966)	62,034	
Premium on Bonds Payable ($56,000 x 2/116)	966	
Cash ($1,400,000 x 9% x 6/12)		63,000

(To record semiannual payment of interest
and amortization of premium for two months)

TIP! A premium or discount is to be amortized over the period the bonds are outstanding (from the date of issuance to the date of maturity). In this case, May 1, 2005 to January 1, 2015 is four months short of 10 years (which is 116 months).

December 31, 2005

Bond Interest Expense ($63,000 – $2,897)	60,103	
Premium on Bond Payable ($56,000 x 6/116)	2,897	
Bond Interest Payable		63,000

($1,400,000 x 9% x 6/12)
(To record accrual of interest since last payment
date and amortization of premium for 6 months)

	Bond Interest Expense				Bond Interest Payable	
7/1/05	62,034	5/1/05	42,000		12/31/05	63,000
12/31/05	60,103					
Balance					Balance	
12/31/05	80,137				12/31/05	63,000

TIP! Bonds are often issued between interest payment dates. When this occurs, the issuer requires the investor to pay the market price for the bonds plus accrued interest since the last interest date. At the next interest payment date, the corporation will return the accrued interest to the investor by paying the full amount of interest due on outstanding bonds. In the situation at hand, the issuer collects from the investor interest from the date the bonds are dated to the date of issuance (from January 1, 2005 to May 1, 2005 is four months). When the next interest date comes around (July 1, 2005), a full interest payment is made to the investor. Thus, the investor receives the two months' interest earned from May 1, 2005 to June 30, 2005, plus the accrued interest for four months that the investor paid in at the purchase date. Accrued interest at the date bonds are sold by an issuer is handled in this manner to expedite the issuer's payment procedures. At any interest payment date, interest for a full interest period is paid to each bondholder, there is no need to calculate the actual time the bond investment was held by a particular bondholder and to prorate the interest because the investor has already paid in any portion of the full interest payment not earned by them during that interest period.

TIP!

The journal entry to record the second interest payment on January 1, 2006 would be as follows (assuming reversing entries are not used):

Bond Interest Payable	63,000	
Cash		63,000
(To record a full interest payment)		

TIP!

Refer to the journal entry made at the date of issuance (May 1, 2005). Rather than credit Bond Interest Expense for $42,000, you may credit Bond Interest Payable for the accrued interest of $42,000. This procedure will then require a modification to the entry on July 1, 2005. That entry would then include a debit to Bond Interest Payable for $42,000 and a debit to Bond Interest Expense for $20,034 rather than a debit to Bond Interest Expense for $62,034.

TIP!

Refer to the journal entry made at December 31, 2005. You may wish to make two separate entries rather than the one compound entry. The equivalent single entries would be as follows:

December 31, 2005

Bond Interest Expense	63,000	
Bond Interest Payable		63,000
(To record accrued interest for the six months)		
($1,400,000 x 9% x 6/12 = $63,000)		
Premium on Bonds Payable	2,897	
Bond Interest Expense		2,897
(To record premium amortization for six months)		
($56,000 x 6/116 = $2,897)		

(b) Accrued interest payable at December 31, 2005:
       $1,400,000 x 9% x 6/12 = <u>$63,000</u>

TIP!

Refer to explanation of part (a) above and balance of T-account for Bond Interest Payable.

(c) Interest paid on July 1, 2006 ($1,400,000 x 9% x 6/12) $ 63,000
     Premium amortized on July 1, 2006 ($56,000 x 6/116)   (2,897)
     Interest accrued on December 31, 2006
         ($1,400,000 x 9% x 6/12)   63,000
     Premium amortized on December 31, 2006 ($56,000 x 6/116)   <u>(2,897)</u>
       Total bond interest expense for the year ending
         December 31, 2006   <u>$ 120,206</u>

Exercise 15-3

PURPOSE: This exercise will illustrate the calculation of the bond price when interest is due semiannually. Additionally, it will present the accounting for bonds where the effective interest method of amortization is used and the end of the accounting period does not coincide with the end of an interest period.

Chase Company sells $500,000 of 10% bonds on November 1, 2005. The bonds pay interest on May 1 and November 1 and are to yield 12%. The due date of the bonds is May 1, 2009. The accounting period is the calendar year. No reversing entries are made. Bond premium or discount is to be amortized at interest dates and at year-end.

Instructions

(a) Calculate the price of the bonds at the issuance date.
(b) Prepare the amortization schedule for this issue.
(c) Prepare all of the relevant journal entries for this bond issue from the date of issuance through May 2007.

Solution to Exercise 15-3

(a) Time diagram:

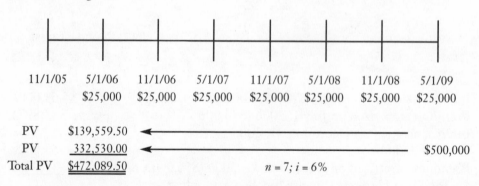

11/1/05	5/1/06	11/1/06	5/1/07	11/1/07	5/1/08	11/1/08	5/1/09
	$25,000	$25,000	$25,000	$25,000	$25,000	$25,000	$25,000

PV $139,559.50 ⟵
PV   332,530.00 ⟵ $500,000
Total PV $472,089.50 $n = 7; i = 6\%$

Factor for present value of a single sum, $i = 6\%$, $n = 7$ .66506
Factor for present value of an ordinary annuity, $i = 6\%$, $n = 7$ 5.58238
$500,000 x 5% = $25,000 interest per period
$500,000 x .66506 = $ 332,530.00
$25,000 x 5.58238 =   139,559.50
Issuance price $ 472,089.50

(b)

Date	5% Stated Interest	6% Interest Expense	Discount Amortization	Carrying Value
11/1/05				$ 472,089.50
5/1/06	$ 25,000.00	$ 28,325.37	$ 3,325.37	475,414.87
11/1/06	25,000.00	28,524.89	3,524.89	478,939.76
5/1/07	25,000.00	28,736.39	3,736.39	482,676.15
11/1/07	25,000.00	28,960.57	3,960.57	486,636.72
5/1/08	25,000.00	29,198.20	4,198.20	490,834.92
11/1/08	25,000.00	29,450.10	4,450.10	495,285.02
5/1/09	25,000.00	29,714.98 *	4,714.98	500,000.00
	$ 175,000.00	$202,910.50	$ 27,910.50	

*Includes a rounding error of $2.12.

There are two interest periods per year; therefore, the stated interest rate per interest period is the annual rate (10%) divided by 2, which is 5%. **TIP!**

If you round all of your calculations to the nearest cent, your rounding error will be small. A small (less than $5.00) rounding error provides some comfort that the amortization schedule is largely correct. A large rounding error (more than $10.00) indicates that one or more mistakes are likely included in the calculation within the schedule or in the determination of the starting point (issuance price of the debt). **TIP!**

The amortization schedule displays amounts according to bond periods. If one interest period overlaps two different accounting periods, the amount of expense and amortization for that interest period must be appropriately allocated to the respective accounting periods. **TIP!**

Instead of just memorizing what goes on an amortization schedule, think about the reason the amounts have been included. That will help you to construct a schedule without much effort. In the date column, start with the issuance date, followed by each interest date. The stated interest amount is calculated by multiplying the face value of the instrument by the stated rate of interest per interest period. Interest expense is calculated by multiplying the carrying value at the beginning of the period (end of the prior line on the amortization schedule) by the market rate of interest per period. The difference between the stated interest and the interest expense for the period is the amount of the amortization for the period. Discount amortization is added to the previous carrying value (or premium amortization is deducted from the previous carrying value) to arrive at the carrying value at the end of the interest period (interest payment date). **TIP!**

(c)   **November 1, 2005**

Cash	472,089.50	
Discount on Bonds Payable	27,910.50	
Bonds Payable		500,000.00

December 31, 2005

Bond Interest Expense	9,441.79	
Discount on Bonds Payable		1,108.46
Interest Payable		8,333.33

     ($28,325.37 x 2/6 = $9,441.79)
     ($3,325.37 x 2/6 = $1,108.46)
     ($25,000.00 x 2/6 = $8,333.33)

May 1, 2006

Interest Payable	8,333.33	
Bond Interest Expense	18,883.58	
Discount on Bonds Payable		2,216.91
Cash		25,000.00

     ($28,325.37 – $9,441.79 = $18,883.58)
     ($3,325.37 – $1,108.46 = $2,216.91)

November 1, 2006

Bond Interest Expense	28,524.89	
Discount on Bonds Payable		3,524.89
Cash.		25,000.00

December 31, 2006

Bond Interest Expense	9,578.80	
Discount on Bond Payable		1,245.47
Interest Payable		8,333.33

     ($28,736.39 x 2/6 = $9,578.80)
     ($3,736.39 x 2/6 = $1,245.46 + $.01 to balance)
     ($25,000.00 x 2/6 = $8,333.33)

May 1, 2007

Bond Interest Expense	19,157.59	
Interest Payable	8,333.33	
Discount on Bonds Payable		2,490.92
Cash.		25,000.00

     ($28,736.39 – $9,578.80 = $19,157.59)
     ($3,736.39 – $1,245.47 = $2,490.92)

Exercise 15-4

PURPOSE: This exercise will enable you to practise identifying data required to perform calculations involving bonds payable and applying the terminology associated with bonds.

    On January 1, 2005, Tuna Fishery sold $100,000 (face value) worth of bonds. The bonds are dated January 1, 2005 and will mature on January 1, 2010. Interest is to be paid annually on January 1. Issue costs related to these bonds amounted to

$2,000, and these costs are being amortized by the straight-line method. The following amortization schedule was prepared by the accountant for the first two years of the life of the bonds:

Date	Stated Interest	Effective Interest	Amortization	Carrying Value of Bonds
1/1/05				$ 104,212.37
1/1/06	$ 7,000.00	$ 6,252.74	$ 747.26	103,465.11
1/1/07	7,000.00	6,207.91	792.09	102,673.02
1/1/08	7000	6160.38	839.62	

@ premium.

Instructions

On the basis of the information above, answer the following questions (round your answers to the nearest cent or percent) and explain the reasoning or calculations, as appropriate.
(a) What is the nominal or stated rate of interest for this bond issue?
(b) What is the effective or market rate of interest for this bond issue?
(c) Prepare the journal entry to record the sale of the bond issue on January 1, 2005 including the issue costs.
(d) Prepare the appropriate entry(ies) at December 31, 2007 the end of the accounting year.
(e) Identify the amount of bond issue costs and the amount of interest expense to be reported on the income statement for the year ended December 31, 2007.
(f) Show how the account balances related to the bond issue will be presented on the December 31, 2007 balance sheet. Indicate the major classification(s) involved.
(g) What is the book value of the bonds at December 31, 2007?
(h) What is the net book value of the bonds at December 31, 2007?
(i) If the bonds are retired for $100,500 (excluding interest) at January 1, 2008 will the bonds be extinguished at a gain or a loss? What is the amount of that gain or loss?

Solution to Exercise 15-4

(a) Stated interest = Stated rate of interest x Par
$7,000 = Stated rate of interest x $100,000
$7,000 ÷ $100,000 = Stated rate of interest
7% = Stated rate of interest

(b) Effective interest = Market rate x Carrying value at beginning of period
$6,252.74 = Market rate x $104,212.37
$6,252.74 ÷ $104,212.37 = Market rate
6% = Market rate

(c) Cash   102,212.37
     Unamortized Bond Issue Costs   2,000.00
         Bonds Payable   100,000.00
         Premium on Bonds Payable   4,212.37

(d) Bond Interest Expense   6,160.38
     Premium on Bonds Payable   839.62
         Interest Payable   7,000.00
             ($102,673.02 x 6% = $6,160.38)

     Bond Issue Expense   400
         Unamortized Bond Issue Costs   400

(e) Bond issue expense* $400
     Bond interest expense** $6,160.38
     *$2,000 ÷ 5 years = $400
     **$102,673.02 x 6% = $6,160.38

(f) **Other assets**
         Unamortized bond issue costs $ 800
     Current liabilities
         Interest payable $7,000
     Long-term liabilities
         Bonds payable, 7%, due 1/1/07 $ 100,000.00
         Unamortized premium*   1,833.40
                                                            $ 101,833.40

     *$4,212.37 – $747.26 – $792.09 – $839.62 = $1,833.40

(g) $101,833.40 [See solution for part (f).]
     Book value is another name for carrying value or carrying amount.

     The amount, $101,833.40, can also be calculated by:
         Carrying value at 1/1/07 [per schedule] $ 102,673.02
         Amortization for 2007 [part (d)]   (839.62)
         Carrying value at 12/31/07   101,833.40

(h) Bonds payable balance $ 100,000.00
     Premium on bonds payable balance   1,833.40
     Book value at 12/31/07   101,833.40
     Unamortized bond issue costs   (800.00)*
     Net book value at 12/31/07 $ 101,033.40

     *[$2,000 – 3($400) = $800]

(i) Gain. A gain will result because the retirement price is less than the net carry-
     ing value at the date of retirement.
         Net carrying value at 1/1/08 [part (g)] $ 101,033.40
         Retirement price   100,500.00
         Gain on extinguishment of debt $ 533.40

Exercise 15-5

PURPOSE: This exercise will illustrate how to account for the redemption of bonds by cash payment prior to maturity.

The balance sheet for Sea Corporation reports the following information on December 31, 2004:

Long-term liabilities

9% Bonds payable, due December 31, 2008	$ 1,000,000
Less: Discount on bonds payable	60,000
	$ 940,000

Interest is payable annually on December 31. The straight-line method of amortization is used. Interest rates have declined in the market place since the above mentioned bonds were issued. Sea decides to borrow money from another source at a lower interest rate to lower its annual interest charges. Therefore, on July 1, 2005, it redeems all of the old outstanding bonds at 102 (recall that bond prices vary inversely with changes in the market rate of interest).

Instructions

Prepare the journal entry(ies) to record the redemption (extinguishment) of these bonds on July 1, 2005.

Solution to Exercise 15-5

Bond Interest Expense	45,000	
Cash		45,000

    (To record the payment of accrued interest at
     July 1, 2005)
    ($1,000,000 x 9% x 6/12 = $45,000)

Bond Interest Expense	7,500	
Discount on Bonds Payable		7,500

    (To record the amortization of discount for six months)
    [($60,000 ÷ 4) x 6/12]

Bonds Payable	1,000,000	
Loss on Bond Redemption	72,500[3]	
Discount on Bonds Payable		52,500[2]
Cash		1,020,000[1]

    (To record the redemption of the bonds
     payable at 102)

[1]$1,000,000 face value x 1.02 = $1,020,000 redemption price.
[2]$60,000 – $7,500 = $52,500 balance at July 1, 2005.
[3]$1,020,000 redemption price – $947,500 carrying value = $72,500 loss on redemption.

EXPLANATION: Break the required entries into three simple parts—payment of accrued interest, update of discount amortization, and extinguishment of the liability. The bond holder is entitled to interest for the months between the last interest payment date and the redemption date, which is six months in this case. The amortization of the discount must be updated to arrive at the carrying value of the debt at the redemption date. In this case, six months of amortization must be recorded. The straight-line amortization method is being used so the $60,000 balance in the discount account at December 31, 2005 applies evenly to the remaining four years of the bond's term. The amortization for six months would, therefore, be one-half of the $15,000 annual amount.

For the entry to record the redemption, do the following: (1) Begin with the easiest part of the journal entry. Credit Cash to record the payment of the redemption price, which is 102% of the face value of the bonds. (2) Remove the carrying value of the bonds from the accounts by debiting Bonds Payable for the face value of the bonds and crediting Discount on Bonds Payable for the balance of the related unamortized discount ($60,000 balance at December 31, 2004 less the $7,500 amortization for the first six months of 2005 = $52,500). (3) Record the difference between the redemption (retirement) price and the carrying value of the bonds as a gain or loss on redemption. An excess of carrying value over redemption price results in a gain. In the case at hand, the redemption price ($1,020,000) exceeds the carrying value of the bonds ($1,020,000 – $52,500 = $947,500). Since it cost $1,020,000 to eliminate a debt that appears on the books at only $947,500, a loss results.

Exercise 15-6

PURPOSE: This exercise will illustrate the accounting for the issuance of a note payable to acquire land when the note bears an interest rate that is unreasonably low in relation to the market rate of interest.

On December 31, 2004, Weiss, Inc. purchased land by giving $40,000 in cash and a 3% interest-bearing note with a face value of $500,000. There was no established exchange price for the land, nor a ready market for the note. The note is due December 31, 2008. Interest is payable each December 31. Weiss incremental borrowing rate is 10%.

Instructions

(a) Draw a time line for the note and determine the amount to record as the cost of the land.

(b) Prepare the amortization schedule for the note payable.
(c) Determine the amount to report as interest expense on the income statement for the fiscal year ending March 31, 2006.
(d) Determine the amount to report as interest paid on the statement of cash flows for the fiscal year ending March 31, 2006.
(e) Determine the amounts to appear (with respect to the above information) on the balance sheet at March 31, 2006, and indicate the proper classification for each item.

Solution to Exercise 15-6

(a) Time line:

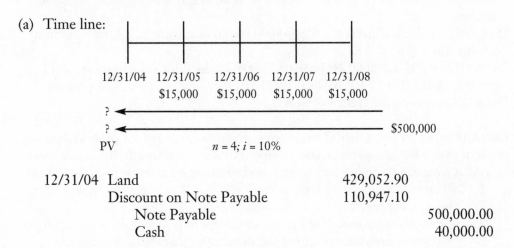

12/31/04	12/31/05	12/31/06	12/31/07	12/31/08
	$15,000	$15,000	$15,000	$15,000

?   (arrow)

?   (arrow) $500,000

PV $n = 4; i = 10\%$

12/31/04	Land	429,052.90	
	Discount on Note Payable	110,947.10	
	Note Payable		500,000.00
	Cash		40,000.00

The market rate of interest is used to calculate the present value of the note which is then used to establish the exchange price for the land. The cash down payment of $40,000.00 plus the present value of the note of $389,052.90 equals the $429,052.90 cost of the land. The market rate of interest should be the rate the borrower normally would have to pay to borrow money for similar activities.

Calculation of the present value of the note:

Maturity value		$500,000.00
Present value of $500,000 due in 4 years		
at 10% ($500,000 x .68301)	$341,505.00	
Present value of $15,000 payable annually		
for 4 years at 10% ($15,000 x 3.16986)	47,547.90	
Present value of the note and interest		389,052.90
Discount on note receivable		$110,947.10

(b)

Amortization Schedule for Note Payable

Date	3% Stated Interest	10% Effective Interest	Amortization of Discount	PV Balance
12/31/04				$ 389,052.90
12/31/05	$15,000.00 [a]	$ 38,905.29 [b]	$ 23,905.29 [c]	412,958.19 [d]
12/31/06	15,000.00	41,295.82	26,295.82	439,254.01
12/31/07	15,000.00	43,925.40	28,925.40	468,179.41
12/31/08	15,000.00	46,820.59 [1]	31,820.59	500,000.00
Totals	$60,000.00	$170,947.10	$110,947.10	

[a] $500,000.00 face value x 3% stated interest rate = $15,000.00 stated interest

[b] $389,052.90 present value x 10% effective interest rate = $38,905.29 effective interest.

[c] $38,905.29 effective interest – $15,000.00 stated interest = $23,905.29 discount amortization.

[d] $389,052.90 PV balance 12/31/04 + $23,905.29 discount amortization for 12 months = $412,958.19 PV balance 12/31/05.

[1] Includes rounding difference of $2.65.

EXPLANATION: When a debt instrument is given in exchange for property, goods, or services in a bargained transaction entered into at arms length, the stated interest rate is assumed to be fair and is thus used to calculate interest revenue unless:

1. No interest rate is stated, or
2. The stated interest rate is unreasonable, or
3. The stated face amount of the debt instrument is materially different from the current cash sales price for the same or similar items or from the current market value of the debt instrument.

In these circumstances, the present value of the debt instrument is measured by the fair value of the property, goods, or services, or by an amount that reasonably approximates the note's market value. If the fair value of the property, goods, or services is not readily determinable, the market value of the note is used to establish the present value of the note. If the note has no ready market, the present value of the note is approximated by discounting all of the related future cash payments (for interest and principal) on the note at the market rate of interest. This rate is referred to as an imputed rate and should be equal to the borrower's incremental borrowing rate (that is, the rate of interest the maker of the note would currently have to pay if it borrowed money from another source for this same purpose). Weiss, Inc. issued a note in exchange for land. No information was given about the fair value of the land or the market value of the note. Thus, the debtor company's incremental borrowing rate of 10% was used to impute interest and determine the note's present value.

(c) Interest from April 1, 2005 through December 31, 2005:

$38,905.29 x 9/12	$29,178.97
Interest from January 1, 2006 through March 31, 2006:	
$41,295.82 x 3/12	10,323.96
Interest for the fiscal year ending March 31, 2006	$39,502.93

| | **TIP!** |

The amount of interest shown on the 12/31/05 line in the amortization schedule is the amount of interest that pertains to the interest period that is just ending on that date (12/31/05 in this case). When interest is payable annually, an interest period is 12 months in length. When interest is payable semi-annually, each interest period is six months long.

TIP!

When the end of an accounting period does not coincide with an interest payment date, interest must be apportioned to the proper periods. For example, we will use the amortization schedule above and assume that the accounting period ends on March 31, 2005. The effective interest of $38,905.29 for the calendar year ending December 31, 2005 must be apportioned between two fiscal years: the one ending March 31, 2005 and the one ending March 31, 2006. 3/12 x $38,905.29 = $9,726.32 would be allocated to the fiscal year ending March 31, 2005 and 9/12 x $38,905.29 = $29,178.97 would be allocated to the fiscal year ending March 31, 2006. The 12 months ending March 31, 2006 would include the 9/12 x $38,905.29 plus three months of the $41,295.82 interest amount shown on the 12/31/06 payment line.

Entering the interest amounts from the amortization schedule into the proper places on a time line should greatly help your comprehension of these calculations. The following pictorial will aid you in following the logic of the calculations.

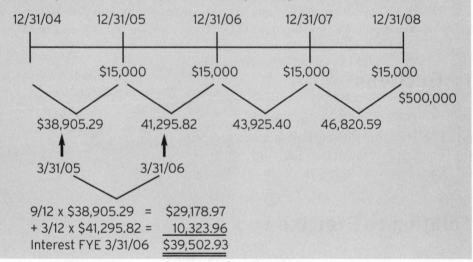

(d) A payment of cash of $15,000 was made for interest on December 31, 2005. Thus, a cash outflow of $15,000 would be reflected in the operating activity section of the statement of cash flows for the fiscal year ending March 31, 2006.

(e)

Balance Sheet (Partial)
March 31, 2006

Property, Plant & Equipment		Current Liabilities	
Land	$429,052.90	Interest Payable	$3,750.00[a]
		Long-term Liabilities	
		Note Payable	$500,000.00
		Less: Discount on	
		Note	80,467.85[b]
			$419,532.15

[a]3/12 x $15,000 = $3,750.00
[b]3/12 x $26,295.82 = 6,573.96 amortization of discount for
  01/01/06 – 03/31/06

$110,947.10	Balance of Discount on Note Payable on 12/31/04
(23,905.29)	Amortization for 01/01/05 through 12/31/05
(6,573.96)	Amortization for 01/01/06 through 3/31/06
$ 80,467.85	Balance of Discount on Note Payable on 03/31/06

Exercise 15-7

PURPOSE: This exercise will illustrate the accounting entries for a long-term note payable.

The Feelgood Clinic issued a $400,000, 10%, 10-year mortgage note on December 31, 2004. The terms provide for semiannual instalment payments of $32,097.03 on June 30 and December 31. The note, along with $80,000 cash, was given in exchange for a new building. The accounting period is the calendar year.

Instructions

Prepare the journal entries to record:
(a) The acquisition of the building and inception of the mortgage loan payable.
(b) The first mortgage payment on June 30, 2005.
(c) The second mortgage payment on December 31, 2005.

Solution to Exercise 15-7

December 31, 2004

(a)	Building	480,000.00	
	Cash		80,000.00
	Mortgage Note Payable		400,000.00

June 30, 2005

(b)	Interest Expense	20,000.00 *	
	Mortgage Note Payable	12,097.03 **	
	Cash		32,097.03

* Principal balance at December 31, 2004	$400,000.00
Semiannual interest rate	x .05
Interest expense for first six months	$ 20,000.00

** First payment	$32,097.03
Interest portion of first payment	(20,000.00)
Reduction in principal—first instalment payment	$12,097.03

December 31, 2005

(c) Interest Expense   19,395.15 *
     Mortgage Note Payable   12,701.88 **
        Cash   32,097.03

* Principal balance at December 31, 2004	$400,000.00
Reduction in principal—first instalment payment	(12,097.03)
Principal balance at June 30, 2005	387,902.97
Semiannual interest rate	.05
Interest expense for second six months	$ 19,395.15

** Second payment	$32,097.03
Interest portion of second payment	(19,395.15)
Reduction in principal—second instalment payment	$12,701.88

EXPLANATION TO PART (A): The cost of the building is determined by the fair market value of the consideration given, which is the $80,000 cash plus the $400,000 present value of the note payable.

EXPLANATION TO PARTS (B) AND (C): The mortgage note payable is recorded initially at its face value ($400,000), which is often referred to as the note's beginning principal, and each instalment payment reduces the outstanding principal amount. The instalment payments are an equal amount each interest period; however, the portion of the payment going to cover interest charges and the portion going to reduce the outstanding principal varies each period. In this exercise, the instalment payments are due semiannually; thus, the length of an interest period is six months and the annual interest rate (10%) must be expressed on a semiannual basis (5%) to perform the interest calculation. Interest is a function of outstanding balance, interest rate, and time. Thus, the interest sustained for the first six months is determined by the note's initial carrying value (the face value of $400,000), the annual rate of 10%, and a six-month time period. The interest sustained for the second six months cannot be determined until the outstanding principal balance is updated for the portion of the first instalment payment that is to be applied to the principal balance. The updated principal balance (carrying value) is used to calculate the interest charges for the second interest period. Although the exercise does not require a complete payment schedule (often called an amortization schedule) for this note, one is presented below for your observation and study. Notice that as subsequent instalment payments are made, a decreasing portion of each payment goes to cover interest and an increasing portion is applied to the principal balance. The reason for this is the fact that interest is calculated by a constant interest rate (5% each interest period) multiplied by a decreasing principal balance (carrying value).

TIP! The stated rate of interest (10% in this case) is assumed to be equal to the market rate of interest; therefore, the present value of the note at its inception is the same as the face value ($400,000) and there is no discount or premium related to this mortgage note payable.

TIP! A mortgage note will usually require the borrower to make monthly payments, and interest is then compounded monthly. In this exercise, semiannual payments are assumed (thus interest is compounded twice a year) in order to simplify the amortization schedule but yet allow you an opportunity to view a situation involving the compounding of interest more than once a year.

Mortgage Instalment Payment Schedule

Semiannual Interest Period	(A) Cash Payment	(B) Interest Expense (D) x 5%	(C) Reduction of Principal (A) – (B)	(D) Principal Balance (D) – (C)
12/31/04				$400,000.00
6/30/05	$ 32,097.03	$ 20,000.00	$ 12,097.03	387,902.97
12/31/05	32,097.03	19,395.15	12,701.88	375,201.09
6/30/06	32,097.03	18,760.05	13,336.98	361,864.11
12/31/06	32,097.03	18,093.21	14,003.82	347,860.29
6/30/07	32,097.03	17,393.01	14,704.02	333,156.27
12/31/07	32,097.03	16,657.81	15,439.22	317,717.05
6/30/08	32,097.03	15,885.85	16,211.18	301,505.87
12/31/08	32,097.03	15,075.29	17,021.74	284,484.13
6/30/09	32,097.03	14,224.21	17,872.82	266,611.31
12/31/09	32,097.03	13,330.57	18,766.46	247,844.85
6/30/10	32,097.03	12,392.24	19,704.79	228,140.06
12/31/10	32,097.03	11,407.00	20,690.03	207,450.03
6/30/11	32,097.03	10,372.50	21,724.53	185,725.50
12/31/11	32,097.03	9,286.28	22,810.75	162,914.75
6/30/12	32,097.03	8,145.74	23,951.29	138,963.46
12/31/12	32,097.03	6,948.17	25,148.86	113,814.60
6/30/13	32,097.03	5,690.73	26,406.30	87,408.30
12/31/13	32,097.93	4,370.42	27,727.51	59,680.79
6/30/14	32,097.03	2,984.04	29,112.99	30,567.80
12/31/14	32,097.03	1,529.23 [a]	30,567.80	0.00
Totals	$641,940.60	$241,940.60	$400,000.00	

[a]Includes rounding difference of 10¢.

TIP! Notice that the total interest to be incurred over the ten-year period is $241,940.60 on the loan of $400,000.00. The pattern of interest charges is one of a decreasing amount each interest period because interest is a function of present value balance, constant rate, and time.

Exercise 15-8

PURPOSE: This exercise will illustrate how an instalment note payable affects the financial statements.

The use of a mortgage note is a common vehicle to finance the acquisition of long-lived tangible assets. A mortgage note usually requires the borrower to repay the loan by equal periodic payments over the life of the loan. Each payment goes to cover the interest accrued during the time segment since the previous payment and to reduce the principal balance.

Instructions

Using the amortization schedule from **Exercise 15-7**, answer the following questions:

(a) How much interest expense would be reported on the income statement for the year ending December 31, 2005?

(b) How would the two payments during the year 2005 of $32,097.03 each be reflected in the statement of cash flows for the year ending December 31, 2005?

(c) How would the balance of $375,201.09 at December 31, 2005 be reported on a balance sheet as of that date?

Solution to Exercise 15-8

(a)
$20,000.00	Interest expense 1/01/05 – 6/30/05
19,395.15	Interest expense 7/01/05 – 12/31/05
$39,395.15	Total interest expense for the year ending 12/31/05

(b) The amounts paid during year 2005 for interest ($20,000.00 + $19,395.15 = **$39,395.15**) should be reported as a cash outflow due to operating activities. The amounts paid during year 2005 for principal reduction ($12,097.03 + 12,701.88 = **$24,798.91**) would be reported as payments on debt which are classified as cash outflows from financing activities on a statement of cash flows for the year ended December 31, 2005.

(c) The balance of the Mortgage Note Payable account is reported as a liability in the balance sheet. The portion of the instalment payments scheduled to be due and paid within the next year (that is, the year that follows the balance sheet date) that represents the reduction of the principal balance is to be reported in the current liability section of the balance sheet; the remaining unpaid principal balance is classified in the long-term liability section.

$ 13,336.98	Amount due June 30, 2006
14,003.82	Amount due December 31, 2006
$ 27,340.80	Current liability as of December 31, 2005
$347,860.29	Long-term liability as of December 31, 2005

TIP!

If Feelgood Clinic **(Exercise 15-7)** had its accounting period end on March 31, 2006 rather than December 31, 2005, the answers to parts "a", "b", and "c" of **Exercise 15-8** would be as follows:

a. $10,000.00 $20,000.00 x 3/6 = Interest expense 3/31/05 to 6/30/05
      19,395.15 $19,395.15 x 6/6 = Interest expense 7/01/05 to 12/31/05
       9,380.03 $18,760.05 x 3/6 = Interest expense 01/01/06 to 03/31/06
    $38,775.18   Total interest expense for the year ending 03/31/06

b. The payments on 6/30/05 and 12/31/05 fall in the year ending March 31, 2006. Therefore, this answer would be the same as in **Exercise 15-8**:
    $20,000 + $19,395.15 = $39,395.15 cash outflow due to operating activities (interest paid)
    $12,097.03 + $12,701.88 = $24,789.91 cash outflow due to financing activity (payment on debt)

c. For the balance sheet:
    $ 13,336.98   Amount due June 30, 2006
       14,003.82   Amount due December 31, 2006
    $ 27,340.80   Current liability as of March 31, 2005
    $347,860.29   Long-term liability as of March 31, 2005

Notice that answers "b" and "c" above are the same as answers "b" and "c" in the **Solution to Exercise 15-8**. This is because the cash payments are made at a point in time and a principal reduction applies at a point in time when a cash payment is made. Fractions (such as 3/12 and 9/12) are applied to interest amounts (which are for a period of time) to apportion interest to the appropriate accounting periods. However, fractions are **never** applied to principal reduction figures.

Illustration 15-4
Summary of Accounting for Impairment and Troubled Debt Restructurings

Event	Accounting Procedure
1. Impairment	**Creditor:** Loss based upon difference between present value of future cash flows discounted at historical effective interest rate and carrying amount of note. **Debtor:** No recognition.
2. Restructuring—Settlement of Debt a. Transfer of noncash assets.	**Creditor:** Recognize loss on restructure. **Debtor:** Recognize gain on restructure and recognize gain or loss on asset transfer.

b. Granting of equity interest.

Creditor: Recognize loss on restructure.
Debtor: Recognize gain on restructure.

3. Restructurings—Continuation of Debt with Modified Terms, examples include one or more of the following
   a. Reduction of stated interest rate;
   b. Extension of maturity date;
   c. Reduction of face amount;
   d. Reduction of accrued interest.

Creditor: Loss based upon difference between present value of future cash flows discounted at historical effective interest rate and carrying amount of note.
Debtor: If a settlement (see TIP below), the old liability is eliminated and a new liability is assumed. The new liability is measured at the present value of the revised future cash flows discounted at the current prevailing market interest rate. A gain will be recorded for the difference. If in substance it is a modification, the old debt still exists, along with any deferrals that may relate to it. A new effective interest rate will be determined based on the original debt and the revised cash flows.

TIP!

When there is a restructuring that involves the continuation of debt with modification of terms, the issue is whether, in substance, the renegotiation is considered a **settlement** or a **modification** regarding the old debt. *CICA Handbook*, EIC Abstract # 88, as well as proposed Section 3855, provides guidance in making this determination. If **one** of the three criteria given is met, there is a substantial change and the debt is considered settled. The three criteria are (a) the PV of the new cash flows discounted at the old interest rate are > 10% different from the PV of the old cash flows at the historic rate, or (b) there is a change in borrowing currency, or (c) there is a change in creditor.

TIP!

When there is a restructuring that involves a settlement of debt by transfer of non-cash assets, the debtor has the following gain-loss calculations:

(1) The excess of the carrying amount of the debt over the fair market value of the assets is recorded as a gain on restructuring.
(2) The difference between the fair market value of the assets and their recorded value (book value) is recorded as a gain or loss on disposition of assets.

Exercise 15-9

PURPOSE: This exercise will illustrate the accounting for a transfer of noncash assets to settle a debt obligation in a troubled debt situation.

Naples Co. owes $194,400 to Morgan Trust Co. The debt is a 10-year, 8% note. Because Naples Co. is in financial trouble, Morgan agrees to accept some property and cancel the entire debt. The property has a cost of $150,000, accumulated amortization of $80,000, and a fair market value of $110,000.

Instructions

(a) Prepare the journal entry on Naples's books for the debt restructure.
(b) Prepare the journal entry on Morgan's books for the debt restructure.

Solution to Exercise 15-9

(a) **NAPLE'S ENTRY:**

Notes Payable	194,400	
Accumulated Amortization	80,000	
Property		150,000
Gain on Property Disposition		40,000 *
Gain on Restructuring of Debt		84,400 **

$$* \quad \$110,000 - (\$150,000 - \$80,000) = \$40,000$$
$$** \quad \$194,400 - \$110,000 = \$84,400$$

EXPLANATION: (1) Begin with the easiest part of the journal entry. Remove the debt amount by a debit to Notes Payable for $194,400. (2) Remove the carrying value of the property by a debit to Accumulated Amortization for $80,000 and a credit to Property for the $150,000 cost. (3) Calculate and record the gain from settlement ($84,400 credit) and, (4) calculate and record the gain from disposition of assets ($40,000). (5) Double check the entry to make sure it balances.

The debtor is required to determine the excess of the carrying amount of the payable ($194,400) over the fair value of the assets transferred ($110,000) and report that difference as an extraordinary gain ($84,400). The difference between the fair value of those assets and their carrying amounts is to be recognized as a gain or loss on disposition of assets. In this case, the fair value of $110,000 exceeds the carrying amount of $70,000; therefore, an ordinary gain of $40,000 is to be recognized. Although the gain on troubled debt restructuring is to be classified as an extraordinary item, the gain (or loss) from disposition of assets is to be classified as other revenues and gains (or other expenses and losses) on the debtor's income statement.

(b) **MORGAN'S ENTRY:**

Property	110,000	
Allowance for Doubtful Accounts	84,400	
(or Loss on Restructuring)		
Notes Receivable		194,400

EXPLANATION: (1) Remove the carrying amount of the receivable from the accounts by a credit to Notes Receivable for $194,400. (2) Record the acquisition of the property by a debit to Property for its fair value of $110,000. (3) Record the loss on settlement of $84,400 by a debit to Allowance for Doubtful Accounts or to a loss account. (4) Double check the entry to make sure it balances.

The creditor is required to determine the excess of the carrying amount of the receivable over the fair value of the assets being transferred to the creditor and record it as a charge against the Allowance for Doubtful Accounts account or to a loss account (such a loss is not to be classified as an extraordinary item).

Analysis of Multiple-Choice Type Questions

Question

1. Bonds for which the owners' names are not registered with the issuing corporation are called:
   a. bearer bonds.
   b. term bonds.
   c. debenture bonds.
   d. secured bonds.

APPROACH AND EXPLANATION: Briefly define each answer selection. Choose the one that is described in the question's stem. **Bearer** (or **coupon**) ° are bonds for which the name of the owner is not registered with the issuer; bondholders are required to send in coupons to receive interest payments and the bonds may be transferred directly to another party. **Registered bonds** are bonds registered in the name of the owner. **Term bonds** are bonds that mature (become due for payment) at a single specified future date. **Debenture bonds** are unsecured bonds. **Secured bonds** are bonds having specific assets pledged as collateral by the issuer. (Solution = a.)

Question

2. The periodic amortization of a premium on bonds payable will:
   a. cause the carrying value of the bonds to increase each period.
   b. cause the carrying value of the bonds to decrease each period.
   c. have no effect on the carrying value of the bonds.
   d. cause the carrying value always to be less than the par value of the bonds.

EXPLANATION: Think about the process of amortizing a premium on bonds payable and how it affects the carrying value of the bonds. The Premium on Bonds Payable account has a normal credit balance. A premium is an adjustment to interest via an adjustment to price. Therefore, the entry to amortize the premium involves a debit to Premium on Bonds Payable and a credit to Bond Interest Expense. The amortization process reduces the balance of the unamortized premium. The carrying value of a bond issued at a premium is calculated by adding the premium balance to the face value of the bond. Thus, the carrying value of bonds payable issued at a premium will decrease each period until the maturity date (at which time the carrying value will equal the face value). (Solution = b.)

Question

3. A large department store issues bonds with a maturity date that is 20 years after the issuance date. If the bonds are issued at a discount, this indicates that at the date of issuance, the:
   a. nominal rate of interest and the stated rate of interest coincide.
   b. nominal rate of interest exceeds the yield rate.
   c. effective yield rate of interest exceeds the coupon rate.
   d. stated rate of interest exceeds the effective rate.

EXPLANATION: Before reading the answer selections, write down the relationship that causes a bond to be issued at a discount: market rate of interest exceeds the stated rate of interest. Then list the synonymous terms for market rate and for stated rate: (1) market rate, effective rate, and yield rate; (2) stated rate, coupon rate, nominal rate, and contract rate. Selection "a" is incorrect because the nominal rate and the stated rate are just different names for the same thing. Selections "b" and "d" are incorrect because an excess of nominal rate (stated rate) over the yield rate (effective rate) will result in a premium, not a discount. Selection "c" is correct because when the yield rate (market rate) exceeds the coupon rate (stated rate), an issuance discount will result. (Solution = c.)

Question

4. Assume the face value of a bond is $1,000. If the bond's current price is quoted at 102 3/4, the bond price is:
   a. $1,000.00.
   b. $1,002.75.
   c. $1,020.75.
   d. $1,027.50.

EXPLANATION: Convert the fraction (3/4) to a decimal (.75). Now take 102.75% of the bonds face value to determine its current price of $1,027.50. (Solution = d.)

Question

5. The amount of cash to be paid for interest on bonds payable for any given year is calculated by multiplying the:
   a. face value of the stated interest rate.
   b. face value by the market interest rate at the date of issuance.
   c. carrying value at the beginning of the year by the market interest rate in existence at the date of issuance.
   d. carrying value at the beginning of the year by the stated interest rate.

EXPLANATION: The amount of cash interest to be paid is the amount promised by the bond contract (indenture) which is the contractual (stated) interest rate multiplied by the face value of the bond. (Solution = a.)

Question

6. The amortization of a discount on bonds payable results in reporting an amount of interest expense for the period which:
   a. exceeds the amount of cash interest for the period.
   b. equals the amount of cash interest for the period.
   c. is less than the amount of cash interest for the period.
   d. bears no predictable relationship to the amount of cash interest for the period.

EXPLANATION: Think about the process of amortizing a discount on bonds payable and how it affects interest expense. The Discount of Bonds Payable has a normal debit balance. Thus, to amortize it, you credit Discount on Bonds Payable and debit Bond Interest Expense. A debit to the expense account increases its balance. Thus, interest expense is comprised of the amount to be paid in cash for interest for the period plus the amount of discount amortization for the period. Another way of viewing this situation is as follows: a discount is an additional amount of interest to be paid at maturity but is recognized (charged to expense) over the periods benefited (which would be the periods the bonds are to be outstanding). (Solution = a.)

Question

7. If bonds are initially sold at a discount and the straight-line method of amortization is used, interest expense in the earlier years of the bond's life will:
   a. be less than the amount of interest actually paid.
   b. be less than it will be in the latter years of the bond's life.
   c. be the same as what it would have been had the effective interest method of amortization been used.
   d. exceed what it would have been had the effective interest method of amortization been used.

EXPLANATION: Quickly sketch the graph that shows the patterns of and relationships between interest paid, interest expense using the straight-line method, and interest expense using the effective interest method. The graph appears in **Illustration 15-3**. Treat each of the possible answer selections as a True-False question. Look at the graph after reading each of the answer selections to determine if it is a correct answer.

Selection "a" is False because interest expense for a bond issued at a discount will be greater than interest actually paid throughout the bond's entire life, regardless of the amortization method used. Selection "b" is False because interest expense is a constant amount each period when the straight-line method is used; hence interest expense will be the same amount in the latter years as it is in the earlier years. Selection "c" is False because in the earlier years of life for a bond issued at a discount, interest expense calculated using the straight-line method is greater than interest expense calculated using the effective interest method. Selection "d" is True. The interest expense will increase over a bond's life when the bond is issued at a discount and the effective interest method of amortization is used. In the earlier years of life, that expense amount is less than interest expense using the straight-line method; and, in the latter years of life, that expense amount is more than interest expense calculated using the straight-line method. (Solution = d.)

Question

8. At the beginning of 2005, the Alston Corporation issued 10% bonds with a face value of $400,000. These bonds mature in five years, and interest is paid semiannually on June 30 and December 31. The bonds were sold for $370,560 to yield 12%. Alston uses a calendar-year reporting period. Using the effective interest method of amortization, what amount of interest expense should be reported for 2005? (Round your answer to the nearest dollar.)
    a. $44,333
    b. $44,467
    c. $44,601
    d. $45,888

APPROACH AND EXPLANATION: Write down the formula for computing interest using the effective method of amortization. Use the data in the question to work through the formula.

	Carrying value at the beginning of the period	$ 370,560.00
x	Effective rate of interest per interest period	6%
=	Interest expense for the first interest period	22,233.60
−	Cash interest for the interest period	20,000.00*
=	Amortization of discount for the first interest period	2,233.60
+	Carrying value at the beginning of the first period	370,560.00
=	Carrying value at the beginning of the second period	372,793.60
x	Effective rate of interest per interest period	6%
=	Interest expense for the second interest period	22,367.62
+	Interest expense for the first interest period	22,233.60
=	Interest expense for the calendar year of 2005	$ 44,601.22

*$400,000 x (10% ÷ 2) = $20,000   (Solution = c.)

TIP! | The interest must be calculated on a per interest period basis. In this question, the interest period is six months. The interest for 2005 is comprised of the interest for the bond's first two interest periods.

Question

9. At December 31, 2005 the following balances existed on the books of the Malloy Corporation:

Bonds Payable	$ 500,000
Discount on Bonds Payable	40,000
Interest Payable	12,500
Unamortized Bonds Issue Costs	30,000

If the bonds are retired on January 1, 2006, at 102, what will Malloy report as a
loss on extinguishment?
   a. $92,500
   b. $80,000
   c. $67,500
   d. $50,000

EXPLANATION: Write down the format for the calculation of the gain or loss on
redemption and plug in the amounts from this question.

	Par value	$ 500,000
−	Unamortized discount	40,000
=	Carrying amount	460,000
−	Unamortized debt issue costs	30,000
=	Net carrying amount	430,000
−	Redemption price	510,000*
=	Gain (Loss) on extinguishment	$ (80,000)

*$500,000 x 102% = $510,000.

(Solution = b.)

Question

10. "In-substance defeasance" is a term used to refer to an arrangement whereby:
    a. a company gets another company to cover its payments due on long-term
       debt.
    b. a governmental unit issues debt instruments to corporations.
    c. a company provides for the future repayment of a long-term debt by
       placing purchased securities in an irrevocable trust.
    d. a company legally extinguishes debt before its due date.

EXPLANATION: **In-substance defeasance** is an arrangement whereby a company
provides for the future repayment of one or more of its long-term debt issues by
placing purchased securities in an irrevocable trust, the principal and interest of
which are pledged to pay off the principal and interest of its own debt securities as
they mature. The company, however, is not legally released from being the primary obligor under the debt that is still outstanding. (Solution = c.)

Question

11. On December 31, 2005, Sugar Products Company borrows $100,000 from
    Candy Factory Company and gives Candy Factory a five-year, noninterest-
    bearing note with a face value of $100,000. The conditions of the note provide
    that Candy Factory can purchase $400,000 of products from the issuer of the
    note at something less than the regular market price over the next five years.
    Sugar Products normally has to pay an interest rate of 10% when it borrows
    money from a bank to finance purchases of raw materials. Which of the fol-
    lowing is **true?**

a. Sugar Products should report the note payable at a carrying value of $100,000 on its balance sheet at December 31, 2005.

b. Sugar Products should record no interest expense over the next five years in connection with this loan.

c. At the inception of the note, Sugar Products should record a debit to Cash for the present value of the note using a 10% interest rate for discounting purposes.

d. At the inception of the note, Sugar Products should record unearned revenue for the excess of the note's face value over its present value.

EXPLANATION: Record the journal entry for Sugar Products for the inception of the note. The difference between the present value of the note and the amount of cash received should be recorded as both a discount on the note and unearned revenue by the issuer of the note. The journal entry would be as follows:

Cash	100,000	
Discount on Notes Payable	37,908	
Notes Payable		100,000
Unearned Revenue		37,908 *

*Present value of $100,000 due five years at 10% = $100,000 x .62092 = $62,092;
$100,000 face value – $62,092 present value = $37,908 discount.

The Discount on Notes Payable will be amortized to interest expense over the five-year term using the effective interest method. The Unearned Revenue will be recognized as revenue from the sale of products and is prorated on the same basis that each period's sales to the lender-customer bear to the total sales to that customer for the term of the note. Thus, in this situation, the amortization of the discount and the recognition of the unearned revenue are at different rates. (Solution = d.)

Question

12. Bandy Rentals borrowed money from a bank to build new mini-warehouses. Bandy gave a 20-year mortgage note in the amount of $100,000 with a stated rate of 10.75%. The lender charged $4,000 (4 "points") to close the financing. Based on this information:

    a. Bandy should debit Interest Expense in recording the points at the date the money is borrowed.

    b. Bandy's effective interest rate is now less than the 10.75% stated rate.

    c. Bandy should record the Mortgage Note Payable for only $96,000 since only $96,000 cash was received.

    d. Bandy should amortize the $4,000 to interest expense over the life of the loan.

EXPLANATION: Bandy will receive $96,000 cash but will have to repay $100,000 plus interest at 10.75% on the $100,000. Thus, the points raise the effective interest rate above the stated rate and should be accounted for as interest expense over the life of the loan. (Solution = d.)

Question

13. A corporation borrowed money from a bank to build a building. The long-term note signed by the corporation is secured by a mortgage that pledges title to the building as security for the loan. The corporation is to pay the bank $80,000 each year for 10 years to repay the loan. Which of the following relationships can you expect to apply to the situation?
   a. The balance of mortgage payable at a given balance sheet date will be reported as a long-term liability.
   b. The balance of mortgage payable will remain a constant amount over the 10-year period.
   c. The amount of interest expense will decrease each period the loan is outstanding, while the portion of the annual payment applied to the loan principal will increase each period.
   d. The amount of interest expense will remain constant over the 10-year period.

EXPLANATION: Mortgage notes payable are recorded initially at face value, and entries are required subsequently for each instalment payment. Each payment consists of (1) interest on the unpaid principal balance of the loan, and (2) a reduction of loan principal. Because a portion of each payment is applied to the principal, the principal balance decreases each period. Interest for a period of time is calculated by multiplying the stated (contract) rate of interest by the principal balance outstanding at the beginning of the period. Thus, the amount of each payment required to cover interest decreases while the portion of the payment applied to the loan principal balance will increase each period. (Solution = c.)

Question

14. The debt-to-total asset ratio measures the:
   a. relationship between interest expense and income.
   b. percentage of total assets financed through creditor sources.
   c. portion of debt used to acquire assets.
   d. relationship between debt and interest expense.

EXPLANATION: Write down the calculation for the debt-to-total asset ratio and think about its components and their relationship. The debt-to-total asset ratio is calculated by dividing total debt by total assets. This ratio measures the percentage of the total assets provided by creditors. The higher the percentage of debt to total assets, the greater the risk that the company may be unable to meet its maturing obligations. (Solution = b.)

Question

15. The times interest earned ratio provides an indication of the:
   a. company's ability to meet interest payments as they become due.

b. relationship between current liabilities and current assets.
c. percentage of assets financed by debt.
d. relationship between debt and interest expense.

EXPLANATION: Write down the calculation for the interest earned ratio and think about the relationship of the components of the ratio. The interest earned ratio is calculated by dividing income before income taxes and interest expense by interest expense. This ratio provides an indication of the relationship between income (before taxes and interest expense have deducted) and the amount of interest expense for the period. It is an indication of the company's ability to meet interest payments as they become due. (Solution = a.)

Question

16. A debtor in a troubled debt restructuring has debt that is settled by a transfer of land with a fair value that is less than the carrying amount of the debt but is more than the book value of the land. Should a gain or loss on restructuring of debt be recognized? Should a gain or loss on the disposition of assets be recognized?

	Gain or Loss on Restructuring of Debt	Gain or Loss on Disposition of Assets
a.	Gain	Gain
b.	Gain	Loss
c.	Loss	Loss
d.	Loss	Gain

EXPLANATION: Assign amounts to the (1) carrying amount of the debt, (2) carrying amount of the loan, and (3) fair value of the land. Be sure your assigned amounts maintain the relationships stated in the question. Then use a journal entry approach to solve. For instance: Fair value of land, $100,000; carrying amount of debt, $127,000; and book value of land, $65,000. For the journal entry, debit the debt account(s) for $127,000; credit Land for $65,000; credit Gain on Disposition of Assets for $35,000 (an excess of the fair value over the book value indicates that a gain has been experienced on the old asset). The rest of the entry is due to a gain or loss on restructuring of debt. A credit for $27,000 is needed for the entry to balance; hence, there is a gain on settlement. If you are able to settle a debt by giving an asset with a value that is less than the carrying amount of the debt, you have an advantageous settlement of debt; hence a gain on restructuring of debt should be recognized.

Debt		127,000	
Land			65,000
Gain on Disposition of Assets			35,000
Gain on Restructuring of Debt			27,000

(Solution = a.)

CHAPTER 16

Shareholders' Equity

Overview

A major source of assets of an entity is owners' equity. Owners' equity of a corporation is called shareholders' equity because the owners of the business hold shares as evidence of their ownership claims. Shareholders' equity typically has two major classifications for reporting purposes: contributed capital and earned capital (retained earnings). Contributed capital includes the subclassifications of share capital and contributed surplus.

The term "earnings" refers to net income for a period. The term "retained earnings" refers to accumulated earnings. That is, retained earnings is the total of all amounts reported as net income since the inception of the corporation less the sum of any amounts reported as net losses and dividends declared since the inception of the corporation. Thus, distributions of corporate profits to shareholders reduce retained earnings.

A corporation may distribute cash, noncash assets, or additional shares to its owners in the form of dividends. A distribution of assets may represent a distribution of income or a return of invested capital. A distribution of a corporation's own shares results in capitalizing retained earnings.

This chapter also discusses the accounting for issuance, reacquisition, retirement, and cancellation of shares.

Study Steps

Understanding the Nature and Purpose of Equity

A company is financed using either debt, equity, or internally generated funds. Ideally, debt and equity are recorded on the balance sheet, although off-balance-sheet financing, where the financing is not recorded on the balance sheet, has become popular.

The different types of financing carry different rights and claims on the company. Debt holders usually have the greatest rights. Generally, they have preferential treatment with respect to a return on their investment (interest) after a specified period of time or on liquidation of the company.

All forms of debt or equity financing fit somewhere on the spectrum noted above. Common shares are residual in nature in that these shareholders get whatever is left after other claims on the company are settled. Further, the common shares carry the votes and therefore the right to make decisions for the company. Common shareholders are therefore seen to have the risks and rewards of ownership.

Common shares are often called residual ownership shares since they get the "residue" or whatever is left after other investors and creditors have had their share in earnings and net assets.

Since the common shareholders are at risk with respect to their original investment and return on that investment, they have the risks of ownership. Note that they also have rewards of ownership since they also stand to gain more and have control over the company through the voting provisions in the shares.

Preferred shares fall somewhere between debt and equity and have characteristics of both. Shares that have a fixed term or requirement to redeem are more debt-like. Shares that are retractable at the option of the holder are also seen as being more debt-like.

The shareholders' equity section on the balance sheet has two basic types of equity included in it: earned equity and contributed equity. Contributed equity is the amount invested in the company by the shareholders or contributed to the company, and earned equity is the amount that has been earned by the company itself (i.e., through net income).

Understanding the Nature of Surplus and Distributions

Contributed versus earned surplus

Firstly, the distinction between contributed capital and retained earnings should be recognized. Retained earnings is effectively surplus net income that has not yet been distributed to shareholders. It is earned by the company. Contributed surplus, on the other hand, is not earned by the company but is contributed usually, although not necessarily, by the shareholders. As such, it is not connected with operations or the earnings process of the company. The distinction is not always so clear, however, and requires some judgement.

Both contributed surplus and retained earnings are forms of surplus in the company. One is contributed however, and one is earned.

Dividends

Dividends are charged to retained earnings and effectively represent the distribution of the excess profits of the company to the shareholders.

There are legal restrictions on how much may be distributed. In general, dividends should not be paid if it would result in the company being unable to pay its liabilities or would result in the realizable value of the assets being less than the liabilities and capital. Often there are other restrictions on how much of retained earnings may be distributed. These arise from contractual arrangements entered into by the company, such as covenants on debt obligations or shares.

Although legal restrictions need not be separately disclosed, since it is presumed that this is public knowledge, other restrictions on dividend payout should be disclosed since this is a decision relevant to users of the financial statements.

Usually dividends are paid in cash; however, sometimes they may take the form of property or stock. These are called dividends in kind and are generally valued at the fair value of the property given up, unless they are seen as a spin-off or restructuring, in which case they are recorded at the carrying value of the assets distributed.

Liquidating dividends occur when the dividend is paid out of equity other than retained earnings. The implication is that the dividend is a return of capital (contributed surplus) to the shareholders rather than a distribution of profits (retained earnings).

Stock dividends versus stock splits

Stock dividends are paid out as a return on capital for shareholders. Stock splits however are normally initiated in order to lower the share value such that shares are more accessible to investors. In general, a 2:1 split means that for every one share there are now two. Therefore the new shares trade at half the value.

While dividends are debited to retained earnings, stock splits are not recorded at all except by adjusting the number of shares (not the dollar value).

When a large stock dividend is issued, it is difficult to judge whether the economic substance is more like a dividend or a split. Professional judgement must be exercised.

Becoming Proficient in Related Calculations

There are no significant calculations or methods that need be mastered here. The par value method of accounting for shares is common in the United States; however, in Canada, most companies would not issue shares with par value since it is not permitted by law (CBCA and most provincial Acts). The journal entries for acquisition of shares and subsequent sale/cancellation may be tricky and a number of the multiple-choice questions and problems below focus on this.

Financial Statement Analysis

Key ratios and their interpretation are discussed in Illustration 16-4.

Understanding Financial Reorganizations

A financial reorganization occurs when a financially troubled company restructures its debt and equity in agreement with existing creditors and shareholders. Often, existing creditors exchange their debt for equity of the company and, in general, the capitalization and financing of the company is adjusted to place less of a financial burden on it. Control of the company changes as a result of the reorganization.

The restructuring involves a change in ownership or voting control. Often it is the creditors who gain control.

Normally, the assets and liabilities would be revalued and any retained earnings or deficit relating to accumulated net losses would be closed out to either contributed surplus or share capital. This gives the company a new start and allows retained earnings to start from zero.

Tips on Chapter Topics

TIP! **Shareholders' equity** is classified into two categories: contributed capital and earned capital.

TIP! **Contributed capital** is comprised of **share capital** and **contributed surplus.** **Earned capital** (commonly referred to as retained earnings) is the undistributed income that remains invested in an enterprise.

TIP! **Share capital** accounts include Common Share, Preferred Share, Common Share Subscribed, Preferred Share Subscribed, and Stock Dividends Distributable.

TIP! **Contributed surplus** can arise from many situations which include the following: capital donations, liquidating dividends, and share subscriptions forfeited.

TIP! There is a tremendous amount of terminology relating to capital transactions. You should have a clear understanding of all of the terms mentioned in this chapter before going on to subsequent chapters.

TIP! Both **par value** and **treasury shares** are **not** allowed under the Canada Business Corporations Act (CBCA). However, for those jurisdictions that allow it, the **par value** of a share is an arbitrary value assigned to a share at the time of incorporation and is printed on the share certificate. Par value usually has **no** direct relationship to the share's issuance price or to its market value at any date subsequent to the issuance date.

TIP! The **market value** of a share at a given point in time is the value at which the share can be bought or sold.

When a corporation issues more than one class of capital share, each contributed surplus account should specify the class of share to which it relates. Although a separate account may be maintained in the general ledger for each source of contributed surplus, the balances of all contributed surplus accounts are typically summed and reported by a single amount on the balance sheet by the caption Contributed Surplus.   **TIP!**

When shares are issued in a nonmonetary exchange, the shares are recorded at the fair value of the shares issued given or the fair value of the noncash consideration received, if the latter is more clearly determinable.   **TIP!**

Treasury shares occur when a company repurchases its own shares and does not cancel or retire them. This is **not allowed** under the CBCA. However, for those jurisdictions that allow it, the single transaction method is used to account for treasury shares.   **TIP!**

Dividends in arrears are **not** to be reported as a liability. Dividends become a liability when they are declared. By definition, dividends in arrears are dividends on cumulative preferred shares which have been passed (not declared). Dividends in arrears should be disclosed, however, in the notes to the financial statements.   **TIP!**

A corporation acquires resources (assets) from new owners by issuing shares; the issuance is recorded on the company's books by an increase in assets and an increase in owners' equity. When that initial owner later sells his (her) shares through the stock market, there is **no** journal entry to be made on the corporation's books; only the shareholders' name is changed in the corporation's records. The assets, liabilities, and owners' equity of the corporation are **not** affected by the purchase (or sale) of shares by investors in the stock market.   **TIP!**

Shareholders' equity is often referred to as **capital**. In accounting for shareholders' equity, the emphasis is on the source of capital. **Retained earnings** is sometimes called **earned capital** because it is the portion of shareholders' equity which has been generated by the entity's operations. **Share capital** is often called **contributed capital** or **invested capital** because it arises from owner contributions. Contributed capital includes share capital accounts and contributed surplus accounts.   **TIP!**

A preferred share's preference as to dividends is either expressed as a percentage of the par or stated value or in terms of dollars per share.   **TIP!**

Retained earnings represents a source of corporate assets. The balance of the Retained Earnings account at any point in time reflects the total unspecified assets which have been obtained through profitable operations of the reporting entity. The balance of the Retained Earnings account has **no** direct relationship to the amount of cash held by the entity; a corporation can have a large balance in the Cash account and a small balance in Retained Earnings or a small balance in Cash and a large balance in Retained Earnings.   **TIP!**

There are three dates associated with the declaration of any dividend: (1) the declaration date, (2) the date of record, and (3) the date of payment (or distribution). A journal entry is required at the date of declaration and at the date of payment.   **TIP!**

Dividends are **not** usually an expense, unless the underlying security that generated the dividend is classified as debt (see Chapter 17). Otherwise, dividends are considered a distribution of income, not a determinant of income. In recording the declara-   **TIP!**

TIP! tion of any dividend (except for a liquidating dividend), the accountant may use a temporary account called Dividends Declared, rather than debiting the Retained Earnings account directly. At the end of the period, in the closing process, the balance of the Dividends Declared account is closed directly to the Retained Earnings account.

TIP! The declaration of a cash dividend reduces working capital; the payment of a previously declared (and unrecorded) cash dividend has no effect on working capital. Unless otherwise indicated, Dividends Payable will require a cash payment to settle the obligation.

TIP! A property dividend (dividend payable in assets of the corporation other than cash) is an example of a nonreciprocal transfer of nonmonetary assets. *CICA Handbook* Section 3830.05 requires that a nonreciprocal transfer of nonmonetary assets be recorded at the fair value of the assets transferred. Thus, any difference between the transferred asset's fair value and its carrying amount is to be recognized as a gain or a loss.

Exercise 16-1

PURPOSE: This exercise will highlight the relationship between authorized, issued, outstanding, and subscribed shares.

The following data are available regarding the common shares of the Daffy Corporation at December 31, 2005:

Authorized shares	200,000
Unissued shares	60,000
Subscribed shares	5,000
Treasury shares	12,000

Instructions

Calculate the number of outstanding shares. Assume treasury shares are allowed in the jurisdiction.

Solution to Exercise 16-1

Authorized shares	200,000
Unissued shares	(60,000)
Issued shares	140,000
Treasury shares	(12,000)
Outstanding shares	128,000

Illustration 16-1 75

EXPLANATION: Write down the formula for determining the number of outstanding shares:

Issued Shares – Treasury Shares = Outstanding Shares

Fill in the data given. Authorized shares are either issued or unissued. Issued shares are either outstanding shares or treasury shares. The number issued can readily be calculated in this situation. Treasury shares are issued shares, but are not outstanding (in the hands of shareholders). Subscribed shares are not issued until they are fully paid, so they are part of the unissued number.

Illustration 16-1
Transactions That May Affect Contributed Surplus

Contributed surplus may be derived from a variety of transactions or events as noted below:

Transactions that may affect Contributed Surplus

- Par value shares—issue, retirement
- Capital donations
- No par shares—repurchase/retirement
- Liquidating dividends
- Financial reorganizations
- Stock rights and warrants
- Issue of convertible debt
- Share subscriptions forfeited
- Redemption or conversion of shares

Exercise 16-2

PURPOSE: This exercise will illustrate how to record selected transactions related to the issuance of share capital.

On February 1, 2005, Bimini Bay Corporation received authorization to issue 400,000 common shares. The following transactions occurred during 2005:

Feb. 24   Issued 100,000 common shares for cash at a price of $18 per share.

Feb. 28   Issued 50,000 shares of common shares in exchange for a group of modular warehouses.

Mar. 28   Received subscriptions for 30,000 common shares at $18 per share. Collected a down payment of 20% of the subscription price.

Apr. 15   Collected 50% of the subscription price from the subscribers.

Apr. 30   Collected the balance from the subscribers of 28,000 shares and issued the related shares. The remaining subscribers (2,000 shares) defaulted. The subscription agreement provides that the corporation will refund only the amount collected in excess of 20% of the subscription price.

Nov. 4   Issued 20,000 common shares at $24 per share.

Instructions

Prepare the journal entries to record the transactions listed above.

Solution to Exercise 16-2

February 24

Cash (100,000 x $18)	1,800,000	
Common Shares (100,000 x $18)		1,800,000

February 28

Warehouses (50,000 x $18)	900,000	
Common Shares (50,000 x $18)		900,000

March 28

Subscriptions Receivable (30,000 x $18)	540,000	
Common Shares Subscribed (30,000 x $18)		540,000

TIP! In accounting for share subscriptions, share capital is increased at the date the subscriptions (contracts) are received, not when the related cash is received. However, because the Subscriptions Receivable account is classified as a contra shareholders' equity account, total shareholders' equity is unaffected by the entry (above) to record the receipt of the subscriptions contract. Total shareholders' equity increases only when cash is received (which reduces the contra equity account).

Cash (20% x 30,000 x $18)	108,000	
Subscriptions Receivable		108,000

April 15

Cash (50% x 30,000 x $18)	270,000	
Subscriptions Receivable		270,000

April 30

Cash (30% x 28,000 x $18)	151,200	
Subscriptions Receivable		151,200

Common Shares Subscribed (28,000 x $18)	504,000	
Common Shares		504,000
Common Shares Subscribed (2,000 x $18)	36,000	
Cash (2,000 x 50% x $18)		18,000
Subscriptions Receivable (2,000 x 30% x $18)		10,800
Contributed Surplus, Forfeited Subscriptions		
(2,000 x 20% x $18)		7,200

November 4

Cash (20,000 x $24)	480,000	
Common Shares (20,000 x $24)		480,000

EXPLANATION:

Feb. 24   The **issuance of shares in exchange for cash** is recorded by crediting common shares for the amount of the cash consideration received ($1.8 million).

Feb. 28   The **issuance of shares in exchange for nonmonetary assets** requires an application of the following principle: The asset and the shares are to be recorded at the fair value of the consideration given (the shares) or the fair value of the consideration received (warehouses), whichever is the more clearly determinable. Because some common shares were issued only four days earlier at $18 per share, the February 24 transaction provides good evidence of the fair value (cash equivalent value) of the shares issued on February 28. No mention of the fair value of the warehouses is made.

Mar. 28   The **receipt of a subscription contract** is recorded by a debit to a receivable account for the total contract (subscription) price, with a credit to a share subscribed account for the same amount. The partial collection increases Cash and reduces the Subscriptions Receivable account. The Common Share Subscribed account is classified as a share capital account; it has a balance only from the date of receipt of the subscription contract until the date the last collection is made on the contract. The Subscriptions Receivable account is classified as a contra shareholders' equity account, similar to the presentation of treasury shares.

Apr. 15   The **collection of cash from subscribers** increases assets (cash). It also increases total shareholders' equity by reducing the contra account— Subscriptions Receivable.

Apr. 30   The **collection of additional cash from subscribers** is recorded in the same manner as previous collections. The **issuance of the subscribed shares** reduces one share capital account (Common Shares Subscribed) and increases another share capital account (Common Shares) by the same amount. The default is recorded by removing the subscription price of the related shares ($18 x 2,000 shares) from the accounts; the

Common Shares Subscribed account is debited for the same amount. Cash is credited for the amount refunded. (Collections of 20% of subscription price on March 28 and 50% on April 15 total 70%, which exceeds 20% by 50%; thus, 50% of the $18 subscription price is refunded to the subscribers of 2,000 shares.) Subscriptions Receivable is credited with the unpaid balance. The portion of the subscription price paid by the defaulting subscribers but not refunded to them (70% − 50% = 20% not refunded) is credited to contributed surplus.

Nov. 4   The **issuance of shares for cash** increases assets and total shareholders' equity by the issuance proceeds.

Exercise 16-3

PURPOSE: This exercise will illustrate how the components of shareholders' equity should be reported in the balance sheet.

Build-It Corporation's charter authorizes 200,000 common shares, and 50,000 6% cumulative and nonparticipating preferred shares.

The corporation engaged in the following share transactions between the date of incorporation and December 31, 2005:
  (1) Issued 40,000 common shares for $1.92 million.
  (2) Issued 10,000 preferred shares in exchange for machinery valued at $1.12 million.
  (3) Took subscriptions for 5,000 common shares and collected 30% of the subscription price of $50 per share.

At December 31, 2005, Build-It's retained earnings balance was $2.2 million.

Instructions

Prepare the shareholders' equity section of the balance sheet in good form.

Solution to Exercise 16-3

Build-it Corporation
PARTIAL BALANCE SHEET
December 31, 2005

Shareholders' equity
    Preferred shares; 6% cumulative and
       nonparticipating; 50,000 shares authorized;
       10,000 shares issued and outstanding $1,120,000
    Common shares; 200,000 shares authorized,
       40,000 shares issued and outstanding   1,920,000

Common shares subscribed; 5,000 shares		250,000
Total share capital		3,290,000
Retained earnings		2,200,000
Total share capital and retained earnings		5,490,000
Less: Share subscriptions receivable		175,000
Total shareholders' equity		$ 5,315,000

APPROACH: Reconstruct the journal entries for the transactions. Use the resulting balances in the accounts to prepare the shareholders' equity section of the balance sheet at December 31, 2005.

EXPLANATION:

(1) Cash	1,920,000	
Common Shares		1,920,000
(2) Machinery	1,120,000	
Preferred Shares		1,120,000
(3) Subscriptions Receivable (5,000 x $50)	250,000	
Common Shares Subscribed (5,000 x $50)		250,000
Cash (30% x $250,000)	75,000	
Subscriptions Receivable		75,000

Exercise 16-4

PURPOSE: This case examines the major classifications within the shareholders' equity section of the balance sheet.

Shareholders' equity is an important element of a corporation's balance sheet.

Instructions

Identify and discuss the general categories of shareholders' equity (capital) for a corporation. Enumerate specific sources included in each general category.

Solution to Exercise 16-4

The general categories of a corporation's capital are:
• Contributed capital (share capital **plus** contributed surplus).
• Earned capital (retained earnings).

Contributed capital represents the amounts paid in for all classes of shares. Contributed capital also includes contributed surplus which may be affected by the following transactions:

- Par value shares—issue, retirement
- Capital donations
- No par shares—repurchase/retirement
- Liquidating dividends
- Financial reorganizations
- Stock rights and warrants
- Issue of convertible debt
- Share subscriptions forfeited
- Redemption or conversion of shares

Retained earnings are the accumulated net earnings of a corporation in excess of any net losses from operations and dividends. There may be appropriations of retained earnings which are restrictions on retained earnings, making a portion of the balance unavailable to serve as a basis for dividends. These restrictions may arise as a result of a restriction in a bond indenture or other formal agreement or they may be created at the discretion of the board of directors.

Accumulated Other Comprehensive Income is the cumulative change in equity due to revenue, expenses, gains or losses that result from nonshareholder transactions which are excluded from the calculation of Net Income.

TIP! The following items may appear as separate components in the shareholders' equity section of the balance sheet:
(1)   Appraisal increase credits.
(2)   Cumulative translation adjustments.

TIP! A **liquidating dividend** is a distribution to shareholders from invested capital. Thus, a liquidating dividend results in a reduction of contributed capital and does not affect retained earnings. A shareholder's investment in the corporation is reduced, but not necessarily eliminated, by this type of dividend. If a dividend is only **partially liquidating**, both contributed capital and retained earnings are reduced.

TIP! Although a stock dividend results in a reduction in retained earnings, it also causes an increase in contributed capital by the same amount. There is **no change in total shareholders' equity** when a stock dividend is declared or distributed. The CBCA requires that companies use fair value in accounting for stock dividends.

TIP! The term **capitalization of retained earnings** refers to the process of transferring an amount from retained earnings to contributed capital. Stock dividends result in the capitalization of retained earnings. Thus, stock dividends are declared as a means of informing shareholders that assets arising from past income will be retained in the business rather than distributed as dividends to the shareholders.

TIP! Stock Dividend Distributable is a share capital account and, therefore, is to be reported as an element of contributed capital. This account only has a balance for the short period of time between the date of declaration and the date of distribution of the dividend.

Illustration 16-2   81

All changes during a period in all shareholders' equity accounts should be disclosed. **TIP!**
Disclosure of such changes may take the form of a separate **statement of shareholders' equity** or may be made in the other general purpose financial statements
or the notes thereto. A popular format for the presentation of changes in shareholders' equity items is illustrated in the **Solution to Exercise 16-8**.

If the return on common shareholders' equity is greater than the return on assets, **TIP!**
the interest rate on debt is less than the average return on total assets; hence, the
entity is **favourably trading on the equity**. However, if the cost of debt exceeds the
return on total assets, the return on common shareholders' equity will be less than
the return on total assets; hence, the entity will be **unfavourably trading on the
equity**.

Illustration 16-2
Journal Entries for Recording Dividends and Splits

Cash Dividend

Data	The board of directors declares a cash dividend of $100,000.		
Date of Declaration	Retained Earnings (or Cash Dividends Declared)	100,000	
	Dividends Payable		100,000
Date of Record	No entry.		
Date of Payment	Dividends Payable	100,000	
	Cash		100,000

Property Dividend

Data	Jones Corporation declares a property dividend on March 1 to be distributed to shareholders on April 15. The property is an investment in shares of Bonnie Corporation and has a carrying value of $11,000. The market value of the Bonnie shares is $14,000 on March 1 and $14,900 on April 15.		
Date of Declaration	Investments in Securities	3,000	
	Gain on Appreciation of Securities		3,000

	Retained Earnings (or Property Dividends Declared)	14,000	
	Property Dividends Payable		14,000

Date of Record   No entry.

Date of Payment	Property Dividends Payable	14,000	
	Investments in Securities		14,000

TIP! | Any change in the fair value of the property between the date of declaration and the date of payment of the dividend is ignored.

Liquidating Dividend

Data   Harness Corporation declares a liquidating dividend of $4,000.

Date of Declaration	Contributed surplus/share capital	4,000	
	Dividends Payable		4,000

Date of Record   No entry.

Date of Payment	Dividends Payable	4,000	
	Cash		4,000

Small Stock Dividend

Data   Henry Corporation has 100,000 common shares outstanding on March 1, 2005. On March 2, the board of directors declares a 10% stock dividend distributable on April 4 to shareholders of record on March 16. The market price per share of common is $24 on March 2, $23 on March 16, and $25 on April 4.

Date of Declaration	Retained Earnings (or Stock Dividend Declared)	240,000	
	Common Stock Dividend Distributable		240,000

Date of Record   No entry.

Date of Distribution	Common Stock Dividend Distributable	240,000	
	Common Shares		240,000

Large Stock Dividend

Data   JJH Corporation has 100,000 common shares outstanding on March 1, 2005. The book value is $10 per share. On March 2, the board of directors declares a 40% stock split-up carried out in the

Illustration 16-2   83

form of a dividend. The dividend shares are to be distributed on April 3 to shareholders of record on March 15. The market price per common share is $24 on March 2, $15 on March 15, and $16 on April 3.

Date of **Declaration**	Retained Earnings (or Stock Dividend Declared)	400,000	
	Common Stock Dividend Distributable		400,000
	(40% x 100,000 = 40,000 shares)		
	(40,000 x $10 book value = $400,000)		

Date of **Record**	No entry.	

Date of **Distribution**	Common Stock Dividend Distributable	400,000	
	Common Shares		400,000

TIP!

Certain acts of incorporation require shares to be issued at market value. In this case, the dividend should be recorded at market value.

TIP!

It may be better, given the significance of the stock dividend, to treat it as a stock split, as illustrated below. Canadian GAAP is not definite on this issue, but in practice, stock dividends greater than 20-25% are treated more like a stock split. See **Exercise 16-5** for more detail on this subject.

Stock Split

Data   Howell Corporation has 100,000 common shares outstanding on March 1, 2005. The book value per share is $10. On March 2, the board of directors declares a 4-for-1 stock split. The split is to be effective April 2 for shareholders of record on March 13.

Date of   No entry.
Declaration

Date of   No entry.
Record

Date of   No entry. The number of shares outstanding is increased to
Distribution 400,000.
   The balance of Common Shares remains at $1 million, but the book value per share drops to $ 2.50 ($1,000,000/400,000).

Exercise 16-5

PURPOSE: This case will compare and contrast a large stock dividend with a small stock dividend.

   Stock splits and stock dividends may be used by a corporation to change the number of shares outstanding.

Instructions

(a) Explain what is meant by a stock split carried out in the form of a dividend.
(b) From an accounting viewpoint, explain how a stock split carried out in the form of a dividend differs from an ordinary stock dividend.
(c) Explain how and why a stock dividend which has been declared but not yet issued should be classified in a statement of financial position (balance sheet).

Solution to Exercise 16-5

(a) A stock split carried out in the form of a dividend is a distribution of corporate shares to present shareholders, in proportion to each shareholder's current holdings, which can be expected to cause a material decrease in the market value per share. Usually a distribution in excess of 20% to 25% of the number of shares previously outstanding would cause a material decrease in market value; a 40% stock dividend, a 50% stock dividend, and a 100% stock dividend are examples.

(b) A stock split carried out in the form of a dividend is accounted for similarly to an ordinary stock dividend in that retained earnings is capitalized. The difference is that retained earnings is charged for the market value of the dividend shares in an ordinary stock dividend but is charged only for the carrying value (or not at all!) of the dividend shares in a stock split carried out in the form of a dividend. A stock split does not involve any transfer of retained earnings to contributed capital; rather, the book value per share is changed in proportion to the multiple of issued shares.

(c) A declared but unissued stock dividend should be classified as part of corporate capital rather than as a liability in a statement of financial position. A stock dividend affects only capital accounts; that is, retained earnings are decreased and contributed capital is increased. Thus, there is no debt to be paid, and, consequently, there is no severance of corporate assets when a stock dividend is distributed. Furthermore, stock dividends declared can be revoked by a corporation's board of directors any time prior to issuance. Finally, the corporation usually will formally announce its intent to issue a specific number of additional shares, and these shares must be reserved for this purpose.

Exercise 16-6

PURPOSE: This exercise will allow you to practise recording various types of dividends.

Scot Corporation has the following shareholder equity items at December 31, 2004:

Common shares, 200,000 shares authorized,	
80,000 shares issued and outstanding	$ 800,000
Contributed surplus	2,400,000
Retained earnings	28,500,000
Total contributed capital and retained earnings	31,700,000
Total shareholders' equity	$ 31,700,000

Instructions

Assume each of the transactions listed below is **independent** of the others unless otherwise indicated. Dividends are declared only on outstanding shares. Record the following transactions at the beginning of 2005:

1. Declared a cash dividend of $0.50 per share.
2. Paid the dividend declared in "1" above.
3. Declared a property dividend. Inventory with a cost of $160,000 and a market value of $200,000 is to be distributed.
4. Distributed the property for the dividend described in "3" above.
5. Declared a 5% stock dividend when the market value was $14 per share.
6. Distributed the shares for the stock dividend described in "5" above.
7. Declared a liquidating dividend of $0.10 per share.
8. Distributed the dividend described in "7" above.
9. Declared a 100% stock dividend when the market value was $14 per share.
10. Distributed the dividend described in "9" above.
11. Declared a 2:1 stock split.

Solution to Exercise 16-6

1. Retained Earnings (or Cash Dividends Declared)   40,000
         Dividends Payable   40,000
          (80,000 outstanding shares x $0.50 = $40,000)

2. Dividends Payable   40,000
         Cash   40,000

3. Inventory   40,000
         Gain on Appreciation of Inventory   40,000
          ($200,000 market value – $160,000 cost = $40,000)

Retained Earnings (or Property Dividends Declared)	200,000	
Property Dividends Payable		200,000

4. Property Dividends Payable   200,000
       Inventory   200,000

5. Retained Earnings (or Stock Dividend Declared)   56,000
       Common Stock Dividend Distributable   56,000
       (5% x 80,000 outstanding shares = 4,000 dividend shares)
       (4,000 shares x $14 market value = $56,000)

6. Common Stock Dividend Distributable   56,000
       Common Shares   56,000

7. Contributed Surplus   8,000
       Dividends Payable   8,000
       ($0.10 x 80,000 outstanding shares = $8,000)

8. Dividends Payable   8,000
       Cash   8,000

9. Retained Earnings (or Stock Dividend Declared)   1,120,000
       Common Stock Dividend Distributable   1,120,000
       (100% x 80,000 shares outstanding x $14 = $1,120,000)

10. Common Stock Dividend Distributable   1,120,000
        Common Shares   1,120,000

11. No entry required except for a memorandum-type entry. The book value per share is reduced to one-half of what it was (from $10 per share to $5 per share) and the number of shares are doubled. Thus, the authorized number increases to 400,000, the issued number increases to 160,000.

Illustration 16-3
Steps in Allocating Dividends to Preferred and Common Shareholders

Step 1: Assign the dividends in arrears to preferred, if any.
If there are any dividends in arrears, the amount of arrearage is first allocated to the preferred shareholders. The remaining amount of dividends to be allocated is calculated. (If the amount declared is not enough to cover the arrearage, all dividends declared go to preferred holders, the remaining arrearage is calculated for disclosure, and the rest of the steps are not performed.)

Step 2: Assign current period preference to preferred.
The amount of the preferred shareholders' current year preference is calculated and that amount is allocated to the preferred shareholders. The remaining amount of dividends to be allocated is calculated. (If the dividends declared are not enough to cover the preferred's current year preference, all of the dividends declared are allocated to the preferred shareholders, the remaining arrearage is calculated for disclosure, and the rest of the steps are not performed.)

Step 3: Assign common an equal percentage dividend.
An amount of dividends to common shareholders to "match" the "percentage-on-par" (i.e., a "like" percentage) dividend given to preferred (for current year preference only) is calculated. If the remaining amount of dividends is sufficient to cover this "matching process," the amount of "matching" is allocated to common and the remaining amount of dividends is the amount in which both preferred and common will "participate." (If the amount declared is not enough to "match" the preferred, whatever is available after the preferred get their portion as calculated in steps "1" and "2" is allocated to common.)

Step 4: Assign the participation amount to preferred and common.
If the preferred share is nonparticipating, any remaining dividends are assigned to the common shareholders. If the preferred shares are participating, the amount of dividends available for "participation" is allocated between preferred and common based on an "equal percentage on par basis." That percentage is determined by dividing the amount of dividends available for participation by the sum of the aggregate par value of the preferred and the aggregate par value of the common.

Step 5: Total the amounts allocated and calculate per share amounts.
The amounts from the previous steps are added for each class. The total amount allocated to preferred shareholders and to common shareholders is often expressed on a per share basis. To calculate the amount per share, divide the total dividends allocated to the class by the number of outstanding shares in that class.

Arrearage refers to the amount of dividends in arrears.	**TIP!**

Exercise 16-7

PURPOSE: This exercise will illustrate the allocation of dividends when a corporation has both preferred and common shares outstanding.

Daly Corporation has the following shares outstanding without any changes for years 2004, 2005, and 2006.

50,000 preference shares, 4%	$ 500,000
200,000 common shares	1,000,000
	$ 1,500,000

Dividends are declared as follows:

2004	$15,000
2005	$50,000
2006	$72,000

Instructions

Calculate the amount of dividends (total and per share) to be allocated to the preferred shareholders and the common shareholders for each of the three years under each of the independent assumptions below:

(a) The preferred shares are noncumulative and nonparticipating.

(b) The preferred shares are cumulative and nonparticipating.

(c) The preferred shares are cumulative and participating.

Solution to Exercise 16-7

APPROACH: Calculate the preferred's current year preference ($500,000 x 4% = $20,000) and the amount to "match" the common holders ($1,000,000 x 4% = $40,000). Then use the steps listed in **Illustration 16-3** to solve.

(a)		**Preferred**	**Common**	**Total**
2004:	Total to distribute			$15,000
	Step 1:			
	Step 2: Less than preference	$15,000		$15,000
	Step 3:			
	Step 4:			
	Step 5:	$15,000	$ -0- .	$15,000
	÷ by	50,000	200,000	
	=	$ .30	$ .00	
2005:	Total to distribute			$50,000
	Step 1:			
	Step 2: 4% x $500,000	$20,000		$20,000
	Step 3: Remainder		$30,000	30,000
	Step 4:			
	Step 5:	$20,000	$30,000	50,000
	÷ by	50,000	200,000	
	=	$ .40	$ .15	
2006:	Total to distribute			$72,000
	Step 1:			
	Step 2: 4% x $500,000	$20,000		$20,000
	Step 3: 4% x $1,000,000		$40,000	$40,000
	Step 4: Remainder		12,000	12,000
	Step 5:	$20,000	$52,000	$72,000
	÷ by	50,000	200,000	
	=	$ .40	$ .26	

(b)

		Preferred	**Common**	**Total**
2004:	Total to distribute			$15,000
	Step 1:			
	Step 2: Less than preference	$15,000		$15,000
	Step 3:			
	Step 4:			
	Step 5:	$15,000	$ -0-	$15,000
	÷ by	50,000	200,000	
	=	$ .30	$ .00	
2005:	Total to distribute			50,000
	Step 1: $20,000 - $15,000	$ 5,000		$ 5,000
	Step 2: 4% x $500,000	20,000		20,000
	Step 3: Remainder		$25,000	$25,000
	Step 4:			
	Step 5:	$25,000	$25,000	50,000
	÷ by	50,000	200,000	
	=	$ .50	$ .125	
2006:	Total to distribute			$72,000
	Step 1:			
	Step 2: 4% x $500,000	$20,000		$20,000
	Step 3: 4% x $1,000,000		$40,000	40,000
	Step 4: Remainder		12,000	12,000
	Step 5:	$20,000	$52,000	$72,000
	÷ by	50,000	200,000	
	=	$ .40	$ .26	

(c)

		Preferred	**Common**	**Total**
2004:	Total to distribute			$15,000
	Step 1:			
	Step 2: Less than preference	$15,000		$15,000
	Step 3:			
	Step 4:			
	Step 5:	$15,000	$ -0-	$15,000
	÷ by	50,000	200,000	
	=	$ .30	$ .00	

		Preferred	Common	Total
2005:	Total to distribute			$50,000
	Step 1: $20,000 – $15,000	$ 5,000		$ 5,000
	Step 2: 4% x $500,000	20,000		20,000
	Step 3: Remainder		$25,000	$25,000
	Step 4:			
	Step 5:	$25,000	$25,000	$50,000
	÷ by	50,000	200,000	
	=	$ .50	$ .125	

TIP! | Notice that in performing step 3, the remaining dividends ($25,000) are not sufficient in amount to allocate a "matching" dividend to the common shareholders (4% x $1,000,000 > $25,000)

		Preferred	Common	Total
2006:	Total to distribute			$72,000
	Step 1:			
	Step 2: 4% x $500,000	$20,000		$20,000
	Step 3: 4% x $1,000,000		$40,000	40,000
	Step 4: To participate at 0.8%*	4,000	8,000	12,000
	Step 5:	$24,000	$48,000	$72,000
	÷ by	50,000	200,000	
	=	$ .48	$ .24	

$$\frac{\text{*Amount to participate}}{\text{Total par}} = \frac{\$12,000}{\$1,500,000} = .008 \text{ or } .8\%$$

.008 x $500,000 = $4,000 allocated to preferred
.008 x $1,000,000 = $8,000 allocated to common

Exercise 16-8

PURPOSE: This exercise will illustrate the preparation of a statement of shareholders' equity and the related shareholders' equity section of the balance sheet.

On January 1, 2005, Hutton Corporation had the following shareholders' equity balances:

Common Shares (800,000 shares authorized, 300,000 issued)	$ 300,000
Contributed Surplus	710,000
Retained Earnings	390,000
Treasury Shares (3,000 shares)	6,000

During 2005, the following occurred:
- Issued 50,000 common shares for $150,000.
- Declared a $70,000 cash dividend.
- Purchased 1,000 treasury shares for $2,000.
- Declared and distributed a 5% stock dividend when the market value was $3 per share.
- Earned net income for the year of $200,000.

Instructions

(a) Prepare a statement of shareholders' equity for the year ending December 31, 2005.

(b) Prepare the shareholders' equity section of the balance sheet as of December 31, 2005.

Solution to Exercise 16-8

(a)

Hutton Corporation
STATEMENT OF SHAREHOLDERS' EQUITY
For the Year Ended December 31, 2005

	Total	Retained Earnings	Common Shares	Contributed Surplus	Treasury Shares
Balance January 1	$1,394,000	$390,000	$300,000	$710,000	$(6,000)
Issued 50,000 common shares for $150,000	150,000		150,000		
Declared a $70,000 cash dividend	(70,000)	(70,000)			
Purchased 1,000 shares for treasury at $2	(2,000)				(2,000)
Declared and distributed a 5% stock dividend		(51,900)	51,900		
Net income for year	200,000	200,000			
Balance, December 31	$1,672,000	$468,100	$501,900	$710,000	$(8,000)

> **TIP!**
> Notice how the columns on this statement foot (add down) and crossfoot (add across).

EXPLANATION: A corporation is to disclose all changes that took place in all shareholder equity items during the reporting period. A convenient and effective way of meeting that requirement is to present a statement of shareholders' equity (sometimes called a shareholders' equity statement). When this statement is presented, it replaces the statement of retained earnings because it contains all the information that a statement of retained earnings would contain plus data regarding changes in other components of shareholders' equity.

The calculations for the stock dividend are as follows:
    350,000 shares issued – 4,000 treasury shares = 346,000 shares outstanding.
    346,000 shares outstanding x 5% = 17,300 dividend shares.
    17,300 shares x $3 market value = $51,900 decrease in Retained Earnings.
    17,300 shares x $3 market value = $51,900 increase in Common Shares.

(b)

Hutton Corporation
BALANCE SHEET (Partial)
As of December 31, 2005

Shareholders' Equity
    Paid-in capital

Common shares, 800,000 shares authorized,	
- 367,300 shares issued,	
- 363,300 shares outstanding	$ 501,900
Contributed surplus	710,000
Total paid-in capital	1,211,900
Retained earnings	468,100
Total paid-in capital and retained earnings	1,680,000
Treasury shares, 4,000 shares, at cost	(8,000)
Total shareholders' equity	$1,672,000

Illustration 16-4
Ratios for Analysis of Shareholders' Equity

The following four ratios use shareholders' equity amounts to evaluate a company's profitability and long-term solvency.

1. **Rate of return on common shareholders' equity.** This widely used ratio measures profitability from the common shareholders' viewpoint. This ratio shows how many dollars of net income were earned for each dollar invested by the owners. The ratio is calculated as follows:

$$\frac{\text{Rate of return on}}{\text{common share equity}} = \frac{\text{Net income} - \text{preferred dividends}}{\text{Average common shareholders' equity}^{a}}$$

[a]The carrying value of preferred shares is deducted from total shareholders' equity to arrive at the amount of common shareholders' equity used in this ratio.

Illustration 16-4 93

TIP!

When the rate of return on common shareholders' equity is greater than the rate of return on total assets, the company is said to be "trading on the equity at a gain" or "favourably trading on the equity." "**Trading on the equity**" describes the practice of using borrowed money at fixed interest rates or issuing preferred shares with constant dividend rates in hopes of using the assets obtained (by use of the money from the borrowing or issuance of preferred shares) in such a way that the rate of return on the assets exceeds the rate of interest or dividends. If this can be done, the capital obtained from bondholders or preferred shareholders earns enough to pay interest or dividends and to leave a margin for the common shareholders. When this condition exists, trading on the equity is profitable.

2. **Payout ratio.** The payout ratio is the relationship of cash dividends to net income; it is a measure of profitability. The ratio is calculated for common shareholders as follows:

$$\text{Payout ratio} = \frac{\text{Cash dividends}}{\text{Net income less preferred dividends}}$$

TIP!

Some investors look for shares that have a payout ratio sufficiently high to provide a good yield on the shares; other investors view the potential appreciation in the market value of the shares as more important than the prospect of high dividends.

TIP!

Another closely watched ratio is the **dividend yield** which is calculated by dividing the cash dividend per share by the market price of the share. This ratio affords investors of some idea of the rate of return that will be received in cash dividends from their investment.

3. **Price earnings (P/E) ratio.** This ratio is often highlighted by an analyst in discussing the investment possibility of a given enterprise. It is calculated by dividing the share's market price by its earnings per share. This ratio is calculated as follows:

$$\text{Price earnings ratio} = \frac{\text{Market price of shares}}{\text{Earnings per share}}$$

TIP!

The P/E ratio is often referred to as a "multiple."

TIP!

When one company has a P/E ratio significantly different than the P/E ratio of another company, the reason for this difference is linked to several factors; relative risk, stability of earnings, trends in earnings, and the market's perception of the company's growth potential and quality of earnings.

4. **Book value per share.** The book value or **equity value per share** is a much-used basis for evaluating the net worth of a corporation. Book value per share is the amount each share would receive if the company were liquidated on the basis of amounts reported on the balance sheet. The ratio loses much of its relevance if the valuations on the balance sheet do not approximate fair market value of the assets. Assuming no preferred shares are outstanding, the ratio is as follows:

$$\text{Book value per share} = \frac{\text{Common shareholders' equity}}{\text{Outstanding shares}}$$

TIP!

To calculate the book value per common share when there are preferred shares also outstanding, use the following steps:

Step 1: Calculate the total book value of preferred shares by multiplying the book value per share by the number of preferred shares outstanding. The book value per share of preferred is one of the following (listed in order of preference):

a. Liquidation value of preferred plus dividends in arrears.

b. Call or redemption price of preferred plus dividends in arrears.

c. Par value of preferred plus dividends in arrears.

Step 2: Calculate the total book value of common shares by deducting the total book value of preferred shares from total shareholders' equity.

Step 3: Calculate the book value per share of common shares by dividing the total book value of common shares by the number of common shares outstanding.

Exercise 16-9

PURPOSE: This exercise will give you an example of how to calculate the return on common shareholders' equity.

	Dec. 31 2004	Dec. 31 2005
Preferred shares, 8%, noncumulative	$250,000	$250,000
Common shares	600,000	800,000
Retained earnings	150,000	370,000
Dividends paid on preferred shares for the year	20,000	20,000
Net income for the year	120,000	240,000

Instructions

(a) Calculate Bradley's return on common shareholders' equity (rounded to the nearest percentage) for 2005.

Solution to Exercise 16-9

$$\text{Return on common shareholders' equity} = \frac{\text{Net income} - \text{Preferred dividends}}{\text{Average common shareholders' equity}}$$

$$\frac{\$240,000 - \$20,000}{1/2\ (\$750,000^1 + \$1,170,000^2)} = \frac{\$220,000}{\$960,000} = \underline{23\%}$$

[1]Beginning total shareholders' equity ($250,000 + $600,000 + $150,000) – carrying value of preferred shares ($250,000) = $750,000 beginning common shareholders' equity.

[2]Ending total shareholders' equity ($250,000 + $800,000 + $370,000) – carrying value of preferred shares ($250,000) = $1,170,000 ending common shareholders' equity.

EXPLANATION: A widely used ratio that measures profitability from the common shareholders' viewpoint is **return on common shareholders' equity**. This ratio shows how many dollars of net income were earned for each dollar invested by the owners. It is calculated by dividing net income applicable to common shareholders (net income – preferred dividends) by average common shareholders' equity.

Exercise 16-10

PURPOSE: This exercise will illustrate the proper procedures to be employed in a financial reorganization.

The following facts pertain to the Keller Corporation at December 31, 2005:
1. Retained earnings has a negative balance of $30,000.
2. The cost of inventory exceeds its market value by $12,000.
3. The carrying value of plant assets exceeds their market value by $28,000.
4. There are 3,000 common shares with a carrying value of $300,000.
5. There is no contributed surplus.

Future prospects for successful operations are good. In order to eliminate the deficit (negative retained earnings balance), a financial reorganization is successfully negotiated, such that the conditions under *CICA Handbook* Section 1625 are met.

Instructions

(a) Record all of the journal entries related to this financial reorganization.
(b) Explain what must be disclosed after the financial reorganization.

Solution to Exercise 16-10

APPROACH: Follow the three easy steps listed below.

Step 1: **The deficit balance is brought to zero.** Any asset writedowns or impairments that existed prior to the reorganization should be recorded first. The deficit is reclassified to Share Capital, Contributed Surplus, or a separately identified account within Shareholder's Equity.

Step 2: **The changes in debt and equity as negotiated are recorded.** Often debt is exchanged for equity reflecting a change in control.

Step 3: **The assets and liabilities are comprehensively revalued.** This step assigns appropriate going concern values to all assets and liabilities as per the negotiations. The difference between the carrying values prior to the reorganization and the new values after is known as a revaluation adjustment. The revaluation adjustment and any costs incurred to carry out the financial reorganization are accounted for as capital transactions and are closed to Share Capital, Contributed Surplus, or a separately identified account within Shareholders' Equity. Note that the new costs of the identifiable assets and liabilities must not exceed the entity's fair value if known.

(a) **ENTRIES:**

Step 1:			
Common shares		70,000	
	Retained earnings		30,000
	Inventory		12,000
	Plant Assets		28,000

Step 2: No additional entry required.
Step 3: No additional entry required.

(b) After a financial reorganization, the following must be disclosed: The date of the reorganization, a description of the reorganization, and the amount of change in each major class of assets, liability of description, and shareholder's equity resulting from the reorganization. For a period of at least three years following the reorganization, the following must be disclosed: The date of the reorganization, the revaluation adjustment, the amount of the deficit that was reclassified, and the measurement basis for the assets and liabilities that were revalued.

TIP! | A financial reorganization is often called a **fresh start**.

Analysis of Multiple-Choice Type Questions

Question

1. Which of the following rights does a preferred shareholder normally possess?
    a.   right to vote
    b.   right to receive a dividend before a common shareholder
    c.   preemptive right
    d.   right to participate in management

EXPLANATION: A preferred shareholder usually has a preference over common shareholders as to dividends and as to distribution of assets upon liquidation. A preferred shareholder normally has to forego other rights because of the preference described above. The rights the preferred shareholder normally forgoes are the right to participate in management (right to vote on operational and financial decisions) and the preemptive right. A common shareholder normally has the right to vote and the preemptive right (right to maintain the same percentage ownership when additional common shares are issued). (Solution = b.)

Question

2. The Powell Corporation has 10,000 common shares authorized. The following transactions took place during 2005, the first year of the corporation's existence:
    - Sold 1,000 common shares for $18 per share.
    - Issued 1,000 common shares in exchange for a patent valued at $20,000.
    - Reported net income of $7,000.
    At the end of Powell's first year, total contributed capital amounted to:
    a. $8,000.
    b. $18,000.
    c. $20,000.
    d. $28,000.
    e. none of the above.

EXPLANATION: (1) Write down the components of paid-in capital: (a) balances of share capital accounts, and (b) balances of contributed surplus accounts. (2) Reconstruct the journal entries for the transactions listed. (3) Calculate the balances of the relevant accounts. (4) Sum the relevant account balances.

Cash	18,000	
Common Shares		18,000
Patent	20,000	
Common Shares		20,000

| Income Summary | | 7,000 | |
| Retained Earnings | | | 7,000 |

Common shares	$ 38,000	
Contributed surplus	0	
Total contributed capital	$ 38,000	(Solution = e.)

TIP! | Retained earnings is considered **earned capital**.

Question

✗ 3. Which of the following represents the total number of shares that a corporation may issue under the terms of its charter?
   a. authorized shares
   b. issued shares
   c. unissued shares
   d. outstanding shares
   e. treasury shares

EXPLANATION: Explain the meaning of each of the terms used as answer selections. Choose the one that matches the stem of the question. Issued shares (ones the corporation has issued to date) **plus** unissued shares (shares that have not been issued yet but may be issued in the future in accordance with the terms of the charter) **equals** total authorized (approved) shares. Outstanding shares are the issued shares which are now in the hands of the public. Treasury shares are issued shares which are not outstanding at the present time. (Solution = a.)

Question

4. If common shares are issued for noncash assets, the amount to be recorded as share capital related to this transaction is determined by the:
   a. fair market value of the noncash assets received.
   b. par value of the shares issued.
   c. legal value of the shares issued.
   d. book value of the noncash assets on the seller's books.

EXPLANATION: Cost is measured by the fair market value (cash equivalent value) of the consideration given or the fair market value of the consideration received, whichever is the more objectively determinable. Assuming equipment with a fair value of $70,000 is received in exchange for common shares, the journal entry to record the transaction would be as follows:

| Equipment | | 70,000 | |
| Common Shares | | | 70,000 |

(Solution = a.)

Question

5. The balance of the Share Subscriptions Receivable account should be classified:
   a. as a current asset.
   b. contra to common shares.
   c. contra to retained earnings.
   d. contra to the sum of share capital and retained earnings.

EXPLANATION: The balance of the Share Subscriptions Receivable account is best classified contra to the subtotal of share capital plus retained earnings. (Solution = d.)

Question

6. Treasury shares are: ✗
   a. shares held as an investment by the treasurer of the corporation.
   b. shares held as an investment of the corporation.
   c. issued and outstanding shares.
   d. unissued shares.
   e. issued but not outstanding shares.

EXPLANATION: Write down the definition of treasury shares. Treasury shares are a corporation's own shares that have been issued, fully paid for, and reacquired by the corporation but **not** retired (cancelled). Treasury shares are shares that have been issued previously (so are not unissued) but are not outstanding now, as they have been subsequently reacquired by the company. Treasury shares refer to a company's own shares so they cannot be an investment. A company cannot own itself. The acquisition of treasury shares represents a contraction of capital (owners' equity) rather than the acquisition of an asset. (Solution = e.)

If and when treasury shares are formally retired, they revert back to an unissued status.	**TIP!**

Question

7. Wheeler Corporation started business in 2005 by issuing 100,000 common shares for $24 each. On April 15, 2005, 10,000 common shares were issued for a piece of land adjacent to some property currently owned by Wheeler. The property had an assessed value of $270,000 on the rolls of the county's property tax assessor. Wheeler's shares are actively traded and had a market price of $40 on April 15, 2005. The total amount of contributed capital resulting from the above events would be:
   a. $640,000.
   b. $240,000.

c. $510,000.

d. $400,000.

EXPLANATION: The issuance of shares is always recorded at the fair value of the consideration given (the shares) or the fair value of the consideration received (the land), if the latter is more clearly determinable. The shares are actively traded in this case so the $40 current market price of a share (the consideration given) is more clearly determinable than the fair value of the land received in exchange. Therefore the shares will be measured at $400,000. Add this to the original issue of shares at $240,000. (Solution = a.)

Question

8. Preferred shares which can be returned to the corporation and exchanged for common shares at the option of the shareholder are referred to as:
   a. cumulative preferred shares.
   b. convertible preferred shares.
   c. participating preferred shares.
   d. callable preferred shares.

EXPLANATION: Holders of **convertible preferred shares** may, at their option, exchange their preferred shares for common shares at a predetermined ratio. Holders of **cumulative preferred shares** are entitled to receive dividends in arrears before any dividends can be paid to common shareholders; dividends in arrears refers to a passed dividend. Thus, dividends not paid in any year on cumulative preferred must be made up in a later year before any profits can be distributed to common shareholders. Holders of **participating preferred shares** rateably share with common shareholders in any dividend distributions beyond the preferred shares' annual preference. With **callable preferred shares**, the issuing corporation can call or redeem at its option the outstanding preferred shares at specified future dates and at stipulated prices. (Solution = b.)

Question

9. Which of the following transactions will cause a net increase in total contributed surplus?
   a. The sale of common shares at a price in excess of what was expected at issue.
   b. The sale of preference shares in excess of what was expected at issue.
   c. The sale of bonds at greater than face value.
   d. Share subscriptions forfeited, due to partial payment.

EXPLANATION: Recall what affects contributed surplus and how. Proceeds received from issuance of common and preferred shares are included in share capital account. No accounting is made for difference between expected and actual proceeds. The premium on bond issuance is accounted for in the liability section, not shareholder's equity. Contributed surplus will be affected (increased) by partially paid share subscriptions being forfeited. (Solution = d.)

Question

10. The date that determines who is considered a shareholder for the purpose of receiving a dividend is the:
    a. declaration date.
    b. record date.
    c. payment date.
    d. distribution date.

EXPLANATION: The date the board of directors formally declares (authorizes) a dividend and announces it to shareholders is called the **declaration date**. The **record date** marks the time when ownership of the outstanding shares is determined for dividend purposes from the records maintained by the corporation. On the **payment date**, the dividend cheques are mailed to the shareholders. (Solution = b.)

Question

11. The declaration and payment of cash dividends by a corporation will result in a(an):
    a. increase in Cash and an increase in Retained Earnings.
    b. increase in Cash and a decrease in Retained Earnings.
    c. decrease in Cash and an increase in Retained Earnings.
    d. decrease in Cash and a decrease in Retained Earnings.

EXPLANATION: Prepare the journal entries required to record the declaration and payment of a cash dividend. Separately analyse each debit and credit to determine the effect on the balance of Cash and on the Retained Earnings account. Assuming cash dividends of $10,000 are declared, the entries and analysis are as follows:

At the date of declaration:			**Effect**
Retained Earnings	10,000		Decrease in Retained Earnings
Dividends Payable		10,000	Increase in current liabilities

At the date of payment:			**Effect**
Dividends Payable	10,000		Decrease in current liabilities
Cash		10,000	Decrease in Cash

The net effect of the declaration and payment of a cash dividend is to reduce retained earnings (and, thus, total shareholders' equity) and Cash (and, thus, total assets). (Solution = d.)

Question

12. Barney's Corporation has an investment in 1,000 common shares of Jones Corporation with a cost of $29,000. These shares are used in a property dividend to shareholders of Barney's. The property dividend is declared on March 23 and scheduled to be distributed on April 30 to shareholders of record on April 15. The market value per share of Jones stock is $42 on March 23, $44 on April 15, and $45 on April 30. The net effect of this property dividend on retained earnings is a reduction of:
    a. $29,000.
    b. $42,000.
    c. $44,000.
    d. $45,000.

EXPLANATION: Write down the journal entries involved in accounting for this dividend. Examine each account in the entries for its effect on retained earnings. Summarize the results. The entries and their effects on retained earnings (RE) would be as follows:

				Effect on RE
3/23	Investments in Securities	13,000		-0-
	Gain on Appreciation of Securities		13,000	$13,000
	[($42 x 1,000) – $29,000 = $13,000]			
	Retained Earnings	42,000		42,000
	Property Dividends Payable		42,000	-0-
4/30	Property Dividends Payable	42,000		-0-
	Investments in Securities		42,000	-0-
	Net effect on retained earnings =			$29,000
				(Solution = a.)

TIP! | Although a property dividend gets recorded at the **fair value** of the asset to be distributed, retained earnings is decreased by the **carrying value** of the asset due to the recognition of the increase or decrease in the fair value of the asset (this increase or decrease goes through net income, which is closed into retained earnings).

Question

13. The net effect of the declaration and payment of a liquidating dividend is a decrease in:
    a. retained earnings and a decrease in total assets.
    b. total paid-in capital and a decrease in total assets.

c. total paid-in capital and an increase in retained earnings.

d. total shareholders' equity and an increase in liabilities.

EXPLANATION: A dividend based on paid-in capital (rather than retained earnings) is termed a **liquidating dividend**, because the amount originally paid in by shareholders is being reduced or "liquidated." (Solution = b.)

Question

Dividends

14. What effect does the declaration and distribution of a 30% stock split-up carried out in the form of a dividend have on the following?

	Retained Earnings	**Total Paid-in Capital**	**Total Shareholders' Equity**
a.	Decrease	Increase	No Effect
b.	Decrease	No Effect	No Effect
c.	Decrease	No Effect	Decrease
d.	No Effect	No Effect	No Effect

EXPLANATION: Write down the journal entries for the declaration and distribution of a large stock dividend. Analyse the accounts in each entry separately to determine the impact on the three items requested.

The journal entry to record the declaration will reduce retained earnings and increase stock dividend distributable (a component of total share capital and, therefore, a component of total paid-in capital). That entry will **decrease retained earnings** and **increase total paid-in capital** by identical amounts, and thus have **no effect on total shareholders' equity**. The entry to record the distribution will reduce the dividend distributable balance (one share capital account) and increase the common shares account. Thus, the distribution entry will have **no effect** on any total within the major classifications of shareholders' equity. (Solution = a.)

Question

15. A 300% stock dividend will have the same impact on the number of shares outstanding as a:

a. 2-for-1 stock split.

b. 3-for-1 stock split.

c. 4-for-1 stock split.

d. 5-for-1 stock split.

EXPLANATION: Set up an example with numbers. For instance, assume we begin with 10,000 shares outstanding. A 300% stock dividend (or stock split-up carried out in the form of a dividend) will mean 30,000 new shares will be distributed and there will then be 40,000 total shares outstanding. A 2-for-1 split will cause 10,000 shares to be replaced by 20,000. A 3-for-1 split will result in 30,000 total shares. A 4-for-1 split will cause the 10,000 shares to be replaced by 40,000 shares. The example proves that a 300% stock dividend (shares are increased **by** 300%) has the same effect on the number of shares outstanding as does a 4-for-1 split (each share is replaced with four shares). (Solution = c.)

Question

16. Trim Corporation declared a stock dividend of 10,000 shares when the market value was $5 per share, and the number of shares outstanding was 200,000. How does the entry to record this transaction affect retained earnings?
    a. No effect
    b. $10,000 decrease
    c. $40,000 decrease
    d. $50,000 decrease

EXPLANATION: Analyse the data to determine the size of the stock dividend. Prepare the journal entry to record the declaration of the stock dividend and analyse the entry's effect on retained earnings. Comparing the 10,000 dividend shares to the 200,000 outstanding shares prior to the dividend yields a 5% relationship; thus, the stock dividend is an ordinary (small) stock dividend. An ordinary stock dividend is recorded by transferring retained earnings equal to the market value of the dividend shares to paid-in capital. Therefore, 10,000 shares multiplied by $5 means retained earnings is to be charged for $50,000. (Solution = d.)

Question

17. A 4-for-1 stock split will cause a decrease in:
    a. total assets.
    b. total shareholders' equity.
    c. retained earnings.
    d. the book value per share.

EXPLANATION: A stock split involves the issuance of additional shares to existing shareholders according to the number of shares presently owned. A stock split does **not** result in the capitalization of any retained earnings; rather, the book value per share is reduced in proportion to the increase in shares. Thus, in a 2-for-1 split, the number of shares are doubled and the book value per share is cut in half. Whereas with a 4-for-1 stock split, the number of total shares is four times what the number was before the split and the book value per share after the split is 1/4 of the par value per share before the split. Assets are not affected. (Solution = d.)

Question

18. The balance of the Retained Earnings account represents:
    a. cash set aside for specific purposes.
    b. the earnings for the most recent accounting period.

    c. the balance of unrestricted cash on hand.

    d. the total of all amounts reported as net income since the inception of the corporation minus the sum of any amounts reported as net loss and dividends declared since the inception of the corporation.

EXPLANATION: Define retained earnings and select the answer that most closely matches that definition. Retained earnings is net income retained in a corporation. Retained earnings is often referred to as earnings retained for use in the business. Thus, net income (earnings for a period) increases the balance of retained earnings. Distributions of earnings to shareholders (owners) are called dividends; they reduce the balance of retained earnings. (Solution = d.)

Question

19. Assume common shares are the only class of shares outstanding in the Burton Corporation. Total shareholders' equity divided by the number of common shares outstanding is called:

    a. book value per share.

    b. par value per share.

    c. stated value per share.

    d. market value per share.

EXPLANATION: Briefly define each of the answer selections. **Book value** per common share represents the equity a common shareholder has in the net assets of the corporation. When only one class of shares is outstanding, book value per share is determined by dividing total shareholders' equity by the number of shares outstanding. **Par value** is an arbitrary value which does not have much significance except in establishing legal capital and in determining the amount to appear in the Common Shares account for each share issued. **Stated value** refers to an arbitrary value that may be placed on shares by the board of directors. Stated value has about the same significance as par value. **Market value** refers to the price for which shares are currently being bought and sold in the open market. (Solution = a.)

Question

20. A corporation has two classes of shares outstanding. The return on common shareholders' equity is calculated by dividing net income:

    a. minus preferred dividends by the number of common shares outstanding at the balance sheet date.

    b. plus interest expense by the average amount of total assets.

    c. by the number of common shares outstanding at the balance sheet date.

    d. minus preferred dividends by the average amount of common shareholders' equity during the period.

EXPLANATION: The return on common shareholders' equity is calculated by dividing the amount of earnings applicable to the common shareholders' interest in the company by the average amount of common shareholders' equity during the period. The amount of earnings applicable to the common shareholders is the amount of net income for the period less the dividends declared on preferred shares during the period. (Solution = d.)

Question

21. A corporation with a $4 million deficit undertakes a financial reorganization on August 1, 2005. Certain assets will be written down by $800,000 to their present market value. Liabilities will remain unchanged. Common shares have a carrying value of $6 million and contributed surplus is $3 million before the reorganization. How will the entries to accomplish these changes on August 1, 2005 affect the following?

	Contributed Surplus	Retained Earnings	Total Shareholders' Equity
a.	Increase	Decrease	No Effect
b.	Decrease	Increase	Decrease
c.	Decrease	Increase	No Effect
d.	No Effect	Increase	Increase

EXPLANATION: Write down the entries to record the procedures involved in the quasi-reorganization. Carefully analyse the effect of each debit and credit on the items requested.

The entry would be as follows:

Contributed Surplus	4,800,000	
Assets		800,000
Retained Earnings		4,000,000

(Solution = b.)

CHAPTER **17**

Complex Financial Instruments

Overview

Complex financial instruments are used by companies in many different industries. These instruments are used to manage risk, raise capital, and minimize the cost of that capital. This chapter expands on the earlier discussion on basic financial instruments (i.e., accounts receivable, accounts payable, loans, and shares) and focuses on complex financial instruments, including derivative financial instruments. Employee compensation plans are also discussed in this chapter.

Study Steps

Understanding the underlying business arrangement relating to complex financial instruments and stock compensation plans

Perpetual debt

Perpetual debt is a financial instrument, legally debt, that will never be repaid. Because of this feature, it is in substance more like equity in that it represents a permanent source of capital. The issue then becomes whether it should be presented as debt or equity. The *CICA Handbook* addresses this issue directly and has concluded that, due to the requirement to pay interest on the debt, despite the fact that the principal will never be repaid, it requires classification as debt. The measurement is the present value of expected interest payments, which, due to the fact that it is in perpetuity, will be equal to the face value of the bond. Because of this conclusion, perpetual debt is no longer a popular method of raising capital.

Convertible securities

Much more popular is the convertible security. This is a security or instrument that is issued by the company to an investor, e.g., convertible debt or convertible preferred shares.

What makes convertible securities unique is that they carry with them an embedded option to convert to common shares. The instrument allows the holder to have limited risks in that the main instrument is a debt instrument or preferred share instrument. Both the debt and the preferred shares usually receive a stable fixed return on their investment that ranks in priority (in terms of pay out) to dividends on common shares. Furthermore, if the company were to go bankrupt, secured creditors and preferred shareholders would get their money out first.

The convertible feature on the preferred shares or debt, however, allows the holder to also participate in the rewards of owning common shares. It allows the holder to share in rewards of ownership of the company since the holder has the option to convert the security to common shares. The option would only be exercised if it was favourable to the holder.

Convertible securities offer holders greater choice and therefore are generally more valuable.

Stock warrants or options

These are instruments that give the holder the right to buy shares at a certain price (exercise price) over a certain period (exercise period) no matter what the market value of the shares is. The purchaser pays money up front for the option.

Why does a warrant have value? It has value because it provides the opportunity to buy the shares at a pre-specified price even if the market price changes. Thus, if an investor pays $1 for an option to buy a share of a company at $10 and the market price of the share goes up to $20, the investor need only pay $10 to acquire the share (plus the price of the option = $1). Therefore, he has paid $11 for a $20 share.

If the market price of the share decreases (e.g., to $5), the option is worthless. But the investor is not committed to buying the shares and therefore only loses $1 (a limited downside risk). So the warrant allows the investor to benefit from increases in value, but limits the exposure to decreases in value to the cost of the warrant.

Stock option plans (SOPs) may be compensatory or not

The intent of top management in setting up the plans may be either to raise money or to compensate their employees or suppliers. Management intent is a critical deciding factor in this issue (i.e., whether an employee plan is compensatory or not) but factors such as who the options are issued to, the discount on the exercise price, and the extent of option features would be considered.

Stock option plans are fairly common for senior executives. They are a benefit awarded to employees for doing a good job, and therefore, form part of the remuneration for the employees.

Stock option plans are put in place for one of two main reasons: i) to raise capital or ii) to provide another source of compensation to management or suppliers.

Management intent often determines whether a stock option plan is compensatory or not; however, the terms of the arrangement must also be reviewed.

Stock appreciation rights

Stock appreciation rights plans (SARs), sometimes called "phantom" stock plans, award the employee with increases in stock prices even though the employee does not own the shares. They are, therefore, always compensatory. For instance, an executive might be enrolled in one of these plans as part of his remuneration package. The more productive he is, hopefully, the better the company will do and, hence, the higher the share price will be. The plan would entitle him to the increase in the market price of the company's shares (above the exercise or base price) times a notional number of shares or the number of SARs held.

The shares are not actually owned by him and have nothing to do with shares he may already own. The notional number of shares or number of SARs held are merely for calculation purposes and may reflect his status in the company (i.e., a more senior executive would presumably have more notional shares). The plans are often in effect for a limited time.

The employee may exercise the right to the increase in price at any time during a pre-specified period (i.e. collect the difference in cash or other).

Stock appreciation rights plans are always compensatory.

Derivatives

Derivatives are complex financial instruments such as options, futures, and forwards. Options were discussed above.

Forward contracts represent contracts entered into today under which both parties agree to exchange something – i.e., cash, foreign currency – at a future point in time at a preset exchange rate. A company might agree to buy $100 U.S. in 30 days for $150 cash.

Futures are standardized forward contracts.

Derivatives are so named since they derive their value from an underlying instrument, i.e., the forward contract above derives its value from the price of the U.S. dollar.

Understanding the presentation and measurement issues for complex financial instruments and stock compensation plans

Convertible securities

The main issues with convertible securities are measurement issues. Since they are seen as compound financial instruments, they are felt to have two distinct components and, therefore, part is booked as debt or preferred shares and part as a warrant or option to purchase a common share. Both components should be measured and shown separately.

Compensatory employee stock option plans

The main issue here is how to measure the costs associated with these plans. Since the compensation is nonmonetary, it is difficult to measure. The *CICA Handbook* prescribes the fair value method. The fair value is measured at the date the options are granted to employees, using an option pricing model. The grant date is therefore the measurement date. No adjustments are made after the grant date in response to subsequent changes in the share price, either up or down. The option pricing model incorporates numerous input measures as follows:

- The exercise price
- The expected life of the option
- The current market price of the underlying stock
- Volatility of the underlying stock
- The expected dividend during the option life
- The risk-free rate of interest during the option life

This fair value is then allocated over the service period, which is usually the same as the vesting period. The vesting period is the period of time required before the options are exercisable.

Stock/Share appreciation rights plans

Stock appreciation rights carry with them different measurement problems. For stock option plans, the employee gets a fixed number of shares when they exercise the option. For SARs, the employee will get cash or a variable number of shares. For SARs to be settled in cash, it is difficult to determine the amount of this future cash payout (the value of the benefit) before the right is exercised by the employee. Therefore, the cost is not measured until the exercise date. However, all periods between the time that the right is granted and the exercise date benefit from the employee's service and, therefore, some attempt is made to measure and accrue the cost in each period. During each period, the difference between the market price and the exercise or base price times the number of SARs is calculated.

This must be re-estimated every year until the employee exercises the right. Each year, a portion of the amount is recognized based on the number of years left in the service period.

Derivatives

The new *CICA Handbook* Sections 3855, 1530, and 3865 will require the following accounting for derivative financial instruments:

- All derivatives will be recognized on the balance sheet
- All derivatives will be classified and presented as held for trading
- All derivatives and all financial assets and liabilities that are held for trading will be valued and measured at fair value
- All gains and losses related to derivatives will be recognized in net income unless they are part of a hedging relationship
- Extensive disclosures

Tips on Chapter Topics

The definition of **financial liability** is any liability that is a contractual obligation: **(a)** to deliver cash or another financial asset to another party, or (b) to exchange financial instruments with another party under conditions that are potentially unfavourable. **TIP!**

The definition of an **equity instrument** is any contract that evidences a residual interest in the assets of an entity after deducting all of its liabilities. **TIP!**

Compound financial instruments consist of both debt and equity components, while **hybrid financial instruments** have characteristics of both debt and equity. **TIP!**

Convertible bonds are the most common example of **compound financial instruments**. They must be split into their debt and equity components and presented as such on the balance sheet. **TIP!**

Preference shares that are redeemable at the option of the holder are a common example of **hybrid financial instruments**. They must be presented in a manner that best reflects their substance, which in this case would be debt. **TIP!**

Examples of **primary financial instruments** include accounts receivable and accounts payable. Examples of **derivative financial instruments** include forward contracts and interest rate swap contracts. **TIP!**

A **derivative financial instrument** is so named since it derives its value from an underlying primary instrument such as the current value of the $U.S. or market interest rates. **TIP!**

Derivative financial instruments are used mainly for hedging against, and managing exposure to, various financial risks. Extreme caution must be used in accounting for derivative financial instruments that are being used for speculative purposes only. **TIP!**

TIP!

Financial risks include **price** risk, **credit** risk, **liquidity** risk, and **cash flow** risk. **Price** risk is the risk that an instrument's price or value will change. The price or value may change due to change in currency (**currency** risk), interest rate changes (**interest rate** risk), and market forces (**market** risk). **Credit risk** is the risk that one of the parties to the contract will fail to fulfill its obligation under the contract and cause the other party loss. **Liquidity** risk is the risk that the company itself will not be able to honour the contract and fulfill its obligation. **Cash flow** risk is the risk that cash flows related to a contract will change over time.

Derivative financial instruments are used mainly for hedging against, and managing exposure to, various **financial risks**. Extreme caution must be used in accounting for derivative financial instruments that are being used for speculative purposes only.

TIP!

Accounting for derivative financial instruments has recently changed. Derivatives were often restricted to note disclosure because of their nature. However, as a result of three new *CICA Handbook* sections:
- All derivatives will be recognized on the balance sheet
- All derivatives will be classified and presented as held for trading
- All derivatives and all financial assets and liabilities that are held for trading will be valued and measured at fair value
- All gains and losses related to derivatives will be recognized in net income unless they are part of a hedging relationship
- All derivatives will be subject to extensive disclosure requirements

Exercise 17-1

PURPOSE: This exercise will illustrate how to record the issuance of convertible debt and its subsequent conversion to common shares.

Oatmeal Corporation has 300,000 common shares outstanding on January 1, 2005 when it issues convertible bonds. The debt issue is comprised of 1,000 bonds at $1,000 face value with a 20-year term and a 10% coupon rate. Each bond is sold at 101 and is convertible into 20 common shares. Oatmeal incurs costs of $80,000 related to the issue. The straight-line method is to be used to amortize any related premium or discount. An underwriter advises the issuer that the bonds would likely have sold for 99 without the conversion feature.

Instructions

(a) Record the issuance of the convertible bonds on January 1, 2005.
(b) Record the conversion of 50% of the bonds on January 1, 2007, assuming the book value method is used.

Solution to Exercise 17-1

(a) Cash   930,000
    Unamortized Bond Issue Costs   80,000
    Discount on Bonds Payable   10,000
        Bonds Payable   1,000,000
        Contributed Surplus—Stock Options   20,000

> **TIP!** The *CICA Handbook* does not mandate specific measurement techniques, but it does provide alternatives in the Appendix to *CICA Handbook* Section 3860. The above method is the book value method, where the easier of the two is valued (usually the debt), and the remainder is allocated to the conversion feature.

(b) Bonds Payable (50% x $1,000,000)   500,000
    Contributed Surplus—Stock Options   10,000
        Unamortized Bond Issue Costs   36,000
          (50% x $80,000 x 18/20)
        Common Shares   469,500
        Discount on Bonds Payable   4,500
          (50% x $ 10,000 x 18/20)

EXPLANATION: The net book value of bonds payable is removed from the accounts and that net amount is recorded in appropriate shareholder equity accounts. The proportionate contributed surplus is reclassified into common shares. No gain or loss is recorded.

> **TIP!** The **book value method** of recording the conversion of bonds payable to common shares simply removes the net book value of the bonds from debt accounts and records that amount in appropriate shareholder equity accounts. **No gain or loss is recorded** when the book value method is used.
>
> **TIP!** Recall that **book value** is synonymous with **carrying value** and **carrying amount**.
>
> **TIP!** Interest, dividends, gains, and losses related to the financial instrument will be consistently treated. For example, if a preferred share has been classified as debt due to its features, the related dividends will be presented as interest expense.

Exercise 17-2

PURPOSE: This exercise will illustrate how to account for convertible preferred shares.

Royal Corporation has 1,000 shares of $50 par, 6% convertible preferred shares outstanding at December 31, 2005. Each share was issued in a prior year at $54. The preferred shares are convertible into common shares.

Instructions

(a) Record the conversion of 100 preferred shares if one share of preferred is convertible into four shares of common.

(b) Record the conversion of 100 shares of preferred if the conversion ratio is 6:1.

Solution to Exercise 17-2

(a) Convertible Preferred Shares (100 x $54)   5,400
      Common Shares   5,400

If contributed surplus accounts had been used to record the difference between the $50 stated value and the $54 issue price, they would also be proportionately closed to the common share account.

(b) Convertible Preferred Shares (100 x $54)   5,400
      Common Shares   5,400

Note that there is no difference in the two situations, depending on the treatment of the original stated value price versus issue price.

Exercise 17-3

PURPOSE: This exercise will review the accounting procedures for the issuance of debt securities with detachable warrants.

A new issue of 1,000 bonds was sold at 102.5 on January 1, 2005. Each bond had a face amount of $1,000 and one detachable warrant attached. One warrant allowed the holder to purchase 10 common shares at $43 per share. The market value of the common shares at January 1, 2005 was $46. Shortly after issuance of the bonds and warrants, quotes were 98.5 for a bond ex-warrant and $48 for a common share warrant. A few months later, 800 warrants were exercised. Two years later, the remaining 200 warrants expired.

Instructions

(a) Record the issuance of the 1,000 bonds with detachable warrants.

(b) Record the exercise of 800 warrants.

(c) Record the expiration of 200 warrants.

(d) Indicate the effect of each of the entries [(a), (b), and (c)] above on (1) assets, (2) total paid-in capital, and (3) number of common shares outstanding. State the direction and amount of each effect.

(e) Explain how the journal entry for part (a) would differ if the market value of a bond ex-warrant was unknown.

Solution to Exercise 17-3

(a) Cash (1,000 x $1,000 x 102.5%)   1,025,000
     Discount on Bonds Payable   22,628[b]
       Bonds Payable (1,000 x $1,000)   1,000,000
       Contributed Surplus—Stock Warrants   47,628 [a]

[a] $\dfrac{\$48,000}{\$48,000 + \$985,000}$ x $1,025,000 = $47,628 amount to allocate to warrants

[b]$1,025,000 total proceeds – $47,628 allocated to the warrants
    = $977,372 allocated to the bonds.
  $1,000,000 face amount of bonds – $977,372 carrying value of bonds
    = $22,628 to record for discount on bonds payable.

EXPLANATION: The proportional method is used; thus, the proceeds are allocated to the two securities based on their relative market values. The amount to be allocated to the warrants is determined by the formula:

$$\frac{\text{MV Warrants}}{\text{Mv Warrants + MV Bonds Ex-Warrants}} \quad x \quad \frac{\text{Total}}{\text{Proceeds}} \quad = \quad \frac{\text{Paid-in Capital}}{\text{To Record}}$$

The remaining proceeds are recorded in bond accounts (the par value of the bonds always goes in the Bonds Payable account). The $22,628 excess of the bonds' par value over the proceeds allocated to the bonds [$1,000,000 – ($1,025,000 – $47,628) = $22,628] represents a discount on the bonds.

Recall from your study of bonds payable that a bond's price is quoted in terms of a percentage of its par value. Carefully calculate the bond's price before proceeding with the formula in this exercise. A very common error would be to use $98.50 for the price of one bond in this situation rather than the **correct** price of $985.00 (98.5% of $1,000 par = $985.00).   **TIP!**

Warrant prices are quoted like share prices—in terms of dollars.   **TIP!**

When using the proportional method, the amount determined for allocation to the warrants should be close (but usually **not** equal) to the market value of the warrants. In part (a) of this problem, $47,628 is close to $48,000 (1,000 x $48); therefore, the amount determined by the formula is reasonable.   **TIP!**

(b) Cash (800 x 10 x $43)   344,000
     Contributed surplus—Stock Warrants
      (800/1,000 x $47,628)   38,102
       Common Shares (800 x 10 x $10)   382,102

The number of shares obtainable upon the exercise of one warrant does **not** affect the calculations and recording in part (a) [issuance date of bonds plus warrants] but it does effect the calculations in part (b) [exercise date of the warrants].   **TIP!**

(c) Contributed surplus—Stock Warrants
       ($47,628 – $38,102)   9,526
            Contributed surplus--from Expired Stock Warrants   9,526

(d) Effect on:

	(1) Assets	(2) Total Contributed Surplus	(3) Number of Common Shares Outstanding
(a)	Increase $1,025,000	Increase $47,628	No effect
(b)	Increase $344,000	Increase $344,000	Increase 8,000
(c)	No effect	No effect	No effect

(e) The incremental method would be used. Thus, the market value of the warrants would be used to record the warrants and the remaining proceeds would be recorded in debt accounts. The entry would be as follows:

Cash (1,000 x $1,000 x 102.5%)   1,025,000
Discount on Bonds Payable   23,000
       Bonds Payable (1,000 x $1,000)   1,000,000
       Contributed Surplus—Stock Warrants (1,000 x $48)   48,000

Illustration 17-1
Types and Accounting for Stock Compensation Plans

Before considering the accounting for stock compensation plans, it is necessary to ensure the plan is to compensate employees, instead of raising capital. Employee stock option plans (ESOPs) are very popular since they allow employees an opportunity to own part of the company they work for. It is also an efficient method of raising capital for the company. Compare this to so-called compensatory stock option plans (CSOPs) where the purpose is primarily to reward employees.

Some of the factors to consider in determining whether it is an ESOP instead of a CSOP are as follows:

- Option terms—non-standard terms giving employees a longer time to enroll and ability to cancel would imply compensatory
- Discount from market price—a larger discount would imply compensatory. Note that a non-compensatory plan would likely also have a discount, but this would be small and represent savings on issue costs
- Eligibility—options that are available to only certain restricted groups of employees (such as executives) would imply compensatory

If non-compensatory, the transactions are treated as capital transactions.

If non-compensatory, the issues revolve around the recognition and measurement of the compensation. A challenging aspect of this type of plan is that money actually flows into the company.

The steps in determining an expense are as follows:

1. The consideration that a corporation receives for shares issued through a stock option, purchase, or award plan consists of cash or other assets, if any, plus services received from the employee.

2. Compensation for services should be measured by the **fair value method**. Using the fair value method, an option pricing model is used to calculate the fair value (at the grant date) of the stock-based compensation paid to employees for their services.

3. Compensation cost should be recognized as an expense of one or more periods in which an employee performs services (often called the **service period**). The grant or award may specify the periods, or the periods may be inferred from the terms or from the past pattern of grants or awards. Unless otherwise specified, the service period is the vesting period—the time between the grant date and the vesting date. The vesting date is the date—the employee's right to receive or retain shares or cash under the award is no longer contingent upon the employee remaining in the service of the employer.

TIP! Although the measurement date for a stock option plan may be the date of grant, sometimes it is later. If the measurement date is later than the date of grant, the employer corporation should record compensation expense each period from the date of grant or award to the measurement date based on the quoted market price of the shares at the end of each period. Adjustment to this estimate may be needed in a later period.

TIP! Assume a stock option plan provides for the company's president to obtain 1,000 common shares between January 1, 2005 and January 1, 2007 at a price equal to 20% of the market price at the date of exercise. The measurement date for this plan will be the date of exercise; the option price is unknown until the options are exercised.

Exercise 17-4

PURPOSE: This exercise will illustrate the application of the fair value method in accounting for a compensatory stock option plan.

Worldwise Corporation granted options for 10,000 common shares to certain executives on January 1, 2002, when it was selling for $52 per share. The options stipulate a price of $44 per 5 shares and must be exercised between January 1, 2007 and December 31, 2009, at which time they expire. The options state that the service period is January 1, 2005 through December 31, 2006. An option pricing model determined that, at the date of grant, the estimated fair value of these options was $500,000.

Instructions

(a) Calculate the total compensation cost.

(b) Explain when the compensation cost should be recognized as an expense.

(c) Prepare the journal entries for the following (items 3 and 4 are independent assumptions):

(1) To record the issuance of the options (grant of options) on January 1, 2005.

(2) To record compensation expense, if any. Date the entry(s). Assume all employees remain employed by the corporation.

(3) To record the exercise of the options, assuming all of the options were exercised on the earliest possible date, January 1, 2007.

(4) To record the expiration of the options, assuming all of the options were **not** exercised because the market price fell below the exercise price before January 1, 2007 and stayed below that level for the balance of the option period.

Solution to Exercise 17-4

(a) Using the fair value method, the total compensation cost is the fair value, as determined at the grant date. In this case equal to $500,000.

TIP! | The **option price** is often called the **exercise price**.

(b) The compensation cost should be recognized as an expense in the periods the employees perform services for which the option is granted. This service period is either stated in the plan or inferred. In this case, the stated service period is from the date of grant (January 1, 2005) to December 31, 2006. Thus, the compensation cost will be recognized evenly over that two-year period. $500,000 ÷ 2 years = $250,000 per year.

TIP! | When answering exam questions over this subject, use the service period stated, if one is clearly indicated. If it is not stated, indicate the period you assume to be the service period (choose from date of grant to the vesting date or to the date the options first become exercisable or from the date of grant to the date the options expire). If the question is of the multiple-choice type and you cannot write in your assumption, use the amount of time from the date of grant to the date the options become exercisable as the service period. If your resulting solution does not match one of the answer selections, redo your calculations using the time span from the date of grant to the date the options expire as the service period. Your new solution should now match one of the answer selections given.

(c)

(1)   **January 1, 2005**
                           No entry

(2)   **December 31, 2005**

Compensation Expense	250,000	
Contributed Surplus—Stock Options		250,000

                   December 31, 2006

Compensation Expense	250,000	
Contributed Surplus—Stock Options		250,000

(3)   **January 1, 2007**

Cash	440,000	
Contributed Surplus—Stock Options	500,000	
Common Shares		940,000

> **TIP!**
>
> The entry to record the exercise of the options is not affected by the date the exercise takes place. Thus, this same entry would record the exercise if it took place on December 31, 2009. If there is a situation in which the options are exercised prior to the end of the service period (therefore, **prior** to the date the total compensation cost has been charged to expense), an unearned compensation cost account is charged. The balance of this Unearned Compensation Cost account is classified as a contra shareholders' equity item.

(4)   **December 31, 2009**

Contributed Surplus—Stock Options	500,000	
Contributed Surplus—From Expired		
Stock Options		500,000

> **TIP!**
>
> The fact that a stock option is never exercised does not nullify the propriety of recording the cost of services received from executives and attributable to the stock option plan. Compensation expense is, therefore, not adjusted upon expiration of the options. However, if a stock option is forfeited because an employee fails to satisfy a service requirement (e.g., leaves employment), the estimate of compensation expense recorded in the current period should be adjusted (as a change in estimate). This change in estimate would be recorded by debiting Contributed Surplus—Stock Options and crediting Compensation Expense, thereby decreasing compensation expense in the period of forfeiture.

Analysis of Multiple-Choice Type Questions

Question

1. For the purpose of inducing conversion, a corporation with convertible bonds offers the bondholders a $15,000 cash premium to convert. Upon conversion, the $15,000 given should be reported as:
   a. an expense of the current period.
   b. an extraordinary item.
   c. a direct reduction of owners' equity.
   d. proportionate amount to debt retirement cost and issue costs.

EXPLANATION: When an issuer offers some form of additional consideration, called a "sweetener," to induce conversion of convertible debt, the issue is the presentation of this cost. EIC # 96 in the *CICA Handbook* requires the allocation to be consistent with the original method upon issuance. In most cases, this will be the residual (book value) method which would require aportion to be expensed as debt retirement costs, with the remaining portion to be attached to the equity as a capital transaction. (Solution = d.)

Question

2. The Good Corporation issued 1,000 8% convertible bonds with a face value of $1,000 each at a price of 102. An underwriter advised the corporation that without the conversion feature, the bonds could not have been issued at a price above 99. At the date of issuance, the amount to be recorded as contributed surplus attributable to the conversion feature is:
   a. $0.
   b. $10,000.
   c. $20,000.
   d. $30,000.

EXPLANATION: Recall that *CICA Handbook* Section 3860 requires convertible instruments to be split into their components and presented separately in the financial statements. The Section does not prescribe a measurement rule, but does suggest either the incremental or proportional method. The incremental method involves valuing one component first and attributing the remainder to the other component. Therefore, since the above bonds would have been issued at a discount (99) without the conversion feature, the reason they were issued at a premium must be due to the conversion feature. The entry would be as follows for the bonds in question:

Cash	1,020,000	
Discount on Bonds Payable	10,000	
Bonds Payable		1,000,000
Contributed Surplus—Stock options		30,000

(Solution = d.)

Question

3. A corporation issued convertible bonds with a face value of $800,000 at a discount. At a date when the unamortized discount was $70,000, and the Contributed Surplus—Stock Options (related to these bonds) balance was $20,000, the bonds were converted to common shares having a market value of $870,000. Using the book value method, the amount of gain/loss to record on the conversion is:
    a. $0.
    b. $70,000.
    c. $120,000.
    d. $670,000.

EXPLANATION: Reconstruct the journal entry to record the conversion. The book value of bonds is removed from the accounts and that book value amount is recorded in appropriate shareholders' equity accounts. There is **never** a gain or loss recognized when the book value method is used to record the conversion of bonds to stock. The journal entry is as follows:

Bonds Payable	800,000	
Contributed Surplus—Stock options	20,000	
Discount on Bonds Payable		70,000
Common Shares		750,000

(Solution = a.)

Question

4. A corporation issues bonds with detachable warrants. The amount to be recorded as Contributed Surplus—Stock Warrants is preferably:
    a. zero.
    b. calculated by the excess of the proceeds over the face amount of the bonds.
    c. equal to the market value of the warrants.
    d. based on the relative market values of the two securities involved.

EXPLANATION: When both the market value of a warrant and the market value of a bond ex-warrant are known, the proportional method is to be employed; hence, the proceeds are allocated to the warrant (Contributed Surplus) and the debt instrument (liabilities), based on the relative market values of the warrants and bonds. The incremental method (answer section "c") would be appropriate in this case if the market value of the bonds' ex-warrants is not known. (Solution = d.)

Question

5. Stock options allowing selected executives to acquire 10,000 common shares are granted on January 1, 2005. The market price at January 1, 2005 is $22. The option price is $10. The options are for services to be performed over four years from the date of grant. The options become exercisable on January 1, 2007 and expire on December 31, 2009. The fair value of the options is determined to be $120,000 at the grant date. The amount of compensation cost related to these options to be charged to expense for 2005 is:
    a. $24,000.
    b. $30,000.
    c. $60,000.
    d. $120,000.

EXPLANATION: (1) Calculate the total compensation cost. It is the fair value of the options, as determined at the grant date=$120,000 total compensation cost. (2) Determine the service period—span of time over which the employees are to provide services in exchange for the options. It is clearly stated in this plan that the service period is the four years 2005, 2006, 2007, and 2008. (3) Divide total compensation cost ($120,000) by the service period (four years) to arrive at $30,000 per year. (Solution = b.)

Question

6. On January 1, 2005 Chandler, Inc. granted stock options to officers and key employees for the purchase of 1,000 common shares at $20 per share as additional compensation for services to be rendered over the next two years. The options are exercisable during a four-year period beginning January 1, 2007 by grantees still employed by Chandler. The fair value of the options, as determined at the grant date is $6,000. The market price of Chandler's common shares was $26 per share at the date of grant. The journal entry to record the compensation expense related to these options for 2005 would include a credit to the Contributed Surplus—Stock Options account for:
    a. $20,000.
    b. $6,000.
    c. $3,000.
    d. $1,000.

EXPLANATION: Reconstruct the journal entry to record the compensation expense for 2005. It would be as follows:

Compensation Expense	3,000	
Contributed Surplus—Stock Options		3,000

The total compensation cost is determined to be the fair value at the grant date, in this case $6,000. The total compensation cost is allocated to the periods included in the service period (two years). $6,000÷2 = $3,000. (Solution = c.)

Question

7. An example of a derivative financial instrument is:
    a. a commodity futures contract.
    b. a forward contract to buy $ US at a fixed rate in the future.
    c. an accounts receivable.
    d. redeemable/retractable preference shares.

EXPLANATION: Per *CICA Handbook* Section 3860, commodity futures contracts are not considered financial instruments since they do not give rise to both a financial instrument of one party and a financial liability or equity instrument of another party. Accounts receivable and redeemable/retractable preference shares would be examples of primary financial instruments. A forward contract is a derivative financial instrument since it will derive its value from an underlying financial instrument, in this case the market price of the $U.S. versus the contract price. (Solution = b.)

Question

8. Price risk is the risk that a financial instruments price or value will change due to:
    a. one of the parties to the contract failing to fulfill its obligation.
    b. the company itself not being able to honour the contract.
    c. change in currency, interest rate, or market forces.
    d. None of the above.

EXPLANATION: Per *CICA Handbook* Section 3860, **price risk** is the risk that an instrument's price or value will change due to changes in currency (**currency risk**), interest rate changes (**interest rate risk**), and market forces (**market risk**). **Credit risk** is the risk that one of the parties will fail to fulfill its obligation. **Liquidity risk** is the risk that the company itself will not be able to honour the contract and fulfill its obligation. (Solution = c.)

Question

9. Albert Company has forward contracts to buy $U.S. 100,000 at a rate of $1.50 in 180 days. The $U.S. exchange rate is currently $1.55 (the balance sheet date). Under Canadian GAAP, Albert Company would show the following on their balance sheet:
    a. An asset of $U.S. 5,000 (in equivalent Canadian dollars).
    b. A liability of $U.S. 5,000 (in equivalent Canadian dollars).
    c. A liability of $150,000 Canadian.
    d. An asset equal to the fair value of the contract at the balance sheet date, with an offsetting credit to income.

EXPLANATION: Per *CICA Handbook* Section 3855, all financial instruments will be recognized on the balance sheet, with fair value as the measure. In this case, the company has a financial asset since it has a contract to settle at potentially favourable terms. This would result in an asset called "forward contract" and a gain on the income statement. It would be measured at fair value. (Solution = d.)

TIP!   The above answer may change if the contract was identified as a hedge. In this case, the gain would likely be deferred to match with the loss on the hedged item. It may still be a part of comprehensive income, which would show unrealized gains or losses.

Question

10. Berry Corporation has $500,000 in long-term debt, in Canadian funds, with a fixed rate of 7%. They have no other long-term debt outstanding. They believe that market interest rates will drop in the next few years. The best way to "manage" or "hedge" this exposure is:
    a. lend money at a floating interest rate.
    b. pay off the debt immediately.
    c. enter into a forward contract to buy sufficient $U.S. at the maturity date to pay off the debt and perhaps gain on the exchange.
    d. enter into an interest rate swap contract with a party who has floating rate debt and who also believes interest rates will go up.

EXPLANATION: While it is always best to pay off debt, it is presumed that the company will be unable to do this. Same for lending money at a floating rate. The most common method for managing interest rate risk is to enter into an interest rate swap contract. Recall that any company that has long-term debt will be exposed to interest rate risk. Those with fixed-rate debt face the risk that the market rates will go down, and those with floating-rate debt face the risk that the market rate will go up. (Solution = d.)

Question

11. Using the facts above, assume Berry enters into an interest rate swap contract to pay the equivalent floating (market) rate of another party based on a notional principal of $100,000, for the next three years. Assume that the market rate averaged 8% for the first year. The interest expense that Berry will record in the first year is:
    a. zero. All interest will be recorded when the contract is up and the rates are definite.
    b. $40,000.
    c. $35,000.
    d. $36,000.

EXPLANATION: In an interest rate swap contract, no principal changes hands. Rather, there is a contract signed to pay the other party's interest rate on an agreed "notional" principal. Therefore, Berry Corporation agreed to pay market rate (versus their own fixed rate) on $100,000 of their long-term debt. The remainder of their debt will incur interest at the fixed rate of 7%. Therefore, the interest calculation is:

$$\$400,000*7\% \text{ plus } \$100,000*8\% = \$36,000. \text{ (Solution = d.)}$$

The interest rate swap contract is a derivative (since it derives its value from the market rate of interest compared to the fixed rate) financial instrument that will have to be disclosed in the financial statements. The fair value at the end of the first year would be approximately the present value of paying 1% more than they otherwise would have times the notional principal, over two years.

TIP!

Question

12. Continuing with the above example, how would the fair value of the contract be treated at the end of the first year?
    a. Note disclosure of details only.
    b. An asset will be recorded at fair value.
    c. A liability will be recorded at fair value.
    d. No disclosure or entry since rates will change frequently over the contract.

EXPLANATION: Under recently changed GAAP, the fair value of the swap contract is recorded on the balance sheet with a corresponding entry to unrealized gains or losses (which will be shown in comprehensive income). In this case a liability is recognized—Held for trading—swap contract at fair value. (Solution = c.)

Question

13. Which of the following is **not** considered a factor in the determination of whether an employee stock option plan is compensatory or non-compensatory?
    a. the discount from market price of the shares
    b. time frame for exercising the warrant
    c. participating parties
    d. option features

EXPLANATION: Using the factors listed in **Illustration 17-1** it is evident that the size of the discount is a factor (the higher the discount, the more likely it is compensatory); those eligible to participate is a factor (if it is restricted to a group of employees, such as executives, it is likely compensatory); finally, the option features would be a factor (the less standard the features, the more likely it is a compensatory plan). (Solution = b.)

Question

14. A phantom stock option plan (stock appreciation rights plan) may be best described as which of the following:
    a. an employee compensation plan whereby the employee is entitled to the increase in value of the company shares without having to actually hold the shares.
    b. an employee compensation plan whereby the employee is entitled to the increase in value of the company shares where the employee must also hold the shares to benefit from them.
    c. an employee compensation plan whereby the employer sets aside shares for employees and employees are allowed to buy the shares later at a fixed price.
    d. an employee compensation plan where the employer sets aside shares in a separate trust for later issue to the employees upon exercise of options.

EXPLANATION: The main feature of a phantom stock option plan is that it entitles the employees to participate in the increases in value of the shares without the employee actually having to buy the shares. (Solution = a.)

Question

15. According to the *CICA Handbook* the cost of a compensatory employee stock option plan must be accounted for as follows:
    a. a capital transaction that is measured at the grant date.
    b. an expense that is measured at the grant date.
    c. an expense that is measured at the exercise date.
    d. none of the above.

EXPLANATION: After much discussion and controversy, the CICA has decided that the cost of a compensatory stock option plan must be measured at the grant date, using fair value option models, and recognized over the service period. (Solution = b.)

Question

16. Which of the following are not ever considered to be dilutive securities?
    a. debt that is convertible into preferred shares
    b. convertible preferred shares
    c. stock options
    d. stock warrants

EXPLANATION: The concept of dilutive pertains to the common shareholders and the act of diluting their respective interest in the company, as well as their share of the earnings. As such warrants, options, and convertible preferred shares are dilutive since, if issued or converted, this would result in more common shares and less earnings for each of the remaining groups of common shareholders. (Solution = a.)

Question

17. When should the cost of a compensatory stock option plan be expensed?
    a. at the time of issue
    b. at the time of exercise
    c. over the period of service
    d. never

EXPLANATION: The cost should be expensed over the period of service since this is the period that the employee is being motivated to work harder due to the plan. This is normally the period between the grant date and vesting date. Any fluctuations in the value of the option during that period are not accounted for, they are considered to be risks to the employee. (Solution = c.)

CHAPTER 18

Earnings Per Share

Overview

Earnings per share (EPS) is typically the most widely quoted financial ratio. It is used by shareholders and potential investors in evaluating a company's profitability and value. The calculation of earnings per share is complicated by situations where dilutive securities, as well as common shares, are outstanding. This chapter examines how basic and diluted earnings per share figures are calculated and what information they contain.

Study Steps

Understand the calculations required in preparing earnings per share information.

Earnings Per Share (EPS)

EPS is a calculation that lets shareholders know what their share of the company's residual value is. Earnings per share shows the residual (or the common) shareholders what their shares have earned during the year. It does not necessarily bear any relationship to the amount of dividends paid out. Rather, it shows the amount of net income available after preferred shareholders have been allocated a return on their capital.

The **basic** calculation is as follows:

(Net income – preferred dividends)/Number of common shares

Preferred dividends are deducted for cumulative preferred shares regardless of whether the dividends have been declared. However, a deduction is only made for non-cumulative preferred shares if a dividend has been declared.

The number of shares is a weighted-average calculation, weighted by the length of time that shares are outstanding. Stock dividends or splits are treated as though they have been outstanding since the beginning of the year, even if they are issued after year-end.

There are two basic types of EPS calculations:

• Basic EPS (covered above)—"actual" scenario.
• Diluted EPS—"what if" scenario.

Diluted EPS

Diluted EPS shows what EPS would look like if all convertible debt or equity were converted and if all options to purchase common stock had been exercised. The numerator of the basic EPS is adjusted for dividends and after-tax interest that would have been avoided had the conversion taken place at the beginning of the year and the denominator assumes that the shares on conversion/option exercise were issued at the beginning of the year.

For warrants and options, if they are exercised, cash would generally be paid into the company since the holder of the option would buy shares. It is assumed that the company would use the cash to buy shares in the open market and then issue shares under the option exercise. The incremental effect on the EPS calculation only affects the denominator.

Only conversions and/or exercise of options that are dilutive (i.e., decrease basic EPS) would be included in the calculation. Conversions that increase EPS are known as anti-dilutive.

Illustration 18-1   131

Tips on Chapter Topics

A **dilutive security** is a security which would reduce earnings per share (EPS) if it became common shares. An **antidilutive security** is one which would result in an increase in the amount reported as EPS or a decrease in the amount reported as a net loss per share.   **TIP!**

In calculating diluted EPS, any antidilutive security is to be excluded. This means that a convertible bond will be assumed to be converted to common shares for the purposes of calculating diluted EPS **if** the effect of that assumption is dilutive. The convertible bond will **not** be assumed to be converted in calculating EPS **if** the effect of that assumption is antidilutive.   **TIP!**

An entity with a **simple capital structure**, that is, one with only common shares outstanding, must report **basic-per-share** amounts for income from continuing operations and for net income on the face of the income statement. An entity with a **complex capital structure** (i.e., a structure with one or more potentially dilutive securities outstanding) must report **basic and diluted per share** amounts for income from continuing operations and for net income on the face of the income statement with equal prominence.   **TIP!**

Securities such as options, warrants, convertible bonds, convertible preferred shares, or contingent share agreements are referred to as "potential common shares" or "potentially dilutive securities."   **TIP!**

Illustration 18-1
Steps in Computing Earnings Per Share (EPS)

Step 1: Calculate the weighted average number of common shares outstanding.

     A.   When common shares are issued for assets during the period, weight them according to the length of time in the period the shares are outstanding in relation to the total time in the period.

     B.   When common shares are issued in connection with a stock split or stock dividend declared during the period, give retroactive treatment to these shares. Give retroactive treatment even if the stock dividend or split is declared after the end of the period (but before the financial statements are published). Restate EPS in financial statements for prior periods presented.

TIP! | See **Illustration 18-2** for a shortcut method of computing the weighted-average number of common shares outstanding.

Step 2: Calculate basic EPS (EPS before any assumptions or adjustments).

Basic Formula: $$\frac{\text{Net Income - Preferred Dividends}}{\text{Weighted Average Number of Common Shares Outstanding}}$$

The numerator should be the income available to common shareholders—net income minus **dividends on senior equity instruments**—which is usually preferred shares, but would include other instruments that in substance are senior equity instruments. We will continue with this illustration assuming preferred share dividends only. Thus, in the numerator, deduct the preferred dividends actually declared. If the preferred share is cumulative, deduct the preferred's current year preference as to dividends, even if no dividends were declared. Dividends in arrears for prior years have no effect on the current year's basic EPS calculation.

TIP! | Dividends declared and/or paid during the year on common shares have no effect on this calculation.

TIP! | If there is a net loss rather than a net income, the amount of the loss is increased by the preferred dividends.

Step 3: Calculate diluted earnings per share.

A.   The basic formula is adjusted as follows:

$$\frac{\text{Net Income - Preferred Dividends} \pm \text{Adjustments}}{\begin{array}{c}\text{Weighted Average Number of Common Shares Outstanding +}\\ \text{Weighted Average Number of Potential Common Shares}\end{array}}$$

B.   Treatment of convertibles: Use the **if converted** method.

1.   Assume the convertible is converted to common shares, if the effect of that assumption is dilutive.

TIP! | Dilution (dilutive) is a reduction in earnings per share. **Antidilution (antidilutive)** is an increase in earnings per share amounts or a decrease in loss per share amounts.

TIP! | A quick test to determine if a convertible debt instrument is antidilutive is as follows: if the amount of interest net of taxes per common share obtainable upon conversion exceeds basic EPS, the effect is antidilutive.

TIP! | A quick test to determine if a convertible preferred share is antidilutive is as follows: if the amount of preferred dividends per common share obtainable on conversion exceeds basic EPS, the effect is antidilutive.

Illustration 18-1   133

2. For a convertible preferred, add back the preferred dividends (that had been deducted in the basic formula) in the numerator and add an appropriate weighted average number of potential common shares (assumed to be outstanding) in the denominator of the diluted EPS formula.

3. For convertible debt, add back interest and deduct tax savings due to interest in the numerator and add an appropriate weighted average number of potential common shares in the denominator.

TIP!

In using the "if converted" method for a convertible bond, interest expense is added back in the numerator of the EPS formula and the related tax effect is deducted. In using the "if converted" method for a convertible preferred share, preferred dividends are added back in the numerator (because they were deducted in the numerator of the basic formula); however, there is **no** related tax effect because preferred dividends are not a tax deductible item.

4. Assume the conversion takes place at the beginning of the period for which EPS is being calculated or at the date of the issuance of the convertible, whichever is later (more recent).

5. If there is a scale of conversion rates, use the rate that is the most advantageous from the standpoint of the security holder.

C. Treatment of options and warrants:

1. Assume the options and warrants are exercised **if** the effect of that assumption is dilutive.

TIP!

An option or warrant is dilutive if the average market price of the common shares during the period is greater than the exercise price of the option or warrant.

2. Use the **treasury stock method**. Assume that the proceeds (from the exercise of the options or warrants) are used to purchase treasury shares at the **average market price** for the period. Thus, shares will be added to the EPS denominator because of the assumed exercise, and then a smaller number of shares will be deducted from the denominator because of the assumed purchase of treasury shares. Weight the resulting **net** number of common equivalent shares according to the time they are assumed to be outstanding.

3. Assume the exercise occurs at the beginning of the period or at the date of the issuance of the options or warrants, whichever is the later.

D. Treatment of contingent issuance agreements.

1. Common shares contingently issuable with the only condition being the mere passage of time should be assumed to be outstanding for computing both basic and diluted EPS.

2. Common shares contingently issuable upon condition of the attainment or maintenance of a level of earnings should be considered outstanding in computing diluted EPS if that level is currently being attained.

3. Common shares contingently issuable upon condition of the attainment of a market price level should be considered outstanding shares if that level is met at the end of the current year.

TIP! The calculation of diluted EPS should not assume conversion, exercise, or **contingent issuance** of securities that would have an **antidilutive** effect on earnings per share. Shares issued on actual conversion, exercise, or satisfaction of certain conditions for which the underlying potential common shares were antidilutive shall be included in the calculation as outstanding common shares from the date of conversion, exercise, or satisfaction of those conditions, respectively. In determining whether potential common shares are dilutive or antidilutive, each issue or series of issues of potential common shares should be considered separately rather than in the aggregate.

TIP! Convertible securities may be dilutive on their own but antidilutive when included with other potential common shares in computing diluted EPS. To reflect maximum potential dilution, each issue or series of issues of potential common shares shall be considered in sequence from the most dilutive to the least dilutive. That is, dilutive potential common shares with the lowest "earnings per incremental share" shall be included in diluted EPS before those with a higher earnings per incremental share. (Options and warrants generally will be included first because use of the treasury stock method does not affect the numerator of the calculation.)

TIP! An entity that reports a discontinued operation or an extraordinary item should use income before discontinued operations and extraordinary items (adjusted for senior equity dividends) as the "control number" in determining whether those potential common shares are dilutive or antidilutive. That is, the same number of potential common shares used in computing the diluted per-share amount for income before discontinued operations and extraordinary items should be used in computing all other reported diluted per-share amounts even if those amounts will be antidilutive to their respective basic per-share amounts.

For example, assume that Corporation A has income before discontinued operations and extraordinary items of $2,400, a loss from discontinued operations of $(3,600), a net loss of $(1,200), and 1,000 common shares and 200 potential common shares outstanding. Corporation A's basic per-share amounts would be $2.40 for income before discontinued operations, $(3.60) for the discontinued operations, and $(1.20) for the net loss. Corporation A would include the 200 potential common shares in the denominator of its diluted per-share calculation before discontinued operations because the resulting $2.00 per share is dilutive. (For illustrative purposes, assume no numerator effect on those 200 potential common shares.) Because income before discontinued operations is the control number, Corporation A also must include those 200 potential common shares in the denominator for the other per-

Illustration 18-2   135

share amounts, even though the resulting per-share amounts [$(3.00) per share for the loss from discontinued operation and $(1.00) per share for the net loss] are antidilutive to their comparable basic per-share amounts; that is, the loss per-share amounts are less.

TIP!

Including potential common shares in the denominator of a diluted per-share calculation for continuing operations always will result in an antidilutive per-share amount when an entity has a loss from continuing operations or a loss from continuing operations available to common shareholders (that is, after any senior equity dividend reductions). Although including those potential common shares in the other diluted per-share calculations may be dilutive to their comparable basic per-share amounts, no potential common shares should be included in the calculation of any diluted per-share amount when a loss from continuing operations exists, even if the entity reports net income.

TIP!

When a company has a complex capital structure and a dual presentation of earnings per share, it must disclose a reconciliation of the numerators and denominators of the basic and diluted per share calculations, including individual income and share amount effects of all securities that affect EPS.

Illustration 18-2
Shortcut Method for Calculating Weighted Average Number of Common Shares Outstanding

Step 1: Begin with the number of common shares outstanding at the beginning of the period. Assume they were outstanding the entire year; multiply the number by 12/12 to get an equivalent amount. Enter the equivalent amount in the Weighted Average column.

Step 2: Take the first transaction that occurred during the year that changed the number of shares outstanding and properly adjust the balance in the Weighted Average column.

    a. **If shares were issued for assets, weight the new shares** by multiplying them by a fraction. The numerator of the fraction is the number of months in the period the shares were outstanding; the denominator is the number of months in the year. Add this equivalent amount in the Weighted Average column; arrive at a new balance.

    b. **If shares were issued in a stock dividend or a stock split, retroactively adjust for these shares** by taking an appropriate multiple of the existing balance in the Weighted Average column. Ignore the date of the stock dividend or split; the multiple is determined by the size of the stock dividend or split. Arrive at a new balance.

c.   **If shares were acquired as treasury** shares **or retired by the corporation, weight** the shares for the time they were not outstanding and deduct this equivalent amount from the existing balance. Arrive at a new balance.

Step 3: Take each of the other transactions that occurred during the year that changed the number of common shares outstanding and properly adjust the balance in the Weighted Average column as shown in Step 2 above. Handle each transaction in order of date.

EXAMPLE:

Data:

January 1, 2005	100,000 shares were outstanding.
April 1, 2005	Issued 40,000 shares for cash.
June 1, 2005	Declared a 40% stock dividend.
October 1, 2005	Declared a 2-for-1 split.
December 1, 2005	Issued 60,000 shares for cash.

Calculation:

Date		Weighted Average
1/1/05	100,000 x 12/12 =	100,000
4/1/05	40,000 x 9/12 =	30,000
	New balance	130,000
6/1/05	40% stock dividend	x 140% **
	New balance	182,000
10/1/05	2-for-1 split	x 2 ***
	New balance	364,000
12/1/05	60,000 x 1/12	5,000
	New balance	369,000

**The appropriate multiple for a stock dividend is 100% plus the percentage used in the dividend. Thus, 100% + 40% dividend = 140% as the multiplier.

***The appropriate multiple for a stock split is the size of the split. Thus, for a 2-for-1 split, multiply by 2.

TIP!

Notice how the calculation for the weighted average number of common shares outstanding for the period differs from the calculation for the actual number of common shares outstanding at the end of the period. The number of common shares actually outstanding at December 31, 2005 can be calculated as follows:

Date		Actual Shares
1/1/05	Balance	100,000
4/1/05	Issued for assets	40,000
	New balance	140,000
6/1/05	40% stock dividend	56,000
	New balance	196,000
10/1/05	2:1 split	196,000
	New balance	392,000
12/1/05	Issued for assets	60,000
	New balance	452,000

> **TIP!**
>
> Assume that in addition to the transactions listed above, a 10% stock dividend was declared on January 7, 2006, before the financial statements for 2005 were issued. The weighted average number of common shares outstanding for purposes of calculating EPS for 2005 would be 405,900 (369,000 x 110% = 405,900) and the actual number of common shares outstanding to be reported on the balance sheet at December 31, 2005 would be 452,000.

Exercise 18-1

PURPOSE: This exercise will apply the guidelines for calculating the weighted average number of common shares outstanding.

When the number of common shares varies during the year, the weighted average number of common shares outstanding must be calculated before the EPS can be calculated.

Listed below are the details regarding common shares outstanding for four different companies:

1. Jackson Corporation had 100,000 common shares outstanding on January 1, 2005. On March 1, 6,000 common shares were issued for cash.

2. Buffet Corporation had 100,000 common shares outstanding on January 1, 2005. On March 1, 6,000 common shares were issued for cash. On July 1, a 4-for-1 split was declared.

3. Harris Corporation had 100,000 common shares outstanding on January 1, 2005. On March 1, 6,000 common shares were reacquired by the corporation.

4. John Corporation had 100,000 common shares outstanding on January 1, 2005. On March 1, 6,000 common shares were issued for cash. On June 1, a 10% stock dividend was declared. On December 1, 12,000 common shares were issued for cash.

Instructions

(a) Calculate the weighted average number of common shares outstanding for 2005 (to be used to calculate EPS) for **each** of the **independent** situations above.

(b) Calculate the number of common shares outstanding to be reported on the balance sheet at December 31, 2005 for John Corporation (situation 4).

Solution to Exercise 18-1

(a) **EXPLANATION**: Use the shortcut method explained in Illustration 18-2

	Date		**Weighted Average**
1.	1/1/05	100,000 x 12/12 =	100,000
	3/1/05	6,000 x 10/12 =	5,000
		New balance	105,000

TIP! The weighted average calculation for common shares uses the same concept that is applied in calculating equivalent units of production for a manufacturing firm. In the situation above, the calculation indicates that having 6,000 shares outstanding for ten months of the year is equivalent to having 5,000 shares outstanding for twelve months. The weighted average number of shares outstanding is sometimes referred to as equivalent shares.

	Date		**Weighted Average**
2.	1/1/05	100,000 x 12/12 =	100,000
	3/1/05	6,000 x 10/12 =	5,000
		New balance	105,000
	7/1/05	4-for-1 split	x 4
		New balance	420,000
3.	1/1/05	100,000 x 12/12 =	100,000
	3/1/05	(6,000) x 10/12 =	(5,000)
		New balance	95,000
4.	1/1/05	100,000 x 12/12 =	100,000
	3/1/05	6,000 x 10/12 =	5,000
		New balance	105,000
	6/1/05	10% stock dividend	x 110%
		New balance	115,500
	12/1/05	12,000 x 1/12 =	1,000
		New balance	116,500

TIP! If you want, you can prove the answer of 116,500 by a more complex procedure as follows:

Dates Outstanding	Actual Shares[a]	Restatement	Fraction	Weighted Shares
1/1/05 to 2/28/05	100,000	1.1	2/12	18,333
3/1/05 to 5/31/05	106,000	1.1	3/12	29,150
6/1/05 to 11/30/05	116,600		6/12	58,300
12/1/05 to 12/31/05	128,600		1/12	10,717
				116,500

[a]See solution to part (b) for calculations.

A stock dividend or a stock split requires retroactive restatement of shares for the calculation of EPS. A 10% stock dividend causes a 10% increase in the number of shares outstanding. Therefore, to restate the number of shares outstanding at a certain date in the past, to give retroactive effect to a subsequently declared 10% stock dividend, the old number of shares is multiplied by 110% (which is 1.1 in decimal form).

TIP!

When shares are issued for assets, they are weighted for the number of months they are outstanding in relation to the number of months in the period for which EPS is being calculated. When shares are issued in a stock dividend or a stock split, they are not weighted; rather, retroactive adjustment is made for these additional shares in the weighted average shares calculation. The reason for the difference in treatment is that when assets are received, the entity has more resources and, therefore, an opportunity to increase the net income figure by earning a rate of return on those new assets for the months the new resources are available. When shares are issued in connection with a stock dividend or stock split, there are no new resources and, therefore, no changes in net income. In order for EPS figures for successive periods for a company to be meaningful, they must all be based on the rearranged capital structure; therefore, stock dividends and stock splits must be handled retroactively. This **retroactive treatment** causes adjustment to the weighted average shares calculation for EPS **for all periods presented**. Therefore, when the financial statements for a prior period are republished in comparative statements, the EPS amounts for the prior period are to be restated for all stock dividends and stock splits occurring subsequent to the prior period. Thus, a stock dividend declared in 2005 calls for retroactive restatement of the 2004 EPS figure when the 2004 income statement is republished in 2005 for comparative purposes.

(b)

Date		Actual Shares
1/1/05	Balance	100,000
3/1/05	Issued for assets	6,000
	New balance	106,000
6/1/05	10% stock dividend	10,600
	New balance	116,600
12/1/05	Issued for assets	12,000
	New balance	128,600

Exercise 18-2

PURPOSE: This exercise will illustrate the application of the treasury stock method.

Sherman Corporation had 200,000 common shares outstanding during 2005. On January 1, 2005, 40,000 stock options were granted. Each option entitles the holder to purchase one common share at $40. The options become exercisable in 2007. Net income for 2005 was $400,000. The average market price of the shares during 2005 was $50; the closing market price was $54.

Instructions

(a) Calculate the amount(s) that Sherman Corporation should report for earnings per share for 2005.

(b) Explain how your answer(s) to Part (a) would change if the options were issued on April 1, 2005 rather than January 1, 2005.

Solution to Exercise 18-2

(a) **Approach:** Follow the steps for calculating EPS as outlined in Illustration 18-1.

Step 1: Calculate the weighted average number of common shares outstanding.

There were no changes in the 200,000 common shares outstanding during 2005. Therefore, the weighted average is 200,000 shares.

Step 2: Calculate basic EPS before any assumptions (basic formula without adjustment).

$$\frac{\$400,000 - \$0}{200,000} = \$2.00$$

Step 3: Calculate diluted earnings per share.

- Use the treasury stock method for the options.
- Use the quick test to determine if these options are dilutive. Compare the option price and the current market price. The option price ($40) is less than the average market price ($50), so the options will have a dilutive effect on EPS.
- Adjust the basic formula:

$$\frac{\$400,000 - \$0}{200,000 + 40,000^a - 32,000^b} = \$1.92$$

[a]Number of shares to be issued upon exercise of options.
[b]Number of shares that could be purchased for the treasury at $50 (average market price for the period) per share from the proceeds of the exercise of the options:
   40,000 x $40 = $1,600,000 proceeds
   $1,600,000 ÷ $50 = 32,000 assumed treasury shares

TIP! Notice the incremental number of shares calculated by use of the treasury stock method is 8,000 in this example (40,000 - 32,000). If the average market price was less than the option price, the number of assumed treasury shares would exceed the number of shares assumed issued upon exercise of the options, and the result would be to decrease the denominator from the figure used in the basic formula. That decrease in the denominator would have an antidilutive effect on EPS; therefore, the exercise of the options would **not** be assumed in that circumstance. **Never make assumptions in calculating diluted EPS that are antidilutive.**

Notice why the treasury stock method is so named; the proceeds from the assumed exercise of stock options are assumed to be used for the purchase of treasury shares.	**TIP!**

Sherman Corporation should report a dual presentation for 2005 as follows:

> $2.00 basic earnings per share, and
> $1.92 diluted earnings per share

(b) The exercise of the options would be assumed to have taken place on April 1 rather than at the beginning of the year. Therefore, the assumed shares in the denominator would have to be weighted as follows:

$$9/12 \ (40{,}000 - 32{,}000) = 6{,}000$$

Therefore, the calculation for diluted EPS would then be:

$$\frac{\$400{,}000}{200{,}000 + 6{,}000} = \$1.94 \text{ diluted EPS.}$$

Exercise 18-3

PURPOSE: This exercise will illustrate the proper treatment of convertible securities in the EPS calculations.

The following data pertain to the Trent Corporation at December 31, 2005:

Net income for the year	$1,600,000
6% convertible bonds issued at par in a prior year, convertible into 200,000 common shares	$3,000,000
8% convertible, cumulative, preferred shares, $100 stated value, issued in a prior year (each share is convertible into 6 shares of common)	$2,000,000
Common shares, issued in prior years (600,000 outstanding)	$6,000,000
Contributed capital	$3,400,000
Retained earnings	$5,200,000
Tax rate for 2005	40%

There were no changes during 2005 in the number of common shares, preferred shares, or convertible bonds outstanding. There are no treasury shares held.

Instructions

(a) Calculate the basic earnings per share for 2005.

(b) Calculate the diluted earnings per share for 2005.

(c) Explain whether a dual presentation should be presented for EPS for 2005.

Solution to Exercise 18-3

(a) $2.40 (See Step 2 below.)

(b) $1.86 (See Step 3 below.)

(c) Yes, a dual presentation must be reported in 2005 because the corporation has some dilutive securities outstanding.

TIP! Whenever a situation involves the EPS calculation(s), follow the steps (in order) listed in **Illustration 18-1**. By using this organized approach to these situations, you are less likely to overlook guidelines that may affect your solution.

Explanation:

Step 1: Calculate the weighted average number of common shares outstanding.

There were no changes in the number of common shares outstanding during 2005. There are no treasury shares; thus, the number of shares outstanding is equal to the number of shares issued, which is given in the question at 600,000.

Step 2: Calculate basic EPS (before any assumptions).

$$\frac{\$1,600,000 - \$160,000^a}{600,000} = \$2.40$$

^{a}8% x $2,000,000 par = $160,000 preferred dividends.

TIP! Recall that with cumulative preferred shares, the preferred's current year preference as to dividends is deducted in the basic EPS formula, whether or not the dividends were declared.

Step 3: Calculate diluted earnings per share.

$$\frac{\$1,600,000 - \$160,000 + \$180,000^a - \$72,000^b + \$160,000}{600,000 + 200,000 + 6(20,000)^c} = \$1.86$$

[a]6% x $3,000,000 par = $180,000 interest expense.
[b]$180,000 interest x 40% tax rate = $72,000 tax effect of interest.
[c]$2,000,000 par ÷ $100 per share = 20,000 shares of preferred issued.

Notice why the "if converted method" is so named; the earnings per share calculation assumes conversion of the convertible securities.	**TIP!**

When there is more than one potentially dilutive security outstanding, the steps for calculating diluted earnings per share are as follows:

1. Determine, for each dilutive security, the per share effect assuming exercise/conversion.
2. Rank the results from step 1 from smallest to largest earnings effect per share; that is, rank the results from most dilutive to least dilutive.
3. Beginning with the earnings per share based upon the weighted average of common shares outstanding ($2.40 in this problem), recalculate earnings per share by adding the smallest per share effects from step 2. If the results from this recalculation are less than $2.40, proceed to the next smallest per share effect and recalculate earnings per share. This process is continued so long as each recalculated earnings per share is smaller than the previous amount. The process will end either because there are no more securities to test or a particular security maintains or increases earnings per share (is antidilutive).

This means that dilutive potential common shares with the lowest "earnings per incremental share" will be included in diluted EPS before those with a higher "earnings per incremental share."	**TIP!**

The three steps are now applied to the Trent Corporation. The Trent Corporation has two securities (6% and 8% convertible bonds) that could reduce EPS.

The first step in the calculation of diluted earnings per share is to determine a per share effect for each potentially dilutive security.

Step 1: Determine the per share effect of each dilutive security.
Convertible bonds:

Interest expense for year (6% x $3,000,000)	$180,000
Income tax reduction due to interest (40% x $180,000)	72,000
Interest expense avoided (net of tax)	$108,000
Number of additional common shares issued assuming conversion of bonds	200,000

Per share effect:

Incremental Numerator Effect: $108,000	$.54
Incremental Denominator Effect: 200,000 shares	

Convertible preferred shares:

Dividend requirement on cumulative preferred (20,000 shares x 8% x $100)	$160,000

Income tax effect (dividends are not a tax deduction)	none
Dividend requirement avoided	$160,000

Number of additional common shares issued assuming conversion of preferred (6 x 20,000 shares)	120,000

Per share effect:

Incremental Numerator Effect:	$160,000	$1.33
Incremental Denominator Effect:	120,000 shares	

Step 2: Rank the results from Step 1.

The ranking of the two potentially dilutive securities is as follows (lowest earnings per incremental share to the largest):

	Effect Per Share
1. 6% convertible bonds	$.54
2. 8% convertible preferred	1.33

Step 3: Determine diluted earnings per share.

The next step is to determine earnings per share giving effect to the ranking above. Starting with the earnings per share of $2.40 calculated previously, add the incremental effects of the options to the original calculation, as follows:

6% Convertible Bonds

Numerator from previous calculation	$1,440,000
Add: Interest expense avoided (net of tax)	108,000
Total	$1,548,000

Denominator from previous calculation (shares)	600,000
Add: Number of common shares assumed issued upon assumed conversion of bonds	200,000
Total	800,000

Recalculated earnings per share ($1,548,000 ÷ 800,000 shares)	$1.94

Since the recalculated earnings per share is reduced (from $2.40 to $1.94), the effect of the 6% bonds is dilutive.

Next, earnings per share is recalculated assuming the conversion of the 8% preferred share. This is shown below:

8% Convertible Preferred

Numerator from previous calculation	$1,548,000
Add: Dividend requirement avoided	160,000
Total	$1,708,000

Denominator from previous calculation (shares)	800,000
Add: Number of common shares assumed issued upon conversion of preferred shares	120,000
Total	920,000
Recalculated earnings per share ($1,708,000 920,000 shares)	$1.86

Since the recalculated earnings per share is reduced, the effect of the 8% convertible preferred is dilutive. Diluted earnings per share is $1.86.

Exercise 18-4

PURPOSE: To illustrate EPS calculations in a more complex environment.

EPS Limited (EL) has the following capital structure at December 31, 2005:

8% convertible bonds, convertible into 2 pre-split common shares for every $100 bond in 2005	$1,000,000
10% bonds, due in annual instalments of $500,000 on January 1 of each year, beginning January 1, 2005	$5,000,000
4% cumulative preferred shares, (125,000 outstanding)	$3,000,000
Common shares—400,000 outstanding	$4,000,000

The following additional information is available:
- During the year, $1 million 6% convertible bonds were converted into 20,000 common shares on June 30, 2005. The 8% convertible bonds were issued at the same time.

At year-end, the shares were trading at $28, a $4 increase over the price at the beginning of the year, once the stock split is taken into account. Once executives exercise their rights under the plan, it is no longer in effect.
- On March 31, 2004, 25,000 warrants were issued for $2 each allowing the holder to purchase one pre-split common share per warrant for $50.
- Income tax rates are 40%.
- On September 30, 2005 there was a 2-for-1 stock split.
- Net income after taxes for the year ended December 31, 2005 was $1.1 million.
- It is a company policy to update all agreements after a stock split, such that arrangements made prior to the split are adjusted to reflect the split. For instance, if a bond was convertible into two pre-split shares, the understanding after the split would be that the bond would be convertible into four post-split shares.

Instructions

(a) Calculate basic EPS for EL for the year ended December 31, 2005.

(b) Calculate fully diluted EPS.

Solution to Exercise 18-4

(a) Earnings = $1,100,000 – ($3,000,000 x .04) = $980,000.
Weighted-average number of shares:

180,000 x 12/12	=	180,000
20,000 x 6/12	=	10,000
		190,000
		x 2
		380,000

Basic EPS = $980,000/380,000 = $2.58

(b) Diluted EPS should be calculated since there are dilutive securities and share options.

First, identify the securities and options.
- 8% bonds
- 6% convertible bonds
- warrants

Second, calculate the incremental effect of conversion on the basic EPS.
8% bonds:

Impact on earnings:

$1,000,000 x .08 x .6 x 6/12 =$24,000

Had the bonds been converted, $24,000 in interest would have been avoided. This is an after-tax number since the basic EPS is based on net income after tax. Also, interest would have been avoided for only half a year because the bonds were only issued in June.

Impact on shares:

1,000,000/100 x 2 =20,000 would have been issued. This must be weighted since the bonds were only issued June 30. If the bonds had been outstanding since the beginning of the year, there would have been no need to weight the shares. Further, the stock split would have to be taken into account. The conversion rate of 2-for-1 is stipulated in pre-split shares. These shares would be worth two new shares each.

20,000 x 6/12 x 2 = 20,000

Incremental impact:

$24,000/20,000 = $1.20

Since this is less than the basic EPS, the potential conversion is dilutive.

6% bonds:

Impact on earnings:

$1,000,000 x .06 x .6 x 6/12 = $18,000

We must consider these bonds even though they had been converted by year-end. Again, the objective is to show all actual and potential dilutive conversions as though they had happened at the beginning of the year (unless the convertible securities or options were issued later).

Impact on shares:

20,000 shares issued x 2 x 6/12 = 20,000

Again, we must account for the stock split. We must weight this calculation because the basic calculation already assumes conversion June 30.

Incremental impact:

$18,000/20,000 = .90

Since this is less than the basic EPS, this is considered dilutive.

Warrants:

Impact on shares:

Average market price of common shares for the year calculated as follows:

Calculate X which is market value at January 1, 2005

$$X + 4 = 28 \text{ so } X = 24$$

$$\text{average for the year } \frac{28 + 24}{2} = 26$$

If the 25,000 warrants were exercised, the company would receive 25,000 * 50 = $1,250,000, which would be used to buy back shares.

$1,250,000/$26 = 48,077 shares

Therefore, the company would have a net increase of 1,923 common shares (50,000 − 48,077).

Since this results in more shares being issued, it is considered to be dilutive.

The final step is to actually calculate the fully dilutive EPS.

	Earnings	Weighted average shares	EPS
Basic $	980,000	380,000	$2.58
Warrants	0	1,923	
	980,000	381,923	2.57
6% bonds	18,000	20,000	
	998,000	401,923	2.48
8 % bonds	24,000	20,000	
	1,022,000	421,923	2.42

The EPS information would be presented at the bottom of the income statement. Basic and diluted would be shown for the current year and the preceding year, if comparative statements are disclosed. Remember that the preceding year calculations would be adjusted to reflect the stock split.

Analysis of Multiple-Choice Type Questions

Question

1. Wong Corporation had net income reported for 2005 of $880,000. During 2005, dividends of $120,000 were declared on preferred shares and another $200,000 were declared on common shares. There were no changes in the 200,000 common shares or the 40,000 preferred shares outstanding during 2005. There were no potentially dilutive securities outstanding. The earnings per share to be reported for 2005 is:
    a. $4.40.
    b. $3.80.
    c. $3.67.
    d. $2.80.
    e. none of the above.

EXPLANATION: Write down the basic EPS formula. Solve using the data in this question.

$$\frac{\text{Net Income} - \text{Preferred Stock Dividends}}{\text{Weighted Average Number of Common Shares Outstanding}}$$

$$\frac{\$880,000 - \$120,000}{200,000} = \$3.80$$

(Solution = b.)

Question

2. The following data pertain to the Colby Corporation:

January 1, 2005	Shares outstanding	500,000
April 1, 2005	Shares issued	80,000
July 1, 2005	Treasury shares purchased	30,000
October 1, 2005	Shares issued in a 100% stock dividend	550,000

The number of shares to be used in calculating earnings per common share for 2005 is:
a. 682,500.
b. 1,090,000.
c. 1,095,000.
d. 1,100,000.
e. 1,130,000.

EXPLANATION: Follow the steps listed in **Illustration 18-2** to calculate the weighted average number of common shares outstanding for 2002.

Date		Weighted Average
1/1/05	500,000 x 12/12 =	500,000
4/1/05	80,000 x 9/12 =	60,000
	New balance	560,000
7/1/05	30,000 x 6/12 =	(15,000)
	New balance	545,000
10/1/05	100% stock dividend	x 200%*
	New balance	1,090,000

*The appropriate multiple for a stock dividend is 100% plus the percentage used in the dividend. Thus, 100% + 100% dividend = 200% as the multiplier. (Solution = b.)

Question

3. Refer to Question 2 above. The number of shares actually outstanding at the end of 2005 is:
a. 550,000.
b. 1,100,000.
c. 1,130,000.
d. 1,160,000.

EXPLANATION:

Date		Weighted Average
1/1/05	Balance	500,000
4/1/05	Issued for assets	80,000
	New balance	580,000
7/1/05	Acquired for treasury	(30,000)
	New balance	550,000
10/1/05	100% stock dividend	550,000
	New balance	1,100,000

(Solution = b.)

Question

4. At December 31, 2004 Opal Company had 200,000 common shares and 5,000 of 8%, $100 stated value cumulative preferred shares outstanding. No dividends were declared on either the preferred or common shares in 2004 or 2005. On February 10, 2006, prior to the issuance of its financial statements for the year ended December 31, 2005, Opal declared a 100% stock split on its common shares. Net income for 2005 was $480,000. In its 2005 financial statements, Opal's 2005 earnings per common share should be:
   a. $2.40.
   b. $2.20.
   c. $2.00.
   d. $1.20.
   e. $1.10.
   f. $1.00.

EXPLANATION:

$$\frac{\$480,000 - 5,000(8\% \times \$100)}{200,000 \times 2} = \$1.10$$

Dividends on **cumulative** preferred shares are deducted in the numerator, whether declared or not. However, only the current year's preference is used; dividends in arrears for prior years do not affect the EPS calculation. Stock dividends and stock splits are given retroactive treatment for all periods presented, even if they occur after the end of the current year, but before the financial statements are issued. (Solution = e.)

Question

5. Tempo, Inc. had 200,000 common shares issued and outstanding at December 31, 2004. On July 1, 2005 an additional 200,000 shares were issued for cash. Tempo also had stock options outstanding at the beginning and end of 2005 which allow the holders to purchase 60,000 common shares at $20 per share. The average market price of Tempo's common shares was $15 during 2005. The market price of Tempo's common shares was $25 at December 31, 2005. What is the number of shares that should be used in calculating diluted earnings per share for the year ended December 31, 2005?

a. 400,000
b. 300,000
c. 360,000
d. 415,000
e. 320,000
f. 280,000

EXPLANATION: Use the treasury stock method to calculate the number of shares to be used in determining diluted EPS. **However**, only make assumptions about the exercise of stock options when those assumptions are **not** antidilutive. A quick test to determine whether these options are dilutive or antidilutive is to compare the average market price ($15) with the option price ($20). The market price is not higher; therefore, the assumed exercise of stock options in applying the treasury stock method when calculating EPS will have an antidilutive effect. Therefore, no assumptions should be made. Only the weighted average actual outstanding shares should be used in calculating EPS in this situation.

Jan. 1	Shares outstanding: 200,000 x 12/12	=	200,000	
July 1	Issued for assets: 200,000 x 6/12	=	100,000	
	Weighted average shares outstanding	=	300,000	(Solution = b.)

TIP!

You could calculate EPS using the basic formula and calculate diluted EPS assuming the exercise of the options and application of the treasury stock method. Because this would entail an assumption of $1.2 million in proceeds being used to buy back shares at $15 (average market price) per share, this would result in making adjustments to the denominator as follows:

- Add 60,000 shares because of assumed exercise of options.
- Deduct 80,000 shares because of assumed purchase of treasury shares with $1.2 million proceeds from assumed exercise of options.

The net result of these assumptions is a **decrease** in the number of shares used to calculate diluted EPS, which indicates an antidilutive effect on EPS. Thus, these assumptions should **not** be made in the scenario described in this question.

Question

6. Refer to the facts of Question 5 above. If the average market price of Tempo's common shares was $25 rather than $15 during 2005, what is the number of shares that should be used in calculating diluted earnings per share for the year ended December 31, 2005?
   a. 330,000
   b. 448,000
   c. 412,000
   d. 320,000
   e. 348,000
   f. 312,000

EXPLANATION: Use the treasury stock method to calculate the number of shares to be used in determining diluted EPS. The weighted average number of shares actually outstanding is 300,000 (see Explanation to Question 5 above for this calculation). The average market price of the common shares ($25) should be used in determining the number of assumed treasury shares in calculating diluted EPS. The average market price ($25) of Tempo's common shares exceeds the option price ($20); thus the effect of assuming the exercise of the options and purchase of treasury shares with the assumed proceeds is dilutive. Thus, the calculation of the number of shares used in calculating diluted EPS is as follows:

Weighted average actual shares outstanding	300,000
Shares assumed issued upon exercise of options	60,000
Assumed shares purchased for the treasury ($1,200,000 ÷ $25)	(48,000)
Shares used for denominator of diluted EPS	312,000

(Solution = f.)

TIP! A comparison of 312,000 shares (determined by use of the treasury stock method) with the weighted average number of common shares actually outstanding (300,000) indicates a dilutive effect on EPS.

Question

7. A convertible bond issue should be included in the diluted earnings per share calculation as if the bonds had been converted into common shares, if the effect of its inclusion is:

	Dilutive	**Antidilutive**
a.	Yes	Yes
b.	Yes	No
c.	No	Yes
d.	No	No

EXPLANATION: A convertible security is a potentially dilutive security. All potentially dilutive securities should be included in the diluted EPS calculation, if the effect of inclusion is dilutive. No antidilutive assumptions are to be made in calculating diluted EPS. (Solution = b.)

Question

8. Which of the following are not ever considered to be dilutive securities?
    a. debt that is convertible into preferred shares
    b. convertible preferred shares
    c. stock options
    d. stock warrants

EXPLANATION: The concept of dilutive pertains to the common shareholders and the act of diluting their respective interest in the company, as well as their share of the earnings. As such warrants, options, and convertible preferred shares are dilutive since, if issued or converted, this would result in more common shares and less earnings for each of the remaining groups of common shareholders. (Solution = a.)

Question

9. When calculating basic EPS the numerator should be adjusted for:
    a. all dividends declared for the year.
    b. dividends declared during the year for preferred shares only.
    c. dividends declared during the year for the current year only.
    d. dividends declared during the year for all preferred shares and undeclared dividends for the year on cumulative preferred shares.

EXPLANATION: Care should be taken to deduct undeclared dividends on cumulative preferred shares for the current year only, as well as any declared dividends for the year. (Solution = d.)

Question

10. Which of the following does not require a retroactive adjustment when calculating weighted average number of shares for the basic EPS calculation?
    a. a stock split
    b. a reverse split
    c. a stock dividend
    d. a share conversion

EXPLANATION: The rationale behind this rule is when shareholder's wealth has not changed, just redistributed, then it should be handled on a retroactive basis. A share conversion would be accounted for prospectively since it would also affect earnings and therefore shareholder's wealth. (Solution = d.)

CHAPTER 19

Income Taxes

Overview

Most revenue type transactions are taxable amounts (they increase taxable income) in some time period, and most expense type transactions are deductible amounts (they decrease taxable income) in some time period. Interperiod income tax allocation procedures are required when a revenue or expense item is reported on the tax return in one year but is reported on the income statement in a different time period. Thus, the income tax consequences of revenues and expenses are reflected on the income statement in the same year that the revenues and expenses are reported on the financial statements, regardless of when the revenues and expenses appear on the tax return.

Study Steps

Understanding the Nature of Income Taxes

Net Income Versus Taxable Income

Income taxes are charged by the government and are calculated based on net income as defined by the Tax Act ("taxable income"). The area is complicated because net income, as defined by GAAP, is not the same as taxable income. Net income for GAAP purposes is calculated according to accounting principles or rules (i.e., GAAP), with the objective being to provide information that is useful for decision making. This objective encompasses principles that deal with when and how to recognize revenues and costs, among others.

Taxable income is calculated according to rules and regulations laid out in the Income Tax Act. The objectives of the Tax Act are quite different from the objectives of GAAP. The Tax Act is more specific (i.e., to provide guidance in the calculation of taxable income). Furthermore, the rules encompassed by the Tax Act were set out for various reasons (e.g., to stimulate spending in certain areas by allowing the expenditures to be tax deductible immediately, to discourage certain expenditures by not allowing them to be deducted in arriving at taxable income [e.g., club dues], to maximize revenues collected by the government from taxes, etc.).

Tax expense per the income statement is based on net income for GAAP or accounting purposes, and taxes actually paid to the government per the tax return are based on taxable income, which must be calculated separately. Differences between the two give rise to future tax assets or future tax liabilities.

Interperiod Versus Intraperiod Tax Allocation

Interperiod tax allocation deals with allocating taxes between different reporting periods, such as this year and future years. Intraperiod tax allocation deals with allocating taxes between different lines on the income statement (e.g., tax expenses may be allocated to net income from continuing earnings, discontinued earnings, and extraordinary items) or on other financial statements (e.g., statement of retained earnings, or changes in share capital). In general, with respect to the latter, the tax expense should be matched with the net income that it relates to. The bulk of this chapter will be devoted to interperiod allocation since this is the more complex of the two.

Special Tax Rules Relating to Loss Years

If a company suffers losses in a given year it does not have to pay taxes. Furthermore, a company may refile its past years' tax returns and deduct the losses from past years' taxable income. By doing this, they reduce past years taxable income and therefore the taxes payable for past years. They are then able to recover the excess of the taxes that they actually paid for these past years over the new taxes payable calculated. The losses may also be carried forward to offset and reduce future taxable income, thereby reducing taxes payable in the future.

To the extent that the company can reduce the amount of taxes either from past or future years, this represents a benefit to the company. According to the Tax Act, a company may carry tax losses back three years and forward seven years.

To the extent that the company can usually recover taxes already paid if it uses the losses to offset past income, it is wise to carry the taxes back first to obtain cash. Any remaining tax loss may be carried forward to offset future income.

Becoming Proficient in Related Calculations

This topic is very complex both theoretically and with the related calculations. Additionally, the terminology is difficult to grasp.

Therefore, a significant amount of time must be devoted to building an understanding. The exercises and illustrations below are structured to gradually take you through the learning process. As with most topics in accounting, failure to understand a fundamental concept will make it more difficult to grasp the complex aspects!

Exceptions for Non-public Companies

This topic is so complex that the CICA recently allowed an exemption for non-publicly accountable companies, citing, amongst other reasons, cost versus benefit. This possible exemption, referred to as "differential reporting," is available to non-publicly accountable enterprises (generally most private companies), provided that the shareholders unanimously agree. The result is simply using the provisions of the Income Tax Act to calculate tax assets and liabilities. This is the so-called "taxes payable" method. Of course all companies have to calculate taxes owing anyway under the Income Tax Act. Therefore, what is avoided is the additional cost of preparing financial information to comply with *CICA Handbook* Section 3465.

The advantage of this exemption is that a company can still attest to having GAAP financial statements, despite using differential reporting. The possible disadvantage is the lack of predictive value that GAAP purportedly provides. Care should be taken in deciding whether to implement differential reporting in situations where it is an option.

Tips on Chapter Topics

TIP!

The term **accounting income (loss)** refers to the difference between revenues earned and expenses incurred (other than income tax expense) on the accrual basis income statement for a given year. The term **taxable income (loss)** refers to the difference between taxable amounts and tax deductible amounts on the tax return for a given year. **Accounting income** appears on the income statement with the caption "Income before income taxes." Accounting income is often referred to as **income for book purposes, pretax financial income, or income for financial reporting purposes**.

TIP!   An excess of tax deductible expenses over taxable revenues on an entity's tax return is often called a **taxable loss**. Tax law provides that a taxable loss may be carried back three years and forward seven years. Although the use of carryback is optional for a corporation, most textbook questions will assume or require full carryback, to the extent possible.

TIP!   **Income tax payable for a period** is also the amount of **current tax expense** and is determined by applying the provisions of the tax law to the taxable income (or loss) figure for the period. In the case where tax loss results in a carryback, the entity will have **income tax refund receivable** (rather than income tax payable) which results in a **current tax benefit** (or recovery).

TIP!   A revenue or an expense amount that appears on the income statement or the tax return in one year but **never** appears on the other report is called a **permanent difference**. Future income taxes are **never** recorded for permanent differences because these differences will never reverse (i.e., they will neither cause future taxable nor future deductible amounts). Examples of permanent differences appear in **Illustration 19-1**.

TIP!   A **temporary difference** is a difference between the tax basis of an asset or liability and its reported amount (book value or carrying amount) in the financial statements that will result in taxable or deductible amounts in future years when the reported amount of the asset is recovered or the liability is settled. Temporary differences that will result in taxable amounts when the related assets are recovered are often called **taxable temporary differences**; temporary differences that will result in deductible amounts in future years when the related liabilities are settled are often called **deductible temporary differences. Taxable temporary differences give rise to recording future tax liabilities; deductible temporary differences give rise to recording future tax assets.**

TIP!   Most temporary differences are caused by reporting a revenue or an expense in one year for financial reporting purposes and reporting the same revenue or expense in a different year for income tax purposes. Examples of these situations appear in **Illustration 19-2**. Other causes of temporary differences are not addressed in this book.

TIP!   **Future tax expense (or benefit) for a period results from changes in the future tax asset and liability accounts**. A **future tax expense** results from an increase in a future tax liability or a decrease in a future tax asset; a **future tax benefit (recovery)** results from an increase in a future tax asset or a decrease in a future tax liability. This is true because the other half of the journal entry dealing with a future tax account (a balance sheet item) is the income tax expense account (an income statement item). A future tax expense **increases** total income tax expense for the period; a future tax benefit or recovery **reduces** total income tax expense for the period.

TIP!   **Total income tax expense (or benefit)** is the sum of **current tax expense (or benefit)** and **future tax expense (or benefit)**. Income tax expense is often referred to as provision for income taxes. Hence, there is usually both a current portion and a future portion of the income tax provision. The meaning of the word "current" in this text bears **no relationship** to the meaning of the term "current" as used to refer to a balance sheet classification of future taxes.

TIP!   A temporary difference originating in the current period that causes an increase in a future tax liability will also cause a debit (charge) to the provision for future income

Illustration 19-1   159

taxes on the income statement; an increase in a future tax asset will result in a credit to the provision for future taxes.

TIP!

Pay close attention to terminology in this chapter and be careful not to confuse the many terms introduced. When describing future taxes from a balance sheet perspective, we speak about future tax assets and future tax liabilities. Whereas, when talking about the effects of future taxes on the income statement, we speak about future tax expense or future tax benefit. There is a correlation, however, because it is changes in future tax assets and liabilities on the balance sheet that result in future tax expense or benefit on the income statement.

TIP!

A corporation often makes estimated tax payments during the year and charges them to an account called Prepaid Income Taxes. The balance of this account is used to offset the balance of the Income Tax Payable account for reporting purposes. The net amount is classified as a current asset if the prepaid account has the larger balance; the net amount is classified as a current liability if the payable account has the larger balance.

TIP!

The **effective tax rate** for a period is calculated by dividing total income tax expense on the income statement by income before income taxes on the income statement. The effective tax rate for a period may differ from the statutory tax rate for the same period because of (a) permanent differences, and (b) changes in cumulative temporary differences that have been tax effected at statutory tax rates enacted for future (or prior) periods.

TIP!

Future tax accounts are **not** to be reported at discounted amounts.

TIP!

Future deductible amounts are often called **future tax deductible amounts**.

TIP!

Illustration 19-1
Examples of Permanent Differences

1. **Revenues that are recognized for financial reporting purposes but are never included for tax purposes:**
   a. Dividends received from other taxable Canadian corporations.
   b. Proceeds from life insurance carried by the company on key officers or employees.

2. **Expenses that are recognized for financial reporting purposes but are never included for tax purposes:**
   a. Golf and social club dues.
   b. Premiums paid for life insurance carried by the company on key officers or employees (company is beneficiary).
   c. Certain fines and penalties.

3. **Revenues that are recognized for tax purposes but are never included in financial statements:**
   a. No examples exist at the current time.

4. **Expenses or other deductions that are recognized for tax purposes but are never included in financial statements:**
   a. Depletion allowance of natural resources in excess of their cost.

Illustration 19-2
Examples of Temporary Differences

1. **Revenues or gains that are taxable after they are included in accounting income.** This situation will result in **future taxable amounts**.
   - An example is the use of the accrual method in accounting for instalment sales for financial reporting purposes and the use of the instalment (cash) method for tax purposes. This situation causes an excess of the reported amount of an asset (receivable) over its tax basis that will result in a taxable amount in a future year(s) when the asset is recovered (when the cash is collected).
   - Other examples include:
     - Contracts which are accounted for under the percentage-of-completion method for financial reporting purposes, but a portion of the related gross profit is deferred for tax purposes.
     - Accrued revenues that are reported on the income statement in the period earned but included on the tax return in the period collected.
     - Unrealized holding gain on investment in trading securities.

2. **Expenses or losses that are deductible after they are included in accounting income.** This situation will result in **future tax deductible amounts**.
   - An example would be the accrual of an expense or loss contingency (e.g., litigation accrual) in calculating accounting income. This item is deductible for tax purposes only when it is realized. This situation causes a liability's reported amount to exceed its tax basis (zero) which will result in deductible amounts in a future year(s) when the liability (estimated litigation obligation) is settled.
   - Other examples include:
     - Product warranty liabilities.
     - Estimated liabilities related to discontinued operations or restructurings.
     - Accrued pension costs.
     - Unrealized holding loss on investment in trading securities.

3. **Revenues or gains that are taxable before they are included in accounting income.** This situation will result in **future tax deductible amounts**.
   - An example would be revenue received in advance for rent or subscriptions. For tax purposes, the revenue is taxable in the period the related cash is received, but the revenue is not included in the calculation of accounting

Illustration 19-3   161

income until the period in which it is earned. This type of case causes the reported amount for a liability (unearned revenue) on the balance sheet to exceed its tax basis (zero) which will result in future tax deductible amounts when the liability is settled.

This situation is said to result in future tax deductible amounts because of the future sacrifices required to provide goods or services or to provide refunds to those who cancel their orders.	**TIP!**

- Other examples include:
  - Sales and leasebacks for financial reporting purposes (income deferral) and sales for tax purposes.
  - Prepaid contracts and royalties received in advance.

4. **Expenses or losses that are deductible before they are included in accounting income**. This situation will result in **future taxable amounts**.
   - An example is the situation where a depreciable asset is amortized faster for tax purposes than it is amortized for financial accounting purposes. This causes the asset's reported value to exceed its tax basis. Amounts received upon the future recovery of the asset's reported value (through use or sale) will exceed its tax basis, and the excess will be taxable when the asset is recovered.
   - Other examples include:
     - Depletable resources and intangibles which may be amortized faster for tax purposes.
     - Deductible pension funding which exceeds the amount of pension expense.
     - Prepaid expenses that are deducted on the tax return in the period paid but are deducted on the income statement in the period incurred.

Illustration 19-3
Reconciliation of Accounting Income to Taxable Income

Accounting income

P	D		
E	I	–	Revenue recognized for books this period, but never recognized for
R	F		tax purposes
M	F	+	Expense recognized for books this period, but never recognized for
A	E		tax purposes
N	R	+	Revenue recognized for tax purposes this period, but never recognized for books

[...]ENT DIFFERENCES *(vertical heading)*

– Expense recognized for tax purposes this period, but never recognized for books

ORIGINATING TEMPORARY DIFFERENCES *(vertical heading)*

– Revenue recognized for books this period, but recognized later for tax purposes *[handwritten: Credit sales]*

+ Expense recognized for books this period, but recognized later for tax purposes *[handwritten: warranty costs]*

+ Revenue recognized for tax purposes this period, but recognized later for books *[handwritten: unearned revenue]*

– Expense recognized for tax purposes this period, but recognized later for books *[handwritten: prepaid expenses]*

REVERSING TEMPORARY DIFFERENCES *(vertical heading)*

– Revenue recognized for books this period, but recognized earlier for tax purposes

+ Expense recognized for books this period, but recognized earlier for tax purposes

+ Revenue recognized for tax purposes this period, but recognized earlier for books

– Expense recognized for tax purposes this period, but recognized earlier for books

= Taxable income

TIP!

No future taxes are to be recognized for permanent differences because they will not have any future tax consequences.

Temporary differences that **originate** in the current period and give rise to **future taxable amounts** are to be **deducted** from accounting income in this reconciliation. These differences will result in an increase in **future tax liabilities** during the current period for the future tax consequences of those future taxable amounts.

Temporary differences that **originate** in the current period and give rise to **future deductible amounts** are to be **added** to accounting income in this reconciliation. These differences will result in an increase in **future tax assets** during the current period for the future tax consequences of those future deductible amounts.

Refer to **Illustration 19-1** for examples of permanent differences; refer to **Illustration 19-2** for examples of temporary differences. The four types of examples addressed in those two illustrations appear in the same order there as they are referenced in this illustration. Thus, the first type of permanent difference listed in **Illustration 19-3** corresponds to the first type described in **Illustration 19-1**. Also, the first type of the temporary differences listed in Illustration 19-3 corresponds to the first type described in **Illustration 19-2**.

This reconciliation will aid you in solving some homework assignments and exam questions, but it is not relevant to all situations. The temporary differences used in this reconciliation are **only** the ones that originated or reversed during the current year. The reconciliation does **not** use cumulative temporary differences. This reconciliation can be used to solve for taxable income, accounting income, or changes in cumulative temporary differences for a given period of time.

TIP!

CASE 19-1

PURPOSE: This case will provide practice in distinguishing between temporary differences and permanent differences. It will also provide practice in distinguishing between taxable-type and deductible-type temporary differences.

In reviewing the records of a client, you find the items listed below pertain to the current year.

Instructions

For each item below, indicate whether it involves:
  a. A temporary difference which gives rise to future deductible amounts. *Tax Asset*
  b. A temporary difference which gives rise to future taxable amounts. *Tax Liability*
  c. A permanent difference.

_B_ 1. A 20% declining-balance method was used for amortization for tax purposes, and 10 year straight-line amortization was used for accounting purposes for some depreciable assets.

_____ 2. The client is a landlord and collected some rents in advance.

_____ 3. An instalment sale of an investment was accounted for by the accrual method for books and the instalment method for tax purposes.

_C_ 4. Dividends received from taxable Canadian corporations.

_____ 5. The costs of guarantees and warranties were estimated and accrued for accounting purposes.

_____ 6. Fines and penalties for nonpayment of income tax were deducted in accounting income.

_____ 7. Proceeds were received from a life insurance company because of the death of a key officer (the company carries a policy on key officers).

_____   8.   For some assets, straight-line amortization was used for both accounting purposes and tax purposes, but the assets' lives were shorter for tax purposes.

_____   9.   Expenses incurred for golf and social dues were expensed in accounting income.

_____   10.   Estimated losses on pending lawsuits and claims were accrued for books. These losses will be tax deductible in the year(s) they are realized.

_____   11.   Intangible assets are amortized over 20 years for accounting purposes and over 15 years for tax purposes.

_____   12.   The company recognized a loss on the income statement due to a decline in the fair value of the trading portfolio of investment in marketable trading equity securities.

_____   13.   The company has a construction division which uses the percentage-of-completion method for books and the completed-contract method for tax purposes.

_____   14.   The company has made a formal plan for discontinuing a segment of business. A loss of $500,000 is expected on the disposal of the assets of the segment to be discontinued.

_____   15.   Prepaid advertising expense is deferred and amortized for accounting purposes and deducted as an expense when paid for tax purposes.

_____   16.   The corporation owns a patent and allows another company to use the rights embodied in the patent in exchange for royalty payments which are collected in advance.

_____   17.   A transaction accounted for as a sale and leaseback for accounting purposes was treated as a sale for tax purposes. A gain resulted from the sale.

_____   18.   The amount funded for the company pension plan this year was less than the amount expensed for financial reporting purposes. Only the amount funded was deductible on this year's tax return.

_____   19.   The company collected subscriptions in advance for a magazine it publishes.

_____   20.   The accrual for post-retirement benefits other than pensions was made in accordance with *CICA Handbook* Section 3461. This amount will be charged to the tax returns of the years in which amounts are paid for these benefits.

     21. Capital assets were acquired in the current year. The amortization taken for book purposes exceeded the amortization reported for tax purposes for the current year.

     22. An accrued revenue was reported on the income statement for the current year; the revenue will be taxable when it is collected.

Solution to Case 19-1

1.   b

2.   a

3.   b   The use of the accrual method for books causes the entire gross profit from the instalment sale to be reflected in the income statement of the period of sale. The use of the instalment method for tax purposes causes the gross profit to be allocated over the collection period; the amount of gross profit recognized in a period is proportionate to the amount of sales price collected in the period.

4.   c   Dividends flow tax-free between corporations.

5.   a

6.   c

7.   c

8.   b

9.   c

10.   a

11.   b   When any asset is amortized faster for tax purposes than it is amortized for book purposes, the cumulative temporary difference existing at a balance sheet date will result in net future taxable amounts.

12.   a   This loss will not be deductible for tax purposes until the future period in which the loss is realized (that is, in the period the securities are sold).

13.   b

14.   a   The loss cannot be deducted for tax purposes until the period of realization.

15.   b

16.   a   The royalty receipts are to be included in taxable income in the period they are received.

17.   a   The gain is generally deferred for accounting purposes but reported currently for tax purposes.

18.   a

19.   a   The collections are included in taxable income in the period received. The related revenue is deferred for financial reporting purposes until it is earned.

20.   a

21.   a

22.   b

Illustration 19-4
Compound Journal Entry to Record Income Taxes

In recording income taxes, the best approach is to perform the following steps in order:

1. **Calculate the amount of income tax payable for the current period.** This is always based on the amount of taxable income and the tax rate for the current year. This amount is also referred to as "current tax expense"; it is recorded by a credit to Income Tax Payable. If there is a taxable loss for the current year, then the benefits of a loss carryback are called "current tax benefit" (or recovery) and are recorded by a debit to a receivable account.

2. **Calculate the change required in the future tax account(s).** To do this, the appropriate balance of the future tax account(s) at the balance sheet date must be determined and this may require a scheduling process. The appropriate balance represents the future tax consequences of cumulative temporary differences and tax loss carryforwards existing at the balance sheet date. The difference between the ending balance and the beginning balance of a future tax account is called "future tax expense" or "future tax benefit" or "benefits of loss carryforward," whichever is appropriate. It is recorded by a debit or a credit to a future tax asset or liability account.

3. **Record income tax expense** which is the total of current tax expense (or benefit) and future tax expense (or benefit). In a compound journal entry, it is the "plug" figure required to make the journal entry balance.

TIP! In calculating future income taxes at a balance sheet date, the amount of cumulative temporary differences must be determined. Information on when those differences originated is **not** needed; some or all of the differences could have originated in prior periods. Information about the individual future years in which these differences are expected to reverse is generally **not** needed because the tax rate is usually the same flat rate year after year. One case in which this information **is** needed is the situation where there are different tax rates enacted for the individual future years in which existing temporary differences are expected to cause taxable and deductible amounts to occur. Thus, if a single tax rate applies to all future years, an aggregate calculation for future income taxes is appropriate. However, if different tax rates apply to individual future years, a scheduling of future taxable and deductible amounts (due to temporary differences at the balance sheet date) with a separate calculation for each future year affected is required.

TIP! In determining the future tax consequences of temporary differences (Step 2) when there is a phased-in change in tax rates, it is necessary to prepare a schedule showing in which future years existing temporary differences will result in taxable or deductible amounts. In determining the applicable tax rate, you must make assumptions about whether the entity will report taxable income or losses in the various future years expected to be affected by the reversal of existing temporary differences. Thus, you calculate the taxes payable or refundable in the future, due to existing temporary differences. In making these calculations, you apply the provisions of the tax law and enacted tax rates for the relevant periods. The following guidelines are used to determine the applicable tax rate:

1. If taxable income is expected in the year that a future taxable (or deductible) amount is scheduled, use the enacted rate for the future year to calculate the related future tax liability (or asset).
2. If a taxable loss is expected in the year that a future taxable (or deductible) amount is scheduled, use the enacted rate of the prior year to which the tax loss would be carried back or the enacted rate of the future year to which the carryforward would apply, whichever is appropriate to calculate the related future tax liability (or asset).

Single entries (rather than one compound journal entry) can be used to record income taxes. With this approach, you could perform Step 1 above and record the results by either a credit to Income Tax Payable (if there is taxable income for the current period) or a debit to Income Tax Refund Receivable (if there is a loss on the current tax return and a carryback is appropriate). The other half of this first entry is a debit or credit (whichever is needed to make the entry balance) to Income Tax Expense. A second entry would be recorded for the results of Step 2 above. In this second entry, a debit or credit would be recorded to Future Tax Asset or Future Tax Liability, whatever is needed to properly report future taxes on the balance sheet. The other half of this second entry would be either a debit or credit to Income Tax Expense, as appropriate, to make the entry balance. Step 2 is repeated (and another single entry is recorded) if there is more than one reason for having temporary differences. Thus, if one entity has three types of temporary differences, Step 2 is performed three times and there would be a total of four single entries to record income taxes for the period. (This single entries approach to recording income taxes is illustrated in parts (a) and (b) of the **Solution to Exercise 19-1**).

TIP!

Case 19-2

PURPOSE: This case examines the focus of the liability method and the steps in the annual calculation of future tax assets and liabilities.

   The objectives of accounting for income taxes are to recognize (a) the amount of taxes payable or refundable for the current year, and (b) future tax liabilities and assets that arise because of the future tax consequences of events that have been recognized in an enterprise's financial statements or tax returns.

Instructions

(a) If a revenue item is reported on the income statement in 2005, but is included on the tax return in 2006, explain whether the related income tax effect should be reflected on the income statement in 2005 or 2006, and why.

(b) Explain whether the liability method of accounting for future taxes focuses on the proper valuation of assets and liabilities (balance sheet orientation) or on income determination (income statement orientation).

(c) List the steps to be included in the annual calculation of future tax liabilities and assets.

Solution to Case 19-2

(a) The tax consequences of a transaction or event are to be recognized in the same period that the transaction or event is recognized in the financial statements. This is the essence of the comprehensive income tax allocation approach. Thus, the income tax effect of revenue recognized in 2005 should also be recognized on the income statement in 2005, even though the payment of the resulting tax is deferred until a later year.

(b) At any given balance sheet date, future income taxes are calculated by applying the applicable tax rate(s) to future taxable and deductible amounts stemming from temporary differences existing at the balance sheet date. Thus, a future tax liability (or asset) is recognized for taxes payable (or a reduction in taxes payable) in future years due to existing temporary differences. The amount of future tax expense (or benefit) for the income statement is determined by the change in future tax accounts from one balance sheet date to another; thus, future income tax expense (or benefit) is a residual figure (commonly called a plug figure). Therefore, the liability method is said to be balance sheet oriented.

(c) The procedures in the calculation of future income taxes are as follows:
  1. Identify (a) the types and amounts of existing temporary differences, and (b) the nature and amount of tax loss available for carryforward and the remaining length of the carryforward period.
  2. Measure the total future tax liability for taxable temporary differences using the applicable tax rate.
  3. Measure the total future tax asset for deductible temporary differences and taxable loss carryforwards using the applicable tax rate.
  4. Measure future tax assets for each type of tax credit carryforward.
  5. Apply the **"more likely than not" rule** (a likelihood of more than 50 percent) to future tax assets, to ensure no asset is set-up that will **not** be realized. (Note, this should be reviewed each reporting period).

Exercise 19-1

PURPOSE: This exercise will illustrate how to record current tax expense and future tax expense when one taxable temporary difference exists. It will also illustrate the effect of the reversal of the same temporary difference on income tax expense.

Gary Winarski Inc. has accounting income for 2005 of $400,000. There were no future taxes at the beginning of 2005. At the end of 2005, temporary differences of $85,000 exist which are expected to result in taxable amounts in 2007. The enacted tax rates are as follows:

Year	Tax Rate
2004	50%
2005–2006	40%
2007 and later	30%

Instructions

(a) Calculate taxable income for 2005 and record income tax payable.
(b) Calculate future taxes at December 31, 2005 and record the change in future taxes, assuming taxable income is expected in all future years.
(c) Draft the income tax expense section of the income statement for 2005 (beginning with "Income before income taxes").
(d) Draft the income tax expense section of the income statement for 2007 assuming taxable income for 2007 is $360,000 (begin with the line "Income before income taxes").

Solution to Exercise 19-1

(a) Accounting income $ 400,000
    Originating temporary difference resulting in future
      taxable amounts   (85,000)
    Taxable income $ 315,000

Current Income Tax Expense	126,000	
Income Tax Payable ($315,000 x 40%)		126,000
(To record current tax expense)		

EXPLANATION: Use the reconciliation format in **Illustration 19-3** to calculate taxable income. Because there was no future taxes (and, thus, no temporary differences) existing at the beginning of 2005, all $85,000 of temporary differences existing at the end of 2005 must have originated (came about) during 2005. Because these originating temporary differences will result in future taxable amounts, they cause taxable income to be lower than accounting income in 2005.

(b) Future taxable amounts $ 85,000
     Enacted tax rate for applicable future year   30%
     Balance needed for future tax liability at December 31, 2005   25,500
     Balance of future tax liability at January 1, 2005   0
     Increase in future tax liability during 2005 $ 25,500

     Future Income Tax Expense   25,500
         Future Income Tax Liability   25,500*
             (To record the change in future taxes)

         *See calculation above.

EXPLANATION: The future tax liability at December 31, 2005 is measured by using the tax rate enacted for the future year (2007) in which the underlying temporary difference will result in future taxable amounts.

TIP!

> Refer to **Illustration 19-4** and the last **TIP** for that illustration. This exercise makes use of the single entry approach to recording income taxes. The entries for parts (a) and (b) of this exercise are often combined for a compound journal entry as follows:
>
> Income Tax Expense   151,500
>   Income Tax Payable   126,000
>   Future Income Tax Liability   25,500

(c) Income before income taxes $ 400,000
     Income tax expense:
         Current tax expense $ 126,000
         Future tax expense   25,500   151,500
     Net income $ 248,500

TIP!

> Notice that the effective tax rate for 2005 is 37.875% ($151,500 ÷ $400,000 = .37875). This rate is lower than the 40% statutory tax rate for 2005 because $315,000 of the $400,000 is tax effected at 40% and $85,000 of the $400,000 is tax effected at 30%.

(d) Income before income taxes $ 275,000 [a]
     Income tax expense:
         Current tax expense $ 108,000 [b]
         Future tax benefit   (25,500) [c]   82,500
     Net income $ 192,500

         [a]Accounting income $ X
            Reversing taxable temporary difference   85,000
            Taxable income $ 360,000
                Solving for X: X + $85,000 = $360,000
                                      X = $360,000 − $85,000
                                      X = $275,000 = Accounting income

[b]Taxable income for 2007 $ 360,000

   Enacted tax rate   30%

   Income tax payable for 2007 $ 108,000

[c]There is no temporary difference existing at the end of 2007, so the balance in the future tax liability account would be eliminated. A decrease in a future tax liability results in a future tax benefit on the income statement.

Notice that the effective tax rate for 2007 is 30% ($82,500 ÷ $275,000 = .30), which equals the statutory tax rate for 2007.   **TIP!**

Think about the journal entry(s) that would be required in 2007 to record income taxes. Using single entries (as opposed to one compound entry), they would appear as follows: **TIP!**

Income Tax Expense	108,000	
Income Tax Payable ($360,000 x 30%)		108,000
(To record current tax expense)		
Future Tax Liability	25,500	
Future Income Tax Expense/Benefit		25,500
(To record the change in deferred taxes)		

Exercise 19-2

PURPOSE: This exercise illustrates how to account for income taxes when there are both permanent and temporary differences involved and a flat tax rate is enacted for all periods affected.

The Monte Corporation has accounting income of $200,000 for 2005 (the first year of operations). The difference between revenues and expenses reported on the tax return for 2005 and the income statement for 2005 are as follows:

	Tax Return	Income Statement
Amortization expense	$ 80,000	$ 62,000
Insurance premiums expense		8,000
Warranty expense	10,000	19,000
Dividends from taxable Canadian Corporations		2,000
Rent revenue	6,200	5,000

The insurance premiums pertain to life insurance on the lives of corporate officers, and the beneficiary is the corporation.

The tax rate for 2005 is 40%, and no new rate has been enacted for future years.

Instructions

(a) Calculate taxable income for 2005.

(b) Prepare the journal entry to record income taxes for 2005.

(c) Prepare the portion of the income statement for 2005 that reports income taxes. Begin with the caption "Income before income taxes."

Solution to Exercise 19-2

(a)
Accounting income for 2005	$ 200,000
Nondeductible expense—life insurance on officers	8,000
Nontaxable revenue—dividends	(2,000)
Excess amortization per tax return for 2005	(18,000)
Excess warranty expense per books for 2005	9,000
Excess rent revenue per tax return for 2005	1,200
Taxable income for 2005	$ 198,200

(b)
Income Tax Expense	82,400 [e]	
Future Tax Asset—Warranties	3,600 [d]	
Future Tax Asset—Rents	480 [c]	
Future Tax Liability—Amortization		7,200 [b]
Income Tax Payable		79,280 [a]

[a]$198,200 x 40% = $79,280.
[b]$18,000 x 40% = $7,200.
[c]$1,200 x 40% = $480.
[d]$9,000 x 40% = $3,600.
[e]$79,280 + $7,200 − $480 − $3,600 = $82,400.

Although this entry presented a combined expense, most businesses would use two accounts as follows:

Current Income Tax Expense	$ 79,280
Future Income Tax Expense	3,120

TIP! | Although some people may choose to use only one future tax asset account in the above entry, the use of a separate future tax account for each type of temporary difference (as illustrated above) is helpful when later classifying future taxes on the balance sheet.

(c)
Income before income taxes		$ 200,000
Provision for income taxes:		
Current tax expense	$ 79,280	
Future tax expense	3,120 *	82,400
Net income		$ 117,600

*Future tax expense of $7,200, future tax benefit of $480, and future tax benefit of $3,600, net to a future tax expense of $3,120.

The amount reported for total income tax expense ($82,400 in this exercise) should agree with the balance of the Income Tax Expense account before closing.	**TIP!**

Exercise 19-3

PURPOSE: This exercise illustrates the steps involved in calculating and recording income taxes when two types of temporary differences exist and there is a phased-in change in tax rates.

Benyon Corporation has the following facts available:
1. Accounting income for Year 1 is $105,000.
2. Year 1 is the first year of operations.
3. One temporary difference exists at the end of Year 1 that will result in deductible amounts of: $20,000 in Year 2.
    $30,000 in Year 3.
4. Another temporary difference exists at the end of Year 1 which will result in taxable amounts of: $11,000 in Year 2.
    $14,000 in Year 3.
5. Tax rates enacted by the end of Year 1 are: 50% for Year 1.
    40% for Year 2.
    30% for Year 3.
6. Taxable income is expected in all future years.

Instructions

(a) Calculate taxable income for Year 1.
(b) Calculate the future taxes to be reported on the balance sheet at the end of Year 1.
(c) Prepare the journal entry to record income taxes for Year 1.
(d) Draft the income tax expense section of the income statement for Year 1.

Solution to Exercise 19-3

(a)
Accounting income for Year 1	$ 105,000
Temporary differences originating:	
Deductible temporary difference	50,000
Taxable temporary difference	(25,000)
Taxable income for Year 1	$ 130,000

(b) At December 31, Year 1, a future tax asset of $17,000 and a future tax liability of $8,600 should be reflected on the balance sheet. Future taxes are calculated by a scheduling process as follows:

| | Current Year | Future Years | | |
	Year 1	Year 2	Year 3	Total
Taxable income	$130,000			
Future deductible amounts		($20,000)	($30,000)	($50,000)
Future taxable amounts		11,000	14,000	25,000
Enacted tax rates	50%	40%	30%	
Future tax (asset) liability		($8,000)	($9,000)	($17,000)
		4,400	4,200	$ 8,600

(c) Future Tax Asset	17,000	
Income Tax Expense	56,600	
Income Tax Payable		65,000
Future Tax Liability		8,600

Calculations:

Step 1:
Taxable income	$ 130,000
Tax rate for Year 1	50%
Income tax payable	$ 65,000

Step 2:   See the scheduling in part (b) for determination of the $17,000 ending balance for future tax asset and $8,600 ending balance for future tax liability.

The change in future taxes is calculated as follows:

Balance of future tax asset at end of Year 1	$ 17,000
Balance of future tax asset at beginning of Year 1	0
Increase in future tax asset (which is a future tax benefit)	$ 17,000

Balance of future tax liability at end of Year 1	$ 8,600
Balance of future tax liability at beginning of Year 1	0
Increase in future tax liability (a future tax expense)	$ 8,600

Step 3:
Future tax benefit	$(17,000)
Future tax expense	8,600
Net future tax benefit/benefit	(8,400)
Current tax expense	65,000
Total income tax expense for Year 1	$ 56,600

TIP! The three following single entries are equivalent to the one compound journal entry above. Notice the first one records the current tax expense and a current tax obligation of $65,000. The second entry adjusts the future tax asset account and records a future tax benefit of $17,000; a future tax benefit reduces total income tax expense. The third one adjusts the future tax liability account and records a future tax expense of $8,600; a future tax expense increases total income tax expense. These three entries can be used in place of the one compound entry.

Income Tax Expense	65,000	
Income Tax Payable		65,000
Future Tax Asset	17,000	
Future Income Tax Expense/Benefit		17,000
Future Income Tax Expense	8,600	
Future Tax Liability		8,600

(d) The relevant section of the income statement would appear as follows:

Income before income taxes		$ 105,000
Income tax expense:		
Current tax expense	$ 65,000	
Future tax benefit	(8,400)	56,600
Net income		$ 48,400

Exercise 19-4

PURPOSE: This exercise will review a situation that involves both a future tax asset and a future tax liability, one with a beginning balance. It also reviews the relationships existing in the reconciliation of accounting income and taxable income.

The following facts relate to the Tasty Bits Corporation:
1. Future tax liability, January 1, 2005, $80,000.
2. Future tax asset, January 1, 2005, $0.
3. Taxable income for 2005, $164,000.
4. There are no permanent differences in 2005.
5. Cumulative temporary difference at December 31, 2005, giving rise to future taxable amounts, $440,000.
6. Cumulative temporary difference at December 31, 2005, giving rise to future deductible amounts, $70,000.
7. Tax rate for all years, 40%.
8. The company is expected to operate profitably in all future years.

Instructions

(a) Prepare the journal entry to record income tax payable, future income taxes, and income tax expense for 2005.
(b) Draft the income tax expense section of the income statement for 2005, beginning with the line "income before income taxes."

Solution to Exercise 19-4

(a) Journal entry:

Future Income Tax Expense	68,000	
Income Tax Expense	65,600	
Future Tax Asset	28,000	
Income Tax Payable ($164,000 x 40%)		65,600
Future Tax Liability		96,000

Calculations:

Temporary Difference	Future Taxable (Deductible) Amounts	Tax Rate	Future Tax (Asset)	Liability
Taxable type	$ 440,000	40%		$176,000
Deductible type	(70,000)	40%	$(28,000)	
Totals	$ 370,000	40%	$(28,000)	$176,000**

**Because of a flat tax rate, these totals can be reconciled:
    $370,000 x 40% = ($28,000) + $176,000

Future tax liability, 12/31/05	$ 176,000
Future tax liability, 12/31/04	80,000
Future tax expense, 2005	$ 96,000
(Net increase required in a future tax liability)	

Future tax asset, 12/31/05	$ 28,000
Future tax asset, 12/31/04	0
Future tax expense (benefit), 2005	$ (28,000)
(Net increase required in a future tax asset)	

Future tax expense for 2005	$ 96,000
Future tax benefit for 2005	(28,000)
Net future tax expense for 2005	68,000
Current tax expense, 2005	65,600
Total income tax expense, 2005	$ 133,600

(b) Income before income taxes $ 334,000*

Income tax expense:		
Current tax expense	$ 65,600	
Future tax expense	68,000	133,600
Net income		$ 200,400

*Because of the flat tax rate for all years, the amount of cumulative temporary difference existing at the beginning of the year can be calculated by dividing the $80,000 beginning balance in Future Tax Liability by 40%, which equals $200,000. This information may now be combined with the other facts given in the exercise to reconcile accounting income with taxable income for 2005 as follows:

Accounting income	$	X
Net originating temporary difference giving rise to future taxable amounts ($440,000 – $200,000)		(240,000)
Originating temporary difference giving rise to future deductible amounts		70,000
Taxable income		$ 164,000

Solving for X: X – $240,000 + $70,000 = $164,000;
                          X = $334,000

Exercise 19-5

PURPOSE: This exercise illustrates the application of guidelines for the classification of future income taxes.

The Chip Corporation has several temporary differences existing at December 31, 2005. The following information pertains:

1. The carrying value of capital assets exceeds the tax basis of those assets by $500,000.
2. A long-term pension liability of $700,000 appears on the balance sheet due to the accrual of pension costs. Only the amounts funded have been deducted on the tax returns over the years.
3. For tax purposes, $400,000 of income on contracts has been deferred until 2006.
4. The company recognized a loss of $80,000 in 2005 associated with a discontinued segment of business. The disposal date is scheduled for 2006; thus, an accrued liability for plant closing costs is classified as a current liability.
5. An allowance for doubtful accounts of $220,000 appears on the GAAP basis balance sheet. Uncollectible accounts are tax deductible only when individual accounts are written off. All accounts receivable are classified as current assets.
6. An estimated liability for litigation settlements of $130,000 appears in the long-term liability section of the balance sheet. This liability has a tax basis of zero.

A flat tax rate of 40% is enacted for all years.

Instructions

Calculate the current and non-current tax assets and/or liabilities to appear on the balance sheet at December 31, 2005. Indicate how they are to be classified.

TIP!

Future income tax assets and liabilities are to be reported on the balance sheet in a **net** current and a **net** noncurrent amount. Future tax liabilities and assets are to be classified as current or noncurrent based on the classification of the related asset or liability for financial reporting. A future tax liability or asset that is **not** related to an asset or liability for financial reporting, including future tax assets related to carryforwards, should be classified according to the expected reversal date of the temporary difference.

Solution to Exercise 19-5

Temporary Difference	Resulting Future Tax (Asset)	Liability	Related Balance Sheet Account	Future Tax Classification
1. Excess amortization for tax purposes.		$200,000	Capital Assets	Noncurrent
2. Excess pension expense for book purposes.	$(280,000)		Pension Liability	Noncurrent
3. Excess contract income for book purposes.		160,000	None	Current
4. Accrual of plant closing costs for books.	(32,000)		Accrued Liability for Plant Closing	Current
5. Accrual of uncollectible accounts for books.	(88,000)		Allowance for Doubtful Accounts	Current
6. Accrual of litigation settlements.	(52,000)	_____	Estimated Obligation for Lawsuits	Noncurrent
	$(452,000)	$360,000		

SUMMARY: The net current amount is a liability of $40,000 [$160,000 – ($32,000 + $88,000) = $40,000]. The net noncurrent amount is an asset of $132,000 ($280,000 – $200,000 + $52,000 = $132,000).

EXPLANATION:

1. $500,000 future taxable amounts x 40% = $200,000 future tax liability. There is a related asset on the books, Capital Assets, and its classification is noncurrent. Therefore, the resulting future tax liability account is noncurrent.

2. $700,000 future deductible amounts x 40% = $280,000 future tax asset. There is a related Pension Liability on the GAAP balance sheet, and its classification is noncurrent. Therefore, the resulting future tax asset is noncurrent.

3. $400,000 future taxable amounts x 40% = $160,000 future tax liability. There is no asset or liability on the balance sheet that is related to the deferral of contract income for tax purposes. The classification of the future taxes is, therefore, dependent on the expected reversal date of the temporary difference. The expected reversal date (2006) is the year immediately following the balance sheet date; hence, the classification of the future tax account is current.

4. $80,000 future deductible amounts x 40% = $32,000 future tax asset. There is a related liability on the balance sheet, Accrued Liability for Plant Closing Costs, and its classification is current. Therefore, the resulting future tax asset is current.

5. $220,000 future deductible amounts x $40% = $88,000 future tax asset. There is a related contra asset account, Allowance for Doubtful Accounts, in the current asset section of the balance sheet. Hence, the related future tax account is a current asset.

6. $130,000 future deductible amounts x 40% = $52,000 future tax asset. There is a related accrued liability account, Estimated Obligation for Lawsuits, reported as a long-term liability on the balance sheet. The related future tax asset is therefore a noncurrent asset.

> A commonly confusing point stems from the fact that the term **current** is used in association with **two totally unrelated amounts** involved with accounting for income taxes. These two amounts are the **current portion of income tax expense on the income statement** and the **current portion of future taxes on the balance sheet**. On the income statement, income tax expense is comprised of both current and future portions. On the balance sheet, future taxes are classified as either current or noncurrent. A change during the period in both current and noncurrent future taxes on the balance sheet results in the future portion of income tax expense for the same period on the income statement. The current portion of income tax expense on the income statement refers to the amount of taxes generated by the tax return for the current period. Taxable income produces a tax due (payable) and, therefore, current tax expense; a taxable loss on the tax return for the current period that calls for a carryback of the loss results in a current tax benefit to be reported as the current portion of income tax expense on the income statement.

TIP!

Exercise 19-6

PURPOSE: This exercise reviews the accounting procedures for a taxable loss (or loss for income tax purposes).

The Evans Corporation has had no permanent or temporary differences since it began operations. Information regarding taxable income and taxes paid is as follows:

Year	Taxable Income (Loss)	Tax Rate	Taxes Paid
1	$ 60,000	40%	$ 24,000
2	100,000	40%	40,000
3	80,000	35%	28,000
4	160,000	35%	56,000
5	(400,000)	30%	
6	100,000	25%	25,000

The tax rate enacted for Year 6 and subsequent years is 25%.

Instructions

(a) Assuming the taxable loss in Year 5 is carried back to the extent possible, prepare the journal entry to record the benefits of the carryback and the journal entry to record the expected benefits of any related tax loss carryforward. Assume it is likely that the benefits of any carryforward will be fully realized.

(b) Explain how all of the accounts in the entries above are to be reported in the financial statements for Year 5. Draft the income tax expense section of the income statement for Year 5, beginning with the line "Operating loss before income taxes."

(c) Assuming taxable income is $100,000 (before considering the tax loss carry-forward) in Year 6, prepare the journal entry to record income taxes. Also, draft the income tax expense section of the income statement for Year 6, beginning with the line "Income before income taxes."

Solution to Exercise 19-6

(a) Income Tax Refund Receivable   124,000
         Current Income Tax Benefits Due to Loss Carryback   124,000
           ($ 40,000 + $28,000 + $56,000 = $124,000)

     Future Tax Asset   15,000
         Future Income Tax Benefits Due to Loss Carryforward   15,000
           ($400,000 – $ 100,000 – $80,000 – $160,000 = $60,000)
             ($60,000 x 25% = $15,000)

TIP! The expected benefits of a tax loss carryforward are recognized in the year of the loss which gives rise to the carryforward. The tax rate enacted for the future year in which the benefits are expected to be realized is used to calculate the related future tax asset.

TIP! Benefits Due to Loss Carryback and Benefits Due to Loss Carryforward are both negative components of total income tax expense; therefore, they are credits to the income statement. The Benefits Due to Loss Carryback represent a current tax benefit, and the Benefits Due to Loss Carryforward are a future tax benefit.

TIP! If it is **more likely than not** that a portion or the entire future tax asset will **not** be realized, it is best that a future tax asset not be set up. If it is, a valuation allowance should be established by a charge to income tax expense and a credit to an allowance account to essentially reduce the asset to its realizable value. For example, in the case above, if one-half of the benefits of the operating loss carryforward were not expected to be realized within the carryforward period, an adjusting entry for $7,500 would be recorded by a debit to Future Income Tax Benefits Due to Loss Carryforward and a credit to Allowance to Reduce Future Income Tax Asset to Expected Realizable Value. For simplicity, most would choose not to set up the asset, only to effectively draw it down again. If the future tax asset is not set up, and the benefit is realized in a later year, it would be accounted for in that year.

(b) The Income Tax Refund Receivable account is to be classified as a current asset on the balance sheet. The Future Tax Asset relates to a tax loss carryfor-ward so it is to be classified as a current asset if the benefits of the carryforward are expected to be realized in the year that immediately follows the balance sheet date. If the benefits are expected in a later year, the Future Tax Asset is to be classified as a noncurrent asset.

The other two accounts are negative components of income tax expense. The income statement would reflect them as follows:

Operating loss before income taxes		$(300,000)
Income Tax Benefit:		
Benefits due to loss carryback	84,000	
Benefits due to loss carryforward	35,000	119,000
Net loss		$(181,000)

(c)

Future Income Tax	15,000	
Income Tax Expense	10,000	
Income Tax Payable		10,000*
Future Tax Asset ($60,000 x 25%)		15,000

*$100,000 – $60,000 = $40,000 taxable income for Year 6.
$40,000 x 25% = $10,000 income tax payable.

Income before income taxes		$ 100,000
Income tax expense:		
Current tax expense	$ 10,000	
Future tax expense	15,000	25,000
Net income		$ 75,000

Exercise 19-7

PURPOSE: This comprehensive exercise will illustrate how the interperiod allocation of income taxes affects the financial statements.

The following facts pertain to the Hess Corporation:
- There were no future taxes on the December 31, 2004 balance sheet.
- Accounting income for 2005 is $113,000.
- Revenue of $20,000 reported on the 2005 income statement will be included on the 2006 income tax return.
- Expense of $7,000 reported on the 2005 income statement will be reported on the 2007 income tax return.
- There are no differences between accounting income and taxable income for 2005, other than the two items mentioned above.
- Enacted tax rates are as follows as of December 31, 2005:

Year	Rate
2005	50%
2006	40%
2007	30%

- Taxable income is expected in all future years.

Instructions

(a) Calculate the amount of taxable income for the year ending December 31, 2005.
(b) Calculate the amount of income tax payable for the year ending December 31, 2005.
(c) Describe how each of the two temporary differences will impact future income tax returns.
(d) Calculate the future taxes to be reported on the balance sheet at December 31, 2005. Describe how they will affect the income statement for the year ending December 31, 2005.
(e) Prepare the journal entry(ies) to record income taxes for 2005.
(f) Describe how the future tax accounts will be reported on the balance sheet at December 31, 2005.
(g) Prepare the section of the 2005 income statement involving income tax expense, beginning with "Income before income taxes."

Solution to Exercise 19-7

(a)

Accounting income for 2005	$ 113,000
Temporary difference originating that gives rise to a future taxable amount	(20,000)
Temporary difference originating that gives rise to a future deductible amount	7,000
Taxable income for 2005	$ 100,000

(b)

Taxable income for 2005	$ 100,000
Enacted tax rate for 2005	50%
Income tax payable for 2005	$ 50,000

(c) The revenue of $20,000 that is being deferred for tax purposes will result in a **taxable amount** (an amount which increases taxable income) on the 2006 income tax return. The expense of $7,000 that is being deferred for tax purposes will result in a **deductible amount** (an amount which reduces taxable income) on the 2007 income tax return.

(d)

	Current Year	Future Years		
	2005	2006	2007	Total
Taxable income	$100,000			
Future taxable (deductible) amounts				
Revenue deferred for tax purposes		$20,000		$20,000
Expense deferred for tax purposes			$(7,000)	$ (7,000)
Enacted tax rate	50%	40%	30%	
Future tax liability		$ 8,000		$ 8,000
Future tax asset			$(2,100)	$ (2,100)

There is no balance in the Future Tax Liability account at the beginning of 2005. Therefore, the journal entry(ies) to record income taxes for 2005 will include an increase in Future Tax Liability (credit) of $8,000. This will cause a corresponding increase in Future Income Tax Expense (debit) of $8,000, which is referred to as **future tax expense** of $8,000. There is no balance in the Future Tax Asset account at the beginning of 2005. Therefore, the journal entry(ies) to record income taxes for 2005 will include an increase in Future Tax Asset (debit) of $2,100. This will cause a corresponding decrease in Future Income Tax Expense Benefit (credit) of $2,100, which is referred to as **future tax benefit** of $2,100. Future tax expense of $8,000 is combined with the future tax benefit of $2,100 on the income statement to produce a net future tax expense of $5,900.

TIP!

Notice that the future tax consequences of the $20,000 revenue item being deferred for tax purposes are recognized in the income statement in 2005 (which is the year in which that revenue item appears in the income statement). Those tax consequences are an increase in taxes of $8,000. Also, notice that the future tax consequences of the $7,000 expense item being deferred for tax purposes are recognized in the income statement in 2005 (which is the year in which that expense item appears in the income statement). Those tax consequences are a reduction in taxes of $2,100.

TIP!

Examine the definition of "taxable temporary difference," "future tax liability," and "future tax expense" and how they apply to this situation. Those definitions and applications are as follows:

Taxable temporary difference: *Definition*—a temporary difference that results in taxable amounts in a future year(s) when the related asset or liability is recovered or settled, respectively. *Application*—a revenue item of $20,000 is being recognized for financial reporting purposes in 2005 but is being deferred for tax purposes. Thus, it may be an accrued revenue for book purposes, which results in recording an account receivable or accrued receivable. In 2006, this asset (receivable) will be recovered (through collection of the receivable) which will result in reporting the $20,000 revenue item on the future (2006) tax return; that is, a taxable amount of $20,000 will appear on the 2006 tax return. Thus, at December 31, 2005, there is a temporary difference giving rise to a future taxable amount of $20,000.

Future tax liability: *Definition*—the future tax consequences attributable to taxable type temporary differences. *Application*—the taxable temporary difference of $20,000 existing at December 31, 2005 will cause an increase of $8,000 in income taxes payable in the future when the related taxable amount is reported on the 2006 tax return. Thus, a future tax liability of $8,000 is to be reported on the balance sheet at December 31, 2005.

Future tax expense: *Definition*—an increase in a future tax liability or a reduction in a future tax asset during the period. *Application*—the increase of $8,000 during 2005 in a future tax liability account on the balance sheet results in a future tax expense of $8,000 on the income statement for 2005.

TIP!

Examine the definitions of "deductible temporary difference," "future tax asset," and "future tax benefit" and how they apply to this situation. Those definitions and applications are as follows:

Deductible temporary difference: *Definition*—a temporary difference that results in deductible amounts in a future year(s) when the related asset or liability is recovered or settled, respectively. *Application*—an expense item of $7,000 is being recognized for financial reporting purposes in 2005 but is being deferred for tax purposes. Thus, it may be an accrued expense for book purposes which results in recording an account payable or accrued payable. In 2007, this accrued payable will be settled (by payment of the payable) which will result in reporting the $7,000 expense item on the future (2007) tax return; that is, a deductible amount of $7,000 will appear on the 2007 tax return. Thus, at December 31, 2005, there is a temporary difference giving rise to a future deductible amount of $7,000.

Future tax asset: *Definition*—the future tax consequences attributable to deductible type temporary differences and loss carryforwards. *Application*—the deductible temporary difference of $7,000 existing at December 31, 2005 will cause a decrease of $2,100 in taxes payable in the future when the related deductible amount is reported on the 2007 tax return. Thus, a future tax asset of $2,100 is to be reported on the balance sheet at December 31, 2005.

Future tax benefit: *Definition*—an increase in a future tax asset or a reduction in a future tax liability during the period. *Application*—the increase of $2,100 during 2005 in a future tax asset account on the balance sheet results in a future tax benefit of $2,100 on the income statement for 2005.

(e) The journal entry to record current tax expense (the amount of income taxes payable) for 2005 as determined by applying the provisions of the enacted tax law to the taxable income for 2005 is as follows:

Current Income Tax Expense	50,000	
Income Tax Payable ($100,000 x 50%)		50,000

The journal entry to record the increase in future tax liability during 2005 is as follows:

Future Income Tax Expense	8,000	
Future Tax Liability		8,000

The journal entry to record the increase in future tax asset during 2005 is as follows:

Future Tax Asset	2,100	
Future Income Tax Expense/Benefit		2,100

TIP!

The three entries above are usually combined to form one compound journal entry as follows:

Income Tax Expense	55,900	
Future Tax Asset	2,100	
Future Tax Liability		8,000
Income Tax Payable		50,000

(f) The future tax accounts on the balance sheet are classified as current or non-current, based on the classification of any related asset or liability. Assuming the $20,000 temporary difference has a related accrued receivable on the books classified as a current asset, the resulting $8,000 future tax liability will be classified as a current liability. Assuming the $7,000 temporary difference has a related accrued payable on the books classified as a noncurrent liability, the resulting $2,100 future tax asset will be classified under "other assets" on the balance sheet. Future tax assets and liabilities are netted for reporting purposes only where they are both current or both noncurrent classification.

(g)

Income before income taxes		$ 113,000
Income tax expense:		
Current expense	$ 50,000	
Future expense	5,900	
Total income tax expense		55,900
Net income		$ 57,100

TIP! Notice that the effective tax rate for 2002 ($55,900 ÷ $113,000) is not equal to the statutory tax rate for 2005 (50%) because a $20,000 revenue item reflected in the $113,000 is tax effected at 40% in determining the related increase in 2005 income tax expense and a $7,000 expense item reflected in the $113,000 is tax effected at 30% in determining the related reduction in 2005 income tax expense.

TIP! Recall the objectives of the asset-liability method of accounting for income taxes and review the solution above to see how these objectives are met. These objectives are:

(1) to recognize the amount of taxes payable (or refundable) for the current year, and

(2) to recognize future tax liabilities and assets for the **future tax consequences** of events that have been recognized in the financial statements or tax returns.

TIP! Think about what will happen in 2006 when the $20,000 taxable temporary difference is eliminated (reverses). In 2006, the $20,000 will appear as a revenue item on the tax return but not on the income statement for that year. Therefore, there will be no future tax liability on the December 31, 2006 balance sheet. The reduction in the future tax liability (a debit) in 2006 will result in a future tax benefit (a credit) of $8,000 on the 2006 income statement and tax expense for 2006 will exceed total income tax expense for that year because the tax consequences of the $20,000 revenue item were reflected in the total income tax expense amount in 2005.

TIP! Think about what will happen in 2007 when the $7,000 deductible temporary difference is eliminated (reverses). In 2007, the $7,000 will appear as an expense item (deduction) on the tax return but not on the income statement for that year. Therefore, there will be no future tax asset on the December 31, 2007 balance sheet. The reduction in the future tax asset (a credit) in 2007 will result in a future tax expense (a debit) of $2,100 on the 2007 income statement and tax expense for that year will be less than total tax expense for 2007 because the tax consequences (a tax savings) of the $7,000 expense item were reflected in the total income tax expense amount in 2005.

Analysis of Multiple-Choice Type Questions

Question

1. A temporary difference arises when a revenue item is reported for tax purposes in a period:

	After it is reported in accounting income	Before it is reported in accounting income
a.	Yes	Yes
b.	Yes	No
c.	No	Yes
d.	No	No

EXPLANATION: Revenue that is taxable **after** it is recognized in accounting income creates a difference between the tax basis of an asset (zero) and its reported amount in the financial statements. This difference will result in a taxable amount in a future period(s) when the reported amount of the asset is settled. (An example is when revenue is earned and accrued to a period in advance of the period in which the related cash is collected and taxed. A receivable is reported on a GAAP basis balance sheet until the period in which the cash collection occurs. The cash collection is a taxable event.)

Revenue that is taxable **before** it is recognized in accounting income creates a difference between the tax basis of a liability (zero) and its reported amount in the financial statements. This difference will result in a deductible amount in a future period(s) when the reported amount of the related liability is settled. (An example situation is when revenue is collected in a period in advance of the period it is earned. The cash collection triggers a taxable event. Unearned revenue is reported on a GAAP basis balance sheet until the period in which the revenue is earned.) (Solution = a.)

Question

2. Which of the following should be recognized for the amount of future tax consequences attributable to temporary differences that will result in deductible amounts in future years?

	Future Tax Asset	Future Tax Liability
a.	Yes	Yes
b.	Yes	No
c.	No	Yes
d.	No	No

EXPLANATION: A temporary difference giving rise to future deductible amounts requires the recognition of a future tax asset for the amount of the future tax consequences related to the existing temporary difference. A temporary difference giving rise to future taxable amounts requires the recognition of a future tax liability for the amount of the future tax consequences related to the existing temporary difference. (Solution = b.)

Question

3. Assuming a 40% tax rate applies to all years involved, which of the following situations will give rise to reporting a future tax liability on the balance sheet?
    I.   A revenue is deferred for financial reporting purposes but not for tax purposes.
    II. A revenue is deferred for tax purposes but not for financial reporting purposes.
    III. An expense is deferred for financial reporting purposes but not for tax purposes.
    IV. An expense is deferred for tax purposes but not for financial reporting purposes.
    a. item II only
    b. items I and II only
    c. items II and III only
    d. items I and IV only

EXPLANATION: Notice that each situation described involves a difference in the timing of revenue or expense recognition for financial reporting purposes (accounting purposes or book purposes) and tax purposes (tax reporting purposes). Thus, each situation involves a temporary difference. For each, determine if future taxable or deductible amounts will occur. Because a constant tax rate applies to all periods involved, a temporary difference resulting in net future taxable amounts will give rise to reporting a future tax liability, and a temporary difference giving rise to net future deductible amounts will result in reporting a future tax asset. Items II and III will give rise to future taxable amounts; items I and IV will give rise to future deductible amounts. (Solution = c.)

Question

4. At the December 31, 2005 balance sheet date, Brooks Corporation reports an accrued receivable for financial reporting purposes but not for tax purposes. When this asset is recovered in 2006, a future taxable amount will occur and:
    a. accounting income will exceed taxable income in 2006.
    b. Brooks will record a decrease in a future tax liability in 2006.
    c. total income tax expense for 2006 will exceed current tax expense for 2006.
    d. Brooks will record an increase in a future tax asset in 2006.

EXPLANATION: The receivable stems from a revenue earned but not received; the revenue has been booked for accounting purposes but not for tax purposes. When this asset (receivable) is recovered through collection of the receivable in 2006, it will result in a taxable amount (taxable revenue on the 2006 income tax return).

Thus, in 2006, accounting income will be less than taxable income because of the elimination (reversal) of the temporary difference. Also in 2006, Brooks will record a decrease in the future tax liability, resulting in a future tax benefit on the 2006 income statement (which causes current tax expense in 2006 to exceed total tax expense for 2006). (Solution = b.)

Question

5. The Colson Corporation collects rent revenue in advance from tenants. The collection of $50,000 in 2005 is reported as revenue for tax purposes; it will be reported on the income statement in 2006 when it is earned. This situation will:
    a. result in future deductible amounts.
    b. result in reporting a future tax liability on the balance sheet at the end of 2005.
    c. cause total income tax expense to be less than income tax payable in 2006.
    d. cause accounting income to exceed taxable income in 2005.

EXPLANATION: The collection and reporting of revenue for tax purposes in a period before it is earned and recognized for book purposes will result in future deductible amounts. A future tax asset is to be recognized for the future tax consequences of the revenue already reflected in the income tax return. In a later period, the unearned revenue per books (a liability) will be settled by delivering goods or services to the customers or by refunding the customers' money; the related outlays are, therefore, tax deductible in the later period in which the revenue is earned. In that later period, accounting income will exceed taxable income. Also, in that later period, total income tax expense will exceed income tax payable (current tax expense) by the amount of the decrease in the related Future Tax Asset account due to the reversal of the temporary difference. (Solution = a.)

Question

6. Kaminsky Company reported future tax expense of $70,000 on its income statement for the year ended December 31, 2005. This could be the result of an increase in a:

	Future Tax Asset	**Future Tax Liability**
a.	Yes	Yes
b.	No	No
c.	Yes	No
d.	No	Yes

EXPLANATION: Think about the journal entry to record future tax expense. The entry involves a debit to Future Income Tax Expense and a credit to a balance sheet account for future taxes. Thus, this credit is either an increase in the Future Tax Liability account or a decrease in the Future Tax Asset account. (Solution = d.)

Question

7. Mix Corporation reported $50,000 in revenues in its 2005 financial statements, of which $22,000 will not be included in the tax return until 2006. The enacted tax rate is 40% for 2005 and 35% for 2006. What amount should Mix report for future income tax liability in its balance sheet at December 31, 2005?
   a. $7,700
   b. $8,800
   c. $9,800
   d. $11,200

EXPLANATION: At the balance sheet date, December 31, 2005, there is a temporary difference of $22,000. That temporary difference will result in a taxable amount of $22,000 in 2006. The taxes payable on that amount will be $7,700 ($22,000 x 35%). The future tax consequences are to be reflected in the financial statements for 2005. The journal entry to record these consequences (assuming no balance of future taxes at the beginning of the period) would include a credit to Future Tax Liability and a debit to Future Income Tax Expense for $7,700. Therefore: (1) revenue of $50,000; and (2) a current tax expense of $11,200 ($28,000 x 40%) and a future tax expense of $7,700 ($22,000 x 35%) will be reflected on the 2005 income statement. Thus, the tax consequences of the full $50,000 appear on the same income statement as the $50,000 revenue, regardless of when the taxes are to be paid. (Solution = a.)

Question

8. Garver Inc. uses the accrual method of accounting for financial reporting purposes and appropriately uses the instalment method of accounting for income tax purposes. Profits of $500,000 recognized for books in 2005 will be collected in the following years:

	Collection of Profits
2006	$ 50,000
2007	100,000
2008	150,000
2009	200,000

   The enacted tax rates are: 40% for 2005, 35% for 2006, 30% for 2007 and 2008, and 25% for 2009. Taxable income is expected in all future years. What amount should be included in the December 31, 2005, balance sheet for the future tax liability related to the above temporary difference?
   a. $0
   b. $17,500
   c. $125,000
   d. $142,500
   e. $200,000

EXPLANATION: The temporary difference will cause future taxable amounts. The future taxable amounts are to be tax effected at the appropriate enacted tax rates for future periods. The calculation is as follows:

2006	$ 50,000 x 35%	=	$ 17,500
2007	100,000 x 30%	=	30,000
2008	150,000 x 30%	=	45,000
2009	200,000 x 25%	=	50,000
Balance of future tax liability, Dec. 31, 2005			$142,500

(Solution = d.)

Question

9. CMP Corporation prepared the following reconciliation for its first year of operations:

Accounting income for 2005	$ 600,000
Tax-free dividends	(50,000)
Originating temporary difference	(150,000)
Taxable income	$ 400,000

The temporary difference will reverse evenly over the next two years at an enacted tax rate of 40%. The enacted tax rate for 2005 is 28%. What amount should be reported in its 2005 income statement for total income tax expense?
   a. $52,000
   b. $112,000
   c. $168,000
   d. $172,000
   e. $192,000

EXPLANATION:

Current tax expense ($400,000 x 28%)	$112,000
Future tax expense ($150,000 x 40%)	60,000
Total income tax expense for 2005	$172,000

The temporary difference is originating and is causing taxable income to be lower than accounting income in the current period; therefore, the temporary difference will result in future taxable amounts. An increase in the related future tax liability account causes a future tax expense to be reported on the income statement. No future taxes are recorded for the tax-free dividends (a permanent difference). (Solution = d.)

Question

10. Refer to the facts of Question 9 above. In CMP's 2005 income statement, what amount should be reported as the future portion of its provision for income taxes?
   a. $80,000 debit
   b. $60,000 debit
   c. $60,000 credit

d. $56,000 credit

e. $42,000 debit

EXPLANATION: The temporary difference existing at December 31, 2005 will result in future taxable amounts and thus gives rise to a future tax liability of $60,000 ($150,000 cumulative temporary difference x 40%) to be reported on the balance sheet at that date. There was no beginning future tax liability (2005 is the first year of operations). Thus, the $60,000 increase in future tax liability results in future tax expense (debit) of $60,000 on the 2005 income statement. No future taxes are recorded for a permanent difference (the dividends) because it will never reverse. (Solution = b.)

Recall that "provision for income taxes" is another name for "income tax expense."	**TIP!**

Question

11. Refer to the facts of Question 9 above. In CMP's 2005 income statement, what amount should be reported as the current portion of its provision for income taxes?
    a. $112,000
    b. $160,000
    c. $168,000
    d. $240,000

EXPLANATION: The taxable income of $400,000 multiplied by the tax rate of 28% for the current year yields a current tax expense of $112,000. (Solution = a.)

Question

12. The Bryan Company has the following cumulative taxable temporary differences:

	12/31/05	**12/31/04**
	$ 450,000	$ 320,000

The tax rate enacted for 2005 is 40%, while the tax rate enacted for future years is 30%. Taxable income for 2005 is $800,000 and there are no permanent differences. Bryan's accounting income for 2005 is:
    a. $350,000.
    b. $670,000.
    c. $930,000.
    d. $1,250,000.

EXPLANATION: Use the format for the reconciliation of accounting income with taxable income (see **Illustration 19-3** and its accompanying **TIP**). Enter the data given. Solve for the unknown. (Solution = c.)

Accounting income $ X
Temporary differences originating this period which
   will result in future taxable amounts
   ($450,000 – $320,000)   (130,000)
Taxable income $ 800,000

Solving for X: X – $130,000 = $800,000
                        X = $930,000

TIP! | No tax rates were used in this solution.

Question

13. Norman Corporation has a future tax asset at December 31, 2005 of $50,000 due to the recognition of potential tax benefits of a tax loss carryforward. The enacted tax rates are as follows: 40% for 2002–2004; 35% for 2005; and 30% for 2006 and thereafter. Assuming that management expects that only 50% of the related benefits will actually be realized, a valuation account should be established in the amount of:
   a. $25,000.
   b. $10,000.
   c. $8,750.
   d. $7,500.

EXPLANATION: Prepare the journal entry to record the necessary valuation account for the portion of the future tax asset that more likely than not will not be realized. That entry is as follows:

Future Income Tax Benefit Due to Loss Carryforward
   (or Future Income Tax Expense)   25,000
      Allowance to Reduce Future Tax Asset
         to Expected Realizable Value   25,000

Because only 50% of the benefits are expected to be realized, a valuation account is needed for the 50% (50% x $50,000 = $25,000) that is not expected to be realized. The tax rates are not relevant in this question. The future tax rate (30%) was used to apply to the tax loss carryforward amount in calculating the $50,000 of potential benefits reflected in the Future Tax Asset account. (Solution = a.)

TIP! | From the facts given, we can determine that the tax loss carryforward amount was $166,666.67 ($50,000 ÷ 30% = $166,666.67).

TIP! | As mentioned previously, many would not set up the asset at all in the situation above. It is a matter of professional judgement.

Question

14. At December 31, 2004 Malcolm Corporation reported a future tax liability of $60,000 which was attributable to a taxable type temporary difference of $200,000. The temporary difference is scheduled to reverse in 2008. During 2005, a new tax law increased the corporate tax rate from 30% to 40%. Which of the following entries will correctly account for the effect of this change on deferred taxes?

    a. Retained Earnings   20,000

            Future Tax Liability   20,000

    b. Retained Earnings   6,000

            Future Tax Liability   6,000

    c. Future Income Tax Expense   6,000

            Future Tax Liability   6,000

    d. Future Income Tax Expense   20,000

            Future Tax Liability   20,000

EXPLANATION: Future tax liabilities and assets are to be adjusted in the period of enactment for the effect of an enacted change in tax laws or rates. The effect is included in income from continuing operations as a component of future income tax expense [$200,000 x (40% – 30%) = $20,000]. (Solution = d.)

Question

15. Freeman Corporation began operations in 2001. There have been no permanent differences or temporary differences to account for since the inception of the business. The following data are available:

Year	Enacted Tax Rate	Taxable Income	Taxes Paid
2001	50%	$100,000	$ 50,000
2002	40%	200,000	80,000
2003	40%	250,000	100,000
2004	30%	300,000	90,000
2005	25%	(510,000)	
2006	20%		

In 2005, Freeman has a loss for tax purposes of $510,000. What amount of income tax benefits should be reported on the 2005 income statement due to this taxable loss?

    a. $198,000

    b. $127,500

    c. $153,000

    d. $102,000

EXPLANATION: The loss is carried back three years and should be applied to the earliest year first as higher tax rates were applied and a higher tax benefit can obtained. The $310,000 loss is therefore applied as follows:

2002	$200,000 x 40%	=	$80,000
2003	250,000 x 40%	=	100,000
2004	60,000 x 30%	=	18,000
	Benefits of loss carryback		$ 198,000

The future rate (2006 and beyond) would only be used to calculate the benefits of a tax loss carryforward. A loss carryforward will result when the loss is larger than the combined taxable income for the three years involved in the carryback period or when a company elects to forego the carryback procedure and use only the carryforward. The tax rate for the current period (2005) is not used to calculate the benefits of a tax loss carryback or carryforward. (Solution = a.)

CHAPTER 20

Pensions and Other Employee Future Benefits

Overview

A pension plan is an arrangement whereby an employer provides benefits to employees after they retire. A defined benefit plan defines the benefits the employees will receive at the time of retirement. The accounting for a defined benefit plan is complex. Pension cost is a function of service cost, interest on the pension liability, return on plan assets, amortization of past service cost, and recognition of gains and losses. Significant disclosures are required. The accounting for health care and other benefits provided to retirees is similar to the accounting for pension plans. The topic "other employee future benefits" is also covered in this chapter.

Study Steps

Understanding the Transaction/Employee Future Benefit Arrangement

What Is a Benefit Plan?

A benefit plan is any arrangement that it is mutually understood by an entity and its employees whereby the entity undertakes to provide its employees with benefits after active service in exchange for their services.

The employer contributes funds to the plan each year based on the agreement, and eventually, the plan will pay out the funds to the employees when they retire. The plan also earns investment income as the funds are invested.

The employee earns the benefit during the service period and gets paid benefits during the retirement period. The employer contributes to the plan during the service period and the plan pays the employee after retirement.

The Employer/Sponsor Financial Statements Versus the Benefit Plan Financial Statements

Accounting and financial reporting for the plan may be viewed from different perspectives:
1. From the perspective of the employer or sponsor company as a separate reporting entity or,
2. From the perspective of the benefit plan itself as a separate reporting entity.

The sponsor company will record an expense and either an asset or liability, depending on funding on its books, in order to recognize the cost of providing the pension benefit. The pension plan, however, will record the plan assets ("PA") and an estimate of the total projected benefit obligation ("PBO") owed to the employee group based on the benefit earned by each employee up to the reporting date. The assets are accumulated from the contributions made by the employer and are held in a benefit fund under the plan. They are usually invested in securities, bonds, or other investments and will be used in settlement of the pension.

The *CICA Handbook* discusses "pension plan financial statements" in Section 4100 and "pension plan accounting as it relates to employer or sponsor financial statements" in Section 3461. This chapter deals with the latter, although it will be seen that changes in the financial statements of the pension plan affect the accounting for the plan on the sponsor financial statements.

The Players In the Transaction

A trustee (e.g., any trust company) often administers the plan, keeps the books and holds the assets. Therefore, the trustee would keep the bank account and the securities/assets that the plan holds as investments. Decisions about which assets to buy, sell, or hold may also be made by the trustee or by an asset manager. An actuary is used to calculate the benefit expense, the benefit obligation, and the cash funding required to meet the obligation. Initially, as the employee earns the benefits, they are not vested. Vesting is the legal entitlement by the employee to the benefits. The benefits become vested once an employee has worked for the company for a certain pre-specified period of time (dictated by company policy and law). If the employee leaves the company prior to the point where the benefits vest, he forfeits the right to the benefits. As long as he waits until the benefits are vested before leaving, he is entitled to receive the full accumulated amount of benefits.

Defined Benefit Versus Defined Contribution Plans

There are two distinct types of plans. One is a defined benefit plan, whereby the employer promises to pay $x to the employee on retirement, and the other is a defined contribution plan, whereby the employer promises only to contribute $x to the plan each year that the employee is employed. The former is preferable to the employee in most cases since the benefit payout is agreed to up-front, whereas with the latter, the employer is not agreeing to the payout, only the annual contribution to the plan. This chapter focuses mainly on accounting for defined benefit plans since accounting for defined contribution plans is relatively straightforward.

Most of the issues arise with accounting for defined benefit plans and revolve around measurement of the estimated cost of the plan to the employer.

Defined Benefit Plans—Details

An example of a defined benefit plan is as follows. The employer promises to pay 2% of an employee's highest paid salary (during the time that the employee works for the company) times the number of years worked. Therefore, if the highest salary is estimated as $40,000 and the employee has worked 10 years to date, she will be entitled to a payout on retirement of:

$40,000 x .02 x 10 = $8,000 per annum

The actuary would then estimate how long the employee would collect the benefit (x years) and discount the stream of payments to determine what the obligation is worth today .This calculation represents an estimate of the pension obligation as of today.

Post-retirement Benefit Plans

These are similar to pension plans except that instead of offering a pension to retired employees, it offers things such as health and legal coverage. The major differences here are that these benefits are generally not funded up-front and the benefits and use of the program are more difficult to predict.

Becoming Proficient in Calculations

This topic involves fairly complex theoretical concepts as well as detailed calculations. It is therefore imperative in mastering this topic to understand **how** to do the calculations as well as why they are being performed.

The work sheet/spreadsheet

The work sheet approach taught in the text is an excellent tool/skill to help you in calculating the numbers that are needed to prepare the journal entry. Therefore, you should familiarize yourself with it as soon as possible.

Remember that you are trying to record the cost associated with the benefit plan in order to accrue it while the employee is providing services to the company and thus match the costs (which are essentially compensatory costs) with revenues generated by the employee.

Remember also that the benefit plan creates a liability to the company that should be recognized.

The work sheet is only used to calculate the benefit expense for defined benefit plans, not defined contribution plans.

The plan creates a liability and should therefore be accrued on the employer financial statements as an expense and a liability. Therefore, assuming that the plan is new, as the employees work and earn their pension benefits, the liability should theoretically be accrued (dr. expense, cr. liability). As the plan is funded, i.e., as the employer contributes funds, it may be appropriate to record the contribution to the plan as a settlement of the liability (dr. liability, cr. cash). To recap, as the employees provide services and earn their pension, the cost gets recorded, as does a liability. As the employer sets aside funds for this liability, the liability reduces.

Incorporating CICA Handbook Section 3461 into the Work Sheet

It is useful to begin to bring in the *CICA Handbook* requirements at this point. The *CICA Handbook* does not require that the full liability be recorded nor the full amount of subsequent changes to the liability. The CICA approach in *CICA Handbook* Section 3461 defers and amortizes many changes to the liability account. The deferred amounts get deferred in a memo account. That is, they do not get recorded on the employer financial statements when they occur. In subsequent years, a portion of the deferred amount (memo account) will get accrued/amortized on the employer financial statements as dr. (cr.) benefit expense and cr. (dr.) liability such that, eventually, the full amount will get recorded. The work sheet helps us track the changes in the accrued benefit obligation, (showing those booked by the employer and those not booked), the plan asset account, and the memo account.

CICA Handbook also gives a formula for calculating pension expense, which is summarized and defined in **Illustration 20-1**.

Settlements/Curtailments

Settlements or curtailments also affect PBO and PA. For example, if an employee leaves and his benefits are vested, the plan must settle with him and actually pay him the value of the benefits. This results in the PBO decreasing (since the obligation is settled), PA decreasing (as there is a cash payout), and there may be a gain or loss which goes straight to pension expense. The gain or loss does not get deferred and amortized since the employee is no longer with the plan.

A settlement is defined in the *CICA Handbook* as a transaction in which an entity substantially discharges or settles all, or part of, a PBO. (i.e., lump sum cash payment to employee or purchasing insurance or annuity contracts.) The employer no longer has the actuarial and investment risks but employees continue to earn benefits.

A curtailment on the other hand is an event which results in a significant reduction of the expected years of future service for active employees or which eliminates the right to earn benefits for future services. Thus employees are no longer able to earn future benefits but the actuarial and investment risks remain with the employer.

A Critical Analysis of *CICA Handbook* Section 3461

The Unrecognized Pension Obligation/Asset

To the extent that the employees have earned more benefits than the employer has funded at any point in time—PBO>PA on the pension plan financial statements—there exists a deficit in the pension plan (assets less obligation). That is, if the employer suddenly liquidated the plan, there would not be enough assets to cover the liability. Should this full deficit be recorded as a liability on the books of the employer? At present, it is not always recorded, as some of it is in the memo account.

The unfunded obligation or deficit would appear to meet the definition of a liability according to Section 1000 in the *CICA Handbook* in that:
- The obligation embodies a duty to others (i.e., to pay the pension).
- There is no discretion to avoid the responsibility in that the arrangement is a legal, binding contract.
- The event obligating the employer has already occurred (i.e., the employees have earned the pension).

However, as noted previously, all changes in the asset and obligation accounts (and the net amount or deficit/surplus) are eventually booked through the pension expense and hence the employer's balance sheet. Despite this, the CICA has adopted the approach of not recognizing these amounts immediately. Instead, the practice is to recognize them over time by amortizing them. This is a compromise position of sorts, which was likely influenced by politics.

The Use of Management Estimates

When the actuary calculates the pension obligation, the current service cost, and the amount that the employer should contribute to the plan, he must determine which underlying assumptions to use (i.e., discount rates, rates of return on assets, mortality rates, etc.). The actuary actually does two separate calculations of the estimated pension obligation:
- to determine the amount of funding or the contribution that the employer should make each year to the plan.
- to determine the best estimate of pension costs and obligation that the employer should book on his financial statements in order to match costs with revenues.

For the calculations, often different assumptions are used. For the latter calculation, management provides what it feels are the best or most realistic assumptions (management best estimate assumptions). For funding purposes, the actuary uses more conservative assumptions since the calculations will determine the amount of cash that the employer contributes. It is better to advise the employer to contribute a bit more to the plan than too little, since the employer is ultimately responsible for providing an agreed upon pension and since he relies on the actuary to advise him how much to contribute each year in order to meet that promise.

The issue really revolves around the management best estimate assumptions. Assumptions with respect to the expected rate of return on the assets and the discount rate are very subjective. Furthermore, there is the issue of whether to use long-term or short-term rates. The *CICA Handbook* gives some guidance; however, significant judgement must be used.

The choice of discount rate can result in PV calculations of the pension obligation that are very different, with a higher rate resulting in a lower PV. In practice, the actual rates used vary widely. The *CICA Handbook* requires significant disclosures to signal the softness of this number.

Tips on Chapter Topics

TIP! The **accumulated benefit obligation (ABO)** measures the pension obligation at a balance sheet date using current salary levels. The **projected benefit obligation (PBO)** measures the same obligation using future salary levels. Notice which of these is used in various calculations in the chapter and whether a beginning-of-period or end-of-period balance is required for a particular purpose. Such as:

1. The **beginning** balance of the **PBO** is used to calculate the interest component of pension expense for the period, on the assumption that all other transactions affecting the PBO take place at year end.

2. The greater of the **beginning** balance of the **PBO or market-related plan asset value** (beginning of period) is used to calculate the 10% corridor in determining the need for amortization of the balance of unrecognized net gain or loss.

3. The **ending** balance of the **PBO** is used to reconcile the funded status of the plan with amounts reported in the employer's balance sheet.

TIP! The **actual return on plan assets** is the increase in plan assets from interest, dividends, and realized and unrealized changes in the market value of the plan assets. The actual return on pension plan assets can be calculated by (1) finding the change in the fair value of plan assets, (2) deducting contributions, and (3) adding benefits paid. It is compared to the **expected return on plan assets**, with the difference being recorded as actuarial gains or losses and subject to the **Corridor Approach**.

TIP! A debit balance in the Prepaid/Accrued Pension Cost account is reported as an asset; whereas, a credit balance is reported as a liability.

TIP! Plan adoptions or amendments often include provisions to increase benefits for employee service provided in prior years. This **past service cost** is allocated to pension expense in the current and future periods.

Changes in the projected benefit obligation caused by changes in actuarial assumptions are also recorded as actuarial gains or losses. The net gain or loss is amortized

Illustration 20-1   201

by the **corridor approach**; the net gain or loss is amortized when it exceeds 10% of the larger of the beginning balances of the projected benefit obligation or the market-related value of the plan assets.

Although the balances of the projected benefit obligation, plan assets, unamortized past service cost, and unamortized net actuarial gain or loss do **not** appear on the employer's balance sheet, they have an impact on the determination of amounts that do appear on the employer's income statement and balance sheet and amounts that appear in the notes to those financial statements.

TIP!

A pension work sheet includes both formal entries and memo entries. The formal journal entry to record pension expense and the annual contribution to the pension fund is a debit to Pension Expense for the appropriate amount calculated, a credit to Cash for the amount funded for the period, and a debit or credit to Prepaid/Accrued Pension Cost for the difference.

TIP!

Illustration 20-1
Components of Pension Expense

CALCULATION OF PENSION EXPENSE:

      SERVICE COST
+   INTEREST ON THE PBO LIABILITY
−   EXPECTED RETURN ON PLAN ASSETS
+   AMORTIZATION OF UNRECOGNIZED PAST SERVICE COST
+/− AMORTIZATION OF NET ACTUARIAL GAIN OR LOSS
+/− AMORTIZATION OF TRANSITIONAL ASSET OR
      OBLIGATION.
=   PENSION EXPENSE

DEFINITIONS OF COMPONENTS:

Service Cost. The expense caused by the increase in pension benefits payable (the projected benefit obligation) to employees because of their services rendered during the current year. Actuaries calculate **service cost** as the present value of the new benefits earned by employees during the year.

Interest on the Liability. Because a pension is a deferred compensation arrangement, there is a time value of money factor. As a result, it is recorded on a discounted basis. Interest accrues each year on the projected benefit obligation just as it does on any discounted debt. *CICA Handbook* Section 3461 requires the use of the current market rate or the current settlement rate.

Expected Return on Plan Assets. The return earned by the accumulated pension fund assets in a particular year is relevant in measuring the net cost to the employer of sponsoring an employee pension plan. The expected rate of return, based on the expected long term rate of return on plan assets, applied to fair value of plan assets, will reduce pension expense in the year. Expected rate of return is used instead of actual to avoid large fluctuations from one year to the next. The difference between expected and actual is recorded as actuarial gains or losses and is subject to the corridor approach for amortization purposes.

Amortization of Unrecognized Past Service Cost. Pension plan amendments (including initiation of a pension plan) often include provisions to increase benefits (in rare situations to decrease benefits) for employee service provided in prior years. Because plan amendments are granted with the expectation that the employer will realize economic benefits in future periods, the cost (past service cost) of providing these retroactive benefits is allocated to pension expense in the future, specifically over the expected period to full eligibility of the affected employee group.

Amortization of the Net Actuarial Gain or Loss. Actuarial gains and losses arise from two sources: (1) a change in actuarial assumptions; that is, assumptions as to the occurrence of future events that affect the measurement of the future benefit costs and obligations; and (2) experience gains and losses—the difference between what has occurred and what was expected to occur, including expected versus actual return on plan assets. The amortization is subject to the corridor method.

Amortization of Transitional Asset or Obligation. A transitional asset or liability will result from adopting the requirements for the first time. It will be amortized over the expected average remaining service life of the employee group covered by the plan.

In summary, the components of pension expense and their effect are as follows:
- Service cost (increases pension expense).
- Interest on the liability (increases pension expense).
- Expected return on plan assets (decreases pension expense).
- Amortization of unrecognized past service cost (increases pension expense).
- Amortization of net actuarial gain or loss (decreases or increases pension expense).
- Amortization of transitional asset or obligation (decreases or increases pension expense).

Exercise 20-1

PURPOSE: This exercise will enable you to practise computing pension expense.

The following data relate to Kleen Company's pension plan for the year 2005:

Accrued pension cost at January 1, 2005	$ 6,000
Actual and expected return on plan assets	60,000
Benefits paid	40,000
Contributions to plan	105,000
Plan assets at January 1, 2005	684,000
Past service cost amortization	15,000
Projected benefit obligation at January 1, 2005	850,000
Service cost	90,000
Unrecognized past service cost at January 1, 2005	160,000
Interest rate	10%

Instructions

Calculate the pension expense for 2005.

Solution to Exercise 20-1

Service cost	$ 90,000
Interest cost ($850,000 x 10%)	85,000
Expected return on plan assets	(60,000)
Amortization of unrecognized past service cost	15,000
Pension expense for 2005	$ 130,000

APPROACH: Whenever you are to calculate pension expense, use the format in **Illustration 20-1**. Select or solve for the data needed.

TIP!
Because the actual return on plan assets equals the expected return on plan assets for 2005, there was no difference (unexpected gain or loss) to include in net actuarial gains and losses, which would be subject to the corridor approach in the following year.

TIP!
The calculation of interest expense may be done on a weighted average basis as well. For example, since the service cost increases the PBO and the benefits paid decrease the PBO, it may be better to average out these changes to calculate interest expense. Either method is acceptable.

Illustration 20-2
Changes in the Projected Benefit Obligation and Plan Assets

> Projected benefit obligation, balance at beginning of the period
> +   Service cost for the period
> +   Interest cost
> −   Benefits paid to employees during the period
> +/−   <u>Actuarial gains and losses in period</u>
> =   <u>Projected benefit obligation, balance at end of the period</u>

> Plan assets, fair value at beginning of the period
> +   Contributions to plan during the period (employer and employees)
> −   Benefits paid to employees during the period
> +/−   <u>Actual return on plan assets during the period*</u>
> =   <u>Plan assets, fair value at end of the period</u>

*Includes realized earnings such as dividends and interest, realized gains and losses due to sales of plan assets, and unrealized asset gains and losses from changes in the fair value of plan assets.

TIP! It is helpful to know the various reasons for changes in the projected benefit obligation and plan assets over the course of time. For example, if you are given the amounts funded by the employer during the year, the benefits paid from the pension fund during the year, and the net increase in fair value of plans assets for the year, you can solve for the actual return on plan assets for the period.

TIP! Although the balance of the projected benefit obligation and the balance of plan assets are **not** reported on the employer's balance sheet, these balances are used in determining certain amounts that do appear in the financial statements.

TIP! One of the reasons for a change in the balance of the projected benefit obligation is "actuarial gains and losses" which are usually due to changes in actuarial assumptions. Actuarial **gains reduce** the PBO balance, whereas liability **losses increase** the PBO balance.

TIP! One of the reasons for a change in the plan assets' fair value balance is the "actual return on plan assets during the period." This actual return includes unexpected asset gains and losses. Asset **gains increase** the plan assets' fair value balance, whereas asset **losses reduce** the plan assets' fair value balance.

Exercise 20-2

PURPOSE: This exercise illustrates the mechanics of the pension work sheet.

Instructions

(a) Using the data in **Exercise 20-1**, prepare a pension work sheet. Insert January 1, 2005 balances and show the journal entry for pension expense for 2005 and the December 31, 2005 balances.

(b) Prepare a reconciliation schedule.

Preparation of pension work sheet and reconciliation schedule:

In using the work sheet, the Prepaid/Accrued Pension Cost account balance equals the net of the balances in the memo accounts. If the net of the memo record balances is a **credit**, the reconciling amount in the prepaid/accrued cost column will be a **credit** equal in amount.   **TIP!**

The "Memo Record" columns maintain balances of the **unrecognized (noncapitalized)** pension items.   **TIP!**

The reconciliation schedule reconciles the balances of the off-balance-sheet items with the prepaid/accrued pension cost balance reported in the balance sheet.   **TIP!**

Solution to Exercise 20-2

(a)

Kleen Company
Pension Work Sheet - 2005*

	General Journal Entries			Memo Record		
	Annual Pension Expense	Cash	Prepaid/ Accrued Cost	Projected Benefit Obligation	Plan Assets	Unrecognized Past Service Cost
Balance, January 1, 2005			6,000 Cr.	850,000 Cr.	684,000 Dr.	160,000 Dr.
(1) Service cost	90,000 Dr.			90,000 Cr.		
(2) Interest cost	85,000 Dr.			85,000 Cr.		
(3) Expected return	60,000 Cr.				60,000 Dr.	
(4) Amortization of PSC	15,000 Dr.					15,000 Cr.
(5) Contributions		105,000 Cr.			105,000 Dr.	
(6) Benefits				40,000 Dr.	40,000 Cr.	
Journal entry for 2005	130,000 Dr.	105,000 Cr.	25,000 Cr.			
Balance, December 31, 2005			31,000 Cr.	985,000 Cr.	809,000 Dr.	145,000 Dr.

*The use of this pension entry work sheet is recommended and illustrated by Paul B.W. Miller, "The New Pension Accounting (Part 2)," Journal of Accountancy (February 1987), pp. 86-94.

(b)

Reconciliation Schedule - December 31, 2005

Projected benefit obligation (Credit)	$(985,000)
Plan assets at fair value (Debit)	809,000
Funded status	(176,000)
Unrecognized past service cost (Debit)	145,000
Prepaid/accrued pension cost (Credit)	$ (31,000)

Exercise 20-3

PURPOSE: This exercise illustrates the use of the corridor approach to amortizing unrecognized gains and losses.

Beginning-of-the-year present values for Learn Company's projected benefit obligation and beginning-of-the-year market-related values for its pension plan assets are:

	Projected Benefit Obligation	Market-Related Value of Plan Assets
2005	$ 3,200,000	$ 3,600,000
2006	3,700,000	3,900,000
2007	4,300,000	4,200,000
2008	5,000,000	4,800,000

The cumulative unrecognized net actuarial gain is $300,000 on January 1, 2005. The unrecognized net gain or loss that occurred during the year is: 2005, $210,000 gain; 2006, $25,000 loss; 2007, $50,000 loss; and 2008, $100,000 gain. The average remaining service period per employee is 12 years in 2005 and 2006, and is 15 years in 2007 and 2008.

Instructions

Set up an appropriate schedule to calculate the amount of unrecognized actuarial net gain or loss to be amortized to pension expense each year using the corridor approach.

Solution to Exercise 20-3

	Projected Benefit Obligation (1)	Corridor Amortization Schedule Market-Related Value of Plan Assets (1)	10% Corridor (2)	Cumulative Unrecognized Net Gain (1)	Minimum Amortization of Gain
Year					
2005	$ 3,200,000	$3,600,000	$360,000	$300,000	$ -0-
2006	3,700,000	3,900,000	390,000	510,000	10,000 (3)
2007	4,300,000	4,200,000	430,000	475,000 (4)	3,000 (5)
2008	5,000,000	4,800,000	500,000	422,000 (6)	- 0-

(1) All as of the beginning of the year.
(2) 10% of the greater of projected benefit obligation or plan assets' market-related value.
(3) ($510,000 – $390,000) ÷ 12 = $10,000.
(4) $510,000 – $10,000 net gain amortized – $25,000 loss = $475,000.
(5) ($475,000 – $430,000) ÷ 15 = $3,000.
(6) $475,000 – $3,000 net gain amortized – $50,000 loss = $422,000.

TIP!

Unexpected gains or losses from changes in the balance of the projected benefit obligation due to changes in actuarial assumptions are called "actuarial gains and losses". These actuarial gains and losses (gains result from unexpected decreases in the liability balance and losses result from unexpected increases) are deferred (unrecognized). They are combined in the same Unrecognized Net Actuarial Gain or Loss account used for asset gains and losses (this is an off-balance-sheet account). (Refer to the "Explanation" in the Solution for Exercise 20-5 for a description of asset gains and losses.) All unexpected gains and losses are accumulated from year to year, off-balance-sheet, in a memo account.

If the balance of the Unrecognized Net Actuarial Gain or Loss account stays within the upper and lower limits of the corridor, no amortization is required—the unrecognized net gain or loss balance is carried forward unchanged. If amortization is required, the minimum amortization amount is the excess (beyond the corridor) gain or loss divided by the average remaining service period to expected retirement of all active employees.

Exercise 20-4

PURPOSE: This exercise requires calculation of actual return on plan assets.

White Company reports the following pension plan data:

Fair value of plan assets, January 1, 2005	$ 3,200,000
Fair value of plan assets, December 31, 2005	3,600,000
Benefits paid during 2005	460,000
Contributions to the plan during 2005	640,000

Instructions

Calculate the actual return on plan assets for 2005.

Solution to Exercise 20-4

Plan assets, fair value at beginning of the year	$3,200,000
Contributions to plan at end of the year	640,000
Benefits paid to employees at end of the year	(460,000)
Actual return on plan assets during the year	X
Plan assets, fair value at end of the year	$3,600,000

Solving for X: X = $220,000

APPROACH: Write down the format for reconciling beginning and ending balances of plan assets at fair value (see **Illustration 20-2**). Enter the data given. Solve for the unknown.

Exercise 20-5

PURPOSE: This exercise requires calculation of the expected return on plan assets and examines its use in determining pension expense.

White Company (from **Exercise 20-4**) also reports:

Market-related asset value, January 1, 2005	$ 3,000,000
Market-related asset value, December 31, 2005	3,300,000
Expected return on plan assets	10%

Instructions

(a) Calculate the expected return on plan assets during 2005 and the unexpected gain or loss.
(b) Explain how the actual return and the unexpected gain or loss enter into the calculation of pension expense for 2005.

Solution to Exercise 20-5

(a) 10% x $3,000,000 = $300,000 expected return on plan assets.

Expected return	$ 300,000
Actual return (Exercise 20-4)	220,000
Unexpected loss	$ 80,000

Illustration 20-3   209

(b) The expected return of $300,000 is the amount actually used to calculate current pension expense. This is to avoid wide fluctuations in pension expense from year to year. The difference between expected and actual is included in net actuarial gains and losses where amortization is subject to the corridor method.

EXPLANATION: The expected return on plan assets is determined by multiplying the expected rate of return on plan assets times the beginning-of-the-year market-related asset value. Another alternative is to "average" the contributions during the year and the benefit payments made. This will calculate the average dollar amount of assets invested in the year, which will then be used to calculate the expected rate of return. The CICA example in *CICA Handbook* Section 3461 appears to favour the weighted average approach. If a contribution is made at the beginning of the year, the method shown in Exercise 20-5 would not reflect the economic reality that more assets were available for investing than was used in the calculation of expected return. However, since the calculation is an estimate anyway, it is unlikely that either approach will result in a material difference in calculations.

The market-related asset value is used in two calculations: (1) the expected return on plan assets, and (2) the determination of the corridor. In both cases, it is the market-related asset value at the beginning of the year (see above discussions concerning use of weighted average calculations for expected return).

TIP!

Illustration 20-3
Pension Reconciliation Schedule

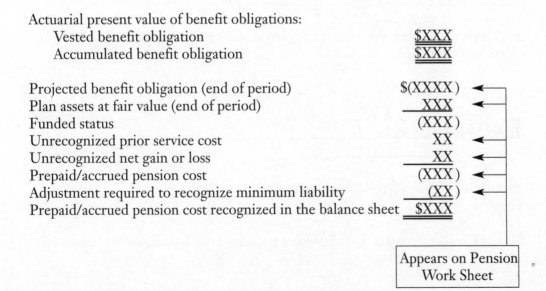

Pension Reconciliation Schedule

Actuarial present value of benefit obligations:
    Vested benefit obligation $XXX
    Accumulated benefit obligation $XXX

Projected benefit obligation (end of period) $(XXXX)
Plan assets at fair value (end of period)   XXX
Funded status   (XXX)
Unrecognized prior service cost   XX
Unrecognized net gain or loss   XX
Prepaid/accrued pension cost   (XXX)
Adjustment required to recognize minimum liability   (XX)
Prepaid/accrued pension cost recognized in the balance sheet $XXX

Appears on Pension Work Sheet

Exercise 20-6

PURPOSE: This exercise illustrates the schedule used to reconcile the funded status of a pension plan with the asset/liability reported on the balance sheet.

Steele Company provided the following data at December 31, 2005:

Market-related asset value	$ 610,000
Plan assets (at fair value)	590,000
Projected benefit obligation	850,000
Unrecognized net actuarial gain	30,000
Unrecognized past service cost	190,000

Instructions

Present the schedule reconciling the funded status with the asset/liability reported on the balance sheet. Assume no prepaid/accrued pension cost existed at the beginning of the year.

Solution to Exercise 20-6

Projected benefit obligation	$(850,000)
Plan assets at fair value	590,000
Funded status	(260,000)
Unrecognized past service cost	190,000
Unrecognized net gain	(30,000)
Pension liability reported on the balance sheet	$(100,000)

APPROACH AND EXPLANATION: This plan is clearly underfunded, since assets are less than obligations. The plan is reconciled to the balance sheet liability by allowing for the unrecognized liabilities and gains. Note that these are unrecognized in the employer balance sheet only; they are already included in the PBO and plan assets as appropriate.

Exercise 20-7

PURPOSE: This exercise is related to post-retirement benefits other than pensions.

Handy Company reports the following data related to post-retirement benefits for 2005:

PBO at January 1, 2005	$ 540,000
Actual return on plan assets in 2005	27,000
Expected return on plan assets in 2005	30,000
Service cost	52,000
Discount rate	10%
Benefits paid	43,000
Contributions (funding)	60,000
Amortization of unrecognized net actuarial gain	2,000
Amortization of transition liability	36,000

Instructions

(a) Calculate the amount of post-retirement expense for 2005.
(b) Prepare the journal entry to record post-retirement expense and Handy's contribution for 2005.
(c) Calculate the amount of PBO at December 31, 2005.

> **TIP!**
> PBO stands for Post-retirement Benefit Obligation. PBO is the actuarial present value of all benefits earned to dare and expected to be paid after retirement to employees and their dependents.

Solution to Exercise 20-7

(a) Service cost	$ 52,000
Interest cost (10% x $540,000)	54,000
Expected return on plan assets	(30,000)
Amortization of unrecognized net gain	(2,000)
Amortization of transition amount	36,000
Post-retirement expense—2005	$ 110,000

EXPLANATION: Post-retirement expense consists of many of the same components used to calculate pension expense.

> **TIP!**
> Service cost is the portion of the PBO attributed to employee service during the period.

> **TIP!**
> Interest cost is the discount rate times the PBO at the beginning of the year. However, similar arguments concerning use of the weighted-average method apply here. See the discussions concerning interest and expected return on asset calculations for pensions above.

> **TIP!**
> A net actuarial gain ultimately reduces the cost to the employer of post-retirement benefits; therefore, the amortization of a net gain reduces post-retirement expense. Note that this is also subject to the corridor approach.

> **TIP!**
> At the beginning of the year of adoption of *CICA Handbook* Section 3461 a **transition amount** (obligation or asset) is calculated as the difference between (1) the PBO and (2) the fair value of the plan assets, plus any accrued obligation or less any

prepaid cost (asset). Because most plans are unfunded and most employers are accruing post-retirement benefit costs for the first time, large transition obligations occur. The amortization of a transition obligation increases post-retirement expense.

(b) Post-retirement Expense (Calculated above)   110,000
       Prepaid/Accrued Cost ($104,000 – $60,000)   50,000
       Cash   60,000

EXPLANATION: The journal entry to record post-retirement expense is similar to the entry to record pension expense.

(c) PBO at January 1, 2005 $ 540,000
    Service cost for 2005   52,000
    Interest cost for 2005   54,000
    Benefits paid in 2005   (43,000)
       APBO at December 31, 2005 $ 603,000

EXPLANATION: Examine the PBO column in a post-retirement benefits work sheet in your text. Note that service cost and interest cost increase the PBO and benefits paid decrease the PBO. A change in actuarial assumptions will also affect the PBO.

Analysis of Multiple-Choice Type Questions

Question

1. The Minnow Corp. has a defined benefit pension plan. Information for the plan for 2005 is as follows:

Service cost	$320,000
Actual and expected return on plan assets	70,000
Amortization of unrecognized past service cost	10,000
Annual interest on pension obligation	100,000

What amount should Minnow report as pension expense in its income statement for 2005?
a. $500,000
b. $420,000
c. $360,000
d. $340,000

EXPLANATION: The pension expense is determined by the following calculation:

Service cost	$320,000
Actual and expected return on plan assets	(70,000)
Amortization of unrecognized past service cost	10,000
Annual interest on pension obligation	100,000
Total pension expense for 2005	$360,000

(Solution = c.)

Question

2.   Which of the following items should be included in the net pension cost calculated by an employer who sponsors a defined benefit pension plan for its employees?

	Fair value of plan assets	**Amortization of unrecognized past service cost**
a.	Yes	Yes
b.	Yes	No
c.	No	Yes
d.	No	No

EXPLANATION: Mentally list the components of pension expense (refer to **Illustration 20-1**). Compare the items in the question with the items in the list. Amortization of unrecognized past service cost is a component of net pension cost. While the expected return on plan assets is a component, the fair value of the plan assets is not used in the net pension cost calculation. (Solution = c.)

Question

3.   The following information is related to the pension plan of Jay, Inc. for 2005.

Actual return on plan assets	$80,000
Amortization of unrecognized net actuarial gain	33,000
Amortization of unrecognized past service cost	60,000
Expected return on plan assets	92,000
Interest on projected benefit obligation	145,000
Service cost	320,000

Pension expense for 2005 is:
a. $400,000.
b. $412,000.
c. $466,000.
d. $478,000.

EXPLANATION: Service cost and interest cost increase pension expense. The expected return on plan assets reduces pension expense. The amortization of the net actuarial unrecognized gain reduces pension expense. Amortization of unrecognized past service cost increases pension expense. The calculation is:

Service cost	$ 320,000
Interest cost	145,000
Expected return on plan assets	(92,000)
Amortization of unrecognized net actuarial gain	(33,000)
Amortization of unrecognized past service cost	60,000
Pension expense for 2005	$ 400,000

(Solution = a.)

Question

4. The following data are for the pension plan for the employees of Chip Company.

	1/1/04	12/31/04	12/31/05
Plan assets (at fair value)	$2,300,000	3,000,000	3,300,000
Accumulated benefit obligation	2,500,000	2,600,000	3,400,000
Projected benefit obligation	2,700,000	2,800,000	3,700,000
Unrecognized net actuarial loss	-0-	480,000	500,000
Market interest rate (for year)		10%	9%
Expected rate of return (for year)		8%	7%

Chip's contribution was $420,000 in 2005 and benefits paid were $375,000. Chip estimates that the average remaining service life is 15 years. The actual return on plan assets in 2005 is:
   a. $155,000.
   b. $200,000.
   c. $255,000.
   d. $300,000.

EXPLANATION: Recall that the actual return is found by (1) calculating the change in plan assets (at fair value), (2) deducting contributions, and (3) adding benefits paid. The calculation is:

Plan assets, 12/31/05	$ 3,300,000
Plan assets, 12/31/04	3,000,000
Increase during 2005	300,000
Deduct contributions	(420,000)
Add benefits paid	375,000
Actual return, 2005	$ 255,000

(Solution = c.)

QUESTION

5. Refer to the data in Question 4. You know that the actual return on plan assets in 2005 is $255,000. The net actuarial gain or loss on plan assets in 2005 is:
   a. $24,000 gain.
   b. $38,000 gain.
   c. $45,000 gain.
   d. $52,000 gain.

EXPLANATION: The expected return is the expected rate of return times the asset value (at fair value) at the beginning of the year. For 2005, the expected return is $231,000 (7% x $3.3 million). Since the actual return is $255,000, there is a net actuarial gain of $52,000 ($255,000 – $231,000) for 2005. (Solution = a.)

QUESTION

6. Refer to the data in Question 4. The corridor for amortization of unreconized net gain or loss in 2005 is:
   a. $280,000.
   b. $290,000.
   c. $300,000.
   d. $370,000.

EXPLANATION: The corridor is 10% of the larger of the beginning balances of the projected benefit obligation ($2.8 million) or the value of the plan assets ($3 million). Chip's corridor in 2005 is $300,000 (10% x $3 million). (Solution = c.)

> The cumulative unrecognized net actuarial gain or loss is the result of both asset gains and losses and liability gains and losses experienced to date.

TIP!

QUESTION

7. Refer to the data in Question 4. You know that the corridor for 2005 is $300,000. The amount of unrecognized net actuarial loss amortized in 2005 is:
   a. $12,667.
   b. $12,000.
   c. $32,000.
   d. $33,333.

EXPLANATION: The amount of unrecognized net actuarial loss that is subject to being amortized is the portion of the unrecognized net actuarial loss at the beginning of the period that is greater than the corridor. The minimum amortization is calculated by dividing the excess over the corridor by the average remaining service life. The amount of net loss in excess of the corridor is $180,000 ($480,000 – $300,000). The net actuarial loss amortized in 2005 is $12,000 ($180,000 ÷ 15). (Solution = b.)

QUESTION

8. A corporation has a defined benefit plan. An accrued pension cost liability will result at the end of the first year if:
    a. The accumulated benefit obligation exceeds the fair value of the plan assets.
    b. The fair value of the plan assets exceeds the accumulated benefit obligation.
    c. The amount of employer contributions exceeds the net periodic pension expense.
    d. The amount of net periodic pension expense exceeds the amount of employer contributions.

EXPLANATION: The journal entry to record the employer contributions and annual pension expense is balanced by either a debit to Prepaid Pension Cost or a credit to Accrued Pension Cost, depending on the relationship of the amount of net periodic pension cost (debit to Pension Expense) and the amount being funded (credit to Cash). For there to be a credit to Accrued Pension Cost, the debit to Pension Expense exceeded the credit to Cash in this entry.

Pension Expense	Expense Calculation
Prepaid Pension Cost	Difference
or Accrued Pension Cost	Difference
Cash	Amount Funded

(Solution = d.)

QUESTION

9. The following pension plan information is for Kent Company at December 31, 2005.

Projected benefit obligation	$ 5,600,000
Plan assets (at fair value)	4,100,000
Unrecognized past service cost	360,000
Pension expense for 2005	2,000,000
Contributions for 2005	1,600,000

Prior to 2005, cumulative pension expense equalled cumulative contributions. The amount to be reported as the total accrued pension cost liability on the December 31, 2005 balance sheet is:

a. $700,000.
b. $900,000.
c. $1,140,000.
d. $1,500,000.

EXPLANATION:

Projected benefit obligation	$5,600,000
Plan assets (at fair value)	(4,100,000)
Funded status (underfunded)	1,500,000
Unrecognized past service costs	360,000
Accrued pension cost liability	$1,140,000

The accrued pension cost liability for pensions in this case is the excess of the projected benefit obligation over the fair value of plan assets, with an adjustment for unrecognized amounts such as past service costs. (Solution = c.)

QUESTION

10. Larson Corp. has a defined benefit plan for its employees. All of the following must be disclosed (either in the body of the financial statements or in the notes) **except:**
    a. All of the major components of pension expense.
    b. A schedule of the changes in employees covered by the plan.
    c. A reconciliation showing how the projected benefit obligation changed from the beginning to the end of the period.
    d. The funded status of the plan.

EXPLANATION: Before reading the answer choices, briefly think of the list of items that must be disclosed with regard to a pension plan. Then compare your list with the answer selections. The disclosure requirements for pensions are extensive. The following information, if not disclosed in the body of the financial statements, should be disclosed in the notes:
    1. A schedule showing all the major components of pension expense.
    2. A reconciliation showing how the projected benefit obligation and the fair value of the plan assets changed from the beginning of to the end of the period.
    3. The funded status of the plan (difference between the projected benefit obligation and fair value of the plan assets) and the amount recognized and not recognized in the financial statements. (Solution = b.)

QUESTION

11. The following data relate to the Shield Company post-retirement plan for 2005:

PBO at January 1, 2005	$ 400,000
Service cost	95,000
Discount rate	10%
Average remaining service periods to full eligibility	20 years
Average remaining service life of employees in plan	25 years

    The amount of post-retirement expense for 2005, assuming they are applying the requirements of Section 3461 on a prospective basis, is:
    a. $111,000.
    b. $151,000.
    c. $155,000.
    d. $161,000.

EXPLANATION: Post-retirement expense on a prospective includes service cost, interest cost, an adjustment for expected return on plan assets, and amortization of the transition amount. The interest cost is the discount rate times the PBO at the beginning of the year. (See weighted average discussion above). There is no actual return or expected return on plan assets for 2005 because there were no plan assets as of the beginning of 2005. The transition amount is amortized over the average remaining service periods to expected retirement.

Service cost	$ 95,000
Interest cost (10% x $400,000)	40,000
Amortization of transition amount ($400,000 ÷ 25)	16,000
Post-retirement expense for 2005	$ 151,000

(Solution = b.)

QUESTION

12. The following data relate to the Boyd Company post-retirement benefits plan for 2005:

PBO at January 1, 2005	$ 300,000
Service cost	82,000
Discount rate	8%
Actual return on plan assets in 2005	13,000
Expected return on plan assets in 2005	17,000

The amount of post-retirement expense for 2005 is (assuming retroactive adoption of Section 3461).

   a. $89,000.
   b. $93,000.
   c. $97,000.
   d. $106,000.

EXPLANATION: Recall that post-retirement expense includes service cost, interest cost, an adjustment for expected return on plan assets, and amortization for the transition amount (if any). The interest cost is the discount rate times the PBO at the beginning of the year. The expected return is deducted in the calculation of expense for the period. Any difference between expected and actual is deferred and accumulated in the net actuarial gains and losses. The amount is subject to the corridor method for amortization. Since Section 3461 was adopted retroactively, the transitional liability is charged to retained earnings in the year. Therefore there is no amortization required.

Service cost	$82,000
Interest cost (8% x $300,000)	24,000
Expected return	(17,000)
Post-retirement expense	$89,000

(Solution = a.)

QUESTION

13. Assumptions used in calculating the pension expense should reflect management's best estimate of the effect of future events on the actuarial present value of accrued pension benefits provided in exchange for services rendered. These assumptions should take into account the following:
    a. Recognition of the past history of the plan, actual experience.
    b. Recognition of the long-term nature of the plan, expected long-term future events.
    c. Recognition of the fact that the estimate is made as of a point in time, recent experience.
    d. All of the above.

EXPLANATION: The assumptions are a matter of professional judgement and should take into account all of the factors mentioned. (Solution = d.)

QUESTION

14. Which of the following would not be considered a defined benefit plan? [x]
    a. Benefit is fixed and based on years of services rendered.
    b. Benefit is based on years of service rendered and the investment earnings earned to date of retirement.
    c. Benefit is based on years of service and compensation earned by employee over entire period of service.
    d. Benefit is based on years of service and compensation over a specified number of years.

EXPLANATION: Under a defined benefit plan, the benefit is fixed, usually by a definite formula. The choices are all in formula (versus an exact dollar amount), but selection "b" has an element of uncertainty tied to investment returns. In this case, the risk is transferred to the employee, which is the essence of a defined contribution plan. (Solution = b.)

CHAPTER 21

Leases

Overview

Many entities lease assets. Leasing will often offer tax and cash flow advantages when compared to the purchase of these assets. Some leases are pure rentals; others are, in substance, an instalment purchase of the asset by the lessee. This chapter will discuss both operating and nonoperating type leases, but will focus on the nonoperating type where we must account for substance over legal form. That is, even though it is legally a rental situation, in substance the transaction is an instalment purchase of the asset by the lessee.

Study Steps

Understanding the Business Arrangement

What is a lease arrangement—the legal form versus the economic substance

A lease is a contractual arrangement whereby one party (the lessor) agrees to the use of an asset (which is owned by the lessor) by another party (the lessee).

The lessor gives up use of the asset for a constant income stream (rent), while the lessee gives up cash over the lease term and has use of the asset.

While the legal form is such that the lessor has legal title to the asset and, therefore, owns it, the economic substance of the arrangement may be different. On the one hand, the lease may represent a pure rental arrangement (e.g., when a tenant signs a lease to rent a one-bedroom apartment in a large building for one year). However, the lease may be such that the economic substance indicates a change in ownership (e.g., when a lessee enters into a "lease to own" arrangement for a new computer).

In the latter case, the lessor is effectively selling the asset and the lessee is effectively buying the asset, even though, legally, the transaction may take the form of a lease contract, where legal title remains (at least initially) with the lessor.

However, many leases fall somewhere in between. Since accounting should ideally follow the substance of the transaction, as opposed to its legal form, the second type of lease where there is an ownership change in substance must be dealt with differently than the first type. It should be accounted for as though the lessor were selling the asset and the lessee purchasing the asset.

Leases often have an option to purchase the asset at the end of the lease term. If this option is at a price that is significantly less than the estimated fair market value (FMV) at the end of the lease (the residual value), then the option is termed to be a bargain—hence the phrase bargain purchase option (BPO). Some leases require that the lessee guarantee the value of the asset when it is returned. If it is not returned in good condition, the lessee must pay an additional amount to make up the amount guaranteed. This is called the guaranteed residual value (GRV).

The lease term is the fixed non-cancellable term and may be extended under a renewal option. The option would again be a bargain if the terms of renewal are more favourable than arm's-length market terms (bargain renewal option).

Becoming Proficient in Lease Calculations and Journal Entries

This topic will be covered first from the lessee's perspective, and then from the lessor's perspective. The following covers only capital, sales-type, and direct financing leases, as these are the most difficult.

Lessee-capital leases

From the lessee's perspective, if the substance is such that there is an ownership change (sale/purchase), the lease is called a capital lease. Therefore, the lessee accounts for the lease just the same as if the lessee had purchased the asset as follows:

Recognition-journal entries

1. Record the asset and the obligation for financing the asset:

>Leased assets
>>Obligation under lease

This is almost the same as if it had been purchased outright, in which case the journal entry would have been:

>Fixed assets
>>Loan payable to bank

Remember, although the substance is the same, the legal rights may be quite different, in which case disclosure is critical.

2. Depreciate or amortize the asset.

There is a choice as to whether to depreciate it over the lease term or the expected useful economic life. If the asset had been purchased outright, it would be depreciated over its useful life. However, under a lease arrangement, the asset may not contribute to revenues over the full useful life (i.e., if the lease term is for a period that is less than the useful life and the lessee intends to return the asset to the lessor at the end of the term). In this case, the choice hinges on whether the asset will be used by the lessee over the economic life of the asset or just over the lease term.

One way to determine this is to look at the terms of the lease. If there is an option to purchase the asset from the lessor at the end of the lease at a price that is less than the fair market value (FMV) of the asset, it is likely that the lessee will exercise this bargain purchase option (BPO) and, therefore, use the asset for its full economic life.

In this case, the depreciation period would be the economic life. If the lease agreement includes a clause that provides for the legal title of the asset to pass to the lessee at the end of the lease term without any payment, again the lessee will use the asset for the economic life and the asset will, therefore, be depreciated over the economic life in order to match costs with revenues.

Depreciate over the lease term unless there is a BPO or title transfer in the lease contract.

3. Accrue interest on the obligation

Interest expense will be booked on the outstanding obligation as though it were a loan payable to the bank. As payments are made, the outstanding obligation will reduce, just as a loan would. The lease payment contains an interest component and a principal component. An amortization table will be used to determine the breakdown between interest and principal. Use an amortization table to determine how much of the lease payment is interest and how much reduces the recorded obligation.

Measurement-calculating the PVMLP (present value of minimum lease payments)

When the lessee records a capital lease, the value is determined by a formula (i.e., the present value of the minimum lease payments [PVMLP]).

Leased assets $PVMLP
    Obligation under lease $PVMLP

PVMLP is defined in the text, however, an attempt should be made to understand what is included in this formula and why. As an overview, the calculation is meant to measure the lease transaction. Purchased assets are normally recorded at historical cost, which is usually determined by an invoice. In the case of a lease, there is no invoice, only the lease contract, which does not include a purchase or sales price. The measurement problem is compounded by the fact that the asset will be "purchased" over time by the lessee and that there is an interest factor included in the monthly payment.

The PVMLP attempts to measure the present value of what the lessee will pay for the asset. In other words, it attempts to approximate the cash exchange price.

This calculation would include the actual lease payments, but what about purchase options or guarantees of residual values (GRV)? One way of looking at it is to determine what the intent is on the part of the lessee. Do they plan to keep the asset at the end of the lease, or give it back? These options are mutually exclusive and therefore should be treated as an either/or situation (i.e., the lessee cannot keep the asset and give it back at the same time). The likelihood of the lessee keeping the asset may be determined by the lease itself (e.g., if the lease contains an option to purchase the asset at the end of the lease at less than FMV, the lessee will likely exercise the option and keep the asset). The intentions of the lessee must also be considered.

In deciding what to include, consider management intent and terms in the lease contract that are inducements to act one way or another.

Whether a purchase option is a bargain or not is a question of professional judgement. In general, it would be a bargain if it were less than the FMV of the estimated residual value at the end of the lease.

When calculating the PVMLP, the payments must be discounted. The question arises as to which rate to use. Since the implicit rate (IR) (i.e., the rate of return required by the lessor) is often not known to the lessee, the lessee must find a substitute discount rate. Therefore, the lessee's incremental borrowing rate (IBR) is often used. If the lessee happens to know the implicit rate, and if this rate is less than the lessee's incremental rate, then the lessee must use the lessor's implicit rate. The lower the discount rate, the higher the obligation under lease. Thus, use of a lower rate would be more conservative as far as recording the obligation is concerned.

The lease term will also affect the calculation of the PVMLP.
The lease term is defined as:

The fixed, non-cancellable period of the lease plus:
i)   all periods covered by bargain renewal option (BRO);
ii) all periods covered by renewal options where there is a large penalty for non-renewal;

iii) all periods covered by renewal options during which lessee guarantees lessor's debt related to the leased asset;

iv) all periods covered by renewal options preceding a date where there is a BPO; or

v) all periods representing renewals or extensions at lessor's option.

The lease term incorporates the base term plus any additional terms where there is an inducement to renew. The PVMLP would then be calculated using the longer period and include any payments made over the longer period.

Lessor-sales-types and direct financing leases

From the lessor's perspective, if the substance is such that there is an ownership change (purchase/sale) then the lease will be accounted for as a direct financing lease or a sales-type lease. A sales-type lease occurs when the lessor makes a profit or loss on the transaction (excluding interest from the financing). The lease arrangement is accounted for as though a sale has taken place and therefore the following entries are booked:

Recognition-journal entries

1. Record the sale of the asset (sales-type lease):
   Lease payment receivable (LPR)
   Cost of goods sold
         Revenues/Sales
         Equipment inventory
         Unearned interest

If the journal entry is rearranged, it is the same as the standard journal entry that would be booked upon the sale of other goods in a standard sale:

    Accounts receivable (LPR)
        Revenues/Sales
        Unearned interest

    Cost of goods sold
        Inventory

The only difference is that some of the account names are different and that the lease transaction produces some revenues that are not yet earned (i.e., interest revenues). The interest will be earned over time, being a function of the length of time that the LPR is outstanding.

For a direct financing lease, omit the sales and cost of goods sold entry, since there is no profit on the deal.

    Accounts receivable (LPR)
        Inventory
        Unearned interest

2. Since the asset has, in effect, been sold, amortization is not necessary.

3. Interest revenues will be earned over time based on the outstanding principal balance in the lease payment receivable account, i.e., the LPR balance in the unearned interest account. The amount of interest earned each year may be calculated with the amortization table. The LPR includes the full amount of the lease payments including interest.

Measurement

The measurement of the transaction is difficult for the lessor for the same reasons as for the lessee. There are, however, two components to measure for the lessor:

1. The cost of the asset sold.
2. The sales price.

The cost

As a general rule, the cost of the asset sold is the laid-down cost that the lessor paid for the asset when it was purchased. Inventory is credited with the cost of the asset in order to remove it from the balance sheet. The cost of sales is usually debited for the same amount (unless there is an unguaranteed residual value, which will be dealt with later).

The sales price

As a general rule, the sales price will be the fair value (FV) of the asset since the lessor will want to ensure that he recovers the FV in a lease transaction, just as he would if it were an outright sale. This amount, however, does depend on how much the lease payments are and if there is any residual value. Just how the lessor determines what the lease payment will be is discussed later.

The amount booked as the LPR is a good starting point and the sales price may be derived from there. The LPR is the sum of all the lease payments (excluding executory costs), including any BPO if there is one. If there is a BPO, the lessee will likely exercise the option to purchase as discussed above. Therefore, this is an additional amount that will be paid by the lessee for the asset and, therefore, it should be included in LPR.

As discussed above, if there is no BPO and the title to the asset does not pass as part of the terms of the lease, it is likely that the asset will return to the lessor and, therefore, the residual value is important. In this case, the residual value should be included in the LPR. If the asset will return to the lessor at the end of the lease, then include the residual value in lease payments receivable whether it is guaranteed or not. This is different from the lessee where you would only include the GRV.

If the asset is returned to the lessor, the lessor will reclassify the residual value from the LPR account to a fixed asset account, since the substance is now that the lessor owns the asset again (dr. fixed asset, cr. LPR). The amounts are not discounted in the LPR calculation. The amount recorded as a sale is simply the discounted value of whatever has been included in the LPR account and the difference between the sales account and the LPR account is the unearned interest. The only exception is if there is an unguaranteed residual value. The present value of this amount should not be included in the sales amount and for that matter, should also be deducted from the cost of goods sold amount.

The unguaranteed residual value should not be included in the sales price or the cost of sales, although it will be included in the lease payment receivable.

The amortization table will be the same for either a guaranteed residual value or an unguaranteed residual value, i.e., the residual value would be included in the table.

The lessor would always discount at the rate implicit in the lease, which is their desired rate of return.

Calculating the lease payment

How does the lessor calculate the lease payment? Basically, the lessor wants to recover the FV of the asset or, for that matter, whatever can be recovered. This is usually capped at FV, as this is all that the lessee is willing to pay.

The lessor, therefore, usually starts with fair value. From this, any special payments that will be made by the lessee—BPO or the residual value—are deducted. Again, the deduction will depend on whether the lessee will likely purchase the asset at the end of the lease or return the asset. If the lessee plans to purchase the asset, then the BPO is relevant. If the asset is expected to be returned, then the residual value, guaranteed or not, is relevant. The remainder is divided by an annuity factor to determine the payments.

The lessor's implicit rate in the lease is the rate of interest that the lessor charges the lessee for providing financing. The lessor not only sells the assets to the lessee but also provides financing. The rate is usually higher than the lessor's own borrowing rate so that the lessor makes a profit on the interest spread. The rate is also adjusted for the risk associated with the particular lessee (i.e., the risk that the lessee will not pay).

The annuity table used depends solely on when the lease payment is made. If the payment is made at the beginning of the lease year, an annuity due table is used. If the payment is made at the end of the lease year, an ordinary annuity table is used.

Initial direct costs

The basic principle that dictates how the initial direct costs should be accounted for is the matching principle (i.e., costs should be matched with the revenues to which they relate). First determine the type of lease and then the type of revenue earned under the lease, e.g., under an operating lease, rental income is earned over the term of the lease and therefore any up-front costs should be deferred and recognized over the term of the lease to match the revenues. Direct financing leases yield interest income and, therefore, any up-front costs should be deferred and amortized to match the costs and revenues. Sales-type leases yield both profit and interest income and the costs could be deferred or recognized when incurred. The latter approach is taken since it is more conservative and since most up-front costs are seen as costs of sales.

Executory costs

All of the lease calculations should be made without making reference to executory costs. The executory costs are not payments for the actual use of the asset. Rather, they are payments made for other expenses that are related to the asset.

Tips on Chapter Topics

TIP! For a nonoperating type lease, **always draw a time line** and enter on that diagram all the cash flows associated with the lease which are expected by the party for whom you are accounting. For a lessee, those will be the minimum lease payments. For a lessor, those will be the minimum lease payments plus any unguaranteed residual value to the lessor.

TIP! **Minimum lease payments** include the following:
1. Regular periodic rental payments, excluding executory costs (an annuity).
2. Bargain purchase option (a single sum), if any.
3. Guaranteed residual value (a single sum), if any.
4. Penalty for failure to renew, if any.

TIP! The **cost** (and initial amount of obligation) **for an asset under a capital lease** is determined by the present value of the minimum lease payments (excluding executory costs included therein). However, the amount recorded should not exceed the fair market value of the asset at the inception date. The rate to use in the discounting process is the lessee's incremental borrowing rate or the lessor's implicit rate. The lessor's rate is used when it is known **and** when it is the lower of the two rates.

TIP! The time period to be used for amortization of an asset under capital lease depends on which criteria the lease meets in determining that it is a capital lease. If there is automatic transfer of title of the asset at the end of the lease term or if there is a bargain purchase option, the asset is expected to be with the lessee for the remainder of its economic life; therefore, to comply with the matching principle, the asset should be amortized over its remaining useful life. If the lease contract does not provide for the automatic transfer of title and there is no bargain purchase option, the asset will be used by the lessee only for the lease term; therefore, to comply with the matching principle, the asset should be amortized over the lease term.

TIP! A **bargain purchase option** is defined as an option to purchase at a bargain price. A bargain price is a price substantially below the expected market value of the asset at the date the option becomes exercisable. If the option price is 30% of the expected market value, accountants would agree that the price constitutes a bargain. If the option price is 90% of the expected market value, accountants would agree that the price does not constitute a bargain. The range that lies between these two extremes provides room for controversy. Professional judgement is required in this area.

TIP! The amount representing gross investment in lease for a lessor is recorded in the lessor's books in the account Lease Payments Receivable; an alternate name for this account is Gross Investment in Lease. Gross investment in lease is defined as mini-

Illustration 21-1 229

mum lease payments plus unguaranteed residual value, if any. Minimum lease payments include a guaranteed residual value, if any. Thus, both guaranteed residual value (because it is included as part of minimum lease payments) and unguaranteed residual value (because it is added in to calculate the gross investment) are included as part of lease payments receivable if a portion of the residual value is guaranteed in the lease agreement and if the unguaranteed portion is relevant to the lessor (that is, if the lessor expects to get the asset back).

TIP!

For an **operating**-type lease, minimum lease payments are recognized as rental expense by the lessee on a **straight-line basis**, even if not payable on a straight-line basis. Thus, situations involving a lease bonus, scheduled rent increases, or free rent must conform to this guideline. For example: a lessee signs a five-year operating lease and receives 10 months of free rent. The cost of the 50 (60 – 10 = 50) rental payments is to be divided by the 60-month lease term to determine the monthly rental expense. See EIC-21, Accounting for Lease Inducements by the Lessee, for more guidance.

TIP!

For an operating lease, rents are recognized as revenue by the lessor on a straight-line basis over the lease term as they are earned. If the cash is not received in the period the revenue is earned, a deferral (or an accrual) type adjustment is required.

Illustration 21-1
Classification of Leases

CLASSIFICATION OF LEASES BY THE LESSEE

From the standpoint of the lessee, all leases may be classified for accounting purposes as follows:
   (a) Operating leases.
   (b) Capital leases.

If at the inception of a non-cancellable lease agreement the lease meets **one or more** of the following three criteria, the lessee shall classify and account for the arrangement as a **capital lease**:
1. The lease transfers ownership of the property to the lessee, or the lease contains a bargain purchase option.
2. The lease term is equal to 75% or more of the estimated economic life of the leased property.
3. The present value of the minimum lease payments (excluding executory costs) equals or exceeds 90% of the fair value of the leased property.

CLASSIFICATION OF LEASES BY THE LESSOR

From the standpoint of the **lessor**, all leases may be classified for accounting purposes as follows:

(a) Operating leases.
(b) Direct financing leases.
(c) Sales-type leases.

If at the inception of a lease agreement the lessor is party to a lease that meets **one or more** of the following Group I criteria (1, 2, and 3) and **both** of the following Group II criteria (1 and 2), the lessor shall classify and account for the arrangement as a **direct financing lease** or as a **sales-type lease**. (If the lessor's net investment at inception equals the asset's carrying value, the lease is a direct financing lease; if the net investment is unequal to the asset's carrying value, the lease is a sales-type lease.)

GROUP I

1. The lease transfers ownership of the property to the lessee, or the lease contains a bargain purchase option.
2. The lease term is equal to 75% or more of the estimated economic life of the leased property.
3. The present value of the minimum lease payments (excluding executory costs) equals or exceeds 90% of the fair value of the leased property.

GROUP II

1. Collectibility of the payments required from the lessee is reasonably predictable.
2. No important uncertainties surround the amount of unreimbursable costs yet to be incurred by the lessor under the lease (i.e., lessor's performance is substantially complete and future costs are reasonably predictable).

TIP! Note that the Group I criteria are identical to the criteria that must be met for a lease to be classified as a capital lease by a lessee.

TIP! In certain cases, the lessee may capitalize the lease while the lessor does not. This situation results because the lease meets one or more Group I criteria, but the lease does not meet both Group II criteria; thus, the lease meets the qualifications required for capitalization by the lessee but the lease does not meet the qualifications required for capitalization by the lessor. Therefore, both parties will report the leased asset on their balance sheets, and both parties will record amortization each period for financial reporting purposes.

Illustration 21-2   231

Illustration 21-2
Steps in Evaluating and Accounting for a Lease Situation for a Lessee

STEP 1:   **Examine the facts regarding the lease agreement.**
Determine if the lease meets the criteria to capitalize the lease (the criteria are listed in **Illustration 21-1**). If so, perform the rest of the steps below; if not, account for the lease as an operating lease.

STEP 2:   **Draw the time line.**

STEP 3:   **Calculate the present value of the minimum lease payments.**
- The minimum lease payments include:
  - (a) periodic rental payments;
  - (b) bargain purchase option, if any;
  - (c) guaranteed residual value, if any residual value is guaranteed by the lessee.
- Use the lessee's incremental borrowing rate or the lessor's implicit rate, whichever is lower. (The lessor's rate must be known for it to be used.)

STEP 4:   **Determine the cost of the asset under capital lease.**
- The cost is the **lower** of the present value of the minimum lease payments (Step 3) or the asset's fair value.
- If the fair value is the lower, a new effective interest rate must be determined. That new rate is the interest rate which sets the minimum lease payments equivalent to the fair value of the asset, giving effect to the time value of money.

STEP 5:   **Prepare the lessee's amortization schedule.**
The beginning obligation balance is the amount determined in Step 4. (The interest rate for Step 5 is the rate used in Step 3, unless that rate was replaced in Step 4.)

STEP 6:   **Prepare journal entries to record the transactions related to the lease on the lessee's books.**

Illustration 21-3

Steps in Evaluating and Accounting for a Lease Situation for a Lessor

STEP 1:   **Examine the facts regarding the lease agreement.**
Determine if the lease meets the criteria for the lessor to capitalize the lease (the criteria are listed in **Illustration 21-1**). If so, perform the rest of the steps below; if not, account for the lease as an operating lease.

STEP 2:   **Determine the periodic rental payments required by the lessor to yield the desired rate of return on the investment if that payment is not given data.**
- The future cash flows to the lessor from the leased asset are to allow the lessor to recover the asset's fair value or its cost.
- The present value of any single sum expected by the lessor at the end of the lease term (bargain purchase option or guaranteed residual value or unguaranteed residual value) is deducted from the asset's fair value (or cost) to arrive at the present value of the periodic rents. The amount of a single rent is determined by solving for Rent in the following formula:

Present Value of an Annuity = Rent x Present Value Factor

STEP 3:   **Draw the time line.**

STEP 4:   **Calculate the net investment at inception.**
- Net investment is the present value of the minimum lease payments plus the present value of any unguaranteed residual value that will be available to the lessor.
- Use the lessor's implicit rate in the discounting process.

STEP 5:   **Prepare the lessor's amortization schedule.**
The beginning net investment (calculated in Step 4) is the starting point for this schedule. Use the lessor's implicit rate to calculate interest revenue.

STEP 6:   **Prepare the journal entries to record the transactions related to the lease on the lessor's books.**

Exercise 21-1

PURPOSE: This exercise illustrates how a lessee and a lessor are to account for a lease when the contract allows for automatic transfer of title to the leased asset at the end of the lease term.

The following facts pertain to a lease between Sun Bank Leasing (lessor) and JMJ Printers (lessee) for an electronic laser printer:

1. The lease is for a five-year term, beginning January 1, 2005. The remaining economic life of the asset is five years.
2. The lessor's implicit rate is 10%; the lessee's incremental borrowing rate is 10%.
3. The fair value of the leased asset is $100,000. The lessor's cost is $100,000.
4. The annual rent payments are $25,981.62; the first one is due on January 1, 2005. This amount includes $2,000.00 for executory costs.
5. The title to the asset automatically transfers to the lessee at the end of the lease term. The asset is expected to have a fair value of $5,000 at that date.
6. Both the lessee and the lessor use the calendar year for their accounting periods.

Instructions

(a) Describe the type of lease from the viewpoint of the: (1) lessee and (2) lessor.
(b) Prepare an amortization schedule for use by the lessee and the lessor. Explain why they could both use the same schedule in this situation. Also, draw a time line for the lessor.
(c) Prepare the journal entry to record the inception of the lease on the lessee's books.
(d) Prepare the journal entry to record the inception of the lease on the lessor's books.
(e) Indicate the amount(s) to appear in the lessee's December 31, 2006 balance sheet for this lease. Also indicate the portion that will appear in the current liability section, and the portion that will appear in the long-term liability classification. Explain how to determine these amounts.
(f) Indicate the amount to appear in the lessor's December 31, 2006 balance sheet for net investment in lease. Also indicate the portion that will appear in the current asset section, and the portion that will appear in the long-term investment section of the balance sheet. Also show the gross investment and unearned interest components of each net investment figure. Explain how to determine these amounts.

Solution to Exercise 21-1

(a) The lease is a capital lease for the lessee because the title to the leased asset automatically transfers to the lessee at the end of the lease term. (The lease also meets two other criteria required by the lessee for capitalization.) Assuming that uncollectible lease payments are reasonably estimable and there are no important uncertainties surrounding future unreimbursable costs to be incurred by the lessor with respect to the lease, the lessor has a nonoperating type lease because of the automatic transfer of the title of the leased asset at the end of the lease term. The lessor has a direct financing type lease because the net investment at inception equals the lessor's carrying value.

Calculations:
$25,981.62 – $2,000.00 executory costs = $23,981.62
$23,981.62 x present value factor for an annuity due for n = 5, i = 10% = net investment
$23,981.62 x 4.16986 = $100,000.00 net investment

(b)　　　　　　　　　　**AMORTIZATION SCHEDULE**

Date	Rent Excluding Executory Costs	10% Interest	Reduction of Present Value	Present Value Balance
1/1/05				$ 100,000.00
1/1/05	$ 23,981.62*	$ -0-	$ 23,981.62	76,018.38
1/1/06	23,981.62	7,601.84	16,379.78	59,638.60
1/1/07	23,981.62	5,963.86	18,017.76	41,620.84
1/1/08	23,981.62	4,162.08	19,819.54	21,801.30
1/1/09	23,981.62	2,180.32**	21,801.30	-0-
	$ 119,908.10	$19,908.10	$ 100,000.00	

*$25,981.62 – $2,000.00 = $23,981.62
**Includes rounding error of $0.19.

The lessor and the lessee can use the same amortization schedule in this situation because they are using the same interest rate to account for the lease, and the lessor has no unguaranteed residual value for which to account. For these same reasons, both parties have the same time line for the lease, which is depicted as follows:

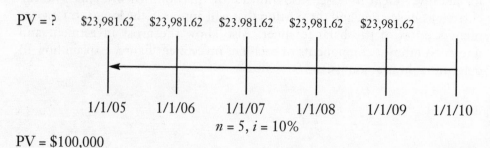

PV = ?　　$23,981.62　$23,981.62　$23.981.62　$23,981.62　$23,981.62

1/1/05　　1/1/06　　1/1/07　　1/1/08　　1/1/09　　1/1/10

n = 5, i = 10%

PV = $100,000

(c) Printer Under Capital Lease   100,000.00
     Obligations Under Capital Leases   100,000.00

(d) Lease Payments Receivable   119,908.10
     Unearned Interest Revenue—Leases   19,908.10
     Printer   100,000.00

(e) The asset Printer Under Capital Lease for $100,000 will appear in the property, plant, and equipment section of the lessee's balance sheet. Accumulated amortization of $38,000 would also appear in that section. In calculating the periodic amortization, the residual value is deducted from the asset's cost because the lessee expects to recover $5,000 from disposal of the asset after the end of the lease term when the title to the asset automatically transfers to the lessee. Thus, ($100,000 – $5,000) ÷ 5 years = $19,000 per year. The present value of the obligation under capital lease at December 31, 2006 is $65,602.46 ($59,638.60 + $5,963.86 = $65,602.46). The present value amount will be reported on the lessee's balance sheet at this date as follows:

Current liabilities
    Interest payable $ 5,963.86
    Obligations under capital leases   18,017.76
Long-term liabilities
    Obligations under capital leases   41,620.84

To determine these amounts, look at the amortization schedule. Find the date on the schedule that is the balance sheet date (December 31, 2006). If the balance sheet date is not on the schedule (as is the case here), locate the date that most recently precedes the balance sheet date. That date is January 1, 2006 in this exercise. Find the balance on that payment line (which is $59,638.60) and add any interest that has accrued since that date (i.e., $59,638.60 x 10% = $5,963.86). The total is the present value of the remaining minimum lease payments at the balance sheet date. The liability due to the accrued interest expense belongs in the current liability classification. The portion of the principal that is to be shown in current liabilities is the amount on the **next** payment line (1/1/07) of the amortization schedule in the "Reduction of Present Value" column ($18,017.76); the portion of the principal that is noncurrent is on that same (1/1/07) line in the "Present Value Balance" column ($41,620.84).

(f) The net investment in lease at December 31, 2006 is $65,602.46 ($59,638.60 + $5,963.86 = $65,602.46). This will appear on the lessor's December 31, 2006 balance sheet as follows:

Current assets
    Lease payments receivable $ 23,981.62
    Unearned interest revenue—leases   -0-
      Net investment in lease $ 23,981.62

Long-term investments

Lease payments receivable	$ 47,963.24
Unearned interest revenue—leases	(6,342.40)
Net investment in lease	$ 41,620.84

TIP! To check on the accuracy of the current and noncurrent portions, add the two portions together; that total ($23,981.62 + $41,620.84 = $65,602.46) should equal the present value of the lease at the balance sheet date ($65,602.46). It does in this case.

TIP! To determine the amounts to appear in the current asset section, refer to the amortization schedule. Look for the balance sheet date or the date that most recently precedes the balance sheet date. The rent on the following line is the amount of gross investment to be classified as a current asset. The interest portion of that rent that is yet unearned at the balance sheet date is to be deducted to arrive at net investment. In the exercise at hand, none of the $5,963.86 interest due on 1/1/07 is unearned at 12/31/06 because it was all earned during 2006; therefore $0 unearned interest revenue is reflected in the current asset section. The rents (and other receipts) appearing on all subsequent lines ($23,981.62 + $23,981.62 = $47,963.24) are to be reflected as gross investment in a noncurrent asset classification. The interest portion of each of those rents ($4,162.08 + $2,180.32 = $6,342.40) is to be deducted as unearned interest revenue to arrive at the noncurrent portion of net investment.

Exercise 21-2

PURPOSE: This exercise is a comprehensive illustration of the accounting procedures for a lease where the leased asset will revert back to the lessor at the end of the lease term and still have some value. This exercise illustrates (1) how the lessor determines the amount of the periodic lease payment, (2) the lessor's calculations for recording the transactions associated with the lease, (4) the meaning of the terms "gross investment" and "net investment," (5) the lessee's calculations for recording the transactions associated with the lease, (6) the journal entries on the lessor's books, and (7) the journal entries on the lessee's books.

On January 1, Year 1, Leaseco has a piece of equipment with a cost of $80,000 and a fair value of $80,000. On that date, Leaseco leases the asset to Rentco for a five-year term at an implicit rate of 10%. The annual lease payment is due at the beginning of each year, and the first payment is to be collected at the inception date. The leased asset will revert back to Leaseco at the end of the lease term; its market value at that date is estimated to be $7,000. Both Leaseco and Rentco have a calendar-year reporting period. Rentco is aware of the lessor's implicit rate; Rentco's incremental borrowing rate is 12%. Leaseco can reasonably estimate uncollectible lease payments and has no important uncertainties regarding future unreimbursable costs associated with this lease.

Instructions

Assuming the lease is a capital lease to the lessee and a direct financing lease to the lessor:

(a) Calculate the amount of the annual lease payment (excluding executory costs) to be collected by the lessor.

(b) Draw the time line for the lessor.

(c) For the lessor, calculate the (1) gross investment in lease at inception, and (2) net investment in lease at inception.

(d) Calculate the amount of interest revenue to be reported by the lessor for: (1) Year 1, (2) Year 2, and (3) Year 5.

(e) Prepare the amortization schedule for the lessor.

(f) Calculate the cost of the lessee's asset under capital lease.

(g) Draw the time line for the lessee.

(h) Calculate the amount of interest expense to be reported by the lessee for (1) Year 1, (2) Year 2, and (3) Year 5.

(i) Prepare the amortization schedule for the lessee.

(j) Explain why the lessee's amortization schedule is different than the lessor's amortization schedule. Under what circumstances would the two parties be able to use the same amortization schedule?

(k) Prepare all of the journal entries for the lessor's books for Years 1 and 2, assuming reversing entries are used.

(l) Prepare all of the journal entries for the lessee's books for Years 1 and 2, assuming reversing entries are used.

(m) Compare and contrast the journal entries for the lessee [part (l)] with the journal entries for the lessor [part (k)].

Solution to Exercise 21-2

(a)

Total amount to be recovered	$80,000.00
Present value of unguaranteed residual ($7,000 x .620921)	(4,346.44)
Present value of annual payments	75,653.56
Factor for present value of an annuity due of 1 for $n = 5$, $i = 10$	÷ 4.16986
Annual rent required	**$18,142.95**

[1].62092 is the factor for present value of 1 for $n = 5$, $i = 10\%$.

> **TIP!**
> In this case, the asset's fair value (or cost) is to be recovered through annual payments by the lessee and through the asset's market value ($7,000) at the end of the lease. Today's cash equivalent of $7,000 due in five years is less than $7,000, due to the time value of money.

(b)

PV = ?

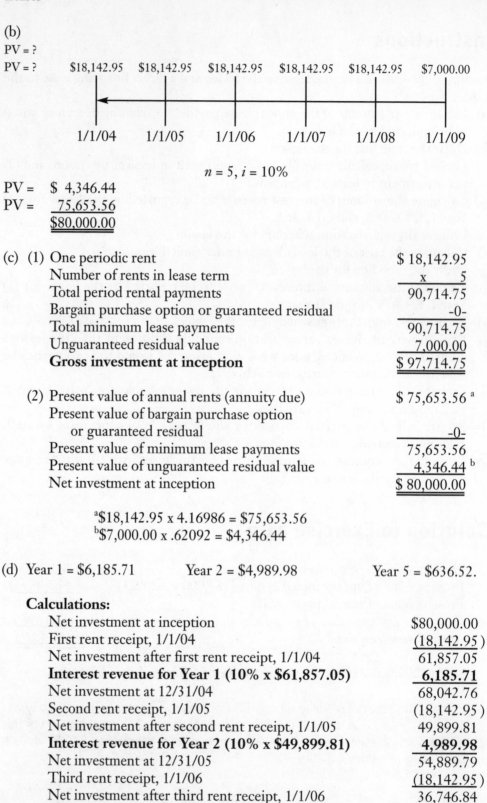

PV = ? $18,142.95 $18,142.95 $18,142.95 $18,142.95 $18,142.95 $7,000.00

1/1/04   1/1/05   1/1/06   1/1/07   1/1/08   1/1/09

$n = 5, i = 10\%$

PV = $ 4,346.44

PV =   75,653.56

$80,000.00

(c) (1) One periodic rent $ 18,142.95

Number of rents in lease term   x   5

Total period rental payments   90,714.75

Bargain purchase option or guaranteed residual   -0-

Total minimum lease payments   90,714.75

Unguaranteed residual value   7,000.00

Gross investment at inception $ 97,714.75

(2) Present value of annual rents (annuity due) $ 75,653.56 [a]

Present value of bargain purchase option

or guaranteed residual   -0-

Present value of minimum lease payments   75,653.56

Present value of unguaranteed residual value   4,346.44 [b]

Net investment at inception $ 80,000.00

[a]$18,142.95 x 4.16986 = $75,653.56

[b]$7,000.00 x .62092 = $4,346.44

(d) Year 1 = $6,185.71   Year 2 = $4,989.98   Year 5 = $636.52.

Calculations:

Net investment at inception	$80,000.00
First rent receipt, 1/1/04	(18,142.95)
Net investment after first rent receipt, 1/1/04	61,857.05
Interest revenue for Year 1 (10% x $61,857.05)	**6,185.71**
Net investment at 12/31/04	68,042.76
Second rent receipt, 1/1/05	(18,142.95)
Net investment after second rent receipt, 1/1/05	49,899.81
Interest revenue for Year 2 (10% x $49,899.81)	**4,989.98**
Net investment at 12/31/05	54,889.79
Third rent receipt, 1/1/06	(18,142.95)
Net investment after third rent receipt, 1/1/06	36,746.84
Interest revenue for Year 3 (10% x $36,746.84)	**3,674.68**
Net investment at 12/31/06	40,421.52
Fourth rent receipt, 1/1/07	(18,142.95)
Net investment after fourth rent receipt, 1/1/07	22,278.57

Interest revenue for Year 4 (10% x $22,278.57)   2,227.86
Net investment at 12/31/07   24,506.43
Fifth rent receipt, 1/1/08   (18,142.95)
Net investment after last rent receipt, 1/1/08   6,363.48
Interest revenue for Year 5 ($7,000.00 – $6,363.48)   636.52 [a]
Net investment at end of lease term before disposal of asset $ 7,000.00

[a]Includes a rounding error of $0.17.

Notice the interest amount for the last period ($636.52 for Year 5, in this case) is a "plug" figure. When the derived amount ($636.52) is compared with what would have been a calculated amount for interest ($6,363.48 x 10% = $636.35), the difference is the amount of rounding error ($636.52 - $636.35 = $.17 rounding error).   **TIP!**

Notice that **net investment in lease is a present value (discounted) amount**.   **TIP!**

Interest is a function of (a) present value balance, (b) rate, and (c) time. As time passes, interest accrues (due to the time value of money). Interest **increases** the present value balance; payments **decrease** the present value balance.   **TIP!**

Notice that there is interest to be earned by the lessor during Year 5, even though the last lease payment is to be received at the beginning of Year 5. This is due to the existence of the single sum (the unguaranteed residual value, in this case) expected by the lessor at the end of the lease term.   **TIP!**

(e)   **LESSOR'S AMORTIZATION SCHEDULE**

Date	Receipts Residual Value	10% Interest Revenue	Net Investment Recovery	Net Investment Balance
1/1/04				$80,000.00
1/1/04	$18,142.95		$18,142.95	61,857.05
1/1/05	18,142.95	$ 6,185.71	11,957.24	49,899.81
1/1/06	18,142.95	4,989.98	13,152.97	36,746.84
1/1/07	18,142.95	3,674.68	14,468.27	22,278.57
1/1/08	18,142.95	2,227.86	15,915.09	6,363.48
12/31/08	7,000.00	636.52 *	6,363.48	-0-
	$97,714.75	$17,714.75 `	$80,000.00	

*Includes a rounding error of $0.17.

The interest included in a rent is the interest for the period that occurs **prior** to the due date of the rent. Thus, the interest shown on the 1/1/06 line on the amortization schedule is the interest charged for the calendar year of Year 2.   **TIP!**

The amounts on the amortization schedule were derived by the calculations performed in part (d) above. However, the components are arranged a little differently on the amortization schedule.   **TIP!**

There is no interest included in the first rent receipt because the first rent is to be received on the inception date (hence, the rents constitute an annuity due). There is   **TIP!**

no passage of time between the inception date and the first rent receipt date; therefore, no interest is earned.

TIP! The rounding error is always to be plugged in the interest column on the last line of the amortization schedule. If all calculations are performed correctly and are rounded to the nearest cent, the rounding error will be small—usually less than $10. Therefore, a rounding error larger than this will generally indicate that there are errors in the schedule. There may be math errors or more serious procedural errors.

TIP! All items that appear on the time line in part (b) are to appear in the "Receipts" column of the amortization schedule.

TIP! The total of the "Net Investment Recovery" column is equal to the beginning figure in the "Net Investment Balance" column.

TIP! The total of the "Receipts" column is the initial gross investment in lease amount [see solution to part (c)].

TIP! Notice how the net investment amount at December 31, Year 1, as derived from the appropriate numbers on the amortization schedule, can be proved by an independent present value calculation as of that date.

Calculations:
From the amortization schedule:

Net investment balance at 1/1/04	$ 61,857.05
Interest for Year 1	6,185.71
Net investment balance at 12/31/04	$ 68,042.76

Present value calculations:
Present value of an annuity due of 1, $n = 4$, $i = 10\% = 3.48685$
Present value of 1, $n = 4$, $i = 10\% = .68301$

$18,142.95 x 3.48685	$ 63,261.75
$7,000.00 x .68301	x 4,781.07
Present value at end of Year 1	$ 68,042.82

The 6 cents difference between $68,042.76 and $68,042.82 is due to rounding errors.

(f)

Annual rent payment	$ 18,142.95
Present value of an annuity due of 1, $n = 5$, $i = 10$	x 4.16986
Present value of annual rents	75,653.56
Present value of bargain purchase option or guaranteed residual	-0-
Present value of minimum lease payments	$ 75,653.56

TIP! The lessee's cost of asset under capital lease is the lower of the asset's fair value or the present value of the minimum lease payments. The interest rate to be used in determining the present value of the minimum lease payments is the lessee's incremental borrowing rate or the lessor's implicit rate, whichever is lower. (The lessor's rate cannot possibly be used if it is unknown.)

TIP! When the leased asset is to revert back to the lessor at the end of the lease term rather than remain with the lessee, and the lessee does not guarantee a residual value, the lessee does not find the residual value of any relevance; hence, under these circumstances, the lessee does **not** use the residual value for any of its accounting.

(g)

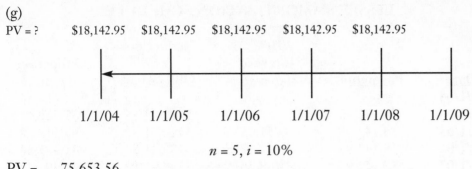

PV = ? $18,142.95 $18,142.95 $18,142.95 $18,142.95 $18,142.95

1/1/04   1/1/05   1/1/06   1/1/07   1/1/08   1/1/09

$n = 5, i = 10\%$

PV =   75,653.56

| The lessee's time line differs from the lessor's time line in this case because the lessor has an unguaranteed residual value that is not relevant to the lessee. | **TIP!** |

(h) Year 1 = $5,751.06   Year 2 = $4,511.87   Year 5 = $0.

Calculations:

Present value of obligation at inception	$ 75,653.56
First rent payment, 1/1/04	(18,142.95)
Present value of obligation after first rent payment, 1/1/04	57,510.61
Interest expense for Year 1 (10% x $57,510.61)	**5,751.06**
Present value of obligation at 12/31/04	63,261.67
Second rent payment, 1/1/05	(18,142.95)
Present value of obligation after second rent payment, 1/1/05	45,118.72
Interest expense for Year 2 (10% x $45,118.72)	**4,511.87**
Present value of obligation at 12/31/05	49,630.59
Third rent payment, 1/1/06	(18,142.95)
Present value of obligation after third rent payment, 1/1/06	31,487.64
Interest expense for Year 3 (10% x $31,487.64)	**3,148.76**
Present value of obligation at 12/31/06	34,636.40
Fourth rent payment, 1/1/07	(18,142.95)
Present value of obligation after fourth rent payment, 1/1/07	16,493.45
Interest expense for Year 4 ($18,142.95 – $16,493.45)	**1,649.50**[a]
Present value of obligation at 12/31/07	18,142.95
Fifth rent payment, 1/1/08	(18,142.95)
Present value after last rent payment, 1/1/08	-0-
Interest expense for Year 5 (10% x $0)	**-0-**
Present value at end of lease term	$ -0-

[a]$18,142.95 – $16,493.45 = $1,649.50 interest including rounding error.
  $16,493.45 x 10% = $1,649.35 interest if there was no rounding error.
  $1,649.50 – $1,649.35 = $0.15 rounding error.

| In this situation, there is no interest expense for the last year of the lease because the obligation is to be fully paid as of the beginning of the fifth year. | **TIP!** |

(i)   **LESSEE'S AMORTIZATION SCHEDULE**

Date	Payments	10% Interest Expense	Reduction of Obligation	Obligation Balance
1/1/04				$75,653.56
1/1/04	$18,142.95		$18,142.95	57,510.61
1/1/05	18,142.95	$ 5,751.06	12,391.89	45,118.72
1/1/06	18,142.95	4,511.87	13,631.08	31,487.64
1/1/07	18,142.95	3.148.76	14,994.19	16,493.45
1/1/08	18,142.95	1,649.50 [a]	16,493.45	-0-
	$90,714.75	$15,061.19	$75,653.56	

[a]Includes rounding error of $0.15.

TIP! The total of the "Payments" column minus the total of the "Interest Expense" column equals the total of the "Reduction of Obligation" column, and the total of the "Reduction of Obligation" column equals the obligation's present value at inception (the beginning amount for the schedule).

(j)   Even though the lessee and the lessor both use the same interest rate in this scenario, the lessee's amortization schedule differs from the lessor's because the $7,000 unguaranteed residual value must be accounted for by the lessor but not by the lessee. The lessor and the lessee can use the same amortization schedule when they use the same interest rate and when there is one of the following: (1) an automatic transfer of title, or (2) a bargain purchase option, or (3) a residual value guaranteed by the lessee to the lessor, or (4) an unguaranteed residual value for the lessor of zero.

(k)	1/1/04	Lease Payments Receivable	97,714.75	
		Equipment		80,000.00
		Unearned Interest Revenue—Leases		17,714.75
		Cash	18,142.95	
		Lease Payments Receivable		18,142.95
	12/31/04	Unearned Interest Revenue—Leases	6,185.71	
		Interest Revenue—Leases		6,185.71
	1/1/05	There are no adjustments appropriate for reversal.		
	1/1/05	Cash	18,142.95	
		Lease Payments Receivable		18,142.95
	12/31/05	Unearned Interest Revenue—Leases	4,989.98	
		Interest Revenue—Leases		4,989.98
(l)	1/1/04	Leased Equipment Under Capital Leases	75,653.56	
		Obligations Under Capital Leases		75,653.56

	Obligations Under Capital Leases	18,142.95	
	Cash		18,142.95

12/31/04	Interest Expense	5,751.06	
	Interest Payable		5,751.06

	Amortization Expense	15,130.71	
	Accumulated Amortization		15,130.71
	($75,653.56 ÷ 5 years = $15,130.71)		

1/1/05	Interest Payable	5,751.06	
	Interest Expense		5,751.06

	Interest Expense	5,751.06	
	Obligations Under Capital Leases	12,391.89	
	Cash		18,142.95

12/31/05	Interest Expense	4,511.87	
	Interest Payable		4,511.87

	Amortization Expense	15,130.71	
	Accumulated Amortization		15,130.71

(m) (1) At the inception date, the lessor records the **gross** amounts to be received in a receivable account (Lease Payments Receivable); whereas the lessee records the **present value** of amounts to be paid in a payable account (Obligations Under Capital Leases). Because receivables and payables are to be reported at present value, the lessor has to set up a contra receivable account (Unearned Interest Revenue—Leases) to reduce the carrying value of its receivable to the present value of all future cash flows associated with the lease.

(2) The lessor accounts for interest as a **deferral** situation, but the lessee accounts for interest as an **accrual** situation. Therefore, the lessor records interest only at the end of an accounting period; this recording is accomplished by an adjusting entry. The lessee records interest when a cash payment is made **and** at the end of an accounting period (by an adjusting entry) because the accounting period ends at a date other than a rent payment date. The lessor's adjusting entry to record the recognition of interest earned is never reversed; the lessee's adjusting entry to accrue interest can be reversed.

(3) The lessor's entry to record a rental receipt is the same each period. (Debit Cash and credit Lease Payments Receivable for the entire rent receipt.) The lessee's entry to record a rental payment is different each period because the amount of the payment attributable to interest versus the amount going to reduce the obligation balance differs for each payment.

(4) Both the lessor and the lessee account for interest, **but** only the lessee accounts for amortization in this scenario.

Exercise 21-3

PURPOSE: This exercise will provide an example of: (1) the accounting procedures for a lessor with a sales-type lease, (2) lease periods that do not coincide with accounting periods, and (3) a lease with a purchase option.

The following facts relate to a lease made by the Wormold Company to the Marina Corporation.

Inception of lease	May 1, 2005
Annual payment due at beginning of each lease year, first payment due May 1, 2005	$10,000
Lease term	5 years
Remaining economic life of asset	7 years
Residual value at end of lease term	$8,000
Purchase option at end of lease term	$2,000
Lessor's cost	$40,000
Lessor's implicit rate	10%
Annual accounting period	Calendar year

Instructions

(a) Prepare the amortization schedule and draw the time line for the lessor.
(b) Answer the following questions from the viewpoint of the lessor:
   (1) What is the gross investment at inception?
   (2) What is the net investment at inception?
   (3) What amount of gross profit should be reported on the income statement for 2005?
   (4) What amount of gross profit should be reported on the income statement for 2006?
   (5) What amount should be reported as interest revenue on the income statement for 2005?
   (6) What amount should be reported as interest revenue on the income statement for 2006?
(c) Prepare the following journal entries for the lessor:
   (1) Inception of the lease on May 1, 2005.
   (2) Rent receipt on May 1, 2005.
   (3) Adjusting entry at December 31, 2005.
   (4) Rent receipt on May 1, 2006.
   (5) Adjusting entry at December 31, 2006.
(d) If the lessee has an incremental borrowing rate of 10%, can the lessee use the same amortization schedule as the lessor in this situation?

(e) Explain how the entry in part (c)(1) would be different for the lessor if there was no purchase option and the estimated residual value to the lessor (unguaranteed) at the end of the lease term was $2,000. Also, explain whether the lessee could use the same amortization schedule as the lessor in this latter instance.

Solution to Exercise 21-3

(a)   **AMORTIZATION SCHEDULE FOR LESSOR**

Date	Rents Plus BPO[a]	10% Interest	Reduction of Present Value	Present Value Balance
5/1/05				$42,940.44
5/1/05	$10,000.00		$10,000.00	32,940.44
5/1/06	10,000.00	$3,294.04	6,705.96	26,234.48
5/1/07	10,000.00	2,623.45	7,376.55	18,857.93
5/1/08	10,000.00	1,885.79	8,114.21	10,743.72
5/1/09	10,000.00	1,074.37	8,925.63	1,818.09
4/30/10	2,000.00	181.91 *	1,818.09	-0-
	$52,000.00	$9,059.56	$42,940.44	

[a]BPO is an abbreviation for "bargain purchase option." The option to purchase is deemed to constitute a bargain purchase option because the option price is only 25% ($2,000 ÷ $8,000 = 25%) of the estimated market value of the asset at the date the option is exercisable.

*Includes a rounding error of $0.10.

PV = ?
PV = ?

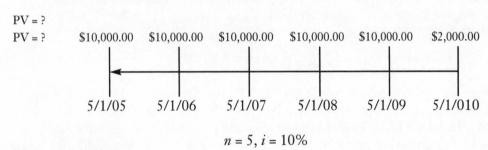

$$n = 5, i = 10\%$$

PV = $ 1,241.84
PV =   41,698.60
        $42,940.44

(b) (1) Total rents: 5 x $10,000 .... $ 50,000.00
          Bargain purchase option 2,000.00
          Minimum lease payments 52,000.00
          Unguaranteed residual value .... -0-
          Gross investment at inception .... $ 52,000.00

     (2) Present value of rents ($10,000 x 4.16986[a]) ... $ 41,698.60
          Present value of BPO ($2,000 x .62092[b]) 1,241.84

Present value of minimum lease payments   42,940.44
Present value of unguaranteed residual value   -0-
Net investment at inception $ 42,940.44

[a]Factor for present value of an annuity due for $n=5$, $i=10\%$.
[b]Factor for present value of a single sum for $n=5$, $i=10\%$.

(3) Sales price $ 42,940.44 [a]
     Cost of goods sold   40,000.00 [b]
     Gross profit to be recognized during 2005 $ 2,940.44

[a]The sale price is equal to the present value of the minimum lease
   payments:
         Present value of rents ($10,000 x 4.16986) $41,698.60
         Present value of BPO ($2,000 x .62092)   1,241.84
         Present value of minimum lease payments $42,940.44

[b]Cost of goods sold is equal to the lessor's carrying value less the
   present value of any unguaranteed residual value for the lessor:
         Carrying value $40,000.00
         Present value of unguaranteed residual value   -0-
         Cost of goods sold $40,000.00

(4) None. All of the gross profit attributable to a sales-type lease is to be
     recognized in the year in which the inception of the lease occurs. In
     this case, that year is 2005.

TIP! Do not confuse this situation with that of a sale-leaseback transaction in which the
profit (gain) on the sale of an asset (that is leased back to the seller) is generally
deferred and amortized.

(5) $3,294.04 x 8/12 = $2,196.03 interest for 2005

There are eight months between May 1, 2005 and December 31, 2005. The interest for those eight months is reflected on the 5/1/06 payment line of the amortization schedule. The $3,294.04 interest showing on that 5/1/06 payment line is for
the 12-month period preceding 5/1/06. The interest for the last eight months of
2005 is therefore 8/12 x $3,294.04.

(6) $3,294.04 x 4/12 $ 1,098.01
     $2,623.45 x 8/12   1,748.97
     Interest for 2006 $ 2,846.98

TIP! The amortization schedule is **always** prepared using the interest dates (which are
dictated by the lease periods). The interest amount appearing on a given payment
line is then apportioned to the appropriate accounting period(s). In examining the
amortization schedule in part (a), the interest appearing on the 5/1/06 line is the
interest for 5/1/05 through 4/30/06. Thus, 8/12 of it belongs on the 2005 income
statement and 4/12 of it is reported on the 2006 income statement. Likewise, the
$2,623.45 appearing on the 5/1/07 payment line reflects the interest for 5/1/06
through 4/30/07. Thus, 8/12 of it is reported on the 2006 income statement.

(c)   (1) 5/1/05

Lease Payments Receivable	52,000.00	
Cost of Goods Sold	40,000.00	
Unearned Interest Revenue—Leases		9,059.56
Inventory		40,000.00
Sales Revenue		42,940.44

    (2) 5/1/05

Cash	10,000.00	
Lease Payments Receivable		10,000.00

    (3) 12/31/05

Unearned Interest Revenue—Leases	2,196.03	
Interest Revenue		2,196.03
($3,294.04 x 8/12 = $2,196.03)		

    (4) 5/1/06

Cash	10,000.00	
Lease Payments Receivable		10,000.00

    (5) 12/31/06

Unearned Interest Revenue—Leases	2,846.98	
Interest Revenue		2,846.98
($3,294.04 x 4/12 = $1,098.01)		
($2,623.45 x 8/12 = $1,748.97)		
($1,098.01 + $1,748.97 = $2,846.98)		

(d) Yes. The lessee will record the asset under capital lease and the obligation under capital lease at $42,940.44. The lessee's amortization schedule will appear exactly like the lessor's amortization schedule.

TIP! The lessee will amortize the entire $42,940.44 cost of the asset under capital lease over the useful life of the asset to the lessee, which is seven years. Due to the existence of the bargain purchase option, the lessee is expected to use the asset for its entire remaining economic life. Thus, the matching principle will dictate that the asset's cost be allocated over the seven years.

(e) If there was no bargain purchase option, but there was a $2,000 unguaranteed residual value relevant to the lessor, the lessor's journal entry at inception would be:

Lease Payments Receivable	52,000.00	
Cost of Goods Sold	38,758.16 [a]	
Unearned Interest Revenue—Leases		9,059.56 [b]
Inventory		40,000.00
Sales Revenue		41,698.60 [c]

[a] Carrying value of the asset $40,000.00
  Present value of unguaranteed residual value ...... (1,241.84) [1]
  Cost of goods sold $38,758.16

    [1] $2,000.00 x .62092 = $1,241.84

[b] Gross investment in lease $52,000.00
  Net investment in lease .... 42,940.44 [2]
  Unearned interest revenue .... $ 9,059.56

    [2] Present value of minimum lease payments $41,698.60
      Present value of unguaranteed residual   1,241.84
      Net investment in lease $42,940.44

[c] Present value of rents .... $41,698.60 [3]
  Present value of BPO or GRV .... -0-
  Present value of minimum lease payments $41,698.60

    [3] $10,000.00 x 4.16986 = $41,698.60

The entry differs from part (c)(1) in that both Sales Revenue and Cost of Goods Sold are reduced by the cash equivalent value of the $2,000 unguaranteed residual value to be received in five years. In this instance, a portion of the asset ($2,000) is considered **not** to be sold to the lessee; the remainder of the asset is treated as a sale.

The lessor's amortization schedule would be the same as it appears now in part (a), except that the column heading "Rents Plus BPO" would be changed to "Rents Plus Residual Value"; however, the lessee's amortization schedule would differ, even if both parties are using a 10% interest rate.

The lessor's amortization schedule would include accounting for the $2,000 unguaranteed residual value. The lessee's schedule would not include any accounting for the $2,000 unguaranteed residual value to the lessor. The lessee's schedule would begin with $41,698.60, rather than $42,940.44.

Illustration 21-4   249

Illustration 21-4
Use of Residual Value in Nonoperating Lease Situations

Residual value is the estimated value of an asset at some given future point in time. Residual value may be estimated at the end of the lease term or at the end of the asset's useful life, depending on which, if either, is relevant to the party for whom you are accounting.

The residual value at the end of the lease term is used by the lessor in determining the amount to charge the lessee as the periodic rent if either of the following is true:

- The asset will revert back to the lessor at the end of the lease and the residual value is guaranteed.
- The asset will revert back to the lessor at the end of the lease and the residual value is unguaranteed.

The residual value at the end of the lease term is used by the lessor in determining the gross investment and the net investment in the lease if either of the following is true:

- The asset will revert back to the lessor at the end of the lease and the residual value is guaranteed.
- The asset will revert back to the lessor at the end of the lease and the residual value is unguaranteed.

The residual value at the end of the lease term is used by the lessee in determining the cost of the asset under capital lease **only** if the following is true:

- The asset will revert back to the lessor at the end of the lease and the residual value is guaranteed by the lessee.

The residual value at the end of the lease term (or at the end of the asset's life) is used by the lessee in determining the periodic amortization if either of the following is true:

- The asset will revert back to the lessor at the end of the lease and the residual value is guaranteed by the lessee. (Use the residual value at the end of the lease term.)
- The asset will transfer to the lessee at the end of the lease term either through an automatic transfer clause or a bargain purchase option. (Use the residual at the end of the asset's life.)

Case 21-1

PURPOSE: This case will review the lessee's and lessor's accounting procedures for a lease with a guaranteed residual value.

Instructions

Refer to the facts of **Exercise 21-3** above. Assume there is no purchase option at the end of the lease term. Further, assume the asset reverts back to the lessor at the end of five years and the lessee guarantees the lessor a residual value of $2,000 at that date.

(a) Explain how the lessor's accounting procedures for a lease with a $2,000 guaranteed residual value will differ from the procedures for a lease containing a $2,000 bargain purchase option.

(b) Explain how the lessee's accounting procedures for a lease requiring the lessee to guarantee a residual value of $2,000 will differ from the procedures for a lease containing a $2,000 bargain purchase option.

Solution to Case 21-1

(a) From the lessor's standpoint, there is no difference in the calculations, time line, or journal entries if the $2,000 is a guaranteed residual value rather than a bargain purchase option. Thus, the **Solution to Exercise 21-3**, parts (a) through (c) would also hold for the $2,000 guaranteed residual value (refer to that solution, and every place you see "bargain purchase option" or "BPO" simply change that phrase to "guaranteed residual value" or "GRV").

(b) From the lessee's standpoint, the time line, journal entries, and most of the calculations are the same for a lease containing a guaranteed residual value as those pertaining to a lease that contains a bargain purchase option. The major difference lies in the calculation of amortization:

- If the lease contains a bargain purchase option, the cost of the asset under capital lease (reduced by any residual value available to the lessee at the end of the asset's economic life) is amortized over the remaining economic life of the asset.
- If the lease contains a guaranteed residual value, the cost of the asset under capital lease reduced by the guaranteed residual value is amortized over the lease term.

Thus, using the data from **Exercise 21-3**, and assuming the lessee uses a 10% interest rate to account for the lease and the straight-line amortization method, amortization calculations for the lessee would be as follows:

Assuming a bargain purchase option of $2,000:

$$\frac{\$42,940.44 - 0^a}{7 \text{ years}} = \$6,134.35 \text{ amortization per year for seven years}$$

^{a}Assumes a zero residual value at the end of seven years.

Assuming a guaranteed residual value of $2,000:

$$\frac{\$42,940.44 - \$2,000.00}{5 \text{ years}} = \$8,188.09 \text{ amortization per year for five years}$$

When the $2,000 is assumed to be a guaranteed residual value and the lessee uses the same interest rate as the lessor, the lessee's amortization schedule is the same as the lessor's amortization schedule.

TIP!

Exercise 21-4

PURPOSE: This exercise will illustrate how to classify receivables and payables related to leases on the balance sheet.

The following amortization schedule is properly being used by a lessee and a lessor. The lease contains a bargain purchase option (BPO). Both the lessee and the lessor have a calendar-year reporting period.

Date	Rent Plus BPO	10% Interest	Reduction of Present Value	Present Value Balance
5/1/05				$ 42,940.44
5/1/05	$ 10,000.00		$ 10,000.00	32,940.44
5/1/06	10,000.00	$3,294.04	6,705.96	26,234.48
5/1/07	10,000.00	2,623.45	7,376.55	18,857.93
5/1/08	10,000.00	1,885.79	8,114.21	10,743.72
5/1/09	10,000.00	1,074.37	8,925.63	1,818.09
4/30/10	2,000.00	181.91	1,818.09	-0-
	$ 52,000.00	$9,059.56	$ 42,940.44	

Instructions

Fill in the blanks that follow. Show calculations.

(1) The amount of gross investment to be reported in the current asset section of the lessor's balance sheet at December 31, 2006 is $_____.

(2) The amount of net investment to be reported in the current asset section of the lessor's balance sheet at December 31, 2006 is $_____.

(3) The amount to be reported in the current liability section of the lessee's balance sheet at December 31, 2006 by the caption "Interest Payable" is $_____.

(4) The amount to be reported in the current liability section of the lessee's balance sheet at December 31, 2006 by the caption "Obligations Under Capital Leases" is $_____.

(5) The amount to be reported in the long-term liability section of the lessee's balance sheet at December 31, 2006 by the caption "Obligations Under Capital Leases" is $_____.

Solution to Exercise 21-4

(1) $\underline{\$10,000}$ gross investment in current assets at December 31, 2006.

The most recent payment prior to the balance sheet date (December 31, 2006) was May 1, 2006. The payment line following that line shows a receipt of $10,000 is due on May 1, 2007, which is within one year of the balance sheet date.

(2)

Gross investment classified in current assets	$ 10,000.00
Unearned interest revenue classified in current assets	(874.48)[a]
Net investment in current assets at December 31, 2006	$ 9,125.52

    [a]$2,623.45 x 4/12 = $874.48

The interest portion of the rent payment due to be received on May 1, 2007 is $2,623.45. That interest is for the twelve months that precedes May 1, 2007. Thus, at December 31, 2006, four months of that interest remains unearned.

TIP!

The net investment reflected in noncurrent assets (in the long-term investments classification) on the lessor's December 31, 2006 balance sheet would be determined as follows:

Gross investment classified in noncurrent assets	$22,000.00 [a]
Unearned interest revenue classified in noncurrent assets	(3,142.07)[b]
Net investment in noncurrent assets at 12/31/06	$18,857.93

    [a]Rents due 5/1/08 and 5/1/09 and BPO = $10,000 + $10,000 + $2,000.00 = $22,000.00
    [b]Interest portion of rents due 5/1/08 and 5/1/09 and interest portion of BPO = $1,885.79 + $1,074.37 + $181.91 = $3,142.07.

(3)

Balance of obligation at May 1, 2006	$26,234.48
Interest rate	10%
Interest for twelve months, 5/1/06 to 4/30/07	2,623.45
Fraction of year from 5/1/06 to 12/31/06	x 8/12

Interest for 5/1/06 to 12/31/06,
which is a current liability at 12/31/06 $ 1,748.97

(4) Current portion of Obligations under Capital Leases
at 12/31/06 $ 7,376.55

The payment line that follows the balance sheet date (12/31/06) is 5/1/07. The principal portion of the rent payment due on that date ($7,376.55) represents the current portion of the lessee's obligation under capital lease [excluding any accrued interest calculated in part (3)] at 12/31/06.

> **TIP!**
>
> The interest portion of a rent payment is for a span of time, so it gets apportioned (allocated) between accounting periods; however, the principal portion of a rent payment falls in only one period and does **not** get allocated. Thus, the interest of $2,623.45 on the 5/1/07 payment line is to be expensed 8/12 in 2006 and 4/12 in 2007. The entire $7,376.55 principal payment appearing on the 5/1/07 rent line becomes due at a point in time and does not get apportioned.
>
> **TIP!**
>
> In published financial statements, the amount of accrued interest payable [solution to part (3)] is often combined with the current portion of the remaining principal [solution to part (4)] and reported as a single line item in current liabilities.

(5) Noncurrent portion of Obligations Under Capital Leases
at 12/31/06 $18,857.93
(This figure is the present value balance on the 5/1/07 rent line.)

Exercise 21-5

PURPOSE: This exercise will review the accounting procedures for an operating lease for both the lessee and the lessor.

On January 1, 2005, Clarence Corp. leased office space to Montreal Service Corp. The following data apply:
1. The lease is appropriately classified as an operating lease by both the lessee and the lessor.
2. The lease term is for five years.
3. The rent payment is $50,000 for 2005 and is scheduled to increase by $10,000 each year.
4. Rent payments are due each January 1 and the first one is paid on January 1, 2005.
5. The lessee paid a $5,000 bonus payment on January 1, 2005 to obtain the lease.
6. The lessor's cost of the asset is $900,000. The lessor uses the straight-line amortization method and estimates the asset has a service life of 25 years with no residual value.

7. The lessor paid an $8,000 finder's fee to a leasing agent for their service.
8. Annual insurance and property taxes on the property amount to $7,200 and are borne by the lessor.

Instructions

(a) Calculate the rental expense for the lessee for (1) 2005 and (2) 2006.
(b) Calculate the lessor's operating profit (loss) on the leased asset for (1) 2005 and (2) 2006.

Solution to Exercise 21-5

(a) (1) $71,000
     (2) $71,000

Calculations:

Average rental	$ 70,000[a]
Amortization of lease bonus	1,000[b]
Rent expense per year	$ 71,000

[a] Rental for 2005	$ 50,000
Rental for 2006	60,000
Rental for 2007	70,000
Rental for 2008	80,000
Rental for 2009	90,000
Total rents	$ 350,000

$350,000 ÷ 5 years = $70,000 per year

[b] $5,000 bonus ÷ 5 years = $1,000 per year

EXPLANATION: For an operating lease, minimum lease payments are recognized as rental expense on a straight-line basis, even if not payable on a straight-line basis. Thus, the lease bonus and scheduled rent increases are amortized to rent expense by the lessee over the lease term on a straight-line basis.

(b) (1) $26,200
     (2) $26,200

Calculations:

Average rental		$ 70,000[a]
Amortization of lease bonus		1,000[b]
Rental revenue		$ 71,000
Less: Amortization	$ 36,000[c]	
Amortization of initial direct costs	1,600[d]	

	Executory costs—taxes and insurance	7,200	44,800
	Operating profit on leased asset		$ 26,200

[a]Same calculation as in part (a) above.
[b]Same calculation as in part (a) above.
[c]($900,000 – 0) ÷ 25 years = $36,000 amortization per year
[d]$8,000 ÷ 5 years = $1,600 amortization per year

EXPLANATION: For an operating lease, each rental receipt by the lessor is recorded as rental revenue. The amount of revenue recognized in each accounting period is a level amount (straight-line basis) regardless of the lease provisions, unless another systematic and rational basis is more representative of the time pattern in which the benefit is derived from the leased asset. Thus, the lease bonus and scheduled rent increases are amortized to rent revenue by the lessor over the lease term on a straight-line basis. The leased asset is amortized in the normal manner. Costs paid to independent third parties such as appraisal fees, finder's fees, and other initial direct costs of the lease are amortized over the life of the lease. Executory costs (taxes, insurance, etc.) are charged to expense in the period to which they pertain.

Analysis of Multiple-Choice Type Questions

Question

1. Wells Ltd. leases an airplane from Kitson Corp. under an agreement which meets the criteria to be a capital lease for Wells Company. The 10-year lease requires payment of $34,000 at the beginning of each year, including $5,000 per year for maintenance, insurance, and taxes. The incremental borrowing rate for the lessee is 15%; the lessor's implicit rate is 12% and is known by the lessee. The present value of an annuity due of 1 for 10 years at 15% is 5.77158. The present value of an annuity due of 1 for 10 years at 12% is 6.32825. According to the accounting guidelines for leases, the lessee should record the leased asset at:
   a. ($29,000) (5.77158) = $167,376.
   b. ($29,000) (6.32825) = $183,519.
   c. ($34,000) (5.77158) = $196,234.
   d. ($34,000) (6.32825) = $215,161.

EXPLANATION: Think through the steps involved in accounting for a lease for a lessee (see **Illustration 21-2**). Calculate the present value of the minimum lease payments (excluding executory costs). Use the lessee's incremental borrowing rate to do the discounting process, unless the lessor's implicit rate is known and is lower. In this scenario, the $5,000 executory costs must be deducted from the $34,000 to arrive at a $29,000 rent excluding executory costs. The lessor's implicit rate of 12% is known by the lessee and is lower than 15%; therefore, the 12% is to be used to calculate the present value of the minimum lease payments. That present value figure is determined by multiplying the rent (excluding executory costs) by the factor for present value of an annuity due of 1 for $n = 10$, $i = 12\%$. There is no indication that the asset's fair value may be lower than the calculated present value amount; therefore, the asset is to be recorded at the present value figure. (Solution = b.)

Question

2. The amount to be recorded as the cost of an asset under capital lease is equal to the:
    a.   present value of the minimum lease payments.
    b.   present value of the minimum lease payments or the fair value of the asset, whichever is lower.
    c.   present value of the minimum lease payments plus the present value of any unguaranteed residual value.
    d.   carrying value of the asset on the lessor's books.

EXPLANATION: For a capital lease, the lessee records an asset and a liability at the lower of (1) the present value of the minimum lease payments or (2) the fair market value of the leased asset at the inception of the lease. An unguaranteed residual value is not relevant to the lessee; the lessee does not account for it. The lessor's carrying value is also irrelevant to the lessee. (Solution = b.)

Question

3. The following list of items relate to lease accounting:
    I.   Annual lease payments
    II.   Bargain purchase option
    III.   Guaranteed residual value
    IV.   Unguaranteed residual value

    A lessor has a direct-financing type lease. Minimum lease payments associated with that lease would include items:
    a.   I and II only.
    b.   I, II, and III only.
    c.   I, III, and IV only.
    d.   I, II, III, and IV.

EXPLANATION: Mentally list the components of minimum lease payments and compare with the list above. Minimum lease payments may include
*   Periodic regular rental payments
*   Guaranteed residual value (if any)

- Bargain purchase option (if any)
- Penalty for failure to renew

The minimum lease payments thus include <u>only</u> items I, II, and III of the list given in the question. (Solution = b.)

> An unguaranteed residual will be involved in the lessor's accounting for the lease, but it is not part of minimum lease payments. For example, gross investment in lease is comprised of minimum lease payments plus unguaranteed residual value and net investment in lease is the present value of the components in gross investment.

TIP!

Question

4. On December 31, 2004, Ryan Corporation leased a yacht from Sean Company for an eight-year period expiring December 30, 2012. Equal annual payments of $80,000 are due on December 31 of each year, beginning with December 31, 2004. The lease is properly classified as a capital lease on Ryan's books. The present value at December 31, 2004 of the eight lease payments over the lease term discounted at 10% is $469,474. Assuming all payments are made on time, the amount that should be reported by Ryan Corporation as the total obligation under capital leases on its December 31, 2005 balance sheet is:
   a. $348,421.
   b. $400,063.
   c. $436,421.
   d. $480,000.
   e. none of the above.

EXPLANATION: Calculate the information for the first three entries on the lessee's amortization schedule. The schedule will appear as follows: (Solution = a.)

Date	Rent	Interest	Principal	Present Value Balance
12/31/04				$469,474.00
12/31/04	$80,000.00	0	$80,000.00	389,474.00
12/31/05	80,000.00	$38,947.40	41,052.60	348,421.40

Question

5. The following facts pertain to a single lease:
   1. A lease provides that the asset will revert back to the lessor at the end of its seven-year term.
   2. The present value of the minimum lease payments is equal to $54,000 and the fair value of the asset at the inception date is $60,000.

3. The remaining economic life of the leased asset is estimated to be 10 years.

✓ 4. Uncollectible lease payments are subject to a reasonable estimation.

✓ 5. The lessor guarantees the asset against obsolescence.

✓ 6. The fair value of the asset exceeds its cost on the lessor's books.

✓ How should the lease be classified on the books of the lessee and lessor, respectively?

	Lessee	**Lessor**
a.	Capital	Sales-type
(b.)	Capital	Operating
c.	Operating	Sales-type
d.	Operating	Operating

EXPLANATION: Review the facts and determine how the lease should be classified on the books of the lessee. Repeat the process to determine how the lease should be classified on the books of the lessor. Refer to **Illustration 21-1**. The lease meets criterion 4 in Group I. Thus, it is a capital lease from the standpoint of the lessee because it meets at least one criterion in Group I. Because the lease does **not** meet **both** of the criteria in Group II, it is an operating lease from the standpoint of the lessor.

The significance of the facts given is as follows:

1. The asset will be returned to the lessor at the end of the lease; therefore, the lease does not meet criterion 1 or 2 of Group I.

2. The present value of the minimum lease payments ($54,000) is equal to 90% of the asset's fair value ($60,000) at the inception date; hence, the lease agreement meets criterion 4 in Group I.

3. The term of the lease is seven years, which is only 70% of the remaining economic life of the asset; hence, criterion 3 of Group I is not met.

4. The lessor can reasonably estimate any uncollectible lease payments; therefore, criterion 1 of Group II is met by the lessor.

5. The lessor guarantees the asset against obsolescence. This means that the costs of meeting this promise are indeterminable, which further means that an important uncertainty exists surrounding the amount of unreimbursable costs yet to be incurred by the lessor under the lease. Thus, criterion 2 of Group II is not met.

6. The fair value of the asset (which usually establishes the lessor's initial amount of net investment in lease) exceeds the lessor's carrying value for the asset. This means that the lease would be a sales-type lease on the books of the lessor **if** the lease met one criterion from Group I and both criterion from Group II. (Solution = b.)

Question

6. Digger Corporation is a lessee with a capital lease. The asset is recorded at $180,000 and has an economic life of eight years. The lease term is five years. The asset is expected to have a market value of $60,000 at the end of five years, and a market value of $20,000 at the end of eight years. The lease agreement provides for the automatic transfer of title of the asset to the lessee at the end of the lease term. What amortizable base and what service life should the lessee use to calculate amortization for the first year of the lease?

	Amortizable Base	Service Life
a.	$180,000 – $20,000	5 years
b.	$180,000 – $20,000	8 years
c.	$180,000 – $60,000	5 years
d.	$180,000 – $60,000	8 years

EXPLANATION: Determine what will provide the best matching of costs with revenues. Because of the automatic transfer of title, the lessee is expected to hold and use the asset for eight years. The benefits to be consumed over the eight years are determined by the difference between the asset's recorded cost ($180,000) and its expected value at the end of its useful life to the lessee ($20,000). (Solution = b.)

Question

7. Three different lease situations are described below:

   1. Lessee's incremental borrowing rate is 12%.
      Lessor's implicit rate is 12%.
      Asset will revert to the lessor at the end of the lease term when the
        asset is expected to have a fair value of $60,000. ↘ unguaranteed residual value

   2. Lessee's incremental borrowing rate is 12%.
      Lessor's implicit rate is 12%.
      Lease requires lessee to guarantee a residual value of $30,000 to
        the lessor.

   3. Lessee's incremental borrowing rate is 12%.
      Lessor's implicit rate is 14%.
      Lease contains a bargain purchase option of $20,000.

In which of the above cases will the lessor and the lessee have the same amortization schedule?
   a. 1 and 2 only.
   b. 2 and 3 only.
   c. 1 and 3 only.
   d. 1, 2, and 3.
   e. None of the above.

APPROACH AND EXPLANATION: The lessee and lessor can use the same amortization schedule when both of the following two conditions exist: (1) the lessee and the lessor both use the same interest rate to account for the lease, and (2) the lessor does **not** have an unguaranteed residual value to account for. The lessee and the lessor have the same rate in case 1 and case 2. The lessee and the lessor will **not** use the same rate in case 3 because the lessee is to use the lower of the two rates, which in this case is **not** the lessor's implicit rate. Therefore, in case 3, the two parties cannot use the same amortization schedule. In case 1, the asset reverts to the lessor at the end of the lease term when the asset has a fair value of $60,000, which constitutes an unguaranteed residual value that will have to be reflected in the lessor's amortization schedule but will not affect the lessee's amortization schedule. Therefore, the two parties cannot use the same amortization schedule for case 1. Thus, case 2 is the only scenario listed in the question in which the two parties can use the same amortization schedule. (Solution = e.)

Question

8. A lessee with a capital lease containing a bargain purchase option should amortize the leased asset over the:
   a. asset's remaining economic life.
   b. term of the lease.
   c. life of the asset or the term of the lease, whichever is shorter.
   d. life of the asset or the term of the lease, whichever is longer.

EXPLANATION: Amortization is a cost allocation process which is done to comply with the matching principle—that is, to match expenses with revenues. The period appropriate for amortization is the period of time the asset will be used in operations. If the lease agreement provides for automatic transfer of title of the asset to the lessee at the end of the lease term or for a bargain purchase option, the assumption is that the lessee will use the asset for its remaining economic life and, therefore, that is the span of time appropriate for amortization. If the lease does not provide for automatic transfer of title of the asset or for a bargain purchase option, the assumption is that the lessee will use the asset only for the term of the lease and, therefore, the lease term is the appropriate period for amortization. (Solution = a.)

TIP! | The cost of leasehold improvements (items such as fences and partitions added to leased premises by a lessee) are to be amortized (amortized) over the life of the asset (the improvement) or the term of the lease, whichever is the shorter.

Question

9. A lessor has a direct financing type lease. The end of the lessor's accounting period does not coincide with a lease payment date. At the end of the lessor's accounting period, the journal entry to record interest earned since the last rental payment date would be:

a.	Cash	XX	
	Interest Revenue		XX
b.	Interest Receivable	XX	
	Interest Revenue		XX
c.	Unearned Interest Revenue	XX	
	Interest Revenue		XX
d.	Interest Expense	XX	
	Interest Payable		XX

EXPLANATION: A lessor accounts for interest as a deferral situation. Thus, at the date of inception, the lessor includes all the amounts ever to be received from the lease (gross investment) in the Lease Payments Receivable account. These amounts include interest to be earned over the term of the lease; hence, a contra account called Unearned Interest Revenue is established in order to reduce the carrying value of the receivable down to the present value of the components of gross investment (that present value amount is called net investment). As interest is earned, it is transferred from the Unearned Interest Revenue account to an earned interest account (Interest Revenue). A confusing aspect of lease accounting often results from the fact that the lessee uses an accrual approach to accounting for interest. Thus, the lessee initially records only the present value of the lease obligation in the Obligations Under Capital Leases account. Thus, at a balance sheet date, an adjusting entry on the lessee's books will include a debit to Interest Expense and a credit to Interest Payable. (Solution = c.)

Question

10. At the inception of a capital lease, a residual value guaranteed by a lessee should be included as part of minimum lease payments on the books of the:

	Lessee	Lessor
a.	Yes	Yes
b.	Yes	No
c.	No	Yes
d.	No	No

EXPLANATION: List the components of minimum lease payments. They are: (a) regular periodic rental payments (excluding executory costs), (b) bargain purchase option, (c) guaranteed residual value, and (d) penalty for failure to renew. If the lessor has a guaranteed residual value, it is included in the lessor's calculation of minimum lease payments, regardless of whether the lessee or a third party is the guarantor. The lessee includes a guaranteed residual value in its calculation of minimum lease payments only if the lessee is the one providing the guarantee. (Solution = a.)

Question

11. A lessor has an operating lease with a five-year term that requires lease payments of $100,000 in 2005, $120,000 in 2006, $140,000 in 2007, $160,000 in 2008, and $180,000 in 2009. In 2007, compared to 2006, the lease will cause the following revenues to increase.

	Rent	Interest
a.	Yes	Yes
b.	Yes	No
c.	No	Yes
d.	No	No

EXPLANATION: The amount of rent revenue recognized in each accounting period covered by the term of an operating lease is a level amount (straight-line basis) regardless of the lease provisions, unless another systematic and rational basis is more representative of the time pattern in which the benefit is derived from the leased asset. In this situation, an average amount of $140,000 would be recognized as rent revenue in each of the five years. Therefore, the amount of rent revenue is a constant amount. An operating lease has no interest associated with it. Thus, there is no increase in rent revenue or interest revenue from one year to another with an operating lease. (Solution = d.)

TIP!

The journal entry to record the receipt of rent in 2005 would appear as follows:		
Cash	100,000	
Rent Receivable	40,000	
Rent Revenue		140,000

Question

12. Hanks Leasing Co. has an operating lease. Rents are a constant amount each year. Rent payments collected in 2005 that pertain to use of the leased asset in 2006 should be reported as:
    a. rent revenue in 2005.
    b. accrued rent on the December 31, 2005 balance sheet.
    c. unearned rent on the December 31, 2005 balance sheet.
    d. rent receivable on the December 31, 2005 balance sheet.

EXPLANATION: Rent revenue received in advance represents a liability at the December 31, 2005 balance sheet date. Revenue received in advance is often called unearned rent revenue or deferred rent revenue. (Solution = c.)

Question

13. A lessor with a sales-type lease involving an unguaranteed residual value available to the lessor at the end of the lease term will report sales revenue in the period of inception of the lease at which of the following amounts?

a.   The minimum lease payments plus the unguaranteed residual value.

b.   The present value of the minimum lease payments.

c.   The cost of the asset to the lessor, less the present value of any unguaranteed residual value.

d.   The present value of the minimum lease payments, plus the present value of the unguaranteed residual value.

EXPLANATION: The unguaranteed residual value is viewed as pertaining to a portion of the asset that is not yet sold. Therefore, the sales revenue figure is the present value (today's cash equivalent) of all future cash flows expected to be received by the lessor for the leased asset **except** for the unguaranteed residual value. Therefore, sales revenue is calculated by determining the present value of the minimum lease payments. Answer section "a" describes the gross investment calculation, answer selection "c" describes the lessor's cost of goods sold calculation, and answer selection "d" describes the lessor's net investment in lease amount. (Solution = b.)

Question

14. A lease has an eight-year term, and the related asset has a remaining economic life of 10 years. The lease is appropriately classified as a sales-type lease on the books of the lessor. The gross profit related to this lease should be:

    a.   recognized wholly in the period of the inception of the lease.

    b.   amortized evenly over eight years.

    c.   amortized evenly over 10 years.

    d.   amortized over eight years using the effective interest method of amortization.

EXPLANATION: The gross profit related to a sales-type lease is recognized wholly in the period in which the lease's inception date occurs. The lessor's journal entry at the date of inception includes a credit to Sales Revenue (for the present value of the minimum lease payments) and a debit to Cost of Goods Sold (for the asset's carrying value less the present value of any unguaranteed residual value). When these two amounts are reported on the income statement, the resulting difference is the amount of gross profit earned on the lease. (Solution = a.)

Question

15. Trim Corporation sold a greenhouse to Laventhall Company for $800,000 and realized a gain of $300,000. The buyer immediately leased the asset back to the seller under a capital lease arrangement for the remainder of the asset's economic life of 10 years. The lessee uses the straight-line amortization method. The profit on the sale of the greenhouse should be:

    a.   recognized in full in the year of sale.

    b.   deferred and amortized over the term of the lease.

c. deferred and recognized in full at the end of the lease term.
d. credited directly to retained earnings.

EXPLANATION: Any profit or loss experienced by the seller-lessee from the sale of the assets that are leased back under a capital lease should be deferred and amortized over the lease term (or the asset's economic life if criterion 1 or 2 is satisfied) in proportion to the amortization of the leased assets. At a balance sheet date, the balance of the deferred gain is reported as an asset valuation allowance. (Solution = b.)

CHAPTER 22

Accounting Changes and Error Analysis

Overview

In order to have comparability of financial statements for successive periods for an entity, the accountant must be consistent in the application of generally accepted accounting principles (quality of consistency). However, sometimes there is justification for a change. The accountant must then meet the requirements of full disclosure in reporting the change. Accounting changes are discussed in this chapter.

The accountant may be consistent in the application of accounting practices but may make some type of error (such as a math mistake or misapplication of generally accepted accounting principles). When the error is discovered, the effects must be properly reported. Error analysis is also discussed in this chapter.

Study Steps

Understanding the Nature of Changes

Changes in accounting policy

CICA Handbook Section 1506, "Changes in Accounting Policies and Estimates, and Errors" permits a voluntary change in policy only if it results in a reliable and more relevant financial statement presentation. Specifically, the change must remain reliable and be more relevant. It cannot produce more reliable but less relevant information. Therefore, a proposed change that remains reliable and is equally relevant would not be allowed.

The change in policy must be on a retroactive basis.

Retroactive application also results in consistency.

The initial adoption of an accounting policy (i.e., new or revised *CICA Handbook* standards) would follow implementation guidance on the specific section. If there is no guidance, it would be done on a retroactive basis.

Change in estimate

A change in accounting estimate usually results from additional new information or a change in circumstances (e.g., a change in the obsolescence provision for inventory might result from an inventory count, or a change in the estimated remaining useful life of an asset may result from real-life experience in that the asset physically lasts longer than originally expected). Therefore, it does not make sense to adjust retroactively since the situation was different in those earlier periods.

If in doubt as to whether something is a change in policy or in estimate, treat it as a change in estimate.

Correction of an error

A correction of an error is accounted for retroactively with restatement since, once the error is found, the previous statements may be incorrect or misleading and should be adjusted.

Be careful to differentiate between changes in estimates from corrections of errors due to the different accounting procedures.

Remember that estimates are made everyday in accounting. And, as long as the estimates are made with care and consider available information, they are acceptable for that time and would not be subsequently adjusted even though they proved to be incorrect in hindsight.

Any type of change or adjustment should be noted in the notes to the financial statements if they are material, except for changes in estimates since they are considered to be a normal part of financial reporting. Even changes in estimates may warrant some additional disclosure, however, depending on how significant the change is.

Tips on Chapter Topics

There are actually only two basic types of **accounting changes**. They are: (1) change in accounting policy, and (2) change in accounting estimate. A change in the reporting entity is a special type of a change in accounting principle (not discussed in this chapter) because while prior period financial statements are to be restated, there is usually no impact on net income. Finally, a correction of an error in previously issued financial statements is not an accounting change; it is a prior period adjustment.

TIP!

A **change in accounting policy** occurs when there is a change from one generally acceptable accounting principle or method to another generally accepted accounting principle or method. Therefore, a change from one generally acceptable inventory pricing method to another generally accepted inventory pricing method is a change in an accounting policy. A change from an accounting method that is **not** generally accepted to a method that is GAAP is not an accounting change—it is a correction of an error.

TIP!

The term **accounting policy** includes not only accounting principles and practices but also the methods of applying them. Thus, a switch from the aggregate basis to the individual basis for determining the lower-of-cost-or-market valuation of inventory constitutes a change in accounting policy.

TIP!

A **change in accounting estimate** occurs when an entity has a change from one good faith estimate to another good faith estimate. Accounting estimates change as new events occur, as more experience is acquired, or as additional information is obtained. A change in estimate results from new information or subsequent developments and not from oversights or misuse of facts, which is a correction of an error.

TIP!

A change from one generally accepted amortization method to another generally accepted amortization method might appear to be a change in an accounting policy. The new Handbook standards identify this situation as a change in estimate because amortization is an estimate of the expected pattern of consumption of the future economic benefits. In addition, a change in the estimated service life or a change in the estimated residual value of a depreciable asset also constitute a change in accounting estimate.

TIP!

Errors include mathematical mistakes, oversights of information available at the time, misapplications of accounting principles, and misuse of facts.

TIP!

Generally, a change in an accounting policy is to be accounted for retroactively with restatement. However, *CICA Handbook* Section 1506, "Changes in Accounting Policies and Estimates, and Errors," indicates that retroactive without restatement is allowed when the information is not practical to obtain, or when a specific *CICA Handbook* section allows it. These situations are expected to be rare. A change in accounting estimate is to be accounted for prospectively. Refer to **Illustration 22-1** for a summary of the relevant reporting requirements.

TIP!

Most errors are **counterbalancing**. Therefore, if a counterbalancing error causes an understatement of net income in one period, the same error will cause an overstatement of net income in the immediately following period by the same amount. This

TIP!

type of error will effect two income statements and one balance sheet (the balance sheet at the end of the period in which the error occurred). The balance sheet at the end of the following period will not be affected as the error will have "offset" itself or been counterbalanced by that date.

TIP! Errors that are not counterbalancing will affect two or more income statements and two or more balance sheets. The error will "wash out" at some point in time, although it may take many years to do so. Conceivably, some may not "reverse" until a particular asset is disposed of, maybe at the point where a business ceases to exist. In the context of error analysis, the terms "offset," "reverse," "self-correct," and "wash out" are synonymous.

TIP! If an error causes an **understatement** in revenue, it will cause an **understatement** of net income for that same year; however, if an error causes an **understatement** of expense, it will cause an **overstatement** of net income for that same year.

TIP! All the error situations discussed in this chapter maintain balance in the basic accounting equation (often called the balance sheet equation). Thus, when you analyse the effects of these errors, always make sure your analysis maintains balance in the balance sheet equation (A = L + OE).

TIP! Most of the errors illustrated in this chapter are the result of using the cash basis of accounting rather than the accrual basis of accounting.

Illustration 22-1
Summary of Reporting Requirements for Accounting Changes

TREATMENT	WHEN TO USE	MANNER OF REPORTING
Retroactive with restatement	On initial adoption of a primary source of GAAP	1. A catch-up adjustment is recorded using the Retained Earnings account.
	Change in accounting policy—voluntary (if more relevant	2. A description of the change and its effect on the current and prior period's financial statements is disclosed.
	Examples: Change from LIFO to any other pricing method such as change from LIFO to FIFO or change from LIFO to average cost.	3. Financial statements of prior periods presented are formally restated to give effect to the new accounting policy.
	Change in method used to account for long-term con-	

Illustration 22-1   269

struction contracts such as change from completed-contract to percentage-of-completion or vice versa.

Retroactive without restatement — If information to restate prior year information is not practical to obtain, or the specific *CICA Handbook* section allows this treatment.

1. A catch-up adjustment is recorded using the Retained Earnings account.
2. A description of the change and its effect on the current year's income is disclosed.

Prospective — Change in accounting estimate. Permitted in rare cases for a change in accounting policy, when the cumulative effect of the change is not possible to determine.

Examples:
Change in the estimated service life of a fixed asset.
Change in the estimated residual value of a fixed asset.
Change in the percentage used for estimate of bad debts.
Change in accounting principle necessitated by a change in estimate.

1. The effect of the change on prior periods will be reflected in the amount of a revenue or expense reported in the income statement for the current period or for the current and future periods, as appropriate.
2. No restatement of financial statements for prior periods is made.
3. Because changes in estimates are considered normal and recurring events in the accounting process, there are no disclosure requirements for such changes.

TIP!

It is sometimes difficult to differentiate between a change in an estimate and a change in an accounting policy. Assume that a company changes from deferring and amortizing certain marketing costs to recording them as an expense as incurred because future benefits of these costs have become doubtful. Is this a change in policy or a change in estimate? **In cases when it is unclear whether a change in policy or a change in estimate has occurred, the change should be considered a change in estimate.** The *CICA Handbook* suggests that a change attributed to "changed circumstances, experience, or new information," should be treated as a change in estimate.

TIP!

The **restatement of financial statements** for a prior period involves making revisions within the previously prepared statements before they are republished in comparative statements. When restatement is appropriate, the accountant will restate only those prior periods that are being published again for readers' use. For example, assume a company used LIFO from the company's inception in 2000 through 2004. In 2005, the company changes to FIFO. This change is to receive retroactive treatment. Thus, if at the end of 2005, the company presents income statements for 2003 and 2004 along with 2005 (comparative statements), the income statements previously published for 2003 and 2004 would be restated (that is, changed or revised) to reflect the individual amounts that would have been reported in the body of the statements in the prior years if the new method (FIFO) had been used. The effect on the periods prior to the first year being republished (2000 through 2002 are the years prior to 2003, which is the earliest year being presented in the set of comparative reports) would be shown as an adjustment to the balance of Retained Earnings at the beginning of 2003, on the statement of retained earnings for 2003, in the comparative statements of retained earnings. Thus, calculations related to this change involve data from several prior years (2000 through 2004), but only two prior years (2003 and 2004) are formally restated because they are the only years being presented in comparative financial statements. Restated financial statements reflect "as if" type amounts in the body of the statements.

Case 22-1

PURPOSE: This case will provide examples of changes in accounting policies, changes in accounting estimates, and changes from non-generally accepted methods to accepted methods (error corrections). It will also identify the proper accounting treatment for each.

Instructions

For each item in the list:
(a) Use the appropriate number to indicate if it is:
    1. A change in accounting policy.
    2. A change in accounting estimate.
    3. An error correction.
    4. None of the above.
(b) Use the appropriate letter to indicate if it is to receive:
    R. Retroactive treatment.
    P. Prospective treatment.
    N. None of the above.

The following is a list of changes.

(a)   (b)

_____ _____   1.   Change in the estimate for obsolescence of inventory.

_____ _____   2.   Change from completed-contract to percentage-of-completion method in accounting for long-term construction contracts.

(a)   (b)

_____ _____   3.   Change from straight-line to double-declining-balance amortization method for all assets held.

_____ _____   4.   Change from sum-of-the-years'-digits amortization method to straight-line method for all assets held.

_____ _____   5.   Change to straight-line amortization method for all new assets acquired; 150% declining-balance method will continue to be used for all assets acquired in prior years.

_____ _____   6.   Change from double-declining-balance method to straight-line amortization method; this change was not planned when the asset was acquired and the accelerated method was adopted.

_____ _____   7.   Change in the estimated residual value for a fixed asset.

_____ _____   8.   Change from the FIFO cost method to the average cost method for inventory pricing.

_____ _____   9.   Change from LIFO to the average cost inventory pricing method.

_____ _____   10.   Change from FIFO to LIFO inventory cost method.

_____ _____   11.   Change from LIFO to FIFO for inventory pricing.

_____ _____   12.   Change to or from the full cost method as used in the extractive industries.

_____ _____   13.   Change from the cash basis to the accrual basis of accounting.

_____ _____   14.   Change from the direct write-off method to the allowance method to account for bad debts, where bad debts have always been (and continue to be) a material amount.

_____ _____   15.   Change from the direct write-off method to the allowance method to account for uncollectible accounts where bad debts have just become a material amount in the current period.

_____ _____   16.   Change from direct costing to full absorption costing for a manufacturing company.

_____ _____   17.   Change from pay-as-you-go to accrual basis in accounting for pension costs.

	(a)	(b)		

   (a)   (b)

_____ _____   18.   Change from the instalment basis to the accrual basis in accounting for instalment sales where uncollectible accounts have always been subject to a reasonable estimation.

_____ _____   19.   Change in the interest rate used to calculate pension expense.

_____ _____   20.   Adoption of a new accounting method because this is the first time a new type of transaction has occurred.

Solution to Case 22-1

Answers			Explanation and/or Comment
(a)	(b)		
2	P	1.	
1	R	2.	Unless due to changed conditions.
2	P	3.	Change in estimate of expected pattern of consumption of benefits.
2	P	4.	
4	N	5.	Only footnote disclosure is required. New method is used only for new assets.
2	P	6.	
2	P	7.	
1	R	8.	If more relevant.
1	R	9.	
1	R	10.	
1	R	11.	
1	R	12.	
3	R	13.	The cash basis of accounting is not GAAP.
3	R	14.	The direct write-off method is not GAAP where bad debts are material.
4	P	15.	Changed circumstances.
1	R	16.	Direct costing is permitted in Canada. Therefore, it is a change in policy.
3	R	17.	The pay-as-you-go approach is not GAAP.
3	R	18.	The instalment basis is not GAAP unless you cannot reasonably estimate uncollectibles.
3	P	19.	Assume both old and new rates are good faith estimates.
4	P	20.	New circumstances.

EXPLANATION: First determine the nature of the change. Then determine how to treat that change. Notice how the answer to part (a) automatically determines the solution to part (b). A change in an accounting policy is to be treated retroactively (with restatement, unless the information is not practical to obtain). A change in an accounting estimate is accounted for prospectively. Therefore, an answer of 1 to (a) means a response of R for part (b), an answer of 2 means a response of P for part (b), and an answer of 3 or 4 for part (a) calls for an answer of R for part (b).

Illustration 22-2   273

Illustration 22-2
How to Calculate and Record the Effects of a Change in Accounting Policy

A. Calculate the effect of a change in accounting method (policy) on income of periods prior to the change and record it as follows:
   1. Determine the effect of the change on retained earnings as of the beginning of the period of change as follows:
       (a) Identify the revenue and/or expense item(s) and amounts that were affected in the prior periods by use of the old method.
       (b) Calculate what the amount of those revenue and/or expense item(s) would have been in the prior periods if the new method was used in all periods. Also consider the effect on the amount of taxes reported.
       (c) Compare the amounts in (a) above with those in (b) above. The net difference is the effect of the change on income of prior periods (net of tax effect).
   2. Record the effect of the change on prior periods as follows:
       (a) Determine if the adjustment for the effect on prior periods is a debit or a credit.
           (1) If use of the new method would have resulted in higher net incomes in prior years, the adjustment needed is a credit.
           (2) If use of the new method would have resulted in lower net incomes in prior years, the adjustment needed is a debit.
       (b) Record the rest of the entry so that asset and liability account balances are restated to balances that would have existed at the beginning of the period of change had the new method been used in all prior periods.

B. Calculate the effect of a change in accounting method on the income of the **current** period (period of change) and report it as follows:
   1. Identify the amount of revenue and/or expense on the income statement for the current period calculated as a result of the use of the new method.
   2. Calculate what the amount of the particular revenue and/or expense item would be in the current period if the old method was used.
   3. Compare the amount(s) in "1" above with the amount(s) in "2" above. The net difference is the effect on the period of change.

The effect on the period of change does **not** include the cumulative effect on prior periods.   **TIP!**

   4. Disclose the effect on the period of change (net of tax effect) in the notes to the financial statements of the period of change.

Exercise 22-1

PURPOSE: This exercise will illustrate the following for a change in accounting policy: (1) calculation of effect on prior periods, (2) calculation of effect on the period of change, and (3) calculation of amounts for restatement purposes.

The Spencer Corp. used the sum-of-the-years'-digits method for the first three years for both book and tax purposes to calculate amortization for its equipment. During the fourth year, the company changed to the straight-line method for book purposes for all assets held. The following facts pertain:

Cost of equipment	$70,000
Date acquired	January 1, Year 1
Estimated service life	10 years
Residual value	$15,000
Tax rate	40%
Number of shares outstanding	10,000

Assume this is a change in accounting policy rather than a change in estimate of how asset benefits will be consumed.

Instructions

(a) Calculate the cumulative effect on periods prior to the year of change.

(b) Prepare the journal entry to record the accounting change.

(c) Calculate the amortization expense for Year 4 and prepare the appropriate adjusting entry.

(d) Calculate the effect of the change on the year of change. Indicate the direction of change (increase or decrease in net income).

(e) Calculate the book value of the equipment to be reported on the balance sheet at the end of Year 4.

(f) Calculate the restated net income figures for Years 1-4, assuming the following amounts were reported prior to the change:

Net income—Year 1	$50,000
Net income—Year 2	55,000
Net income—Year 3	60,000
Income before cumulative effect—Year 4	68,000

Solution to Exercise 22-1

(a)

	Amortization Using OLD (SYD) Method	Amortization Using NEW (Straight-line) Method
Year 1	$10,000 [a]	$ 5,500 [d]
Year 2	9,000 [b]	5,500
Year 3	8,000 [c]	5,500
	$27,000	$16,500

Amortization expense was $27,000 for Years 1–3 using old method.
Amortization would have been 16,500 for Years 1–3 using new method.
Difference is $10,500 cumulative effect on prior periods.
Net-of-tax rate x 60% (100% – 40% tax rate)
Cumulative effect, net of tax $ 6,300

[a]
$$\frac{10}{\frac{10(10+1)}{2}} \times (\$70,000 - \$15,000) = \$10,000$$

[b]
$$\frac{9}{\frac{10(10+1)}{2}} \times (\$70,000 - \$15,000) = \$9,000$$

[c]
$$\frac{8}{\frac{10(10+1)}{2}} \times (\$70,000 - \$15,000) = \$8,000$$

[d]
$$\frac{\$70,000 - \$15,000}{10 \text{ years}} = \$5,500$$

Refer to the guidelines in **Illustration 22-2** in performing the relevant calculations required in this exercise.   **TIP!**

EXPLANATION: The current year (year of change) is Year 4. Therefore, the prior years affected are Years 1, 2, and 3. The total amount that was reported as amortization in the prior years (as determined by using the old amortization method) is compared to what would have been reported as amortization in those same years if the new method had been used for all periods. The difference is the total effect on the prior periods' income before taxes ($10,500) which is commonly called the cumulative effect on prior periods. The net-of-tax answer for the cumulative effect ($6,300) is determined by multiplying the cumulative effect by the 60% net-of-tax rate (100% minus the 40% tax rate).

(b) Accumulated Amortization   10,500
    Cumulative Effect of Change in Accounting Policy—
      Retained Earnings   6,300
    Future Tax Liability (40% x $10,500)   4,200

EXPLANATION: The new method (straight-line) would have yielded less amortization expense and more net income if it had been used in prior periods; therefore, the adjustment to record the cumulative effect on periods prior to the change is a credit. The adjustment is to retained earnings.

The rest of the journal entry restates balances for a contra asset account and a liability account to balances that would have existed at the beginning of the year of change (Year 4) if the new method had been used in all prior periods. At the end of Year 3, accumulated amortization would have been less by $10,500 if the straight-line method had been used since the acquisition date of the asset. Use of an accelerated amortization method for tax purposes would have resulted in a temporary difference that would have given rise to future taxable amounts of $10,500 and a future tax liability at the end of Year 3 of $4,200 ($10,500 x 40% = $4,200).

TIP! | The old method is assumed to be continued for tax purposes.

(c) Straight-line amortization: $\dfrac{\$70,000 - \$15,000}{10 \text{ years}}$ = $\underline{\$5,500}$ Amortization for Year 4

Amortization Expense	5,500	
Accumulated Amortization		5,500

TIP! | Do not confuse this calculation with the procedures employed for a change in accounting estimate. This calculation for amortization ignores what was actually amortized in prior periods because the journal entry in part (b) restated the accounts to balances that would have existed if the new method had been used in all prior periods.

(d)

Amortization Year 4 using new method	$5,500
Amortization Year 4 using old method	7,000 *
Increase in income before income taxes, Year 4	1,500
Net-of-tax rate	60%
Increase in income Year 4, net of tax	$ 900

*7/55 ($70,000 – $15,000) = $7,000

(e)

Cost of equipment	$70,000
Accumulated amortization, end of Year 4	(22,000)*
Book value, end of Year 4	$48,000

*This balance is best determined by reconstructing the entries that would be reflected in the Accumulated Amortization account as follows:

Accumulated Amortization			
		Amortization for Year 1	10,000
Adjustment for cumulative		Amortization for Year 2	9,000
Effect of change in method	10,500	Amortization for Year 3	8,000
		Amortization for Year 4	5,500
		Balance, end of Year 4	22,000

> Notice that because the journal entry in part (b) has put the books on a basis as if the new method (straight-line) had been used in all periods, the balance of Accumulated Amortization at the end of Year 4 is four years worth of $5,500 (straight-line amortization for one year).

TIP!

(f)

	Year 1	Year 2	Year 3	Year 4
Amortization reported	$10,000	$ 9,000	$ 8,000	$ 5,500
Amortization using new method	5,500	5,500	5,500	5,500
Increase in income before taxes	4,500	3,500	2,500	0
Net-of-tax rate (100% – 40%)	60%	60%	60%	--
Increase in net income	2,700	2,100	1,500	--
Net income reported	50,000	55,000	60,000	--
Income before cumulative effect	--	--	--	68,000
Restated net income	$52,700	$57,100	$61,500	$68,000

Exercise 22-2

PURPOSE: This exercise provides an example of the accounting procedures for a change in accounting policy that is to be handled retroactively with restatement.

The Buildaway Construction Company enters into long-term construction contracts. The following data relate to gross profit figures determined first by use of the completed-contract method, and second by use of the percentage-of-completion method for Years 1 through 3:

	Completed-Contract	Percentage-of-Completion
Year 1	$ 40,000	$ 140,000
Year 2	160,000	280,000
Year 3	270,000	350,000

The company used the completed-contract method in Years 1 and 2 for both book purposes and tax purposes. In Year 3, the company changed to the percentage-of-completion method for book purposes only. The tax rate is 40% for all years.

Instructions

(a) Calculate the effect of the change on periods prior to the change.
(b) Prepare the journal entry to record the accounting change.
(c) Calculate the effect of the change on the year of change.

Solution to Exercise 22-2

(a) Total gross profit for Years 1 and 2 using the old method $200,000 [1]
     Total gross profit for Years 1 and 2 using the new method   420,000 [2]
     Cumulative (total) effect on prior periods   220,000
     Net-of-tax rate   60%
     Cumulative effect on prior periods, net of tax $132,000

     [1]$40,000 Year 1 + $160,000 Year 2 = $200,000
     [2]$140,000 Year 1 + $280,000 Year 2 = $420,000

(b) Construction in Process   220,000
     Future Tax Liability ($220,000 x 40%)   88,000
     Retained Earnings   132,000

TIP!

> The new method would have resulted in reporting higher net incomes if it had been used in prior periods; thus, the adjustment required to record the cumulative effect is a credit.

(c) Gross profit for Year 3 using the new method $ 350,000
     Gross profit for Year 3 using the old method   270,000
     Increase in income before income taxes for Year 3   80,000
     Net-of-tax rate   60%
     Increase in net income for Year 3 $ 48,000

Illustration 22-3
Accounting for a Change in Estimate for a Plant Asset

Whenever there is a change in the estimate of service life or salvage value for a depreciable asset, the following format will aid in the calculation of amortization.

    Original Cost
− Accumulated Amortization[a]
= Book Value
+ Additional Expenditures Capitalized, If Any[b]
= Revised Book Value
− Current Estimate of Residual Value
= Remaining Depreciable Cost to be Allocated Over Remaining Life of Asset

[a]Total amortization taken prior to beginning of the year of change.

[b]Sometimes an extension of life is obtained by a major overhaul or other expenditure capitalized subsequent to the acquisition of the original asset.

Exercise 22-3

PURPOSE: This exercise will illustrate the proper accounting procedures for a change in an accounting estimate.

Mitten Corporation acquired a plant asset costing $300,000 at the beginning of Year 1. After amortizing it for four years using the straight-line method, a 10-year service life, and an expected residual value of $30,000, Mitten estimated the asset would be useful for a total of 12 years and have a residual value of $20,000. The tax rate is 40% for all years.

Instructions

(a) Calculate the amortization expense to report for Year 5. Prepare the appropriate journal entry to record it.

(b) Prepare the journal entry, if any, to record the accounting change. Also, explain the type of treatment to give this situation.

(c) Calculate the effect of the change on the year of change. Explain where it is to be reported.

Solution to Exercise 22-3

(a) **APPROACH:** Apply the format outlined in **Illustration 22-3** to calculate amortization where there has been a change in the estimate of service life and/or the estimate of salvage value for plant assets.

Original cost	$ 300,000
Accumulated amortization	(108,000)*
Book value, beginning Year 5	192,000
Additional costs capitalized	-0-
Revised book value	192,000
Current estimate of residual value	(20,000)
Remaining depreciable cost	172,000
Divide by the remaining life	÷ 8 **
Amortization per year for Year 5 and subsequent years	$ 21,500

$$*\frac{\$300,000 - \$30,000}{10 \text{ years}} = \$27,000 \text{ per year using old estimates}$$

$27,000 x 4 years = $108,000

**12 years total – 4 years gone = 8 years remaining

ENTRY:

Amortization Expense	21,500	
Accumulated Amortization		21,500

TIP! An accounting change is always made as of the beginning of the year of change, even though it is not recorded until the end of the period of change.

(b) **No entry.** There is no journal entry to record this change because a change in estimate is to receive prospective treatment. Therefore, there is no calculation of the total effect on prior periods; there is no entry for the effect on prior periods. The total effect on the past is, in this case, spread over the current (Year 5) and future periods (Years 6 through 12).

(c) Amortization to be reported for Year 5 (part a) $ 21,500
    Amortization for Year 5 if old estimate were used   27,000
    Increase in income before income taxes for Year 5   5,500
    Net-of-tax rate   60%
    Increase in net income for Year 5 $ 3,300

The $3,300 effect on the current year is to be disclosed in the footnotes.

Illustration 22-4
Common Relationships and Assumptions Inherent in Error Situations

1. An accrued expense that is **not** recorded at the end of one period is assumed to have been paid (and recorded as expense) in the following period.

2. An accrued revenue that is **not** recorded at the end of one period is assumed to have been received (and recorded as revenue) in the following period.

3. A prepaid expense that is omitted in Year 1 is assumed to have been recorded as expense in Year 1 when the cash was disbursed. Unless otherwise indicated, it is assumed to have become an expired cost in Year 2 (although not correctly recorded as such, due to the omission of the prepaid item at the end of Year 1).

4. An unearned revenue that is omitted in Year 1 is assumed to have been recorded as revenue in Year 1 when the cash was received. Unless otherwise indicated, it is assumed to have become earned in Year 2 (although not correctly recorded as such, due to the omission of the unearned item at the end of Year 1).

5. The ending inventory of one period is the beginning inventory of the following period.

6. If purchases of inventory which are made near the end of Year 1 are not recorded and the merchandise is also omitted from the ending inventory for Year 1, there is no net effect on net income of Year 1 or Year 2.

7. If the amortization expense for Year 1 is omitted in Year 1, the amortization expense for Year 2 is assumed to be recorded correctly in Year 2 (but only for the amount belonging in Year 2) unless otherwise mentioned.

Illustration 22-5
Guide for Preparing Correcting Entries for Errors

SHORT METHOD

Step 1: Adjust any current revenue and/or expense (or gain or loss) account affected by the error.

Step 2: Adjust any asset and/or liability account to its proper balance, if needed.

Step 3: Adjust revenue and/or expense items of prior periods by an entry to retained earnings.

OR

LONG METHOD

Step 1: Reconstruct the erroneous entry that was actually made (sometimes no entry was made).

Step 2: Reconstruct the entry that should have been made. Analyse it to determine the effects (what was understated, overstated, etc.). Remember: $A = L + OE$.

Step 3: Make a correcting entry to bring accounts to the balances that should be shown at a current point in time. You can do so by "reversing" the entry that was made and by recording the entry that should have been made and by doing three additional steps:

    Step 3(a): If any revenue or expense accounts of prior periods are involved, cross them out and replace them with Retained Earnings.

    Step 3(b): Clean up the entry by combining like items.

    Step 3(c): Make an adjusting entry for the current year, if necessary.

Exercise 22-4

PURPOSE: This exercise will provide examples of errors, their effects on net income, and their effects on the balance sheet.

The Keith Corporation discovered errors during a recent audit. The company has a calendar-year reporting period. The errors are as follows:

Error 1   Accrued interest on notes payable of $3,500 was omitted at the end of 2004.

Error 2   Prepaid insurance expense of $1,800 was overlooked at the end of 2004. (The premium paid in advance relates to coverage in 2005.)

Error 3   Accrued interest on investments of $5,100 was understated at the end of 2004.

Error 4   Unearned rent revenue of $4,500 was understated at the end of 2004.

Error 5   A truck with a cost of $10,000, a service life of four years, and a residual value of $4,000 was expensed when it was purchased at the beginning of 2004.

Error 6   Amortization of patent, $700, was omitted in 2004.

Instructions

(a) Assuming net income of $50,000 was reported for 2004, and net income of $72,000 was reported for 2005 (before discovery of the errors), calculate the correct net income figures for 2004 and 2005.

(b) For each error, describe the following:
1. Effect on net income for 2004.
2. Effect on the elements of the basic accounting equation at December 31, 2004.
3. Effect on net income for 2005.
4. Effect on the elements of the basic accounting equation at December 31, 2005.

(c) Prepare the correcting entry for each error, assuming the errors are discovered at the end of 2005 before closing.

Solution to Exercise 22-4

(a)

	2004	2005
Net income as previously reported	$ 50,000	$ 72,000
Failure to accrue interest expense in 2004	(3,500)	3,500
Failure to defer insurance expense in 2004	1,800	(1,800)
Failure to accrue interest revenue in 2004	5,100	(5,100)
Failure to defer rent revenue in 2004	(4,500)	4,500
Failure to capitalize truck in 2004 and amortize	8,500	(1,500)
Failure to amortize a patent in 2004	(700)	-0-
Net income, as corrected	$ 56,700	$ 71,600

TIP!   To correct a net income figure that is understated, add the amount in error; to correct a net income figure that is overstated, deduct the amount in error.

(b) and (c)   The solution and explanation for each error is presented below:

> **TIP!** Notice how the analysis of the effects of each error maintains balance in the basic accounting equation (A = L + OE).
>
> **TIP!** When you are asked to describe the effects of an error, you are to describe the effects on all periods affected, assuming the error is allowed to run its course. Do not assume the error is corrected. To assume correction would mean there are no effects remaining.

APPROACH TO PART (B): Reconstruct what was done. Compare that with what should have been done. The effects of the error should then be readily determinable.

APPROACH TO PART (C): Follow the three easy steps in the "short method" in **Illustration 22-5** to prepare the correcting entries. Refer to the Explanation to part (b) of the Solution to analyse what corrections are needed.

ERROR 1

(b) **Effects of Error 1:** Failure to accrue interest expense in 2004:

1. Net income for 2004 is overstated (because interest expense is understated).
2. Liabilities are understated, and owners' equity is overstated at 12/31/04.
3. Net income for 2005 is understated (because interest expense is overstated).
4. There is no effect on the balance sheet at 12/31/05.

> **TIP!** All income statement accounts are closed to owners' equity; therefore, if net income is affected in the year that an error originates, owners' equity is misstated in the same direction and by the same amount as net income.

Explanation:

What Was Done			*What Should Have Been Done*		
12/31/04	No Entry		Interest Expense	3,500	
			Int. Payable		3,500
During	Int. Expense	3,500	Interest Payable	3,500	
2005	Cash	3,500	Cash		3,500

An adjusting entry to record an accrued interest expense of $3,500 was omitted in 2004. The interest would, therefore, have been paid and recorded as an expense in 2005. The disbursement in 2005 should have been recorded as a reduction in a liability, but the liability was never reflected on the books.

> **TIP!** This is an example of a counterbalancing error. Therefore, two successive income statements and the balance sheet in between them are affected. The balance sheet at the end of the second period is unaffected because by that time the error has counterbalanced (or washed out).

(c) **Correcting entry for Error 1 at 12/31/05 before closing:**

Retained Earnings	3,500	
Interest Expense		3,500

Error 1: Explanation for entry:

Step 1: Interest Expense in 2005 will be overstated unless a correcting entry is made; Interest Expense for 2005 is reduced by a credit.

Step 2: No assets or liabilities are affected at 12/31/05.

Step 3: Interest Expense for 2004 was understated. The Interest Expense for 2004 cannot be debited because all income statement amounts for 2004 have been closed to Retained Earnings. Therefore, debit Retained Earnings to correct for the error.

ERROR 2

(b) **Effects of Error 2:** Failure to defer insurance expense in 2004:

1. Net income for 2004 is understated (because insurance expense is overstated).
2. Assets are understated, and owners' equity is understated at 12/31/04.
3. Net income for 2005 is overstated (because insurance expense is understated).
4. There is no effect on the balance sheet at 12/31/05.

Explanation:

What Was Done	*What Should Have Been Done*		
12/31/04 No Entry	Prepaid Insurance	1,800	
	Insurance Expense		1,800
12/31/05 No Entry	Insurance Expense	1,800	
	Prepaid Insurance		1,800

In 2004, insurance premiums for 2005 were paid in advance. The payment must have been recorded by a charge to expense. An adjusting entry at the end of 2004 to record the deferral of a portion of the expense to a future period (2005) was omitted. The omission of that adjustment caused the failure to record any expense in 2005, even though some benefits were consumed in 2005.

(c) **Correcting entry for Error 2 at 12/31/05 before closing:**

Insurance Expense	1,800	
Retained Earnings		1,800

Error 2: Explanation for entry:

Step 1: Insurance Expense in 2005 will be understated unless a correcting entry is made; Insurance Expense for 2005 is increased by a debit.

Step 2: No assets or liabilities are affected at 12/31/05.

Step 3: Insurance Expense for 2004 was overstated. The Insurance Expense account for 2004 cannot be credited because all income statement amounts for 2004 have been closed to Retained Earnings. Therefore, credit Retained Earnings to correct for the error.

ERROR 3
(b) **Effects of Error 3: Failure to accrue interest revenue in 2004:**
1. Net income for 2004 is understated (because interest revenue is understated).
2. Assets are understated, and owners' equity is understated at 12/31/04.
3. Net income for 2005 is overstated (because interest revenue is overstated).
4. There is no effect on the balance sheet at 12/31/05.

Explanation:

What Was Done			*What Should Have Been Done*		
12/31/04	No entry		Interest Receivable	5,100	
			Int. Revenue		5,100
During	Cash	5,100	Cash	5,100	
2005	Int. Revenue	5,100	Int. Receivable		5,100

An adjusting entry to record accrued revenue of $5,100 was omitted in 2004. Therefore, the interest would have been received and recorded as a revenue in 2005. The receipt in 2005 should have been recorded as a reduction in a receivable, but the receivable was never reflected on the books.

(c) **Correcting entry for Error 3 at 12/31/05 before closing:**

Interest Revenue	5,100	
Retained Earnings		5,100

Error 3: Explanation for entry:
Step 1: Interest Revenue in 2005 will be overstated unless a correcting entry is made; Interest Revenue for 2005 is reduced by a debit.
Step 2: No assets or liabilities are affected at 12/31/05.
Step 3: The Interest Revenue account for 2004 cannot be credited because all income statement amounts for 2004 have been closed to Retained Earnings. Therefore, credit Retained Earnings to correct for the error.

ERROR 4
(b) **Effects of Error 4:** Failure to defer rent revenue in 2004:
1. Net income for 2004 is overstated (because rent revenue is overstated).
2. Liabilities are understated and owners' equity is overstated at 12/31/04.
3. Net income for 2005 is understated (because rent revenue is understated).
4. There is no effect on the balance sheet at 12/31/05.

Explanation:

What Was Done		*What Should Have Been Done*		
12/31/04	No Entry.	Rent Revenue	4,500	
		Unearned Rent Revenue		4,500
12/31/05	No Entry.	Unearned Rent Revenue	4,500	
		Rent Revenue		4,500

In 2004, rental receipts were collected in advance. The receipt must have been recorded by a credit to revenue. An adjusting entry at the end of 2004 to record the deferral of a portion of the revenue to a future period (2005) was omitted. The assumption is that the revenue was earned in 2005 or there would have been a description of another error.

(c) **Correcting entry for Error 4 at 12/31/05 before closing:**

Retained Earnings	4,500	
Rent Revenue		4,500

Error 4: Explanation for entry:

Step 1: Rent Revenue in 2005 will be understated unless a correcting entry is made; Rent Revenue is increased by a credit.

Step 2: No assets or liabilities are affected at 12/31/05.

Step 3: Rent Revenue for 2004 was overstated. The Rent Revenue account for 2004 cannot be debited because all income statement accounts for 2004 have been closed to Retained Earnings. Therefore, debit Retained Earnings in the correcting entry.

ERROR 5

(b) **Effects of Error 5:** Failure to capitalize a fixed asset in 2005 and amortize:

1. Net income for 2005 is understated by $8,500.
2. Assets are understated by $8,500, and owners' equity is understated by $8,500 at 12/31/04.
3. Net income for 2005 is overstated by $1,500.
4. Assets are understated by $7,000, and owners' equity is understated by $7,000 at 12/31/05.

Explanation:

	What Was Done			*What Should Have Been Done*		
Beginning of 2004	Truck Expense	10,000		Truck	10,000	
	Cash		10,000	Cash		10,000
12/31/04	No Entry.			Amortization Exp.	1,500	
				Acc. Amort.		1,500
				[($10,000 − $4,000) ÷ 4 = $1,500]		
12/31/05	No Entry.			Amortization Exp.	1,500	
				Acc. Amort.		1,500

The acquisition of a truck in 2004 was incorrectly recorded as an expense of $10,000. The truck should have been amortized by charging $1,500 to expense over each of four years, beginning with 2004. This means that the income statements for 2004, 2005, 2006, and 2007 will be affected by the error if it is not detected and corrected. The balance sheet at the end of each of those four years will also be in error. This error will turnaround or offset in the period of the disposal of the truck (a gain will be overstated in that period and only then will the error self-correct on the balance sheet).

EFFECTS: Truck Expense is overstated by $10,000 in 2004 and Amortization Expense is understated by $1,500 in each year the truck is held. Therefore: Net income for 2004 is understated by $8,500; owners' equity at 12/31/04 is understated by $8,500; assets at 12/31/04 are understated by $8,500; net income for 2005 is overstated by $1,500; owners' equity at 12/31/05 is understated by $7,000; assets at 12/31/05 are understated by $7,000.

(c) **Correcting entry for Error 5 at 12/31/05 before closing:**

Truck	10,000	
Amortization Expense	1,500	
Accumulated Amortization		3,000
Retained Earnings		8,500

Error 5: Explanation for entry:

Step 1: Amortization Expense in 2005 will be understated unless a correcting entry is made; Amortization Expense of $1,500 is recorded by a debit.

Step 2: The asset Truck will be understated at 12/31/05 by the cost of $10,000 unless a correcting entry is made. Likewise, Accumulated Amortization will be understated by two years worth of amortization unless a correcting entry is made. Therefore, debit Truck for $10,000 and credit Accumulated Amortization for $3,000.

Step 3: Truck Expense for 2004 was overstated by $10,000 and Amortization Expense for 2004 was understated by $1,500. All income amounts for 2004 have been closed to Retained Earnings. Therefore, credit Retained Earnings for $8,500 (i.e., the amount by which Retained Earnings is understated at the beginning of the year in which the error is corrected).

ERROR 6

(b) **Effects of Error 6: Failure to amortize an intangible asset in 2004:**

1. Net income for 2004 is overstated by $700 (because patent amortization is understated).
2. Assets are overstated by $700 and owners' equity is overstated by $700 at 12/31/04.
3. Net income for 2005 is not affected
4. Assets are overstated by $700 and owners' equity is overstated by $700 at 12/31/05.

Explanation:

What Was Done	*What Should Have Been Done*	
12/31/04 No Entry.	Patent Amortization Expense 700	
	Patent	700

The failure to record amortization of a patent is **not** a counterbalancing error. This error will self-correct when the patent is fully amortized (it will be amortized one year after it should have been fully amortized) or when the patent is disposed of (through sale or writeoff). There is no mention of a similar omission in 2005 so the assumption is that the 2005 amortization was recorded properly. Therefore, this error will affect the income statement of 2004 and the income statement of the period of disposal (or of the last period amortized) and every balance sheet prepared between these two periods.

(c) **Correcting entry for Error 6 at 12/31/05 before closing:**

Retained Earnings	700	
Patent		700

Error 6: Explanation for entry:

Step 1: Amortization Expense for 2005 is apparently recorded correctly.

Step 2: The asset Patent will be overstated at 12/31/05 unless a correcting entry is made. Therefore, credit Patent.

Step 3: Amortization Expense for 2004 was understated. The Patent Amortization Expense account for 2004 cannot be debited because all income statement amounts have been closed to Retained Earnings. Therefore, debit Retained Earnings.

TIP! If the amortization expense or amortization expense for 2004 is omitted in 2004, the amortization or amortization expense for 2005 is assumed to be recorded correctly in 2005 unless otherwise indicated. Thus, the carrying value of the long-lived asset will remain overstated on the balance sheet until the asset is disposed of (through sale or abandonment and written off) or completely amortized.

TIP! Very often students have a more detailed approach to correcting entries. The following pairs of entries are alternate answers to some of the correcting entries presented above. Both entries in each pair must be included to be equivalent to the entries shown above.

Error 2:	Prepaid Insurance	1,800	
	Retained Earnings		1,800
	Insurance Expense	1,800	
	Prepaid Insurance		1,800

Error 4:	Retained Earnings	4,500	
	Unearned Rent Revenue		4,500
	Unearned Rent Revenue	4,500	
	Rent Revenue		4,500

Error 5:	Truck	10,000	
	Accumulated Amortization		1,500
	Retained Earnings		8,500
	Amortization Expense	1,500	
	Accumulated Amortization		1,500

Exercise 22-5

PURPOSE: This exercise will illustrate the effects of various errors involving purchases and ending inventory.

Smith Sports Equipment Company sells sporting goods. By taking a physical count and pricing its inventory using the FIFO cost method, inventory was determined to be $430,000 and $572,000 at December 31, 2004, and December 31, 2005, respectively. Net income was reported to be $200,000 and $218,000 for 2004 and 2005, respectively. The following errors occurred with regard to accounting for inventory transactions:

Error 1: Purchases of $30,000 made near the end of 2004 were shipped f.o.b. shipping point by the vendor on December 29, 2004; they were not received by Smith until January 3, 2005. These purchases were omitted from the physical count at December 31, 2004, and were not recorded as purchases until January 3, 2005.

Error 2: Merchandise costing $21,000 was on the premises but was overlooked during the physical inventory count at December 31, 2004.

Error 3: Merchandise costing $32,000 was double-counted during the physical inventory count at December 31, 2005.

Error 4: Sales made near the end of 2005 were shipped f.o.b. destination by Smith on December 28, 2005; they were not received by the customers until January 4, 2006. These items, costing $17,000, were omitted from the inventory sheets of the physical count taken on December 31, 2005, and were treated as sales for $28,500 in 2005.

Instructions

Calculate the correct net income amounts for 2004 and 2005.

Solution to Exercise 22-5

	2004	2005
Net income as previously reported	$200,000	$218,000
Both purchases and ending inventory for 2004 understated	--	--
Ending inventory for 2004 understated	21,000	(21,000)
Ending inventory for 2005 overstated	--	(32,000)
Sales for 2005 overstated	--	(28,500)
Ending inventory for 2005 understated	--	17,000
	$221,000	$153,500

Explanation: Analyses of effects of errors on cost of goods sold:

Error 1:

		2004	2005
	Beginning inventory	No effect	Under $30,000
+	Net cost of purchases	Under $30,000	Over $30,000
=	Goods available for sale	Under $30,000	No effect
−	Ending inventory	Under $30,000	No effect
=	Cost of goods sold expense	No effect	No effect

Error 2:

		2004	2005
	Beginning inventory	No effect	Under $21,000
+	Net cost of purchases	No effect	No effect
=	Goods available for sale	No effect	Under $21,000
−	Ending inventory	Under $21,000	No effect
=	Cost of goods sold expense	Over $21,000	Under $21,000

Error 3:

		2004	2005	2006
	Beginning inventory	No effect	No effect	Over $32,000
+	Net cost of purchases	No effect	No effect	No effect
=	Goods available for sale	No effect	No effect	Over $32,000
−	Ending inventory	No effect	Over $32,000	No effect
=	Cost of goods sold expense	No effect	Under $32,000	Over $32,000

Error 4:

		2004	2005	2006
	Beginning inventory	No effect	No effect	Under $17,000
+	Net cost of purchases	No effect	No effect	No effect
=	Goods available for sale	No effect	No effect	Under $17,000
−	Ending inventory	No effect	Under $17,000	No effect
=	Cost of goods sold expense	No effect	Over $17,000	Under $17,000

Also:

	2004	2005	2006
Sales revenue	No effect	Over $28,500	Under $28,500

TIP! An error involving purchases and/or ending inventory and/or beginning inventory should be analysed in terms of its effect on components of the cost of goods sold calculation in order to then determine its effect on net income. That calculation is:

	Beginning inventory
+	Net cost of purchases
=	Goods available for sale
-	Ending inventory
=	Cost of goods sold

TIP! The ending inventory for Year 1 is the beginning inventory for Year 2. Thus, when the ending inventory for Year 1 is overstated, it will cause an overstatement in the net income for Year 1 and an understatement in net income for Year 2. This error will cause retained earnings at the end of Year 1 to be overstated because net income for Year 1 (which is overstated) is closed into retained earnings. The balance of retained earnings at the end of Year 2 will be unaffected by this error because the net income for Year 2 (which is understated by the same amount as the overstatement in retained earnings at the end of Year 1) is closed into retained earnings; the error at this point counterbalances. Working capital at the end of Year 1 is overstated (because inventory is a current asset), but working capital at the end of Year 2 is unaffected because the inventory figure at the end of Year 2 is determined by a physical inventory counting and pricing procedure. No new error in this process is assumed unless otherwise indicated.

TIP!

An understatement in ending inventory of Year 1 will cause an understatement in net income for Year 1 and overstatement in net income for Year 2. Thus, retained earnings and working capital at the end of Year 1 are understated. However, assuming no more errors are committed at the end of Year 2, retained earnings and working capital are not affected at the end of Year 2.

TIP!

If purchases for Year 1 are understated by the same amount as an understatement in inventory at the end of Year 1, there is no net effect on net income of Year 1 and no net effect on net income of Year 2. The balance sheet at the end of Year 1, however, has errors because assets (inventories) are understated and liabilities (accounts payable) are understated.

TIP!

When more than one error affects the net income amount for one year, analyse each error separately and write down its effects before you attempt to summarize all the effects on one given year.

TIP!

When analysing an error situation involving inventory, assume a periodic inventory system is in use unless otherwise indicated.

Exercise 22-6

PURPOSE: This exercise will allow you to practise analysing the effects of errors on income determination.

The Avery Corporation calculated net income of $22,000 and $30,000 for Years 1 and 2, respectively. The following errors were later discovered:

Error 1:   Amortization on computers was omitted in Year 1, $900.

Error 2:   Deferred (prepaid) expenses were understated at the end of Year 1, $400.

Error 3:   Accrued revenues were omitted at the end of Year 1, $600.

Error 4:   Deferred (unearned) revenues were understated at the end of Year 1, $980.

Error 5:   Accrued expenses were overlooked at the end of Year 1, $650.

Instructions

Calculate the corrected net income figures for Year 1 and Year 2.

Solution to Exercise 22-6

	Year 1	Year 2
Net income as previously reported	$22,000	$30,000
Amortization omitted—Year 1	(900)	--
Deferred expenses understated—Year 1	400	(400)
Accrued revenues understated—Year 1	600	(600)
Deferred revenues understated—Year 1	(980)	980
Accrued expenses understated—Year 1	(650)	650
Corrected net income	$20,470	$30,630

TIP! The benefits from the prepaid expense (error 2) are assumed to be consumed in Year 2 and the unearned revenue (error 4) is assumed to be earned in Year 2 because there is no mention of similar errors existing at the end of Year 2.

Analysis of Multiple-Choice Type Questions

Question

1. A manufacturing company changes from the FIFO cost method to the average cost inventory pricing method for all inventories held. Generally, how should this change be accounted for?
   a. Retroactive with restatement
   b. Retroactive without restatement
   c. Prospectively
   d. As a correction of an error.

EXPLANATION: This is a change in accounting policy and therefore the general rule is that it must be accounted for retroactively with restatement. Retroactive without restatement is allowed only in rare cases if information is impractical to obtain, or if the specific *CICA Handbook* section allows it. (Solution = a.)

Question

2. A change from one generally accepted accounting method to another generally accepted accounting method is usually accounted for:
   a. Retroactive with restatement
   b. Retroactive without restatement
   c. Prospectively
   d. As a correction of an error.

EXPLANATION: A change from one generally accepted accounting method to another generally acceptable accounting method constitutes a change in accounting policy. The general rule for a change in accounting policy is to account for it retroactively with restatement. Retroactive without restatement is allowed only if detailed information to restate is impractical or if the specific *CICA Handbook* section allows it. (Solution = a.)

Question

3. A change from a nongenerally accepted accounting principle to a generally accepted accounting principle should be accounted for:
    a. Retroactive with restatement
    b. Retroactive without restatement
    c. Prospectively
    d. As an initial adoption of an accounting policy.

EXPLANATION: A change from a non-GAAP method to one that is GAAP constitutes an error correction. The correction of an error is not an accounting change; it is a prior period adjustment. Prior period adjustments are to receive retroactive with restatement treatment. (Solution = a.)

Question

4. The Mayer Corporation purchased a computer system on January 1, 2003 for $210,000. The company used the straight-line method and no salvage value to amortize the asset for the first two years of its estimated six-year life. In 2005, Mayer changed to the sum-of-the-years'-digits amortization method for this asset. The following facts pertain:

	2003	2004	2005
Straight-line	$35,000	$35,000	$35,000
Sum-of-the-years'-digits	60,000	50,000	40,000

Mayer is subject to a 40% tax rate. In the journal entry to record this as a change in policy, Retained Earnings will be:
    a. credited for $24,000.
    b. debited for $24,000.
    c. credited for $27,000.
    d. debited for $27,000.
    e. none of the above.

EXPLANATION: Follow the procedures described in **Illustration 22-2** to calculate the cumulative effect of the change in accounting principle, net of the related tax effect.

Amortization was	$ 70,000[a] for 2003 and 2004 using old method
Amortization would have been	<u>110,000</u>[b] for 2003 and 2004 using new method

Difference is	40,000	cumulative effect on prior periods
Net-of-tax rate	60%	
Cumulative effect, net of tax	$ 24,000	

[a]$35,000 for 2003 + $35,000 for 2004 = $70,000 total for prior periods.
[b]$60,000 for 2003 + $50,000 for 2004 = $110,000 total for prior periods.

The new method would have resulted in lower net incomes if it had been used in prior years; hence, the "catch-up" adjustment needed is a debit. (Solution = b.)

TIP! | If comparatives are presented, the opening retained earnings of the earliest period presented must be adjusted for the effects of the policy change before that period.

Question

5. Refer to the facts in Question 4 above. The amount that Mayer should report for amortization expense on its 2005 income statement is:
    a. $40,000.
    b. $35,000.
    c. $24,000.
    d. $21,000.
    e. none of the above.

    APPROACH AND EXPLANATION: Calculate the amortization for 2005 (the year of change) using the new method (sum-of-the-years'-digits method) as if the new method had been used in all prior periods. The calculation is:

    $$\frac{4}{21^a} \times (\$210,000 - 0) = \$40,000 \text{ amortization for 2005 using SYD method.}$$

    $$^a\frac{6(6+1)}{2} = 21$$
    (Solution = a.)

TIP! | The journal entry to record the change in accounting policy will adjust balance sheet account balances to what they would have been had the new policy (method) been used in all prior periods.

Question

6. Refer to the facts of Question 4 above. If Mayer prepares comparative financial statements in 2005, the income statement for 2004 included therein will reflect amortization expense of:
    a. $50,000.
    b. $40,000.

c. $35,000.
d. $30,000.

EXPLANATION: A change from one generally acceptable amortization method to another generally acceptable amortization method constitutes a change in accounting policy that is to receive retroactive with restatement treatment. Therefore, the amortization expense for 2004 will appear in 2005 comparative reports as if the new policy had been used in that period. This amount, per the information given, is $50,000. (Solution = a.)

Question

7. A change from the LIFO inventory costing method to the FIFO inventory costing method is to be accounted for:
    a. Retroactive with restatement
    b. Retroactive without restatement
    c. Prospectively
    d. As a correction of an error.

EXPLANATION: A change from one generally accepted accounting method to another generally acceptable accounting method constitutes a change in accounting policy. The general rule for a change in accounting policy, provided the resulting information is more relevant than before, is to account for it retroactively with restatement. Retroactive without restatement is allowed only if detailed information to restate is impractical or if the specific *CICA Handbook* section allows it. (Solution = a.)

Question

8. During 2005, a construction company changed from the completed-contract method to the percentage-of-completion method for accounting purposes but not for tax purposes. Gross-profit figures under both methods for the history of the company appear below:

	Completed-Contract	**Percentage-of-Completion**
2003	$ 190,000	$ 320,000
2004	250,000	380,000
2005	280,000	410,000
	$ 720,000	$ 1,110,000

Assuming an income tax rate of 40% for all years, the affect of this accounting change on prior periods should be reported by a credit of:
a. $156,000 on the 2005 income statement.
b. $234,000 on the 2005 income statement.
c. $156,000 on the 2005 statement of retained earnings.
d. $234,000 on the 2005 statement of retained earnings.

296 CHAPTER 22 Accounting Changes and Error Analysis

EXPLANATION: Identify the type of accounting change and the method of treatment. It is a change in accounting policy; it is to get retroactive with restatement treatment, unless the information is not readily available, which is not the case here. Therefore, the total effect on prior periods (net of tax) is to be recorded as an adjustment to the beginning balance of retained earnings and reported on the statement of retained earnings. Identify the prior years and the effect of the change on those prior years. (Solution = c.)

	Old Method	New Method	Difference
2003	$ 190,000	$ 320,000	$ 130,000
2004	250,000	380,000	130,000
	$ 440,000	$ 700,000	260,000
Net-of-tax rate			60%
Effect net of tax			$ 156,000

Question

9. A change in accounting estimate should be accounted for:
    a. as an adjustment to the beginning balance of retained earnings.
    b. by restating the relevant amounts in the financial statements of prior periods.
    c. in the period of change or in the period of change and future periods, if the change affects both.
    d. by reporting restated amounts for all periods presented.

EXPLANATION: Think about the treatment to be accorded a change in accounting estimate before you read the answer selections. A change in accounting estimate receives prospective treatment; therefore, it is accounted for in the current period or in the current and future periods, whichever is applicable. (Solution = c.)

Question

10. When a change in estimate creates the need for a change in policy (such as when a manufacturing company changes from the policy of deferring and amortizing preproduction costs to the policy of expensing such costs because the estimate of the periods benefited has changed and any future benefits now appear doubtful), the change is accounted for:
    a. retroactively with restatement.
    b. retroactively without restatement.
    c. prospectively.

EXPLANATION: A change in an accounting estimate that necessitates a change in an accounting policy is to be accounted for as a change in estimate. (Solution = c.)

Question

11. A machine was purchased at the beginning of 2002 for $68,000. At the time of its purchase, the machine was estimated to have a useful life of six years and a salvage value of $8,000. The machine was amortized using the straight-line method of amortization through 2004. At the beginning of 2005, the estimate of useful life was revised to a total life of eight years and the expected salvage value was changed to $5,000. The amount to be recorded for amortization for 2005, reflecting these changes in estimates, is:
    a. $7,875.
    b. $7,600.
    c. $6,600.
    d. $4,125.

EXPLANATION: Write down the model to calculate amortization whenever there has been a change in the estimated service life and/or salvage value of a plant asset. Fill in the data of the case at hand and solve:

Cost	$68,000
Accumulated amortization	(30,000)[a]
Book value	38,000
Additional expenditure capitalized	-0-
Revised book value	38,000
Current estimate of salvage	(5,000)
Remaining depreciable cost	33,000
Remaining years of useful life at 1/1/05	÷ 5[b]
Amortization expense for 2005	$ 6,600 (Solution = c.)

[a]Cost	$68,000
Original estimate of salvage	(8,000)
Original depreciable cost	60,000
Original service life in years	÷ 6
Original amortization per year	10,000
Number of years used	3
Accumulated amortization1/1/05	$30,000

[b]Total life as revised	8
Number of years used	(3)
Remaining part of useful life at 1/1/05	5

Question

12. Merchandise inventory was overstated at December 31, 2004. How would this error affect earnings for 2004, earnings for 2005, working capital at December 31, 2004, and owners' equity at December 31, 2004?

	Earnings 2004	Earnings 2005	Working Capital 12/31/04	Owners' Equity 12/31/04
† a.	Overstate	Understate	Overstate	Overstate
b.	Understate	Overstate	Understate	Understate
c.	Overstate	No effect	No effect	Overstate
d.	Overstate	Understate	Understate	Understate

EXPLANATION: This is a counterbalancing error. The overstatement of 2004 ending inventory will cause net income of 2004 to be overstated (because of the understatement of cost of goods sold) and net income of 2005 to be understated. The overstatement of 2004 net income will cause owners' equity to be overstated. Inventory is a current asset. Therefore, working capital at December 31, 2004 will be overstated. (Solution = a.)

TIP! | **Earnings** is synonymous with **net income**.

Question

† 13. Accrued interest expense of $7,500 was omitted at December 31, 2004. Accrued interest expense of $10,000 was omitted at December 31, 2005. The net effect of these errors on net income for 2005 is:
   a. overstatement of $10,000.
   b. understatement of $2,500.
   c. understatement of $7,500.
   d. overstatement of $2,500.
   e. none of the above.

EXPLANATION: Handle each error separately. Fully describe the effects of each error. Write these effects down, then summarize the effects. (If necessary, draft the entries that were made and the entries that should have been made to analyse the effects on interest expense.) (Solution = d.)

Error 1:   Interest expense for 2004 is understated by $7,500.
             Net income for 2004 is overstated by $7,500.
             Interest expense for 2005 is overstated by $7,500.
             Net income for 2005 is understated by $7,500.

Error 2:   Interest expense for 2005 is understated by $10,000.
             Net income for 2005 is overstated by $10,000.
             Interest expense for 2006 is overstated by $10,000.
             Net income for 2006 is understated by $10,000.

Net effects on 2005 net income:
Understatement	$ 7,500
Overstatement	10,000
Net overstatement	$ 2,500

Question

14. Under which of the following situations would a change in accounting policy not be acceptable under GAAP?
    a. To conform with industry practice.
    b. To avoid breaking a debt covenant.
    c. To conform to new *CICA Handbook* recommendation.
    d. To conform to legislative requirements.

EXPLANATION: A change in policy may have to be done to conform with industry practice, a new *CICA Handbook* section or for legislative reasons. A voluntary change in policy is only permitted if it results in more relevant information and remains reliable. Clearly, this rule is to prevent manipulations of results to suit an objective such as meeting a debt covenant. To conclude, it is not acceptable to change accounting policies in order to bias financial reporting. (Solution = b.)

Question

15. Gus Incorporated discovered a balance sheet classification error in its prior year's financial statements. The error does not materially affect financial statement presentation. It is now in the process of preparing its current year financial statements. What, if any, adjustments should be made?
    a. No adjustment is required since it does not affect net income of current or prior year.
    b. Adjustment is required to the prior year. Reclassify comparative numbers and note that the numbers have been restated.
    c. No adjustment is required since the error is not material.
    d. Adjustment is required to the prior year. Reclassify comparative numbers, but do not note that the numbers have been restated, due to immateriality.

EXPLANATION: Alterations to prior year financial statements should be limited to the specific rules of *CICA Handbook* Section 1506. Materiality is an overriding concept for the *CICA Handbook*. Therefore, anything that is not material should not be adjusted. (Solution = c.)

CHAPTER 23

Statement of Cash Flows

Overview

A business enterprise that provides a set of financial statements that report both financial position and results of operations is also required to provide a statement of cash flows for each period for which results of operations are provided. The primary purpose of a statement of cash flows is to provide relevant information about the cash receipts and cash payments of an enterprise during a time period. The information provided in a statement of cash flows, if used with related disclosures and information in the other financial statements, should help investors, creditors, and others to: (a) assess the enterprise's ability to generate positive future net cash flows; (b) assess the enterprise's ability to meet its obligations, its ability to pay dividends, and its needs for external financing; (c) assess the reasons for differences between net income and associated cash receipts and payments; and (d) assess the effects on an enterprise's financial position of both its cash and noncash investing and financing transactions during the period.

Study Steps

Understanding the Value of the Cash Flow Statement

The primary value of the statement of changes is to show where a company gets its cash (e.g., from operations, by selling off assets, by borrowing, etc.) and how it spends its cash (e.g., on operations, paying off debt, buying assets, etc.). The focus is on liquidity and solvency. A company may be profitable according to the income statement but may be having cash flow problems. This is highlighted by the cash flow statement.

Just because a company is profitable does not mean that it is generating cash from its operations.

The key number on the statement is the line that shows cash provided by operations. Ideally, the greater the cash from operations, the stronger the company, since it can use these internally generated funds for expansion, dividends, and other activities. The point is that if the company is able to generate these funds internally, then it does not have to rely on external funding, such as borrowing or issuing shares. External funding often carries with it commitments for paying out a return to outside parties (e.g., interest) and for repayment of principal, which can put an undue strain on the cash flows of the company.

Users put great value on this statement since it is felt to be more objective than the income statement (cash is cash). The measurement of net income is felt to be very subjective and dependent on the accounting principles and procedures selected by financial statement preparers.

Becoming Proficient in Related Calculations

This topic involves learning how to prepare the statement and learning how to interpret it. There are two different approaches for the preparation of the statement:
- the work sheet approach
- analysis of cash G/L account

Since the statement only includes cash (and cash equivalents) transactions, the easiest way to identify these is through analysis of the cash G/L account. All that needs to be done is to group the cash transactions into operating, investing, or financing transactions and then to decide how much detail to present on the statement.

Note that all companies would code cash transactions when they are recorded in the G/L, in order to have sufficient information to produce the cash flow statement later.

This would likely be accomplished by having separate G/L accounts for Cash-Operating, Cash-Investing, and Cash-Financing.

An alternate way to calculating the statement involves analysing changes in the balance sheet (the worksheet approach). This approach is useful for double-checking the cash flow statement.

The objective of the statement is to show changes in cash and cash equivalents over the period. Where the company gets its cash and where it spends it is important and, therefore, the statement is divided into three main areas as follows:
- Cash provided from/used in operations
- Cash provided from/used in investing
- Cash provided from/used in financing

Operating activities are the principal revenue-producing activities of the enterprise and all other activities that are not investing or financing activities.

Investing activities are the acquisition and disposal of long-term assets and other investments not included in cash equivalents.

Financing activities are activities that result in changes in the size and composition of the equity capital and borrowings of the enterprise.

Defining cash and cash equivalents

Cash is made of cash on hand and demand deposits.

Cash equivalents are short-term, highly liquid investments that are readily convertible into known amounts of cash and which are subject to an insignificant risk of changes in value.

Short-term is generally less than three months.

Equity investments are not included as cash equivalents since their value changes all the time.

In preparing the statement, the objective is to first identify all cash transactions and then to classify them as operating, investing, or financing activities.

Identifying Transactions

Which transactions should be on the statement and how do we know that we have included all the ones that should be there? This is where the work sheet approach comes into play.

Theoretically, all transactions end up affecting the balance sheet because the general ledger consists of balance sheet accounts and income statement accounts. Since the income statement is closed out to retained earnings at year-end, and retained earnings is a balance sheet account, all transactions are eventually booked to the balance sheet.

Therefore, if we identify changes in the balance sheet from one period to the next, we will ensure that all transactions are identified. The problem is that looking at the net change in an account (e.g., land), does not give us detailed information about individual transactions that have happened. For instance, if land increased by $100,000 from one year-end to the next, this may be due to one transaction (e.g., a purchase of land costing $100,000) or multiple transactions (including off-setting purchases and disposals). Therefore, although changes in balance sheet accounts are a good starting point, information is required from other sources as well. This will be discussed later.

Classifying Transactions

Earlier, we defined operating, investing and financing transactions. These definitions may be used to classify the transactions. Another way to determine the classification is to break the balance sheet down into quadrants as follows:

I	II
Current assets	Current liabilities
(excluding cash)	(except current LTD)
III	IV
Long-term assets	Long-term debt
	(including current portion)
	and equity

Any transactions that affect quadrant I or II are classified as operating activities. Those affecting quadrant III are investing activities, and those affecting quadrant IV are financing activities. There are some exceptions to this general rule. For instance, the current portion of long-term debt is included in current liabilities; however, it is really a financing activity since it relates to the financing of the company.

A purchase of land involves the purchase of long-term assets and, hence, is an investing activity. The borrowing of money on a long-term basis affects quadrant IV and is, therefore, a financing activity. The process of earning net income is an operating activity (intuitively and since sales and purchases affect accounts such as AR, AP, inventory, etc.).

Dividends paid are financing activities as long as the instrument is classified as equity.

Care must be taken since a balanced statement is not necessarily correct. There are three other things to consider:

1. Have all transactions been identified (i.e., there may be some transactions that offset each other that have not been identified)?

2. Also, transactions may be incorrectly classified on the statement (e.g., classified as operating instead of investment activity).

3. The manner in which the statement is presented must also be considered and will often be a function of user needs (i.e., how much detail and which numbers are emphasized or de-emphasized).

Presentation

The direct and indirect methods are different ways of presenting the same information in the operating activities section. Either way is acceptable, although the *CICA Handbook* encourages the use of the direct method. Many companies use the indirect approach. Under both methods, the objective is to reconcile net income, which is accrual based, to cash from operations.

The Direct Method

The direct method shows the following detail under "Cash from Operating Activities."

    Cash from customers

    Cash paid to suppliers

    Cash from interest/dividends

    Cash paid—other operating expenses

    Cash paid for taxes

The Indirect Method

This method adjusts for the same items adjusted for under the direct method. The main difference is that this method begins with net income and adds/deducts cash and non-cash items.

Extraordinary items should be dealt with as separate line items and income from discontinued operations should also be segregated.

Interpretation of the statement

The final, and perhaps most important study step is to learn how to interpret the results. Usually the best place to start when analysing a company's financial position is with the statement of cash flows. The focus is on cash from continuing operations, since this indicates whether the operations are self-standing and able to pay dividends and interest and repay debt.

As previously discussed, the statement also offers insight into where a company received its cash during the year and where it spent its cash.

Tips on Chapter Topics

TIP!

Homework and examination problems related to the subject of the statement of cash flows very often involve comparative balance sheet data. Although sometimes the older year's information is listed first so that the data is in chronological order, it is a common practice to list the current year's data first. Before beginning to work a problem, carefully note the order of the data so that you properly interpret the changes in accounts as being increases or decreases. These comparative balance sheets are often accompanied by additional information. If no additional information is given about an account, but the account balance has changed, assume that (1) only one transaction is responsible for the change in the balance, (2) the most common transaction occurred to change that particular account balance, and (3) cash was involved in the transaction.

TIP!

In studying this chapter on the statement of cash flows and preparing homework assignments, you will encounter transactions for which you may not recall the proper accounting procedures. One of the challenging aspects about this chapter is that it draws on your knowledge of **all** of the chapters that precede it. Use this opportunity to look up the items you don't recall and refresh your memory. The procedures you review in this manner will likely be easier to recall the next time you need to use them.

TIP! Every transaction affecting the Cash account is to be reflected either as an inflow (receipt) or outflow (payment) on the statement of cash flows. Furthermore, the receipts and payments are to be classified by activity. The three activity classifications are: (1) operating, (2) investing, and (3) financing.

TIP! In determining if a cash transaction is related to an operating activity, investing activity, or financing activity, first see if it meets the definition of investing activities. If not, see if it meets the definition of financing activities. If not, then it is an operating activity. (Refer to **Illustration 23-1** for these definitions and examples.)

TIP! The statement of cash flows emphasizes reporting gross cash receipts and payments. Thus, if long-term debt is issued for $2 million and payments of $300,000 on long-term debt occur during the same period, it is **not** permissible to just show the net inflow of $1.7 million. Rather, the inflow of $2 million and the outflow of $300,000 must be separately shown in the financing activity section of the statement of cash flows. Similarly, if acquisitions and disposals of plant assets occur in the same period, the gross cash effects must be reported; they are not to be netted.

TIP! Cash includes not only currency on hand but demand deposits with banks or other financial institutions. **Cash equivalents** are short-term highly liquid investments that are readily convertible to known amounts of cash and are subject to insignificant risk of changes in value. Examples of items commonly considered to be cash equivalents are Treasury bills, guaranteed investment certificates, and money market funds. Cash equivalents may be combined with cash for presentation on the balance sheet and for reporting cash flows on the statement of cash flows.

TIP! When a homework or exam problem requires use of the indirect method but does not give the net income figure, the amount of net income (or net loss) can usually be derived by analysing the changes that took place in the balance of retained earnings.

Illustration 23-1   307

Illustration 23-1
Operating, Investing, and Financing Activities

DEFINITIONS:

Investing Activities: include (a) making and collecting loans and (b) acquiring and disposing of investments and productive long-lived assets.

Financing Activities: include (a) obtaining capital from owners and providing them with a return on, and a return of, their investment; (b) obtaining cash through the issuance of debt and repaying the amounts borrowed.

Operating Activities: are the enterprise's principal revenue-producing activities and other activities that are not defined as investing or financing activities. Cash flows from operating activities are generally the cash effects of transactions and other events that enter into the determination of net income.

EXAMPLES:

Investing Activities:
    Cash inflows:
        From sale of property, plant, and equipment and other productive assets.
        From sale of debt or equity securities of other entities or return of investments in those instruments.
        From collection of principal on loans to other entities or sale of loans made to others.
    Cash outflows:
        To purchase property, plant, and equipment (plant assets).[a]
        To purchase debt or equity securities of other entities.
        To make loans to other entities.

Financing Activities:
    Cash inflows:
        From sale of equity securities (company's own shares).
        From issuance of debt (bonds and notes).
    Cash outflows:
        To pay dividends to shareholders.
        To reacquire share capital.
        To pay debt (both short-term and long-term).

Operating Activities:
    Cash inflows:
        From cash sales and collections from customers on account.
        From returns on loans (interest) and on equity securities (dividends).
        From receipts for royalties, rents, and fees.
    Cash outflows:
        To suppliers on account.
        To employees for services.

To government for taxes.
To lenders for interest.
To others for expenses.

^a **Incurring directly related debt to the seller is considered a significant noncash transaction that will not be shown on the statement of cash flows, but will be disclosed elsewhere in the financial statements.**

TIP! | The statement of cash flows summarizes all of the transactions occurring during a period that have an impact on the cash balance. The activity format is used whereby cash inflows and cash outflows are summarized by the three categories: operating, investing, and financing.

Exercise 23-1

PURPOSE: This exercise will give you practice in classifying transactions by activity.

The Wolfson Corporation had the following transactions during 2004:

1. Issued common shares for $100,000 in cash.
2. Issued $22,000 worth of common shares in exchange for equipment.
3. Sold services for $52,000 cash.
4. Purchased securities as a long-term investment for $18,000 cash.
5. Collected $9,000 of accounts receivable.
6. Paid $14,000 of accounts payable.
7. Declared and paid a cash dividend of $12,000.
8. Sold a long-term investment in securities with a cost of $18,000 for $18,000 cash.
9. Purchased a machine for $35,000 by giving a long-term note in exchange.
10. Exchanged land costing $20,000 for equipment costing $20,000.
11. Paid salaries of $6,000.
12. Paid $1,000 for advertising services.
13. Paid $8,000 for insurance coverage for a future period.
14. Borrowed $31,000 cash from the bank.
15. Paid $11,000 interest.
16. Paid $31,000 cash to the bank to repay loan principal.
17. Issued $40,000 of common shares upon conversion of bonds payable having a face value of $40,000.
18. Paid utilities of $4,000.
19. Loaned a vendor $6,000 cash.
20. Collected interest of $2,000.
21. Collected $6,000 loan principal from borrower.
22. Purchased treasury shares for $4,000.
23. Sold treasury shares for $6,000 (cost was $4,000).
24. Paid taxes of $20,000.

Instructions

Analyse each transaction above and indicate whether it resulted in a(n):
(a) inflow of cash from operating activities,
(b) outflow of cash from operating activities,
(c) inflow of cash from investing activities,
(d) outflow of cash from investing activities,
(e) inflow of cash from financing activities,
(f) outflow of cash from financing activities, or
(g) noncash investing and/or financing activity.

Solution to Exercise 23-1

1.	e	6.	b	11.	b	16.	f	21.	c
2.	g	7.	f	12.	b	17.	g	22.	f
3.	a	8.	c	13.	b	18.	b	23.	e
4.	d	9.	g	14.	e	19.	d	24.	b
5.	a	10.	g	15.	b	20.	a		

APPROACH: Write down the definitions for investing activities, financing activities, and operating activities. (These definitions can be found in **Illustration 23-1**.) Analyse each transaction to see in which classification the transaction would be included. Watch for any transactions that do not result in a cash flow; they are noncash items. Most noncash items are to be disclosed elsewhere in the financial statements.

EXPLANATION:
1. Issuance of share capital for cash results in a cash inflow from financing activities.
2. Issuance of share capital in exchange for plant assets does not involve any flow of cash; The transaction is a noncash financing and investing activity.
3. The sale of services is a revenue transaction. The sale of services for cash results in an inflow of cash from operating activities.
4. The cash purchase of a security as an investment results in an outflow of cash from investing activities.
5. The collection of accounts receivable constitutes a cash inflow from a customer for a prior revenue transaction. A collection of cash from a customer is an inflow of cash from operating activities.
6. The payment of accounts payable constitutes a payment to a supplier for inventory or other goods or services. There will be a related expense transaction either before the cash payment or after the time of cash payment. A payment to a vendor is an outflow of cash from operating activities.
7. The payment of cash dividends to shareholders is an outflow of cash from financing activities.
8. The sale of an investment constitutes an inflow of cash from investing activities.
9. The acquisition of a plant asset is an investing activity. The issuance of a debt instrument is a financing activity. The purchase of a plant asset by issuance of

a note payable does **not** involve a cash flow. Hence, the transaction is a non-cash financing and investing activity.

10. The acquisition of land (a plant asset) is an investing activity. The sale (disposal) of equipment (plant asset) is an investing activity. The exchange of one plant asset for another plant asset does **not** involve any flow of cash; the transaction is a noncash investing activity.

11. The payment of salaries is a payment to employees for services rendered; it results from an expense transaction. The payment to employees for services is a cash outflow from operating activities.

12. The payment for advertising services is an example of a payment to suppliers of goods and services used in operations; it is a cash outflow from operating activities.

13. The payment for insurance coverage is an example of a payment to suppliers of goods and services used in operations. There will be an expense recognized in a future period. It does not matter in what period the expense recognition takes place; the cash flow occurred in the current period and results in a cash outflow from operating activities.

14. The borrowing of cash from a bank causes an issuance of a debt instrument (i.e., note payable). The borrowing of cash is a cash inflow from financing activities.

15. The payment to lenders for interest will cause an expense to be recognized on the income statement in the period the interest is incurred. The payment of interest is a cash outflow for operating activities in the period the cash is paid.

16. The payment of a loan (debt) is a cash outflow from financing activities.

17. The issuance of common shares is a financing activity and the liquidation (redemption) of bonds payable is a financing activity. However, the redemption of bonds by issuance of shares is a **noncash** financing activity because no cash is received or given in the exchange.

18. The payment of utilities is a payment to a supplier for a service used in operations. The related expense will appear on the income statement in the period the services are consumed. The payment will appear on a statement of cash flows as an outflow of cash from operating activities in the period the cash payment is made.

19. The payment of cash to another entity in the form of a loan to that other entity is a cash outflow from investing activities.

20. The collection of cash for interest is a cash inflow from operating activities.

21. The collection of cash for the principal on a loan to another entity is a cash inflow from investing activities.

22. The cash payment to reacquire a company's own shares (treasury shares) is a cash outflow from financing activities.

23. The sale of treasury shares for cash results in a cash inflow from financing activities.

24. The payment of cash to the government for taxes is a cash outflow from operating activities.

TIP! | In determining if a cash transaction is an operating activity, investing activity, or financing activity, it is usually helpful to reconstruct the journal entry used to record the transaction. The following observations are also helpful:

1. The journal entry to record a transaction that is an investing activity which results in a cash flow will generally involve: (1) Cash and (2) an asset account other than Cash, such as Investment (short-term or long-term), Land, Building, Equipment, Patent, etc.
2. The journal entry to record a transaction that is a financing activity which results in a cash flow will generally involve: (1) Cash and (2) a liability account or an owners' equity account such as Bonds Payable, Notes Payable, Dividends Payable, Common Shares, Contributed Capital, Treasury Shares, etc.
3. The journal entry to record a transaction that is an operating activity which results in a cash flow will generally involve: (1) Cash and (2) a revenue account or an expense account; or, a prepaid expense or an unearned revenue; or, a receivable or a payable account.

Exercise 23-2

PURPOSE: This exercise will provide you with an opportunity to prepare a statement of cash flows using the indirect method.

A comparative balance sheet for Herman Pictures appears below:

	December 31		
Assets	**2005**	**2004**	**Change**
Cash	$ 61,000	$ 35,000	$ 26,000
Accounts receivable	66,000	50,000	16,000
Inventory	155,000	96,000	59,000
Equity investments	100,000	70,000	30,000
Equipment	170,000	100,000	70,000
Accumulated amortization	(31,000)	(20,000)	(11,000)
	$521,000	$331,000	$190,000
Liabilities and Shareholders' Equity			
Accounts payable	$ 32,000	$ 40,000	$ (8,000)
Long-term note payable	72,000	60,000	12,000
Bonds payable	100,000	0	100,000
Common shares	60,000	10,000	50,000
Contributed surplus	190,000	190,000	0
Retained earnings	67,000	31,000	36,000
	$521,000	$331,000	$190,000

Additional information:
1. New equipment costing $80,000 was purchased for cash.
2. Old equipment was sold at a loss of $4,500.
3. Bonds were issued for cash. *financing*

4. An investment costing $30,000 was acquired by issuing a long-term note payable.
5. Cash dividends of $14,000 were declared and paid during the year.
6. Amortization expense for 2005 was $15,000.
7. Accounts Payable relate to operating expenses.
8. Equity investments are intended to be held for the long term.

Instructions

Prepare a statement of cash flows for 2005 using the indirect method.

TIP! | In this exercise, you must analyse the changes in the Retained Earnings account balance to determine the net income figure for 2005.

Solution to Exercise 23-2

HERMAN PICTURES
Statement of Cash Flows
For the Year Ending December 31, 2005

Cash flows from operating activities		
Net income		$ 50,000
Adjustments to reconcile net income to net cash provided by operating activities:		
Increase in accounts receivable	$ (16,000)	
Increase in inventory	(59,000)	
Amortization expense	15,000	
Loss on sale of equipment	4,500	
Decrease in accounts payable	(8,000)	(63,500)
Net cash used by operating activities		(13,500)
Cash flows from investing activities		
Purchase of equipment	(80,000)	
Sale of equipment	1,500	
Net cash used by investing activities		(78,500)
Cash flows from financing activities		
Payment on long-term note payable	(18,000)	
Issuance of bonds	100,000	
Issuance of share capital	50,000	
Payment of dividends	(14,000)	
Net cash provided by financing activities		118,000
Net increase in cash		26,000
Cash at beginning of period		35,000
Cash at end of period		$ 61,000

Noncash investing and financing activities
Acquisition of equity investment by issuance of long-term debt $ 30,000

Examine the statement and notice the major reasons for inflows and outflows of cash during the period.   **TIP!**

APPROACH: Glance through the balance sheet data and additional information to get a feel for the facts given. Set up the format for the statement of cash flows by placing the major headings for the three activity classifications approximately where they go. Leave space to fill in the details later (allow about one-fourth page for investing activities, about one-fourth page for financing activities, and approximately one-half page for the operating activities section). Then take each fact in order and process it by placing it where it belongs on the statement of cash flows.

1. Find the net change in cash by comparing the balance of Cash at the end of the period with the balance of Cash at the beginning of the period. Use the net change in cash to reconcile beginning and ending cash balances.

2. Analyse every change in every balance sheet account other than Cash. Reconstruct the journal entries for the transactions that caused the balance sheet accounts to change. Examine each entry to identify if (a) there is an inflow of cash (debit to Cash) or an outflow of cash (credit to Cash) or no effect on cash; (b) if the transaction involves an operating, investing, or financing activity, and (c) where it goes on the statement of cash flows.

3. To help identify the activity classification for each transaction, write down the definitions for investing activities, financing activities, and operating activities. Analyse each transaction to see if it meets one of these definitions. (Refer to **Illustration 23-1** for these definitions.)

4. To help identify investing activities, recall that transactions involving investing activities typically cause changes in noncurrent asset accounts (or changes in current asset accounts such as short-term investments and nontrade receivables).

5. To help identify financing activities, recall that transactions involving financing activities typically cause changes in noncurrent liability accounts or shareholders' equity accounts (or changes in current liability accounts such as short-term nontrade notes payable).

6. To help identify transactions involving operating activities, recall that operating activities typically result in recording revenues or expenses in some period of time. Thus, the journal entry to record the transaction either involves revenue earned, expense incurred, a receivable, a prepaid expense, a payable, or an unearned revenue. When the indirect method is used, the net income figure is used as a starting point for the calculation of "net cash flows provided by operating activities." The net income figure must then be converted from the accrual basis to a cash basis amount. To help identify the transactions requiring an adjustment to net income, find the transactions whose journal entries involve an income statement account and a balance sheet account other than Cash (such as amortization) or that involve Cash and accruals or deferrals of revenues or expenses (such as the entry to record the payment of expense in advance of its incurrence).

7. If the reasons for changes in balance sheet accounts are not fully explained in the additional information, assume the most common reason for a change. Assume purchases and sales of assets are for cash unless otherwise indicated.

8. When more than one transaction accounts for the net change in an account balance, it is wise to draw a T-account for the account in question and reflect all transactions occurring during the period.

EXPLANATION:

1. There was an increase of $26,000 in the Cash account. The net change goes near the bottom of the statement and reconciles the $35,000 beginning cash balance with the $61,000 ending cash balance.

2. The journal entry to record the increase in Accounts Receivable is reconstructed as follows:

Accounts Receivable	16,000	
Sales		16,000

   Net income is increased but Cash is not increased; thus, using the indirect method, this increase in receivables is deducted from net income to arrive at the net cash provided by operating activities. An increase in accounts receivable indicates that sales revenue for the period exceeds the cash collections from customers during the period; therefore, net income is greater than net cash provided by operating activities.

3. The journal entry to record the increase in Inventory is reconstructed as follows:

Inventory	59,000	
Cash		59,000

   Payments to suppliers are an operating outflow. This outflow is not reflected in the net income figure so, using the indirect method, the increase in inventory is deducted from net income to arrive at net cash provided by operating activities. An increase in inventory indicates that cost of goods sold expense is less than cash payments to suppliers; therefore, net income is greater than net cash provided by operating activities.

4. The journal entry to record the increase in Share Investments is reconstructed as follows:

Equity Investments (Long term)	30,000	
Long-term Note Payable		30,000

   The acquisition of an equity security is an investing activity, and the issuance of debt is a financing activity; however, there is no effect on cash. This non-cash investing and financing activity must be disclosed elsewhere in the financial statements. It is not to be reported in the body of the statement of cash flows.

5. The T-accounts for Equipment, Accumulated Amortization, and Loss on the Sale of Equipment would appear as follows:

Equipment

Jan. 1, 2005 Balance	100,000	Unexplained transaction	
Acquisition during 2005	80,000	during 2005	10,000
Dec. 31, 2005 Balance	170,000		

Accumulated Amortization

Unexplained transaction		Jan. 1, 2005 Balance	20,000
during 2005	4,000	Amortization for 2005	15,000
		Dec. 31, 2005 Balance	31,000

Loss on Sale of Equipment	
	Sale of equipment during 2002 4,500

The problem states that Equipment costing $80,000 was purchased. Amortization expense amounted to $15,000, and old equipment was sold at a loss of $4,500. We can solve for the missing data—an unexplained credit of $10,000 to Equipment and an unexplained debit of $4,000 to Accumulated Amortization. The most common reason for a credit to the Equipment account is the disposal of an asset. That transaction also explains the $4,000 reduction in the Accumulated Amortization account and the recording of a $4,500 loss. Thus, it appears that an asset with a cost of $10,000 and a book value of $6,000 ($10,000 – $4,000 = $6,000) was sold at a loss of $4,500. This means the cash proceeds amounted to $1,500 ($6,000 book value – $4,500 loss = $1,500 proceeds).

The journal entries to record the transactions mentioned above would be reconstructed as follows:

Equipment	80,000	
Cash		80,000

Cash decreased. The purchase of plant assets is an investing activity. Therefore, an outflow is reported in the investing section.

Amortization Expense	15,000	
Accumulated Amortization		15,000

There is no effect on Cash but net income was reduced. Using the indirect method, amortization expense is added to net income to calculate the net cash provided by operating activities.

Cash	1,500	
Loss on Sale of Equipment	4,500	
Accumulated Amortization	4,000	
Equipment		10,000

There is an inflow of $1,500 cash due to the disposal of plant assets, which is an investing activity. When the indirect method is used, the loss must be added to net income; there was no corresponding outflow of cash.

6. The journal entry to record the decrease in Accounts Payable is reconstructed as follows:

Accounts Payable	8,000	
Cash		8,000

Payments to suppliers for goods and services consumed in operations are an operating activity. Using the indirect method, this decrease in Accounts Payable must be deducted from net income because a decrease in Accounts Payable indicates expenses incurred were less than cash payments to suppliers; hence, net income was more than the net cash provided by operating activities.

7. The T-account for a Long-term Note Payable would appear as follows:

Long-term Note Payable

Unexplained transaction during 2005	18,000	Jan. 1, 2005 Balance	60,000
		Issued for investment in 2005	30,000
		Dec. 31, 2005 Balance	72,000

The most common reason for a debit to a liability account is a payment. The journal entries for the transactions affecting this account are reconstructed as follows:

Equity Investments (Long term)	30,000	
Long-term Note Payable		30,000

This transaction was analysed and handled in point 4 above.

Long-term Note Payable	18,000	
Cash		18,000

This represents an $18,000 cash outflow due to the payment of a nontrade note payable which is a financing activity.

8. The journal entry to record the increase in Bonds Payable is reconstructed as follows:

Cash	100,000	
Bonds Payable		100,000

There is a cash inflow of $100,000 due to borrowing which is a financing activity.

9. The most common reason for an increase in the Common Shares account is the issuance of shares for cash. The journal entry to record that transaction is reconstructed as follows:

Cash	50,000	
Common Shares		50,000

There is an inflow of cash of $50,000 due to the issuance of common shares. Obtaining resources from owners is a financing activity.

10. The Retained Earnings T-account would appear as follows:

Retained Earnings

Declaration of Cash Dividends during 2005	14,000	Jan. 1, 2005 Balance	31,000
		Unexplained transaction during 2005	50,000
		Dec. 31, 2005 Balance	67,000

The most common reason for having a credit to Retained Earnings is net income. Because the indirect method is used, the net income figure is needed as the starting point for the calculation of net cash provided by operating activities.

The journal entries to record the declaration and payment of cash dividends are reconstructed as follows:

Retained Earnings	14,000	
Dividends Payable		14,000
Dividends Payable	14,000	
Cash		14,000

Cash decreases by $14,000. Providing owners with a return on their investment constitutes a financing activity. The declaration of dividends has no effect on cash. The payment of a previously declared dividend reduces cash. The payment of cash dividends is to be reported as a financing outflow.

> The last step in the preparation of the statement of cash flows is to subtotal each of the three activity classifications. Inflows are shown as positive amounts; outflows are shown as negative amounts. An excess of inflows over outflows in a category results in a net inflow; an excess of outflows over inflows is captioned as a net outflow. The subtotals of the three activities are then summarized to determine the net change in cash during the year. This net change must agree with your analysis of the change in the Cash account balance (Step 1); otherwise, one or more errors exist and must be corrected to make the statement balance.

TIP!

Case 23-1

PURPOSE: This case will help you to classify transactions as being an operating activity, an investing activity, or a financing activity.

There are four situations described below:
1. A company purchased a machine priced at $100,000 by issuing a cheque for $100,000.
2. A company purchased a machine priced at $100,000 by giving a down payment of $20,000 and by issuing a note payable to the seller for $80,000. During the same year, the company made principal payments of $12,000 on the note and interest payments of $7,000.
3. A company purchased a machine for $100,000. Of that amount, $80,000 was obtained by borrowing from a local bank. During the same year, principal payments of $12,000 and interest payments of $7,000 were made to the bank on this loan.
4. A company acquired a machine by a capital lease agreement. The present value of the minimum lease payments at the inception date was $100,000. The first lease payment of $2,000 was made at the inception date. During the year, additional lease payments of $24,000 were made, which included interest of $15,000.

Instructions

For each situation above, explain how it would be reflected in a statement of cash flows. That is, indicate if it is reported in the operating, investing, or financing section of the statement of cash flows or separately disclosed as a noncash investing and financing activity. Also, indicate the amount reported and if it is a cash inflow or outflow.

Solution to Case 23-1

1. Investing outflow of $100,000

2. Investing outflow of $20,000
    Financing outflow of $12,000
    Operating outflow of $7,000

It would be disclosed elsewhere in the financial statements that machinery was acquired by the issuance of note payable for $80,000.

3. Financing inflow of $80,000
    Investing outflow of $100,000
    Financing outflow of $12,000
    Operating outflow of $7,000

4. Financing outflow of $11,000 ($2,000 + $24,000 – $15,000)
    Operating outflow of $15,000

It would be disclosed elsewhere in the financial statements that machinery was acquired by capital lease for $100,000.

APPROACH: Refer to **Illustration 23-1** for a description of the three classifications of activities.

TIP! Note that all interest payments are classified as operating outflows. Also, note that in situations 2 and 4, all payments of principal on seller-financed debt are classified as financing outflows.

Illustration 23-2   319

Illustration 23-2
Conversion from Accrual Basis to Cash Basis

ACCRUAL BASIS
Revenues Earned
– <u>Expenses Incurred</u>
= Net Income

CASH BASIS
Cash Received from Operations
– <u>Cash Paid for Operations</u>
= Net Cash Provided by Operating Activities

DIRECT METHOD

To Calculate Net Cash Provided by Operating Activities:

    Cash Received From Customers
+ Interest and Dividends Received
+ Other Operating Cash Receipts
– Cash Paid for Operating Expenses and Merchandise Inventory
– Interest Paid
– Income Taxes Paid
– <u>Other Operating Cash Payments</u>
= Net Cash Provided by Operating Activities

EXPLANATION: The major classes of cash receipts and cash payments from operating activities (for which selected calculations are shown below) are listed and summarized on the face of the statement of cash flows when the direct method is used.

To Convert Revenues Earned to Cash Received:

    Revenues Earned
– Increase in Accounts Receivable
+ <u>Increase in Unearned Revenues</u>
= Cash Received from Customers

EXPLANATION: An increase in Accounts Receivable from one balance sheet date to the next indicates that revenues earned exceed cash collections from customers; hence, subtract the increase in Accounts Receivable from sales revenue to obtain the amount of cash received from customers. (A decrease in receivables would indicate cash collections exceed revenues earned and would be added to revenues earned to calculate cash collections.) An increase in Unearned Revenues indicates that cash collections from customers exceed revenues earned; hence, add the increase in Unearned Revenues to Revenues Earned to obtain the amount of cash received from customers. (A decrease in Unearned Revenue indicates opposite relationships.)

OR

Revenues Earned
+ Beginning Accounts Receivable
− Ending Accounts Receivable
− Beginning Unearned Revenues
+ <u>Ending Unearned Revenues</u>
= Cash Received from Customers

EXPLANATION: The balance of Accounts Receivable at the beginning of the period represents revenues earned in a prior period that are collected in the current period; ending Accounts Receivable stem from revenues earned in the current period that are not yet collected. Beginning Unearned Revenues represent cash collections in a prior period (not the current period) that are for revenues earned in the current period. Ending Unearned Revenues come from collections during the current period that are not recognized as earned revenues.

To Convert Cost of Goods Sold to Cash Paid:

Cost of Goods Sold Expense
+ <u>Increase in Inventory</u>
= Purchases
− <u>Increase in Accounts Payable</u>
= Cash Paid for Merchandise
    Inventory

EXPLANATION: An increase in Inventory means purchases for the period exceed cost of goods sold. An increase in Accounts Payable indicates purchases exceed cash payments for merchandise. (Decreases indicate opposite relationships.)

OR

Cost of Goods Sold Expense
− Beginning Inventory
+ <u>Ending Inventory</u>
= Purchases
+ Beginning Accounts Payable
    (for purchases of merchandise)
− Ending Accounts Payable (for
    <u>purchases of merchandise)</u>
= Cash Paid for Merchandise
    Inventory

EXPLANATION: Beginning Inventory represents items purchased in a prior period that were consumed (sold) in the current year. Ending Inventory represents items purchased in the current period that are not reported in the cost of goods sold expense (because they are on hand at the balance sheet date). Beginning Accounts Payable come from purchases of a prior period (as opposed to purchases of the current period) that require cash payment during the current period. The ending Accounts Payable balance stems from purchases in the current period that are not paid for in the current period.

To Convert Operating Expenses to Cash Paid:

Operating Expenses Incurred
    (**Excluding** Amortization and
    Bad Debt Expense)
+ Increase in Prepaid Expenses
− <u>Increase in Accrued Payables</u>
= Cash Paid for Operating
    Expenses

EXPLANATION: An increase in a prepaid expense indicates expenses incurred are less than cash payments for those items. Therefore, the increase in the prepaid is added to the expense total to obtain the amount of related cash payments. An increase in Accrued Payables indicates the expense total exceeds the cash payments for these items; hence, the increase in Accrued Payables is deducted from the expense balance to arrive at cash payments. (A decrease is handled in the opposite manner.)

Illustration 23-2   321

OR

Operating Expenses Incurred
(**Excluding** Amortization and
Bad Debt Expense)
− Beginning Prepaid Expenses
+ Ending Prepaid Expenses
+ Beginning Accrued Payables
− <u>Ending Accrued Payables</u>
= Cash Paid for Operating
Expenses

EXPLANATION: Beginning Prepaid Expenses represent amounts recognized as expense in the current period for which cash payments are not made in the current period. (The cash payments occurred in a prior period.) Ending Prepaids stem from cash payments in the current period for expenses not recognized in the current period. (The expense recognition is being deferred to a future period.) Beginning Accrued Payables come from expenses recognized in a prior period (not the current year) that require cash payments during the current period. Ending Accrued Payables stem from expenses recognized during the current year that have not yet been paid.

To Convert Interest Expense to Interest Paid:

Interest Expense
− Increase in Interest Payable
− Amortization of Discount on Debt
+ <u>Amortization of Premium on Debt</u>
= Interest Paid

EXPLANATION: An increase in an accrued payable indicates that expense exceeds the related cash payments. (A decrease in an accrued payable would indicate the opposite relationship—that expense is less than cash payments.) The amortization of discount on a debt increases total interest expense but does not cause a cash outlay; the amortization of premium on a debt instrument decreases total interest expense but does not reduce the cash outlay required for the interest.

OR

Interest Expense
+ Beginning Interest Payable
− Ending Interest Payable
− Amortization of Discount on Debt
+ <u>Amortization of Premium on Debt</u>
= Interest Paid

EXPLANATION: The balance of Interest Payable at the beginning of the period comes from interest expense accrued in a prior period. Therefore, that amount requires a cash outlay in the current period that relates to an expense of a prior period. The ending balance of Interest Payable comes about from interest accrued in the current period. Therefore, this amount is part of the total interest expense for the current period but it is not part of the cash paid for interest this period. The amortization of discount on a debt instrument increases total interest expense but does not cause a cash outlay; the amortization of premium on a debt instrument decreases total interest expense but does not decrease the corresponding cash outflow.

To Convert Income Tax Expense to Income Taxes Paid:

    Income Tax Expense
+   Increase in Prepaid Income Taxes
−   Increase in Income Tax Payable
+   Increase in Future Tax Asset
−   <u>Increase in Future Tax Liability</u>
=   Income Taxes Paid

EXPLANATION: An increase in Prepaid Income Taxes and/or an increase in Future Tax Asset indicates that the amount of income tax expense is less than the amount paid for income taxes during the period. An increase in Income Tax Payable and/or an increase in Future Tax Liability indicates that the amount of income tax expense exceeds the amount paid for income taxes during the period.

OR

    Income Tax Expense
−   Beginning Prepaid Income Taxes
+   Ending Prepaid Income Taxes
+   Beginning Income Tax Payable
−   Ending Income Tax Payable
−   Beginning Future Tax Asset
+   Ending Future Tax Asset
+   Beginning Future Tax Liability
−   <u>Ending Future Tax Liability</u>
=   Income Taxes Paid

EXPLANATION: A beginning prepaid income tax amount represents taxes recognized as expense in the current period for which a cash payment was made in a prior period. An ending prepaid income tax amount stems from cash payments in the current period for taxes to be expensed in a future period (rather than in the current period). A beginning Income Tax Payable balance stems from income tax expense recognized in a prior period (not the current period) that requires cash payments during the current period. An ending balance in Income Tax Payable stems from income taxes recognized as expense in the current period that have not yet been paid. Changes in the balances of future tax assets or liabilities cause the Income Tax Expense figure to change without a corresponding impact on cash. The treatment of the balance of Future Tax Asset in this reconciliation is the same as for Prepaid Income Taxes, and the treatment of the balance of Future Tax Liability is the same as for Income Tax Payable.

TIP! | For all of the items above, a **decrease** in an account balance will be handled in a manner **opposite** of the way an **increase** is to be treated.

Illustration 23-2   323

INDIRECT METHOD

To Calculate Net Cash Provided by Operating Activities:

Net income

Add noncash charges (such as amortization expense and amortization of intangibles)

Add losses due to writedown of assets

Add losses on sale of assets, settlement of debt, and discontinued operations

Add (deduct) decrease (increase) in net accounts receivable

Add (deduct) decrease (increase) in accrued receivables

Add (deduct) decrease (increase) in inventory

Add (deduct) decrease (increase) in prepaid expenses

Add (deduct) decrease (increase) in future tax assets

Add (deduct) increase (decrease) in accounts payable

Add (deduct) increase (decrease) in accrued payables

Add (deduct) increase (decrease) in unearned revenues

Add (deduct) increase (decrease) in future tax liabilities

Add (deduct) increase (decrease) in accrued pension liability

Deduct noncash credits (such as amortization of premium on bonds payable and income recognized under equity method in excess of dividends received)

Deduct noncash gains (such as unrealized holding gain on investment in trading securities)

Deduct gains on sale of assets, settlement of debt, and discontinued operations

= Net cash provided by operating activities

EXPLANATION: Noncash charges (such as amortization) and losses due to writedown of assets are **added** to net income because they are expense or loss items that do not require an outlay of cash. Losses (or gains) from the sale of assets, settlement of debt, and discontinued operations are **added** to (or deducted from) net income because they relate to transactions for which the related cash flows are to be classified as investing or financing activities. An increase in receivables indicates that revenues earned **exceed** cash inflows; therefore, net income **exceeds** net cash provided by operating activities. An increase in inventory or prepaid expenses indicates that expenses are **less** than cash outflows; hence, net income is **more** than net cash provided by operating activities. Increases in accounts receivable, accrued receivables, inventory, and prepaid expenses must therefore be **deducted** from net income to obtain the amount of cash generated by operations. On the other hand, an increase in accounts payable or accrued payables indicates that expenses incurred **exceed** the amount of cash paid for merchandise inventory and operating expenses; hence, net income is **less** than net cash provided by operations. An increase in unearned revenues indicates that revenue earned is **less** than the cash received and net income is **less** than net cash generated by operations. Therefore, increases in accounts payable, accrued payables, and unearned revenues must be **added** to net income to calculate the amount of cash generated by operations. Noncash credits (such as the recognition of income using the equity method) are **deducted** from net income because they increase net income without having a corresponding cash inflow.

SUMMARY OF TREATMENT FOR ACCRUALS AND DEFERRALS

The treatment of increases during the period for deferred revenues, deferred expenses, accrued expenses, and accrued revenues can be summarized for both the direct method and the indirect method as follows:

	Direct Method		Indirect Method
	Revenues	Expenses	Net Income
Increase in Unearned Revenues	+		+
Increase in Prepaid Expenses		+	−
Increase in Payables		−	+
Increase in Receivables	−		−
	Cash Received From Operations	Cash Paid For Operations	Net Cash Provided by Operating Activities

TIP! In examining the summary above, notice the mathematical signs are the **same** for both the direct method and indirect method for handling a change in unearned revenues or a change in receivables. The reasons for this are (1) changes in unearned revenues and receivables are items which explain the difference between revenues earned during a period and cash received from operations; and (2) revenues earned are a **positive** component of net income, and cash received from operations is a **positive** component of net cash provided by operating activities.

Also notice that the mathematical signs are **different** for the direct method and the indirect method for handling a change in prepaid expenses and payables. The reasons for this are (1) changes in prepaid expenses and payables are items which explain the difference between expenses incurred during a period and cash paid for operations; and (2) expenses incurred are a **negative** component of net income, and cash paid out for operations is a **negative** component of net cash provided by operating activities.

TIP! "Cash provided by operating activities" (or "cash provided by operations") is another name for "net income on a cash basis."

Exercise 23-3

PURPOSE: This exercise will test your ability to convert accrual basis information to cash basis information.

The Fuller Corporation reported the following on its income statement for 2005:

Sales revenue	$600,000
Cost of goods sold	400,000
Salaries expense	42,000
Insurance expense	3,000
Amortization expense	50,000
Other operating expenses	60,000
Income tax expense	18,000
Net income	27,000

The comparative balance sheets reported the following selected information:

	12/31/05	12/31/04	Increase (Decrease)
Cash	$26,000	$12,000	$14,000
Accounts Receivable	37,000	41,000	(4,000)
Inventory	76,000	74,000	2,000
Prepaid Insurance	4,380	4,200	180
Accounts Payable	27,100	24,200	2,900
Salaries Payable	500	800	(300)
Income Taxes Payable	18,000	12,500	5,500
Future Tax Liability	5,400	5,000	400

All of the operating expenses reflected in the "other operating expenses" category were paid in cash during 2005. Accounts payable relate to purchases of merchandise inventory.

Instructions

Calculate the following amounts for 2005:
(a) Cash collections from customers.
(b) Cash payments for merchandise.
(c) Cash payments to employees.
(d) Cash payments for insurance.
(e) Cash payments for income taxes.
(f) Net cash provided by operating activities.

Solution to Exercise 23-3

(a) Sales revenue $600,000
Decrease in accounts receivable 4,000
Cash collections from customers $604,000

OR

Sales revenue $600,000
Beginning accounts receivable 41,000
Ending accounts receivable .... (37,000)
Cash collections from customers $604,000

(b) Cost of goods sold expense $400,000
Increase in inventory 2,000
Purchases 402,000
Increase in accounts payable .... (2,900)
Cash payments for merchandise $399,100

OR

Cost of goods sold expense $400,000
Beginning inventory .... (74,000)
Ending inventory 76,000
Purchases 402,000
Beginning accounts payable 24,200
Ending accounts payable .... (27,100)
Cash payments for merchandise $399,100

(c) Salaries expense $42,000
Decrease in salaries payable 300
Cash payments to employees $42,300

OR

Salaries expense $42,000
Beginning salaries payable 800
Ending salaries payable .... (500)
Cash payments to employees $42,300

(d) Insurance expense $3,000
Increase in prepaid insurance 180
Cash payments for insurance $3,180

OR

Insurance expense $3,000
Beginning prepaid insurance .... (4,200)
Ending prepaid insurance 4,380
Cash payments for insurance $3,180

(e) Income tax expense $18,000
Increase in income taxes payable .... (5,500)
Increase in future tax liability .... (400)
Cash payments for income taxes $12,100

OR

Income tax expense	$18,000
Beginning income taxes payable	12,500
Ending income taxes payable	(18,000)
Beginning future tax liability	5,000
Ending future tax liability	(5,400)
Cash payments for income taxes	$12,100

(f)	Cash received from customers	$604,000
	Cash payments for merchandise	(399,100)
	Cash payments to employees	(42,300)
	Cash payments for insurance	(3,180)
	Cash payments for income taxes	(12,100)
	Cash payments for other operating expenses	(60,000)
	Net cash provided by operating activities	$ 87,320

The change in the cash balance ($14,000 increase) had no effect on the calculations requested. The net cash provided (used) by the total of the three activity classifications (operating, investing, and financing) should net to this $14,000 increase. **TIP!**

Refer to **Illustration 23-2** for explanations to the above calculations. **TIP!**

Exercise 23-4

PURPOSE: This exercise will allow you to practise identifying how to classify transactions on a statement of cash flows using the direct method.

The Salter Corporation uses the direct method for preparing the statement of cash flows. The following summarized transactions took place in 2005:

Collected cash from customers on account	$ 75,000
Paid interest on debt	3,000
Paid principal of note payable	30,000
Sold services for cash	19,000
Paid salaries and wages	27,000
Paid other operating expenses	41,000
Recorded amortization expense	7,000
Paid dividends	6,000
Purchased machinery	60,000
Sold equipment for book value	12,000
Issued common shares in exchange for cash	45,000
Issued long-term debt	52,000
Amortized patents	1,000
Purchased treasury shares	4,000
Accrued salaries	800
Purchased an investment	38,200

Acquired a computer in exchange for Salter common shares	10,000
Received dividends from investee	700
Paid income taxes	6,500
Sold an investment (and recognized a gain of $3,300)	24,000

Instructions

(a) Calculate the following:
   (1) Net cash provided (used) by operating activities.
   (2) Net cash provided (used) by investing activities.
   (3) Net cash provided (used) by financing activities.
   (4) Net increase (decrease) in cash for the period.
(b) If any transactions are **not** used in the required calculations in (a), explain why.
(c) Based on the information given, prepare a statement of cash flows using the direct method. Assume the cash balance at the beginning of the year was $23,000.

Solution to Exercise 23-4

(a) (1)

Collected cash from customers on account	$75,000
Sold services for cash	19,000
Received dividends from investee	700
Paid interest on debt	(3,000)
Paid salaries and wages	(27,000)
Paid other operating expenses	(41,000)
Paid income taxes	(6,500)
Net cash provided by operations	$17,200

(2)

Purchased machinery	$(60,000)
Sold equipment for book value	12,000
Purchased an investment	(38,200)
Sold an investment	24,000
Net cash used by investing activities	$(62,200)

(3)

Paid principal of note payable	$(30,000)
Paid dividends	(6,000)
Issued common shares	45,000
Issued long-term debt	52,000
Purchased treasury shares	(4,000)
Net cash provided by financing activities	$57,000

(4)

Net cash provided by operating activities	$17,200
Net cash used by investing activities	(62,200)
Net cash provided by financing activities	57,000
Net increase in cash	$12,000

(b) (1) Recorded amortization expense, $7,000, was not used because it is a non-cash charge to income. It is an expense which did not require a cash payment. (The cash outlay occurs at the date that payment is made to acquire the related depreciable assets.)

(2) Amortized patents, $1,000, was not used because it is a noncash charge against income. It is an expense which did not require a cash outlay this period. (The cash outlay occurs at the date that cash payment is made for the acquisition of related intangible assets.)

(3) Accrued salaries, $800, was not used because it relates to an expense recognized this period for which the related cash payment is being deferred until next period.

(4) Acquired a computer in exchange for shares, $10,000, was not used because this is a noncash financing and investing activity.

> **TIP!**
>
> If the indirect method was used: (1) the amortization of $7,000 and the amortization of $1,000 would be added to net income, (2) an increase in the Salaries Payable account of $800 (due to the accrued salaries) would also be added to net income, and (3) the $3,300 gain on sale of investment would be deducted from net income in the process of reconciling net income to net cash provided from operations.

(c)

Salter Corporation
Statement of Cash Flows
For the Year Ending December 31, 2005
(Direct Method)

Cash flows from operating activities		
Cash receipts from customers	$94,000[a]	
Dividends received from investee	700	
Interest paid	(3,000)	
Cash paid to employees	(27,000)	
Cash paid for operating expenses	(41,000)	
Income taxes paid	(6,500)	
Net cash provided by operating activities		$17,200
Cash flows from investing activities		
Purchase of machinery	(60,000)	
Sale of equipment	12,000	
Purchase of investment	(38,200)	
Sale of investment	24,000	
Net cash used by investing activities		(62,200)
Cash flows from financing activities		
Payment of note payable	(30,000)	
Payment of dividends	(6,000)	
Issuance of common shares	45,000	

Issuance of long-term debt	52,000	
Purchase of treasury shares	(4,000)	
Net cash provided by financing activities		57,000
Net increase in cash		12,000
Cash at beginning of period		23,000
Cash at end of period		$35,000 [b]

Noncash investing and financing activities

Acquired a computer in exchange for common shares	$10,000

[a]$75,000 + $19,000 = $94,000.

[b]$12,000 net increase in cash + $23,000 beginning cash balance = $35,000 ending cash balance.

TIP! An additional schedule reconciling net income to net cash provided by operating activities should be presented as part of the statement of cash flows when using the direct method. The information with this exercise is insufficient to prepare that complete schedule.

Exercise 23-5

PURPOSE: This exercise will provide examples of transactions and their treatment on a statement of cash flows using the indirect method.

CODE FOR FORMAT OF STATEMENT OF CASH FLOWS
FOR USE WITH EXERCISE 23-2
(Read Instructions for use below)

Code Items	Format of the Statement
	Cash flows from operating activities:
	Net income (loss).
A	Add noncash expenses (charges), losses, and changes in certain accounts needed to convert income to a cash basis.
D	Deduct noncash revenue (credits), gains, and changes in certain accounts needed to convert income to a cash basis.
	Net cash provided (used) by operating activities.
	Cash flows from investing activities:
II	Add amount for an **investing** activity that produced a cash **inflow**.
IO	Deduct amount for an **investing** activity that resulted in a cash **outflow**.
	Net cash provided (used) by investing activities.
	Cash flows from financing activities:
FI	Add amount for a **financing** activity that produced a cash **inflow**.

FO   Deduct amount for a **financing** activity that produced a cash **outflow**.
       Net cash provided (used) by financing activities.

       Net increase (decrease) in cash and cash equivalents.
       Cash and cash equivalents at beginning of year.
       Cash and cash equivalents at end of year.

NI   Use this code for a transaction which is an operating activity and a com-
       ponent of net income. The transaction has the same effect (positive or
       negative) on cash as it has on the net income calculation (thus, it is part
       of net income and no adjustment to net income for this item is appropri-
       ate).

NC   Use this code for a noncash financing and/or investing activity to be
       reported elsewhere in the financial statements.

C   Use this code to refer to a transaction which only affects cash and cash
       equivalents.

X   Use this code for a transaction or event which is not reported or other-
       wise reflected on the statement of cash flows.

Instructions

For each of the following transactions and events, indicate how it should be
reported in a statement of cash flows using the indirect approach. Use the code
from the format above for short-hand notations for your responses. Include the
appropriate dollar amount with each code. A transaction or event may require
more than one code for a complete answer.

_____ $_____   1.   Borrow $50,000 by issuance of a short-term note
                           payable.

_____ $_____   2.   Sell land used in operations: Selling price,
                           $15,000;
_____ $_____   cost, $3,500.

_____ $_____   3.   Exchange long-term mortgage note receivable
                           for shares in
_____ $_____   another company: Carrying value of receivable,
                           $38,000; fair value of the shares, $36,000. The
                           investment in shares is intended to be short term.

_____ $_____   4.   Repay short-term nontrade note payable, $5,100.

_____ $_____   5.   Declare and distribute 10% stock dividend. Market
                           value, $18,000.

_____ $_____   6. Pay administrative salaries for the current period, $56,000.

_____ $_____   7. Accrue interest expense, $1,500.

_____ $_____   8. Accrue rent revenue, $1,800.

_____ $_____   9. Collect magazine subscription revenue in advance, $9,000.

_____ $_____   10. Recognize revenue of $5,000 from investment using the equity method of accounting. Collect $1,800 dividends from that investee.

_____ $_____   11. Acquire machine by exchange of treasury shares: Cost of treasury shares, $18,000; market value of shares, $22,000.

_____ $_____   12. Acquire machinery by issuance of long-term note payable to the seller: Face amount of note, $50,000; stated interest rate 2%; fair value of machinery, $40,000.

_____ $_____   13. Amortize premium on bonds payable, $200.

_____ $_____   14. Record increase in future income tax asset, $1,000.

_____ $_____   15. Use $1,000 cash to purchase a 90-day guaranteed investment certificate.

_____ $_____   16. Record bad debt expense of $7,000.

_____ $_____   17. Settle long-term debt by transfer of a noncurrent investment:
_____ $_____   Carrying value of debt, $77,000; fair value of assets, $70,000; book value of assets, $70,000.

_____ $_____   18. Amortize deferred service revenue of $600.

_____ $_____   19. Sell a plant asset for $1,000: Cost, $7,000; accumulated amortization, $4,000.

_____ $_____   20. Exchange old truck for new truck and also give cash of $11,000:
_____ $_____   Cost of old truck, $10,000; book value of old truck, $3,000; fair
_____ $_____   value of old truck, $2,200; list price of new truck, $14,500.

____ $_____   21. Recognize temporary decline of $7,000 in fair value of investment in equity securities classified as trading securities.

____ $_____   22. Sell merchandise for $400 cash.

____ $_____   23. Pay advertising fees of $1,600 for the current period.

____ $_____   24. Purchase treasury shares: Cost, $7,500; original issuance price, $7,000; cost method is used.

____ $_____   25. Pay accounts payable, $5,700.

____ $_____   26. Acquire a machine by a capital lease: Present value of minimum lease payments at inception, $75,000; first annual payment made at inception, $10,000.

____ $_____   27. Extinguish long-term debt prior to maturity by cash payment of $78,000: Carrying value of debt, $88,000.

Solution to Exercise 23-5

1.	FI	$50,000
2.	II	$15,000; & D $11,500
3.	NC	$36,000; & A $2,000
4.	FO	$5,100
5.	X	$18,000
6.	NI	$56,000
7.	A	$1,500
8.	D	$1,800
9.	A	$9,000
10.	D	$5,000; & A $1,800
11.	NC	$22,000
12.	NC	$40,000
13.	D	$200
14.	D	$1,000
15.	C	$1,000
16.	A	$7,000
17.	NC	$70,000; & D $7,000
18.	D	$600
19.	II	$1,000; & A $2,000
20.	IO	$11,000; & A $800; & NC $2,200
21.	A	$7,000
22.	NI	$400
23.	NI	$1,600
24.	FO	$7,500
25.	D	$5,700
26.	NC	$75,000; & FO $10,000
27.	FO	$78,000; & D $10,000

APPROACH:
1. Reconstruct the journal entry for each transaction. Examine each entry to identify if there is an inflow of cash, an outflow of cash, or no effect on cash. Assume purchases and sales of items are for cash, unless otherwise indicated.

The journal entry to record a transaction that is an investing activity which results in a cash flow will involve: (1) Cash and (2) an asset account other than Cash, such as Investment, Land, Building, Equipment, Patent, Franchise, etc.   **TIP!**

TIP! The journal entry to record a transaction that is a financing activity which results in a cash flow will involve: (1) Cash and (2) a liability account or an owners' equity account such as Bonds Payable, Notes Payable, Dividends Payable, Common Shares, Contributed Surplus, Treasury Shares, etc.

2. Write down the definitions for investing activities and financing activities (see below). Analyse each transaction to see if it fits one of these definitions:

   a) **Investing activities:** include (1) making and collecting loans; (2) acquiring and disposing of investments and productive long-lived assets.

   b) **Financing activities:** include (1) obtaining capital from owners and providing them with a return on, and a return of, their investment and (2) obtaining cash through the issuance of debt and repaying the amounts borrowed.

3. Identify the items requiring adjustments to net income in order to convert net income to net cash provided by operating activities by identifying the reconstructed journal entries that involve: (a) an income statement account and a balance sheet account other than Cash (for example the entry to record amortization), or (b) the Cash account and a noncash asset or liability account that relates to operating activity (accounts receivable, inventory, accounts payable, etc.), or (c) a gain or loss that has no cash effect or a gain or loss stemming from a transaction that is classified as an investing or financing activity.

4. Identify the items which are noncash financing and investing activities by identifying transactions which fit the definitions of investing activities and/or the definition of financing activities but do not affect Cash.

EXPLANATION: The journal entries to record each transaction are reconstructed and analysed below:

1.	Cash	50,000	
	Short-term Note Payable (Nontrade)		50,000

There is an inflow of cash due to a financing activity.

2.	Cash	15,000	
	Land		3,500
	Gain on Sale of Land		11,500

The cash proceeds from the sale of any asset are to be reflected as a cash inflow. Proceeds of $15,000 from the sale of a plant asset should be reported as an investing inflow. The proceeds of $15,000 represents a recovery of the asset's book value of $3,500 and a gain of $11,500. The gain of $11,500 is also a component of net income. When using the indirect method, the gain must be deducted from net income in reconciling net income with net cash from operating activities, so that the $11,500 is not double counted.

3. Equity Investment   36,000
   Loss on Disposal of Investment   2,000
     Investment in Mortgage Note Receivable   38,000

Cash is not affected. This exchange of one noncash asset for another noncash asset is an investing activity that must be disclosed. Regardless of whether this is a similar or dissimilar exchange of nonmonetary assets, a loss on the disposal of the receivable should be recognized on the income statement. That loss is added to net income when the indirect method is used for the statement of cash flows.

4. Short-term Note Payable (Nontrade)   5,100
   Cash   5,100

There is an outflow of cash due to a financing activity.

5. Retained Earnings   18,000
   Common Stock Dividend Distributable   18,000

  Common Stock Dividend Distributable   18,000
   Common Stock   18,000

Cash is not affected. There is no financing or investing or operating activity. This transaction is ignored in reporting the statement of cash flows. Other accounting requirements call for disclosure of this item in another financial statement or in the notes to financial statements because it changes shareholders' equity.

6. Salaries Expense   56,000
   Cash   56,000

There is a $56,000 decrease in cash due to an operating outflow. There is a reduction of $56,000 reflected in the net income figure due to the expense recognition. When the indirect method is used, no adjustment is needed because this transaction reduced both net income and cash.

7. Interest Expense   1,500
   Interest Payable   1,500

Net income is reduced but cash is not. This item is added to net income when the indirect method is used.

8. Rent Receivable   1,800
   Rent Revenue   1,800

Net income is increased but cash is not. This transaction caused an increase in rent receivable which must be deducted from net income when the indirect method is used.

9. Cash   9,000
        Unearned Subscription Revenue   9,000

Cash is increased because of collections from customers; this is an operating activity. The inflow is not reflected in net income so the $9,000 increase in unearned revenue is added to net income when the indirect method is used.

10. Investment in Affiliate   5,000
        Revenue from Investment   5,000

    Cash   1,800
        Investment in Affiliate   1,800

There is a cash flow of $1,800; it is an operating inflow because all dividends received are operating inflows. The first entry increases revenue (and net income) but does not affect cash. The second entry increases cash but does not effect net income. Using the indirect method, the $5,000 credit to income which is not accompanied by a corresponding cash inflow is deducted from net income and the $1,800 cash receipt for dividends is added to net income. Thus, the net $3,200 undistributed earnings of the investee is deducted from net income.

11. Machinery   22,000
        Treasury Shares   22,000

Cash is not affected. This is a significant investing activity (acquisition of equipment) and financing activity (disposal of treasury shares) that must be disclosed outside the body of the statement of cash flows.

12. Machinery   40,000
    Discount on Note Payable   10,000
        Long-term Note Payable   50,000

A note payable is issued at an unreasonably low interest rate for a noncash asset; it is to be recorded at the fair value of the asset received. Thus, a discount is established. Cash is not affected. This is a significant investing and financing activity that must be disclosed in the footnotes or in a schedule of noncash investing and financing activities.

13. Premium on Bonds Payable   200
        Interest Expense   200

There is an increase in net income without any corresponding cash inflow. Therefore, this credit to income is deducted from net income in the reconciliation of net income to net cash flow from operating activities.

14. Future Tax Asset   1,000
        Income Tax Expense   1,000

This entry causes net income to increase, but it does not affect cash. The increase in the future tax asset is deducted from net income when the indirect method is used.

15. Guaranteed investment certificate—90 Day   1,000
       Cash   1,000

There is a decrease in cash and an increase in cash equivalents. Therefore, there is no change in the total of cash and cash equivalents.

16. Bad Debt Expense   7,000
       Allowance for Doubtful Accounts   7,000

Net income decreases but cash does not. This noncash charge to income is added to net income when using the indirect method.

17. Long-term Debt   77,000
         Long-term Investment   70,000
         Gain on Extinguishment of Debt   7,000

Cash is not affected. This is a transaction that is a noncash financing and investing activity, to be separately disclosed. When using the indirect method, the gain must be deducted from net income because the gain is a credit to net income that relates to a (noncash) financing activity.

18. Unearned Service Revenue   600
       Service Revenue   600

There is an increase in net income, but no corresponding cash inflow. The $600 decrease in Unearned Service Revenue must be deducted from net income when using the indirect method.

19. Cash   1,000
    Accumulated Amortization   4,000
    Loss on Disposal of Plant Asset   2,000
       Plant Asset   7,000

There is a cash inflow of $1,000 related to an investing activity. When using the indirect method, the loss of $2,000 must be added back to net income because it is an effect of a transaction (sale of plant asset) that is an investing activity. That activity resulted in a cash inflow, not an outflow.

20. Truck ($11,000 + $2,200)   13,200
    Accumulated Amortization ($10,000 – $3,000)   7,000
    Loss on Disposal of Truck ($3,000 – $2,200)   800
       Truck   10,000
       Cash   11,000

There is an $11,000 cash outflow related to an investing activity (acquisition of property, plant, and equipment). This exchange of similar productive assets results in a loss of $800 which must be added back to net income using the indirect method. The exchange of one noncash asset (book value of $2,200 after the writedown for impairment) for another must be disclosed as a noncash investing activity.

| 21. Unrealized Holding Gain or Loss—Income | 7,000 | |
| Allowance to adjust Trading Securities to Market | | 7,000 |

There is a noncash charge to income. It is added to net income under the use of the indirect method.

| 22. Cash | 400 | |
| Sales Revenue | | 400 |

There is an inflow of cash due to an operating activity. The effect on cash is the same as the effect on net income; no adjustment to net income is made.

| 23. Advertising Expense | 1,600 | |
| Cash | | 1,600 |

There is an outflow of cash due to an operating activity. The effect on cash is the same as the effect on net income; no adjustment to net income is made.

| 24. Treasury Shares | 7,500 | |
| Cash | | 7,500 |

There is an outflow of cash for a financing activity (return of investment to owner).

| 25. Accounts Payable (Trade) | 5,700 | |
| Cash | | 5,700 |

The payment of a trade payable is an operating activity. The outflow is not reflected in net income. The $5,700 decrease in the accounts payable is, therefore, deducted from net income to calculate net cash flow from operating activities.

26. Machine Under Capital Lease	75,000	
Obligation Under Capital Lease		75,000
Obligation Under Capital Lease	10,000	
Cash		10,000

The inception of the lease is a transaction that qualifies as a noncash investing and financing activity that requires disclosure. The first lease payment results in a cash outflow due to a financing activity.

27. Long-term Debt	88,000	
Cash		78,000
Gain on Extinguishment of Debt		10,000

The payment of $78,000 to the creditor results in an outflow of cash for a financing activity. The gain of $10,000 must be deducted from net income when the indirect method is used for the statement of cash flows. The $78,000 payment to the creditor is shown as a financing outflow. The $4,000 payment of taxes is reflected in the net cash flow from operating activities figure because a net gain of $6,000 is part of net income and the gross gain of $10,000 is deducted in the reconciliation of net income to net cash flow from operating activities.

Analysis of Multiple-Choice Type Questions

Question

1. At the end of 2005 a company acquired a hotel by paying a portion of the purchase price in cash and issuing a mortgage note payable to the seller for the balance. In a statement of cash flows for 2005, what amount is included in financing activities for this transaction?
    a.) Zero
    b. Cash payment
    c. Mortgage amount
    d. Acquisition price

EXPLANATION: The portion of the building acquired by the cash down payment should be reported as a cash outflow due to an investing activity. The portion of the building acquired by the issuance of a mortgage note payable to the seller (i.e., a seller-financed debt) is a noncash investing and financing activity. This would be disclosed elsewhere in the financial statements. Payments of principal on the debt will be financing outflows; none have occurred yet because the purchase happened at the end of the period. (Solution = a.)

Question

2. Smith Corporation had the following transactions occur in the current year:
    1. Cash sale of merchandise inventory.
    2. Sale of delivery truck at book value. ✓
    3. Sale of Smith common shares for cash.
    4. Issuance of a note payable to a bank for cash.
    5. Sale of a security held as a long-term investment. ✓
    6. Collection of a loan receivable. ✓

    Which of the above items will appear as a cash inflow from investing activities on a statement of cash flows for the current year?
    a.   All six items
    b.   Five items

c.   Four items
d.   Three items
e.   Two items

EXPLANATION: Define investing activities. Compare each transaction above with the definition. Investing activities include (a) making and collecting loans; (b) acquiring and disposing of debt and equity instruments of other entities; and (c) acquiring and disposing of property, plant, and equipment and other productive assets. The sale of a delivery truck (regardless of the relationship of selling price and carrying value), the sale of a long-term investment, and the collection of a loan receivable are three items that produce cash inflows from investing activities. The cash sale of merchandise inventory results in a cash inflow from operating activities. The sale of the corporation's own common shares and the issuance of the note payable both produce inflows of cash from financing activities. (Solution = d.)

TIP! Recall that transactions classified as investing activities involve assets (delivery equipment, equity investments, loan receivable, for the examples above) whereas transactions classified as financing activities involve liabilities (note payable, for example) or owners' equity (common shares, for example).

Question

3. A corporation had the following transactions occur during the current year:
    1. Reclassification of debt from long-term liabilities to current liabilities.
    2. Payment of principal on mortgage note payable.
    3. Payment of interest on mortgage note payable.
    4. Purchase of treasury shares.
    5. Payment of cash dividend.
    6. Payment of property dividend.
    7. Distribution of stock dividend.
    In a statement of cash flows, which of the above items is reported as a cash outflow from financing activities?
    a. Seven items
    b. Six items
    c. Five items
    d. Four items
    e. Three items

EXPLANATION: The payment of principal on a note payable, the purchase of treasury shares, and the payment of a cash dividend are the three items that will be reflected as cash outflows from financing activities. The reclassification of debt does not affect cash. It may be included in the schedule of noncash investing and financing activities. The payment of interest is to be reported as a cash outflow from operating activities. The payment of a property dividend is a noncash transaction to be disclosed elsewhere in the financial statements. Neither the declaration nor the distribution of a stock dividend affects cash. Because the declaration and distribution of a stock dividend is neither an investing nor a financing activity, a stock dividend is not reported anywhere on a statement of cash flows. (Solution = e.)

Question

4. During 2005, Pullman Inc. had the following activities related to its financial operations:

Proceeds from the sale of treasury shares (on books at cost of $86,000)	$100,000
Carrying value of convertible preferred shares in Pullman, converted into common shares of Pullman	120,000
Distribution in 2005 of cash dividend declared in 2004 to preferred shareholders	62,000
Payment for the early retirement of long-term bonds payable (carrying amount $740,000)	750,000

The amount of <u>net cash used in financing activities</u> to appear in Pullman's statement of cash flows for 2005 should be:
a. $716,000.
b. $712,000.
c. $592,000.
d. $530,000.

EXPLANATION: The net cash used in financing activities is calculated as follows:

Proceeds from sale of treasury shares	$100,000
Payment of cash dividends	(62,000)
Retirement of bonds payable	(750,000)
Net cash flow from financing activities	(712,000)

The conversion of preferred shares to common shares of $120,000 is a noncash transaction and would be disclosed elsewhere in the financial statements. (Solution = b.)

The $10,000 loss on retirement of bonds payable ($750,000 retirement price exceeds carrying value of $740,000 by $10,000) would be a component of net income. If the indirect method is used to present the net cash provided (used) by operations, the $10,000 loss would be added to net income in this calculation. | **TIP!**

Question

+ 5. During 2005, Jackson Corporation had the following activities related to its financial operations:
  ✓ 1. Purchased equipment for cash, which was borrowed from a bank.
  ◦ 2. Acquired treasury shares for cash.
  3. Declared a cash dividend payable in 2006.
  4. Appropriated retained earnings for possible loss from lawsuit.
  5. Purchased a 2-month guaranteed investment certificate.
  ✓ 6. Acquired a 5-year guaranteed investment certificate from a bank.
  7. Made interest payments on bonds payable.
  8. Converted preferred shares to common shares.
  9. Received dividends from an investment in equity of another corporation.

  In a statement of cash flows, how many of the above transactions are reported as a cash **outflow** from investing activities?
  a. One
  (b.) Two
  c. Three
  d. Four
  e. Five
  f. Six

EXPLANATION: Identify each item as being reported as one of the following:
  - A cash inflow from operating activities
  - A cash outflow from operating activities
  - A cash inflow from investing activities
  - A cash outflow from investing activities
  - A cash inflow from financing activities
  - A cash outflow from financing activities
  - An investing or financing activity not affecting cash

Refer to the definitions in **Illustration 23-1** if you need to do so. Count the number that you identify to be reported as a cash outflow from investing activities.

Item 1:	The purchase of equipment for cash is an investing outflow. The borrowing of cash from a bank is a financing inflow.
Item 2:	The acquisition of treasury shares for cash is a financing outflow.
Item 3:	The declaration of a cash dividend is a transaction not affecting cash and does not get reported on a statement of cash flows. The subsequent payment of the cash dividend will be a financing outflow.
Item 4:	The appropriation of retained earnings is a transaction not affecting cash; it is not reported on a statement of cash flows.
Item 5:	The purchase of a two-month guaranteed investment certificate is a transaction where cash is exchanged for a cash equivalent. It is not reported on a statement of cash flows.
Item 6:	The acquisition of a five-year guaranteed investment certificate is an investing outflow.
Item 7:	Interest payments are an operating outflow.

Item 8:   The conversion of preferred shares to common shares is a financing activity that does not affect cash; this transaction is to be disclosed elsewhere in the financial statements.

Item 9:   The receipt of dividends (and interest) are cash inflows from operating activities.

Transactions 1 and 6 are reported as cash outflows from investing activities. (Solution = b.)

Question

6. Refer to the facts of Question 5 above. In a statement of cash flows, how many of the transactions are reported as a <u>cash outflow from financing activities</u>?
    a. One
    b. Two
    c. Three
    d. Four
    e. Five
    f. Six

EXPLANATION: Refer to the explanation for Question 5 above. Only Item 2 is reported as a cash outflow from financing activities. (Solution = a.)

Question

7. Which of the following would be classified as a <u>financing activity</u> on a statement of cash flows?
    a. Declaration and distribution of a stock dividend
    b. Deposit to a bond sinking fund
    c. Sale of a loan receivable
    d. Payment of interest to a creditor

EXPLANATION: Write down the definitions for investing, financing, and operating activities. Take each of the transactions and see if it meets the definition for a financing activity. Declaration and distribution of stock dividend does not meet any of the definitions. It is an example of an item that is not reported anywhere on a statement of cash flows. Although the journal entry to record the deposit to a bond sinking fund results in an increase in the fund, which is often classified as a long-term investment, most accountants emphasize the purpose of the deposit, which is to ultimately pay for amounts borrowed; thus, it is usually classified as a financing activity. The sale of a loan receivable is clearly an investing activity, and the payment of interest to a creditor is an operating activity. (Solution = b.)

Question

8. The following information was taken from the 2005 financial statements of the Laurel Corporation:

Bonds payable, January 1, 2005	$ 100,000
Bonds payable, December 31, 2005	400,000

During 2002
- Bonds payable with a face amount of $40,000 were issued in exchange for equipment.
- A $90,000 payment was made to retire bonds payable with a face amount of $100,000.

In its statement of cash flows for the year ended December 31, 2005, what amount should Laurel report as proceeds from issuance of bonds payable?
   a. $300,000
   b. $360,000
   c. $160,000
   d. $340,000
   e. $170,000
   f. $240,000

EXPLANATION: Draw a T-account for Bonds Payable. Enter the data given and solve for the unknown.

Bonds Payable			
Retired	100,000	100,000	Bal., Jan. 1, 2005
		40,000	Issued for equipment
		360,000	Issued for cash
		400,000	Bal., Dec. 31, 2005

(Solution = b.)

Question

9. In a statement of cash flows, using the indirect method, which of the following are subtracted from net income to determine net cash provided by operating activities?

I.	Amortization of premium on bonds payable
II.	Loss on sale of equipment +
III.	Amortization expense +

   a. I only
   b. II only
   c. I and II
   d. I and III
   e. II and III
   f. I, II, and III

EXPLANATION: Think about how each item (1) affects net income and (2) affects cash. Then reason what is needed to reconcile net income to net cash provided by operating activities. The amortization of premium on bonds payable increases net income (because it reduces interest expense), but does not affect cash; thus it is deducted from net income in the reconciliation of net income to net cash provided by operating activities. The loss on sale of equipment reduces net income but does not affect cash; hence, it is added to net income in the reconciliation under discussion. Amortization expense reduces net income but does not affect cash; thus, it is added to net income in this reconciliation. (Solution = a.)

Question

10. Alley Corporation had net income for 2005 of $5 million. Additional information is as follows:

Amortization of plant assets	$2,000,000
Amortization of intangibles	$400,000
Increase in accounts receivable	$700,000
Increase in accounts payable	$900,000

Alley's net cash provided by operating activities for 2005 was:
a. $2,800,000.
b. $7,200,000.
c. $7,400,000.
d. $7,600,000.

EXPLANATION: The amortization amounts are items that reduce net income but do not cause a decrease in cash during the current period. The increase in accounts receivable indicates that sales revenue earned for the period exceeded the cash collections from customers, and therefore net income exceeded the net cash provided by operating activities. The increase in accounts payable indicates that expenses incurred exceeded cash payments for expense type items, which caused net income to be less than net cash provided by operating activities. The solution is as follows:

Net income	$5,000,000
Amortization of plant assets	2,000,000
Amortization of intangibles	400,000
Increase in accounts receivable	(700,000)
Increase in accounts payable	900,000
Net cash provided by operating activities	$7,600,000

(Solution = d.)

Question

11. Net cash flow from operating activities for 2005 for Graham Corporation was $75,000. The following items are reported on the financial statements for 2005:

Amortization	5,000
Cash dividends paid on common shares	3,000
Increase in accrued receivables	6,000

    Based only on the information above, Graham's net income for 2005 was:
    a. $64,000.
    b. $66,000.
    c. $74,000.
    d. $76,000.
    e. None of the above.

EXPLANATION: Write down the format for the reconciliation of net income to net cash flow from operating activities. Fill in the information given. Solve for the unknown.

Net income	$ X
Amortization	5,000
Increase in accrued receivables	(6,000)
Net cash flow from operating activities	$ 75,000

Solving for X, net income = $76,000.

Cash dividends paid on common shares have no effect on this calculation because cash dividends paid are not a component of net income, and they are not an operating activity. They are a financing activity. (Solution = d.)

Question

12. A change in accounts receivable is used to convert sales revenue to cash receipts from customers when the direct method is used. A change in accounts receivable is also used to convert net income to net cash from operating activities when the indirect method is used. Do you use a change in gross accounts receivable or net accounts receivable?

	Direct	**Indirect**
a.	Gross	Gross
b.	Net	Net
c.	Net	Gross
d.	Gross	Net

EXPLANATION: The change in net accounts receivable includes the change in the Accounts Receivable account and the change in the Allowance for Doubtful Accounts account. The Accounts Receivable account changes because of credit sales, write-offs of individual accounts, cash collections, and the reinstatement of accounts previously written off. The allowance account changes because of the recognition of bad debts expense, write-offs of individual accounts, and the reinstatement of accounts previously written off.

When the direct method is used, only the change in gross receivables is used to convert sales revenue to cash collections from customers. The change in the allowance account is not a factor in this conversion because the related bad debts expense has no impact on this calculation. When the indirect method is used, the change in net receivables is used to convert net income to net cash provided by operating activities because it reflects the bad debts expense (which does not require a cash outlay) as well as the difference between the accrual basis revenue amount and the cash collections from customers. (Solution = d.)

Question

13. Donald Company reported salaries expense of $95,000 for 2005. The following data were extracted from the company's financial records:

	12/31/04	12/31/05
Prepaid Salaries	$20,000	$23,000
Salaries Payable	70,000	85,000

On a statement of cash flows for 2005, using the direct method, cash payments for salaries should be:
a. $77,000.
b. $83,000.
c. $107,000.
d. $113,000.

EXPLANATION: Think of the relationship between salaries expense and cash payments for salaries when there is (1) an increase in prepaid salaries, and (2) an increase in salaries payable. Convert the expense amount to a cash paid figure.

Salaries expense	$ 95,000
Increase in prepaid salaries	3,000
Increase in salaries payable	(15,000)
Cash payments for salaries	$ 83,000 (Solution = b.)

Question

14. The following information was taken from the 2005 financial statements of Gardner Corporation:

Inventory, January 1, 2005	$ 30,000
Inventory, December 31, 2005	40,000
Accounts payable, January 1, 2005	25,000
Accounts payable, December 31, 2005	40,000
Sales	200,000
Cost of goods sold	150,000

If the direct method is used in the 2005 statement of cash flows, what amount should Gardner report as cash payments for goods to be sold?

a. $175,000
b. $165,000
c. $155,000
d. $145,000
e. $125,000

APPROACH AND EXPLANATION: Draw T-accounts. Enter the information given.

Cost of Goods Sold	Inventory	Accounts Payable
150,000	Beg. Bal. 30,000	25,000 Beg. Bal.
	150,000 CGS	
	End. Bal. 40,000	40,000 End. Bal.

Assume all purchases of inventory are on account. Solve for the amount of purchases. Then solve for the amount of cash payments for goods to be sold (assuming all accounts payable arise from purchases of inventory).

Cost of Goods Sold	Inventory	Accounts Payable
150,000	Beg. Bal. 30,000	Cash Payments 145,000	25,000 Beg. Bal.
	Purchases 160,000 150,000 CGS	160,000 Purchases
	End. Bal. 40,000	40,000 End. Bal.

(Solution = d.)

Question

15. Selected information for 2005 for the Green Company follows:

Total operating expenses (accrual basis) (includes amortization)	$200,000
Beginning prepaid expenses	10,000
Ending prepaid expenses	12,000
Beginning accrued liabilities	16,000
Ending accrued liabilities	19,000
Amortization of plant assets	28,000
Amortization of intangible assets	7,500
Payment of cash dividends	5,000

The amount of cash payments made during 2005 for operating expenses is:
a. $234,500.
b. $165,500.
c. $163,500.
d. $160,500.
e. None of these.

EXPLANATION: Use one of the relevant formats in **Illustration 23-2** to convert operating expenses to cash paid.

Total operating expenses (accrual basis)	$200,000
Increase in prepaid expenses	2,000

Increase in accrued liabilities	(3,000)
Amortization of plant assets	(28,000)
Amortization of intangibles	(7,500)
Cash paid for operating expenses	$163,500

(Solution = c.)

> **TIP!** Notice that the amount given in the question for "total operating expenses" includes amortization whereas the format calls for exclusion of these items. Amortization expenses are both expense items that do not require a cash outlay at the time the expense is recorded. Thus, they are deducted from the operating expense total to arrive at the amount of cash paid for operating expense items this period.
>
> **TIP!** Dividends paid are neither an operating expense nor an operating activity. Payment of dividends is a financing activity (outflow). The receipt of dividends from an investee is an operating activity (inflow).

Question

16. The following information was taken from the 2005 financial statements of Nelson Corporation:

Income tax payable, January 1, 2005	$ 50,000
Income tax payable, December 31, 2005	40,000
Future tax liability, January 1, 2005	15,000
Future tax liability, December 31, 2005	30,000
Income tax expense	200,000

If the direct method is used in the 2005 statement of cash flows, what amount should Nelson report as cash payments for income taxes?
   a. $225,000
   b. $210,000
   c. $205,000
   d. $195,000
   e. $190,000
   f. $175,000

EXPLANATION: Draw T-accounts. Enter the information given and solve for the missing amounts.

Income Tax Expense				Income Tax Payable		
Curr. Tax Exp.[2]	185,000				50,000	Beg. Bal.
Fut. Tax Exp.[1]	15,000		Taxes Pd.[3]	195,000	185,000	Cur. Tax Exp.[2]
End. Bal.	200,000				40,000	End. Bal.

Future Tax Liability		
	15,000	Beg. Bal.
	15,000	Fut. Tax Expense[1]
	30,000	End. Bal.

[1]$ 30,000   Future tax liability, 12/31/05
  (15,000)   Future tax liability, 1/1/05
 $ 15,000   Future tax expense for 2005

[2]$200,000   Total income tax expense for 2005
  (15,000)   Future tax expense for 2005
 $185,000   Current tax expense for 2005

[3]$ 50,000   Income taxes payable, 1/1/05
  185,000   Current tax expense for 2005
  235,000
  (40,000)   Income taxes payable, 12/31/05
 $195,000   Income taxes paid in 2005

(Solution = d.)

TIP! The use of T-accounts is a good solutions approach because it requires only that you recall the normal balance of relevant accounts and the transactions that affect certain accounts. Picturing the accounts helps you to readily determine the amounts of any debits or credits that affected an account. Another approach that requires more analysis of the relationship of accounts appears as follows:

Income tax expense for 2005	$ 200,000
Increase in future tax liability (future tax expense)	(15,000)
Current tax expense for 2005	185,000
Decrease in income taxes payable	10,000
Income taxes paid during 2005	$ 195,000

Question

✝ 17. The following facts are available for the Pace Company:

Sales revenue for 2005	$ 450,000
Accounts receivable, January 1, 2005	35,000
Accounts receivable, December 31, 2005	29,000
Allowance for doubtful accounts, January 1, 2005	5,000
Allowance for doubtful accounts, December 31, 2005	3,500
Bad debt expense for 2005	42,000
Write-off of accounts receivable during 2005	43,500

The amount of cash collections from customers during 2005 was:
a. $498,000.
b. $496,500.
c. $487,500.
d. $412,500.
e. none of the above.

EXPLANATION: The calculation for cash collections is as follows:

Sales revenue	$ 450,000
Decrease in accounts receivable	6,000

Write-off of accounts receivable	(43,500)
Cash collections from customers	$ 412,500

(Solution = d.)

TIP!

TIP!

TIP!

TIP!

An alternative solution is as follows:

Sales revenue	$ 450,000
Decrease in accounts receivable	6,000
Decrease in allowance for doubtful accounts	(1,500)
Bad debt expense	(42,000)
Cash collections from customers	$ 412,500

Another way of solving for the above is as follows:

Sales revenue	$ 450,000
Decrease in net accounts receivable	4,500 [a]
Bad debt expense	(42,000)
Cash collections from customers	$ 412,500

[a]			
$35,000 - $5,000	=	$30,000	Beginning net receivables
$29,000 - $3,500	=	$25,500	Ending net receivables
$30,000 - $25,500	=	$ 4,500	Decrease in net receivables

You may also solve for the cash collections by drawing T-accounts for Sales Revenue, Accounts Receivable, Allowance for Doubtful Accounts, and Bad Debt Expense. Enter the information given and solve for the missing amount. The T-accounts would appear as follows:

Sales Revenue		Accounts Receivable		
		Beg. Bal.	35,000	
				43,500 Write-offs
	450,000	Sales	450,000	
				412.500 Cash collections
	450,000	End. Bal.	29,000	

Allowance for Doubtful Accounts			Bad Debt Expense	
	5,000	Beg. Bal.		
Write-offs 43,500	42,000	Bad Debt Expense	42,000	
	3,500	End. Bal.	42,000	

Assume all sales were on account. Even if some sales were cash sales, the answer will be the same for total cash collections.

Question

18. When the indirect method is used for a statement of cash flows, should the gross amount or net-of-tax amount of an extraordinary gain be added to or deducted from net income in calculating cash provided by operating activities?
   a. Gross amount of an extraordinary gain should be added to net income.
   b. Gross amount of an extraordinary gain should be deducted from net income.

c. Net-of-tax amount of an extraordinary gain should be added to net income.

d. Net-of-tax amount of an extraordinary gain should be deducted from net income.

EXPLANATION: All income taxes paid are to be classified as operating cash outflows. No income taxes are to be allocated to investing and financing transactions. Assume an extraordinary gain from an investing activity is tax affected at 40%:

Cash received	$ 50,000
Gain	10,000
Taxes paid	4,000

Net income includes the net gain of $6,000 ($10,000 gain less income tax effect of $4,000). By deducting the gross gain of $10,000 from net income, an outflow of $4,000 (due to income taxes paid) is reflected in the operating activity section of the statement of cash flows. The $50,000 would be classified as an inflow in the investing activity section. (Solution = b.)

It is useful to look at cash flow patterns in the statement, i.e., note where the cash comes from (operating, investing, or financing) and where it goes.

Question

19. The *CICA Handbook* allows either the direct or the indirect method of presenting the statement to be used; however, the use of the direct method is preferred. Which of the following statements is most true under the direct method (i.e., as compared to the indirect method)?
   a. Cash flow from operations is greater
   b. Cash flow from operations is less
   c. Details under cash flow from investing and financing activities are different
   d. The statement is the same except for details under operating activities.

EXPLANATION: The only difference is the amount of detail shown in the operating activities section. The direct method gives more detail as to operating cash inflows and outflows and this is why it is the preferred method. (Solution = d.)

CHAPTER 24

Other Measurement and Disclosure Issues

Overview

Financial statements often contain information for which more detail and/or explanation is desired by the users of the statements. Additional detail may be provided in the notes to the statements. Explanation of management's view may be included in the MD&A (management's discussion and analysis) section of the annual report. These and other measurement and disclosure issues are discussed in this chapter.

Study Steps

Understanding the Importance of Disclosures

The full disclosure principle dictates what information should be provided in financial reporting. It states that anything that will influence or change a user's decision should be disclosed in the financial statements. This is a very broad statement and is certainly open to interpretation.

As a general rule, if in doubt, disclose.

Think about what users are expecting to see in the financial statements. If the preparer is presenting something unexpected, then more disclosure is generally better.

Because financial statement preparers do not always follow the spirit of general principles like this one, especially if it is not in their own or the company's best interests, the CICA has begun to mandate increasing amounts of disclosures.

It is the general "catch-all" nature of the full disclosure principle that makes this area one of constant evolution and change. Users want more disclosures, preparers often want to give less. During the last few years, securities exchange commissions have also become involved and are changing the face of financial reporting by mandating their own disclosures that must be followed by any company whose shares are listed on a stock exchange.

The notes to the financial statements are an integral part of the statements and often incorporate additional valuable information. However, it is important to remember that note disclosure is not a substitute for proper financial statement presentation.

Never analyse financial statements without reading the notes.

A key note is the accounting policy note. It is usually note 1 and sometimes is presented before the statements to encourage users to read it first. All significant accounting policies should be disclosed here, especially ones where there is a choice in what policy could be utilized.

The accounting policy note gives important information about choices made by the financial statement preparers.

Related party transactions

Disclosure of related party transactions is mandated by the CICA since the transactions often do not reflect arm's-length terms. Since users expect that transactions are to be carried out at arm's length (reflecting market terms), it is wise to disclose those that are not.

Required disclosures under *CICA Handbook* Section 3840 are:
- A description of the nature and extent of the transaction.
- A description of the relationship.
- The recorded amount and measurement basis of the transaction.
- Amounts due to or from related parties and, if not otherwise apparent, the terms of settlement.
- Contractual obligations involving related parties.
- Contingencies involving related parties.

There is some judgement required in determining just who the related parties are. Note that the CICA has gone one step farther with these transactions, requiring that the transactions be revalued to carrying value in some cases.

As a general rule, if the transaction is in the normal course of business, is monetary, and there is support for the price, the transaction is not revalued. If, however, these conditions are not present, the transaction gets revalued to book value and any gain/loss gets booked to equity.

If the transaction is remeasured, any difference between the carrying amounts of items exchanged, together with any tax amounts related to the items transferred, should be included as a charge or credit to equity.

See Illustration 24-1 for a summary of measurement issues.

Post-balance sheet events

Subsequent events happen subsequent to the balance sheet date. The issue is whether to adjust the financial statements or not.

Segmented information

Segmented information is also mandated by the CICA. Detailed information about sales, operating profits, and invested funds should be disclosed for different industry and geographic segments. This is encouraged because different operative segments carry different risks.

Users need information about risks in order to make decisions.

See the Solution to Case 24-2 for a detailed account of what must be disclosed.

Interim financial reporting

Interim financial reporting is governed by *CICA Handbook* Section 1751. It is important since information is often no longer relevant by the time the annual financial statements are issued.

CICA Handbook Section 1751 requires that the same accounting principles be used for interim reporting as for annual financial reporting. There are two approaches to interim reporting: the discrete approach and the integral approach. The discrete approach treats each period as a distinct, separate reporting period and states that transactions occurring in the period should be reported in the period. The integral approach treats the periods as an integral part of the year. The latter approach favours calculating certain things on an annual basis and then allocating them.

The *CICA Handbook* favours the discrete approach; however, there are some exceptions.

Required disclosures are listed in Section 1751 and include comparatives. See Case 24-3 to see how this is applied in a case study.

Differential Reporting

This is an option for non-publicly accountable enterprises to avoid some complex GAAP measurement and disclosure issues that are required for public companies. Most companies should qualify, but unanimous consent is required from all shareholders. Additionally, care should be taken in making this decision to ensure major users (such as a bank) agree to the exemptions. The statements will disclose very clearly when differential reporting has been adopted. Note that it is still considered GAAP—just different given the particular environment the company may be in.

One of the basic principles in allowing this differential reporting option is cost versus benefit. It is widely accepted that owners of private business do not necessarily need (or use) some of the complex accounting that is required to be in accordance with GAAP. Further, it is accepted that owners have access to all available information; therefore the cost of providing the information is clearly in excess of the benefit.

The differential reporting options relate to the following areas:

- Subsidiaries: may elect to use the cost or equity methods for subsidiaries that would otherwise be consolidated.
- Long-term investments: may elect to use the cost method rather than the equity method for investments where significant influence exists.
- Interests in joint ventures: may elect to use the cost or equity methods to account for joint ventures that would otherwise be consolidated using the proportionate consolidation method.
- Goodwill and other intangible assets: may elect to test goodwill for impairment when an event occurs that might signal potential impairment (versus annually).
- Share capital: may elect to provide fewer details in terms of disclosures.
- Income taxes: may elect to use the taxes payable method to account for taxes.
- Financial instruments: may elect to treat certain preferred shares as equity rather than debt.

Tips on Chapter Topics

TIP! The initial note to the financial statements should be a **summary of significant accounting policies**. This disclosure should identify principles applied by the entity that are: (a) selections from existing alternatives, (b) principles peculiar to a particular industry, or (c) unusual or innovative applications. This disclosure may precede the notes to the financial statements.

TIP! **Notes to the financial statements** are sometimes called **footnotes**. They are an integral part of the financial statements.

TIP! **Related party transactions** require separate **detailed** disclosures because transactions involving related parties cannot be presumed to be carried out on an arms'-length basis because the requisite conditions of competitive, free-market dealings may not exist. The substance rather than the form of these transactions should be reflected in the financial statements. Furthermore, special measurement principles exist for related party transactions that may require the transaction to be remeasured. Of particular concern is when the transaction is not in the normal course of business.

Subsequent events can be classified into two types: those that provide additional evidence about conditions that existed at the balance sheet date (commonly referred to as a Type I subsequent event), and those that result from new information that may be useful to those reading the financial statements (commonly referred to as a Type II subsequent event). Type I subsequent events require an adjustment to the financial statements and Type II subsequent events would normally be disclosed. Note that there will be many subsequent events that would not fit into either category and therefore not be accrued or disclosed. **TIP!**

In general, the same accounting principles used for annual reports should be employed for interim reports. However, **an interim period is to be treated as a separate accounting period**. Therefore, accruals and deferrals would therefore follow the principles employed for annual reports. Accounting transactions should be reported as they occur, and expense recognition should not change with the period of time covered. **TIP!**

Income taxes for an interim period are to be calculated using an **estimated annual effective tax rate**. The estimated annual effective tax rate is to be applied to the year-to-date "ordinary" income at the end of each interim period to calculate the year-to-date tax. The interim period tax related to "ordinary" income shall be the difference between the amount so calculated and the amounts reported for previous interim periods of the fiscal year. **TIP!**

For interim reporting purposes, extraordinary items are to be reported in the interim period in which they occur rather than arbitrarily allocated over multiple periods. **TIP!**

A **financial forecast** and a **financial projection** are both prospective financial statements that present, to the best of the responsible party's knowledge and belief, an entity's financial position, results of operations, and cash flows for a future time. The difference between a financial forecast and a financial projection is that a forecast attempts to provide information on what is expected to happen; whereas, a projection may provide information on what is not necessarily expected to happen, but might take place. **TIP!**

The MD&A section of the annual financial report will cover three financial aspects of the business: liquidity, capital resources, and results of operations. It is mandated by securities commissions. It is not covered under existing Canadian GAAP. **TIP!**

Differential reporting is an option for non-publicly accountable enterprises (most private companies should qualify) to avoid some of the more complex measurement and disclosure requirements that public companies must follow. To implement differential reporting, unanimous consent of all shareholders is required. **TIP!**

Case 24-1

PURPOSE: This exercise will review the meaning or significance of a number of terms used in this chapter.

Instructions

Select the letter of the item that most directly relates to the numbered statements. Use the letter of the item to identify your response.

A. Summary of significant accounting policies.
B. Related party transactions.
C. Reporting of segment information.
D. Subsequent events.
E. Errors.
F. Differential reporting.
G. Full disclosure principle.
H. Interim reports.
I. Notes to the financial statements.
J. Auditor's report.
K. Management's discussion and analysis
L. Financial forecast.
M. Financial projection.

_____ 1. Calls for financial reporting of any financial facts significant enough to influence the judgement of an informed reader.

_____ 2. Information that is an integral part of the financial statements and serves as a means of amplifying or explaining the items presented in the body of the statements.

_____ 3. Disclosure of the accounting methods employed in the preparation of the financial statements.

_____ 4. A business enterprise engages in transactions in which one of the transacting parties has the ability to influence significantly the policies of the other, or in which a nontransacting party has the ability to influence the policies of the two transacting parties.

_____ 5. Unintentional mistakes.

_____ 6. An option for non-publicly accountable enterprises.

_____ 7. Information related to revenues, operating profit or loss, and identifiable assets of different product lines of an entity.

_____ 8. Reports that cover periods of less than one year.

_____ 9. Section of an annual report that covers three financial aspects of an enterprise's business—liquidity, capital resources, and results of operations.

_____ 10. Information related to events occurring after the balance sheet date but before the financial statements are released.

_____ 11. A report that states whether or not the financial statements are presented in accordance with generally accepted accounting principles.

_____ 12. Prospective financial statements based on a company's assumptions reflecting conditions it expects would exist in the future, given one or more hypothetical assumptions.

13. Prospective financial statements based on a company's assumptions reflecting conditions it expects will exist in the future and the course of action it expects to take.

Solution to Case 24-1

1.	G	6.	F	11.	J
2.	I	7.	C	12.	L
3.	A	8.	I	13.	M
4.	B	9.	K		
5.	E	10.	D		

Case 24-2

PURPOSE: This case will review the tests applied in determining the reportable segments of an entity.

Diversified Galore Inc. has several reportable industry segments that account for 80% of its operations.

Instructions

(1) Explain the term "operating segment" as it applies to an entity diversified in its operations.
(2) Explain when the information about two or more operating segments may be aggregated.
(3) Explain what criteria are to be used to determine Diversified's reportable segments.
(4) Indicate what information is to be disclosed for each operating segment.

Solution to Case 24-2

(1) An **operating segment** is a component of an enterprise:
   (a) that engages in business activities from which it earns revenues and incurs expenses;
   (b) whose operating results are regularly reviewed by the company's chief operating decision maker to assess segment performance and allocate resources to the segment; and,
   (c) for which discrete financial information is available.

(2) Information about two or more operating segments may be aggregated only if the segments have the same basic characteristics in **each** of the following areas:

(a) The nature of the products and services provided.

(b) The nature of the production process.

(c) The type or class of customer.

(d) The methods of product or service distribution.

(e) If applicable, the nature of the regulatory environment.

(3) After the company decides on the segments for possible disclosure, a quantitative materiality test is made to determine whether the segment is significant enough to warrant actual disclosure. An operating segment is regarded as significant and therefore identified as a reportable segment if it satisfies **one or more** of the following quantitative thresholds.

  • Its **revenue** (including both sales to external customers and intersegment sales or transfers) is 10% or more of the combined revenue of all the enterprise's operating segments.

  • The absolute amount of its **profit or loss** is 10% or more of, in absolute terms, the greater of

    (a) the combined operating profit of all operating segments that did not incur a loss, or

    (b) the combined loss of all operating segments that did report a loss.

  • Its **assets** are 10% or more of the combined assets of all operating segments.

In applying these tests, two additional factors must be considered. First, segment data must explain a significant portion of the company's business. Specifically, the segmented results must equal or exceed 75% of the combined sales to unaffiliated customers for the entire enterprise. This test prevents a company from providing limited information on only a few segments and lumping all the rest into one category.

Second, the profession recognizes that reporting too many segments may overwhelm users with detailed information. The CICA (*CICA Handbook* Section 1701) has proposed that 10 is a reasonable upper limit for the number of segments that a company should be required to disclose.

(4) The CICA now requires that an enterprise report:

  (a) **General information about its reportable segments.** This includes factors that management considers most significant in determining the company's reporting segments, and the types of products and services from which each operating segment derives its revenues.

  (b) **Segment profit and loss, assets, and related information.** Total profit or loss and total assets for each reportable segment. In addition, the following specific information about each reportable segment must be reported if the amounts are regularly reviewed by management:

    • Revenues from transactions with external customers.

    • Revenues from transactions with other operating segments of the same enterprise.

    • Interest revenue.

    • Interest expense.

- Amortization of capital assets and goodwill.
- Unusual items.
- Equity in the net income of investees subject to significant influence.
- Income tax expense or benefit.
- Extraordinary items.
- Significant noncash items other than amortization expense.

(c) **Reconciliations.** An enterprise must provide a reconciliation of: the total of the segments' revenues to total revenues: a reconciliation of the total of the operating segments' profits and losses to its income before income taxes, discontinued operations, and extraordinary items; and a reconciliation of the total of the operating segments' assets to total assets. Other reconciliations for other significant items disclosed should also be presented and all reconciling items should be separately identified and described for all of the above.

(d) **Information about geographic areas.** Revenues from external customers (Canada versus foreign), capital assets and goodwill (Canada versus foreign). Disclose foreign information by country if material.

(e) **Major customers.** If 10 percent or more of the revenues is derived from a single customer, the enterprise must disclose the total amount of revenues from each such customer by segment.

Case 24-3

PURPOSE: This case will review the reporting requirements for interim financial statements.

Sally's Sweater Shop is located in Burnaby B.C. It sells sweaters, jackets, and other related merchandise. Some shareholders have requested management to distribute quarterly financial statements to shareholders.

Instructions

(a) Discuss the accounting principles that should be employed for interim reports.
(b) Indicate whether or not it is a requirement to include a statement of cash flows in an interim report. Also list the minimum data to be disclosed in an interim report.

Solution to Case 24-3

(a) **The profession indicates that the same accounting principles used for annual reports should be employed for interim reports.** Revenues should be recognized in interim periods on the same basis as they are for annual periods. Also, costs directly associated with revenues (product costs), such as materials, labour and related fringe benefits, and manufacturing overhead should be treated in the same manner for interim reports as for annual reports.

Companies generally should use the same inventory pricing methods (FIFO, LIFO, etc.) for interim reports that they use for annual reports. However, the following exceptions are appropriate at interim reporting periods:

1. When LIFO inventories are liquidated at an interim date and are expected to be replaced by year end, cost of goods sold should include the expected cost of replacing the liquidated LIFO base and not give effect to the interim liquidation.

2. Planned variances under a standard cost system, which are expected to be absorbed by year end, ordinarily should be deferred.

Costs and expenses other than product costs, often referred to as period costs, are often charged to the interim period as incurred. But they may be allocated among interim periods on the basis of an estimate of time expired, benefit received, or activity associated with the periods.

(b) At a minimum, the balance sheet, income statement, statement of retained earnings, statement of cash flows, and notes are required. Comparative information is required.

Regarding disclosure, the following interim data should be reported as a minimum:
1. When the statements do not comply with GAAP for the annual statements, so disclose. Disclose also that the statements should be read in conjunction with the annual statements.
2. A statement that the company follows the same accounting policies and methods as the most recent annual financial statements except for: any new policy or method; any policies adopted to address the preparation of interim statements only, but where there is no impact on the annual financial statements; any special accounting methods adopted to address temporary costing fluctuations.
3. A description of any seasonality or cyclicality of interim period operations.
4. The nature and amount of changes in estimates.
5. Information about reportable segments.
6. Events subsequent to the interim period.
7. Specific information about business combinations, plans to exit any activ-

ity, restructure, integrate or reorganize, discontinued operations, and extraordinary items.

8. Information about contingencies.
9. Any other information required for fair presentation.

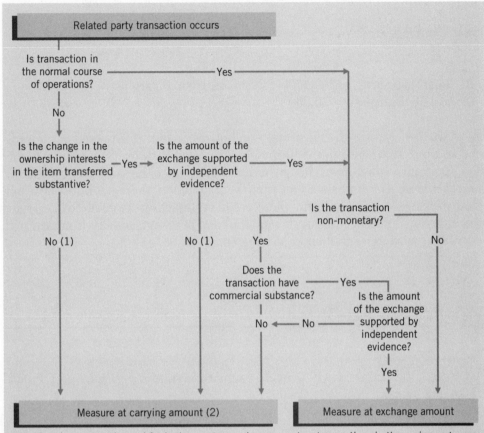

(1) Carrying amount is used for both monetary and non-monetary transactions in these circumstances.
(2) In rare circumstances, when the carrying amount of the item received is not available, a reasonable estimate of the carrying amount, based on the transferor's original cost, may be used to measure the exchange.

Exercise 24-1

PURPOSE: This exercise will give you practice in accounting for related party transactions.

Ellis and Associates is a large multinational company with related companies all over the world. During 2005, their fully owned subsidiary Treat Company sold a building to another fully owned subsidiary company, Trick Company. The building has a fair market value of $100,000, a net book value of $60,000. Trick Company paid Treat Company $80,000 in cash for the building. You may assume that these transactions are outside the normal course of business.

REQUIRED

For the above transaction, give the journal entries required for both Trick and Treat Company.

Solution to Exercise 24-1

Treat Company:

Cash	$ 80,000
Building (net)	60,000
Contributed surplus	20,000

Trick Company:

Building	$ 60,000
Contributed surplus	20,000
Cash	80,000

EXPLANATION: Review the illustration on how to account for related party transactions. Since this is not in the normal course of operations, we look to whether there has been a substantive change in ownership. Since the same company (Ellis) controls the assets both before and after the transaction, there has not been a substantive change in ownership and therefore the transaction is measured at carrying amounts. Any difference in carrying amount and exchange amount is put through contributed surplus or another equity account.

Exercise 24-2

PURPOSE: This exercise will provide you with examples of Type I and Type II subsequent events.

REQUIRED

Analyse the following subsequent events and determine the correct accounting treatment.

(a) Fire destroys an office building that is fully covered by insurance.
(b) A significant customer declares bankruptcy.
(c) A major contract is lost.
(d) The union decides to go on strike.
(e) The market value of short-term investments drops by a material amount.
(f) A new business segment is purchased.
(g) A lawsuit outstanding for two years is finally settled.
(h) The company issues new common shares.
(i) A new company president is appointed.

Solution to Exercise 24-2

(a) Since the condition did not exist at the balance sheet date, this event would not require an adjustment. It would likely be disclosed, depending on the significance of the building to overall operations. The fact that no loss is likely to result would also influence the decision. It would be a matter of professional judgement, but it is likely that it would be disclosed.

(b) Assuming there is an amount owing at year end, this would likely require an adjustment to the financial statements. An argument may be made based on whether the condition existed at the balance sheet date, not just the receivable. Specifically, if the receivable was not in doubt at year end, it may be argued that this is a Type II event that would be disclosed only. Most accountants, using the principle of conservatism would likely adjust the year-end statements.

(c) The loss of a major contract would likely be treated as an event of the subsequent year. It would be neither adjusted nor disclosed on the previous year's financial statements.

(d) Similar to (c) above.

   Since the condition did not exist at the balance sheet date, there would be no adjustment to the financial statements. However, this would be considered significant enough to disclose in the notes as a type II subsequent event.

(f) Similar to (e) above.

(g) The condition existed at year end, therefore the financial statements will be adjusted to reflect the settlement.

(h) Similar to (e) above.

(i) Similar to (c) above.

Analysis of Multiple-Choice Type Questions

Question

1. Which of the following should be disclosed in the summary of significant accounting policies:

	Amortization Method	Composition of Property, Plant, & Equipment
a.	Yes	Yes
b.	Yes	No
c.	No	Yes
d.	No	No

EXPLANATION: The amortization method for plant assets is a commonly required disclosure with respect to accounting policies. The composition of plant assets should **not** be in the summary of significant accounting policies because that information is required elsewhere in the statements. The accounting policy disclosures are **not** to duplicate information presented elsewhere in the financial statements.

Examples of accounting policies to be disclosed include:

a. Inventory pricing method.
b. Depreciation and amortization methods.
c. Revenue recognition policies.
   (Solution = b.)

Question

2. Night Corporation has six operating segments:

Segments	Total Revenue (Unaffiliated)	Operating Profit (Loss)	Assets
A	$ 30,000,000	$ 5,250,000	$ 60,000,000
B	24,000,000	4,200,000	52,500,000
C	18,000,000	3,600,000	37,500,000
D	9,000,000	1,650,000	22,500,000
E	12,750,000	2,025,000	21,000,000
F	4,500,000	675,000	9,000,000
	$ 98,250,000	$ 17,400,000	$ 202,500,000

For which of the segments would information have to be disclosed in accordance with generally accepted accounting principles?
a. segments A, B, C, and D
b. segments, A, B, C, and E

c. segments A, B, C, D, and E
d. All six segments.
e. None of the segments.

EXPLANATION: Write down the criteria to be applied in determining reportable segments. Test each segment to see if it meets **one** of the criteria.
   Criteria applied in determining reportable segments are:
1. Operating segment revenue (from unaffiliated customers and other segments) is ≥ 10% of combined revenue of all operating segments.
2. Operating segment's absolute operating profit/loss is ≥ 10% of the greater, in absolute amount, of:
   (a) combined operating profit of all operating segments that did not incur a loss, or
   (b) combined operating losses of all operating segments that did report a loss.
3. Operating segment's assets are ≥ 10% of the combined identifiable assets of all operating segments.

Segments A, B, C, and E pass the revenue and operating profit tests, but A, B, C, D, and E all pass the asset test. Since an operating segment only has to pass one of the three 10% tests to be considered a reportable segment, Night Corporation has five reportable segments—A, B, C, D, and E. (Solution = c.)

Question

3. Donald Manufacturing Company employs a standard cost system. A planned volume variance in the first quarter of 2005, which is expected to be absorbed by the end of the fiscal year, ordinarily should:
   a. be deferred at the end of the first quarter, regardless of whether it is favourable or unfavourable.
   b. never be deferred beyond the quarter in which it occurs.
   c. be deferred at the end of the first quarter if it is favourable; unfavourable variances are to be recognized in the period incurred.
   d. be deferred at the end of the first quarter if it is unfavourable; favourable variances are to be recognized in the period incurred.

EXPLANATION: Companies generally should use the same inventory pricing methods and procedures for interim reports that they use for annual reports. One of a few exceptions, however, is that planned variances under a standard cost system that are expected to be absorbed by year end ordinarily should be deferred. (Solution = a.)

Question

4. For interim financial reporting, a company's income tax expense for the second quarter should be calculated by using the:

a. statutory tax rate for the year.
b. effective tax rate expected to be applicable for the second quarter.
c. estimated average annual tax rate as estimated at the end of the first quarter.
d. estimated average annual tax rate as estimated at the end of the second quarter.

EXPLANATION: *CICA Handbook* Section 1751 requires that, at the end of each interim period, an enterprise makes its best estimate of the estimated average annual income tax rate. That rate should be used to determine income tax expense on a current year-to-date basis. (Solution = d.)

Question

5. With regard to interim financial statements, the CICA has concluded that interim reporting be viewed as:
    a. reporting for a separate accounting period.
    b. reporting for an integral part of an annual period.
    c. a "special" type of reporting that need not conform to generally accepted accounting principles.
    d. requiring a cash basis approach.

EXPLANATION: *CICA Handbook* Section 1751 views each interim period primarily as a separate accounting period (the so called **discrete** view), with few exceptions. Generally, the preparation of interim reports should be based on the same accounting principles the enterprise uses in preparing annual financial statements. However, certain principles and practices used for annual reporting may require modification at interim dates so that interim reports may relate more closely to the results of operations for the annual period. (Solution = a.)

Question

6. For interim financial reporting, an extraordinary loss occurring in the second quarter should be:
    a. disclosed only in the footnotes in the second quarter.
    b. recognized in the second quarter.
    c. recognized rateably over the last three quarters.
    d. recognized rateably over all four quarters, with the first quarter being restated.

EXPLANATION: *CICA Handbook* Section 1751 requires that extraordinary items be disclosed separately and included in the determination of net income in the interim period in which they occur. Gains and losses that would not be deferred at year end should not be deferred to later interim periods of the same year. Therefore, the extraordinary loss should not be prorated. (Solution = b.)

Question

7. Events that occur after the December 31, 2005 balance sheet date (but before the balance sheet is issued) and provide additional evidence about conditions that existed at the balance sheet date and affect the realizability of accounts receivable should be:
    a. discussed only in the MD&A (Management's Discussion and Analysis) section of the annual report.
    b. disclosed only in the Notes to the Financial Statements.
    c. used to record an adjustment to Bad Debt Expense for the year ending December 31, 2005.
    d. used to record an adjustment directly to the Retained Earnings account.

EXPLANATION: Notes to the financial statements should explain any significant financial events that took place after the formal balance sheet date, but before it is finally issued. These events are referred to as **subsequent events**. Two types of events or transactions occurring after the balance sheet date may have a material effect on the financial statements or may need to be considered to interpret these statements accurately:
1. Events that provide additional evidence about conditions that existed at the balance sheet date, affect the estimates used in preparing financial statements, and, therefore, result in needed adjustments. (Type I)
2. Events that provide evidence about conditions that did not exist at the balance sheet date but arose subsequent to that date and do not require adjustment of the financial statements. However, some of these events may have to be disclosed in the notes to keep the financial statements from being misleading. (Type II)

The subsequent event described in the question encompasses information that would have been recorded in the accounts had it been available at the balance sheet date. This type of event requires adjustments to be made before the financial statements are issued. (Solution = c.)

Question

8. The MD&A section of an enterprise's annual report is to cover the following three items:
    a. income statement, balance sheet, and statement of owners' equity.
    b. income statement, balance sheet, and statement of cash flows.
    c. liquidity, capital resources, and results of operations.
    d. changes in the share price, mergers, and acquisitions.

EXPLANATION: Management's discussion and analysis (MD&A) section of the annual report covers three financial aspects of an enterprise's business—liquidity, capital resources, and results of operations. It requires management to highlight favourable or unfavourable trends and to identify significant events and uncertainties that affect these three factors. This approach obviously involves a number of subjective estimates, opinions, and soft data. However, securities commissions have mandated this disclosure, believing the relevance of this information exceeds the potential lack of reliability. (Solution = c.)

Question

9. The significant difference between a financial forecast and a financial projection is:
    a.   A forecast uses one or more hypothetical assumptions.
    b.   A projection uses one or more hypothetical assumptions.
    c.   A forecast has a greater likelihood of being correct.
    d.   A projection has a greater likelihood of being correct.

EXPLANATION: Recall the definitions for financial forecasts and financial projections:

FINANCIAL FORECAST: Prospective financial statements that present, to the best of the responsible party's knowledge and belief, an entity's expected financial position, results of operations, and cash flows. A financial forecast is based on the responsible party's assumptions, reflecting conditions it expects to exist, and the course of action it expects to take.
FINANCIAL PROJECTION: Prospective financial statements that present, to the best of the responsible party's knowledge and belief, *given one or more hypothetical assumptions*, an entity's expected financial position, results of operations, and cash flows. A financial projection is based on the responsible party's assumptions reflecting conditions it expects would exist and the course of action it expects would be taken, given one or more hypothetical assumptions.   (Solution = b.)

Question

10. A related party cash transaction in the normal course of operations is measured at the following amount:
    a.   exchange amount
    b.   fair market value
    c.   carrying value
    d.   replacement cost

EXPLANATION: Refer to the Illustration elsewhere in this chapter. Recall that related party transactions can only be recorded at exchange value or carrying value. If they are in the normal course of operations, they are recorded at exchange value (Solution = a.)

Question

11. A related party cash transaction not in the normal course of operations and without a substantive change in ownership will be measured at the following amount:

a. exchange amount
b. fair market value
c. carrying value
d. replacement cost

EXPLANATION: Refer to the Illustration elsewhere in this chapter. Recall that related party transactions can only be recorded at exchange value or carrying value. If they are not in the normal course of operations, and they do not result in a substantive change in ownership (usually defined as less than 20%), they are recorded at carrying value. Any differences between exchange values and carrying values are put through the equity accounts. (Solution = c.)

Question

12. Which of the following would **not** be considered a related party to A Company.
    a. A controls B Company
    b. A major shareholder of A (owns 55%)
    c. Management of A
    d. C Company, where A and C have a joint venture together but are otherwise unrelated.

EXPLANATION: Per *CICA Handbook* Section 3840, the definition of a related party includes parent-subsidiary relationship (a), shareholders (b), and even extends to management (c). However, as long as the parties in the venture are not otherwise related, they would not be considered a related party. (Solution = d.)

Question

13. Jutland Company is in the process of having its financial statements audited. The audit partner has called a meeting to discuss the fact that the company has not followed GAAP in accounting for advertising costs. The impact on net income is material but not so material that it renders the statements useless. This situation, if not fixed, could result in which type of audit opinion?
    a. an unqualified opinion
    b. a qualified opinion
    c. an adverse opinion
    d. a denial of opinion

EXPLANATION: A qualified opinion would be issued since this is an exception. The problem is not so material as to render the statements useless. Hence, an adverse or denial would not be issued. (Solution = b.)